Love

Love

A NEW UNDERSTANDING OF
AN ANCIENT EMOTION

Simon May

OXFORD
UNIVERSITY PRESS

OXFORD
UNIVERSITY PRESS

Oxford University Press is a department of the University of Oxford. It furthers
the University's objective of excellence in research, scholarship, and education
by publishing worldwide. Oxford is a registered trade mark of Oxford University
Press in the UK and certain other countries.

Published in the United States of America by Oxford University Press
198 Madison Avenue, New York, NY 10016, United States of America.

© Simon May 2019

First issued as an Oxford University Press paperback, 2022

CIP data is on file at the Library of Congress
ISBN 978-0-19-088483-3 (hardback)
ISBN 978-0-19-765053-0 (paperback)

9 8 7 6 5 4 3 2 1

Paperback printed by Marquis, Canada

In memory of my parents, with gratitude.

Nearly all life's misfortunes come from our false notions about the things that befall us.

—STENDHAL[1]

CONTENTS

ACKNOWLEDGMENTS

I am deeply grateful to the many colleagues with whom I have had rich and stimulating exchanges about topics in this book, most of whom commented on various chapters. I thank in particular Edward Adams, Rachel Adelman, Clare Carlisle, John Cottingham, Armand D'Angour, Fiona Ellis, William Fitzgerald, Jessica Frazier, Stephen Frosch, Sebastian Gardner, Ken Gemes, Anthony Giddens, Andrew Godfrey, Sacha Golob, Lenn Goodman, Beatrice Han-Pile, Edward Harcourt, Colin Heywood, Edward Howells, Andrew Huddleston, Eva Illouz, Luce Irigaray, Robert Jackson, Susan James, Christopher Janaway, Menachem Kellner, Sharon Krishek, David Lancy, Antony Makrinos, David McPherson, Heather Montgomery, Alexander Nehamas, Joshua Neoh, Oliver O'Donovan, George Pattison, Bernard Reginster, Margaret Rustin, Christopher Ryan, Joseph Rykwert, Daniel Rynhold, Roger Scruton, Kenneth Seeskin, Michael Silk, Tom Stern, Alison Stone, Gudrun von Tevenar, John Took, Jeremiah Unterman, Dimitrios Vasilakis, Robert Vilain, Keith Ward, Sarah Young, Nick Zangwill, Semir Zeki, and Viviana Zelizer.

Clare Carlisle, John Cottingham, Sebastian Gardner, Ken Gemes, Sacha Golob, Beatrice Han-Pile, Edward Harcourt, Andrew Huddleston, David McPherson, George Pattison, Daniel Rynhold, Roger Scruton, Kenneth Seeskin, Gudrun von Tevenar, and Keith Ward reviewed the entire manuscript; and it is impossible to express adequate gratitude for their extraordinary generosity with their time and expertise.

I am indebted in so many ways to Ansia Naidoo, who has been unstinting in her encouragement.

My research assistant, Sarah Pawlett-Jackson, checked all the footnotes and references with unwavering attention to detail, compiled the bibliography, and made numerous valuable suggestions. I cannot thank her enough for her meticulous work.

Finally, I extend my warm gratitude to my agent in New York, Peter Bernstein; to my superb editor at Oxford University Press USA, Peter Ohlin, for his advice, support, and confidence in this project; to Christina Nisha Paul for overseeing the production of the book with such efficiency; to my copy editors Karen Jameson and Sangeetha Vishwanathan; and to Sylvia Cannizzaro for her careful proofreading and fruitful suggestions.

INTRODUCTION

What is love?

In particular, what is love's aim and motivation? What is the good that love, uniquely, realizes or constitutes?

Despite our immense focus on love, such questions about its ultimate purpose, motivation, and value are seldom answered in a way that can account for love's tremendous specificity: in what it seeks, in what inspires it, in the kinds of relationships it nurtures, in its choice of loved ones. For the reality is that, of all the people and things and vocations we value or desire, we love very few. And although love can be expressed in many ways—in passionate romance, benevolence, attachment, devotion, intimacy, valuing, caring, compassion, sexual and reproductive desire, or some combination of these—it cannot be equated to any of these things, and not all instances of them are animated by love. If "love" were really just another name for one or more of them, we could dispense with the word altogether. We could call benevolence "benevolence," and sexual intimacy "sexual intimacy." Why call them "loving"?

The remarkable silence on these questions concerning love's specificity is reflected in the fact that much, perhaps most, writing on love—whether by philosophers, or sociologists, or psychologists—is preoccupied instead with the dispositions, behavior, virtues, and social conditions that make for success and inclusiveness in relationships of love, and especially in romantic love. These are vital questions, but treatments of them all too often fail to indicate, more than cursorily, what they take love—the subject of their investigations—to be; or indeed why they assume they are studying love at all, as distinct from, for example, instances of sexual attraction or altruism or esteem that have nothing to do with love.

Only an understanding of love that does justice to the specificity of its aim and motivation—its ground—as well as to the very particular good that it realizes or constitutes can tell us in virtue of what so many diverse yearnings, attachments, dispositions, and attractions can be called "loving." When we speak of loving friends, children, God, parents, spouses, romantic partners—or art, nature, a country, or an ideal—or when we designate altruism, erotic desire, devotion, and valuing as instances of love, only such an understanding of the nature of love can explain in virtue of what all these uses of the word "love" and all these determinate manifestations of the love relationship resemble each other.

———

Why, then, is the specificity of love's ground and good so neglected today?

The reason, I will suggest, is that, consciously or unconsciously, we increasingly rely on human love to supply the consolations of the God in whom so many no longer believe—or, even if they do, no longer necessarily hold to be the source or catalyst of *all* genuine love. And, to that extent, we resist asking fundamental questions about love in a way that would challenge this dominant ideal of it. In particular, human love—of almost any type, from romantic to parental—is widely expected to be unconditional, disinterested, enduring, and affirming of the loved one in just the all-encompassing manner (of remarkably recent origin) in which God is said to love.

This secularized form of divine "*agape*," with its four characteristic features, has now become a dominant ideology of love: one of the most influential ways of understanding human love and the expectations we have of it. As we will see, great effort is directed, by philosophers in particular, at better explaining, justifying, and fulfilling this particular ideology of love, which dates from no further back than the mid-nineteenth century and which demands from human love what was once ascribed only to divine love.

To be clear: the problem here isn't to attribute supreme value to love. It isn't to regard love as sacred—and thus to see love in a religious way, in the sense, say, of Paul Tillich's view that religious faith is "the state of being ultimately concerned."[2] For to love—even more than to be loved—belongs to the most fundamental conditions of a well-lived life, though, I will argue, for different reasons to those given hitherto.

The problem is rather to see any of those four features of divine *agape* as intrinsic to genuine human love—and so as entirely within the scope of human agency—though each can coherently be ascribed only to how God is said to love. For such features constitute an ideal for human love that is unintelligible unless buttressed by a theology—and in particular a theology of grace, as articulated by thinkers from Paul to Augustine to Thomas Aquinas to Luther to Kierkegaard and beyond—in which they are taken to be the gifts of a God who, to a greater or lesser degree, is their source. To strip them of that theology and instead to see any of them—for example, unconditional love, in the sense of love that is ungrounded in, or unmotivated by, any qualities of the loved one, but is rather spontaneously bestowed—as expressing fully sovereign human powers is hubris, which can issue only in disappointment. To conceive love in such terms is, therefore, to undermine the very thing we claim to value.

This is why the overriding purpose of this book is to develop a new understanding of love—an alternative way of characterizing that unique structure of experience common to love's many expressions, whatever objects it takes and whatever relationships it fosters—that, I suggest, *can* better account for its distinctive aim and motivation; an understanding of love that can, therefore, explain why we love only the particular people and things that we do, indeed why we love at all.

In *Love: A History*, I surveyed what I take to be the principal ways in which, over the last two and a half millennia, love has been conceived in those parts of the world that are heir to the confluence of biblical and ancient Greek thought—parts of the world that today centrally constitute the West (and that I will refer to as "the West" here, though they extend beyond Europe and North America). I then introduced, though only in outline, an alternative way of understanding love, another direction in which we might look to identify the nature of love, namely as the joy inspired by whomever or whatever we experience as rooting, or as promising to root, our life.[3]

This joy can be rapturous or quiet; unqualified or admixed with pain, hate, jealousy, and even disgust. It is born of self-interest: to be at home in a world that we supremely value, which I take to be among the greatest of all goods and of all human needs. It sets us on a trajectory of seeking to attain such rootedness in and through a relationship with the loved one. And it can motivate the most devoted self-giving of which humans are capable.

On this picture, therefore, love is grounded in a promise of "ontological rootedness," a promise of home in the world—or, as we will see, in a very particular world that we supremely value—toward the attainment of which our lives become powerfully oriented, though the promise can never be perfectly fulfilled, for no final state of groundedness is available in a human life. Unlike the immensely influential tradition descending from Plato and Aristotle, I do not see beauty or goodness or virtue as the ground of love; rather, we will almost certainly come to see beauty or goodness in an object that holds out such a promise.

In this book, I have four new aims: to address the question "What is love?" by developing in detail my conception of love as our joyful response to a promise of ontological rootedness; to illustrate that conception with two "case studies" drawn from foundational myths of the Western world—Abraham's call by God to Canaan in the Bible's Book of Genesis and Odysseus's return to Ithaca in Homer's *Odyssey*—both of which may be interpreted as connecting love with the search for, or promise of, home in a world that the lover supremely values; to use it to investigate afresh such ancient questions as the relationship between love and beauty, sex, virtue, fear, and destructiveness; and to argue that, at least in Europe and North America, the privileged *object* of love is undergoing a historical change, from the romantic partner to the child.

In Part I, I set the scene by picking up on and developing a major theme of *Love: A History*, namely that what has today become a dominant conception of genuine love is incoherent. For example, by insisting that genuine love is unconditional—that it is in no way grounded in qualities of our loved ones—this conception of love cannot possibly answer the question "why do we love just these people and not others?" On this account, if a loved one were to ask us why we love her we would be forced to reply that *nothing* about her grounds our love for her: that, to this extent, we don't love her for her intrinsic or unique qualities. (And we would need, moreover, to concede that our love might have been bestowed, just as mysteriously, on someone else, or on an unknowable number of other people.)

I then summarize what I take to be the six principal ways of understanding love—the six basic conceptions of love—that have emerged in Western history since biblical and ancient Greek thought, all of which appear in my survey in *Love: A History* and all of which *do* propose grounds for love and so offer an answer to this "why" question. Yet can any of these, I ask, adequately account for the selectivity of passionate human love, whether for friends, children, spouses, works of art, landscapes, God, or any of its other many possible objects and expressions? (Even love for the monotheistic God is experienced as selective in that it explicitly rejects all other idols; for genuinely to love this God is to take oneself to be unable to love *any* others.)

In Part II, I ask what it is to glimpse a promise of ontological rootedness in those we love. This is the heart of the book; for my principal intent is to add to the accumulated store of conceptions of love a new one, which I propose as a way of capturing the very specific intentions and needs that, taken together, are unique to love in its manifold expressions—and so of distinguishing attachments and valuings and desires and virtues that are loving from those that are not. And although my alternative way of characterizing love's master aim—namely to secure a promise of ontological rootedness that it glimpses in another—is new, it can nonetheless accommodate certain motifs to be found within the six traditional conceptions, such as the motif of "return" that we read about from Plato to Augustine to Freud and Proust, or the notion of ethical compatibility articulated by theorists of friendship love from Aristotle to Montaigne and beyond. For, in briefest summary, to glimpse a promise of ontological rootedness in a loved one is to experience them in four ways (which, in any given case of love, may each obtain to very different degrees).[4]

First, we discover in them a source of life, a very particular lineage or heritage or origin (which needn't be our own), with whose sensibility we deeply identify.

Second, we have the sense that they offer us an ethical home: that they embody supreme values and virtues that echo our own, or that we would like to make our own, *and* that we believe we can attain only in and through them.

Third, we feel that they possess decisive power to deepen our sense of existing—power to intensify the reality and vitality, and therefore the validity, of our existence, as we experience it. This is the power—a power that at the limit feels like one of life or death—by which love is always inspired and to which it is unfailingly attracted—one of the reasons why hostages can fall in love with their captors.

And fourth, we experience them as calling us to our so far unlived life or destiny.

One we love offers such a promise of ontological rootedness through who they are for us—through their presence-to-us—and not necessarily in anything they explicitly say or do to us, including how they esteem or value or recognize us. Indeed, their very presence will fortify our sense of existing, as I will explain in Part II, even if they set out to attack our self-esteem.

Though love can be expressed in very diverse relationships and can take very different objects, I will argue that all love, such as for a romantic partner, a child, a parent, a friend, a sibling, or God, has a similar structure. (But because love is a relation to such a grounding presence, which promises us a home—a horizon of possibilities; a source of life—that we cannot find within the compass of our own self, however multiple, sprawling, and fluid we take that self to be, there is no such thing as self-love. We can esteem, recognize, take pride in ourselves and our values, virtues, and accomplishments—indeed, much historical discussion about self-love has, in reality, been about such affirming dispositions; but we cannot, strictly speaking, love ourselves—for love, in the very structure of its experience, is directed at one who breaks into our life from the outside.)

As we will see, these four experiences, taken together, are so specific—in other words, the kinds of qualities of the loved one that arouse our love and the deep needs that they meet in us as lovers are so particular—that we will be fortunate to find, throughout our lives, just one or a few people in whom we discover a powerful promise of ontological rootedness. And so, when we do, we will tend to experience them as irreplaceable, especially after a history of relationship—of interwoven lives, mutual devotion, and shared memories—and the intense attachment it engenders. Such irreplaceability increasingly focuses us on, and engages us with, the larger individuality of loved ones—a focus that causes the specific promise of ontological rootedness that grounds our love correspondingly to retreat into the background of our awareness, though it is no less powerfully at work there than it was when that love was born, though there is no terminus at which the promise is fully and finally attained, and though it never ceases to be a motivating condition of our love.

This rootedness or home that grounds love in my conception of it is nothing like a domestic cocoon that shuts out the world and in particular the public sphere. On the contrary. Instead of offering a realm of fixity, whether conceived as worldly (as in some conceptions of the romantic union) or as otherworldly (such as the *quies*, or eternal rest, that Augustine sees as the consummation of love for God), the loved one—and so love—creates a potentially unsettling place where the lover is called to their destiny: the sort of place that, as we will see, God creates for Abraham and his descendants.

Such a home is, therefore, not akin to a protected sphere of childrearing that we abandon in early adulthood, but is rather a habitat that we might spend our whole life seeking to discover, reach, and make our own. Thus, I characterize relationships of love in terms of *inhabiting*, rather than, as more traditionally, in terms of either possessing or submitting (where possession and submission are often considered mutually exclusive—wrongly, for real possession in love is not appropriation but rather surrender in which the loved one can flood their lover with who they are: with the force of their presence). Indeed, to inhabit a home does not assume sovereignty either over it or over the loved one who has promised it.

In Part III, I then suggest that my conception of love is strikingly exemplified by two archetypal narratives of love, each to be found in one of the West's founding texts: first, the covenant between God and Abraham in the Bible, in which Abraham learns that his true home and destiny are not where he was born or now lives, nor where his kin are, nor in his father's house, but rather far away in Canaan; and, second, Odysseus's journey home from Troy to Ithaca, recounted in Homer's *Odyssey*. In the first case, home is an entirely new territory, which is distant from Abraham's habitual or ancestral habitat, and which is where his true destiny is to be enacted. In the second case, the journey takes the lover back to a fresh encounter and renewed relationship with the place where he started—a return to the beloved that, as we will see, is a way of going forward with one's love and, to that extent, with one's life. In both cases, love involves a displacement—and in the case of Abraham, a radical displacement—from the *status quo ante* and is nourished by a complex experience of exile. Such experience of displacement and exile—of being remote from one's true home, which can be attained only with the greatest dedication—is, I argue, fundamental to love's motivation and development: to why we love and to the effects that love can have on us.

Both these exemplifications of love as our joyful response to a promise of ontological rootedness underline how love is structured by notions such as "promise," "trajectory," "search" for home, "hope," "journey," "attentiveness," "striving" for relationship, "overcoming" exile—all of them speaking of, and freighted with, love's rich intentionality, the object of which is the loved one experienced in the four ways just mentioned; and all of them pointing to a key reality of love: that it has no terminus, no point at which its searching is complete (let alone one that could be specified in advance). For there is no perfect groundedness, no state of ontological invulnerability available to us—and not only, as we will see, because there is none that contingency cannot sabotage.

In Part IV, I go on to use this idea of love as grounded in a promise of ontological rootedness to investigate the relationship between love and beauty, sex, and goodness; and I claim that my way of understanding love helps account for its remarkable specificity: for example, for the fact that we do not love as many people as we find beautiful or good or sexually desirable or reproductively suitable; or that we can encounter people (and things) we find neither beautiful nor good nor attractive, and yet powerfully love them. In doing so, I propose that though sex is one of the main expressions or languages of romantic love, it is never the ultimate ground of love; and that, *contra* the immensely influential view articulated by Plato and many after him, nor is beauty (or creation in beauty). Instead, beauty and sex rivet us to another so powerfully that we are better able to see their promise of ontological rootedness, if it exists.

If this is so, then beauty has a twofold relation to love: it draws our attention toward others, so that we are more likely to notice a promise of rootedness; and it is also a consequence of seeing the promise—a consequence of loving—in that we will attribute beauty to those who root us. As a result, in coming to see what roots us as beautiful, love is able to see beauty in another whom it also finds ugly. Indeed, ugliness—like evil—can be loved, without in any way being imaginatively transformed into beauty, if it speaks of a world in which we seek to be at home.

Finally, in Part V, I suggest that what we in the Western world, or at least in much of Europe and North America, take to be the supreme *object* of love is undergoing a historic change. For Plato's Diotima it was absolute and eternal beauty—or creation of, and in, beauty; for Aristotle it was the perfect friend; for Plotinus it was the "One," the source of everything; for the Christian worldview that dominated for many centuries it was God; for the troubadours of medieval Europe it was the (usually unattainable) Lady, seen as a repository of virtue; for Spinoza it was nature considered as a whole; from the late eighteenth century it became the romantic-erotic partner—or, more rarely, nature or art; for psychoanalytic thinking it is the parent, or rather some internal representation of the parent; but now it is coming to be the child.

In other words, romantic love is gradually giving way to parental love as the *archetypal* love: namely the love without which one's life cannot be deemed to be complete or truly flourishing; the love that traces, or points to, the domain of the sacred. As a result, to violate the child—or the parent–child bond—is now the ultimate sacrilege, the contemporary equivalent of desecrating the divine.

In suggesting that the child is becoming the supreme object of love, I am in no way implying that in previous ages parents didn't love or protect their children, or accord them intrinsic rather than merely instrumental value. Many, of course, did, indeed fiercely so; and evidence for this is to be found all the way back to biblical and classical sources. Still less am I proposing that the elevation of the child to the archetypal object of love means that no parents are now neglectful, resentful, violent, or otherwise abusive toward their children. Clearly some are. Ideals inevitably draw attention to the degree to which they are betrayed—just as, in the centuries when God was unquestionably taken to be the supreme object of love, believers surely took the divine name in vain again and again.

So why, in our era, might the child be elevated to the supreme object of love?

Not, I will argue, because we are seeking immortality in a world that has ceased to believe in an afterlife. Nor because we crave a lost innocence. Nor because of a new fertility cult. Nor, indeed, because the drastic decline in infant mortality has made it "safe" for parents to become lovingly attached to their children. Rather this development is the result of a concatenation of typically modern impulses that have slowly taken powerful root since the late eighteenth century. (And so we might expect it to be most marked in those countries and social groups in which such impulses are strongest.)

Among these impulses is the desire to locate the sacred in the everyday world, instead of in transcendence of it, such as in God or in a romantic union that is taken to abolish the distinct individuality of the lovers; the war on risk and suffering that marks our age, a war in which the security of the child has become totemic; the unprecedented degree to which childhood has come to be seen as *the* key to a flourishing life; the value placed on individual autonomy, to which love for the child is (*pace* harassed parents!) far more attuned than is, say, romantic love; and a turn away from the belief that love can have a final goal, such as union with the loved one, or be marked by an event that "consummates" it, in the sense that it could have in traditional conceptions of love for God or the romantic partner (a development that is one symptom of the long struggle to abandon teleological ways of thinking).

Though it is far too early to tell whether the gathering supremacy of parental love will effect a revolution in the empowerment of women in the realm of love and perhaps, as a result, more widely—it could, I will argue, be both a step forward and a step back—it is the first archetypal love that genuinely reflects what Nietzsche called "the death of God": the first that is no longer marked even by shadows of the divine.

PART } I

Dead Ends

WHY WE NEED A NEW UNDERSTANDING OF LOVE

The Neglected Question: What Is Love's Specific Aim?

Few, if any, ages can have been more preoccupied with love than ours is.

Enormous effort is devoted by psychologists, sociologists, anthropologists, artists, novelists, filmmakers, philosophers, and psychoanalysts, among others, to investigating the nature of love and especially to characterizing those virtues, behaviors, and personal histories that mark genuine love and promote its flourishing, as well as social trends, technologies, and therapies that help and hinder it. Neurobiologists give us fascinating insight into the neural networks, neurochemistry, and brain centers that are activated when we say we love. Evolutionary biologists speculate on the reproductive and social purposes for which love—and its virtues, notably altruism—might have evolved.

Above all, there is our tremendous focus on understanding the ways in which romantic love can unfold; on how to succeed in relationships through the right skills of listening, compromising, and connecting; on whether love works best inside marriage or outside, or indeed in polyamorous relationships; on why we are sexually attracted to some people and not to others; on whether Internet dating is debasing our relationships into a market for quick satisfaction or, on the contrary, multiplying the chances of finding the right person; and on how love is shaped by childhood experience and especially by the template of our relationships to mother and father.

And yet at the core of this great conversation there is, in our time and unlike in most previous periods of Western thought, near silence on whether existing conceptions of love adequately address the single most fundamental question about love: What is its specific ground and aim? And so: What is peculiar to our experience of love as distinct from how we experience any other relationship of devotion, intimacy, attachment, benevolence, affirmation, respect, valuing, caring, or sexual intoxication that takes us out of ourselves into the other person? What is the difference between altruism when it expresses love and when it expresses a virtue of character? What is the nature of sexual intoxication when it involves love, and when it doesn't? How do we experience what we most deeply care about or wholeheartedly value when we love it—say, when we love our child—and, by contrast, when would it not make (the same kind of) sense to call our devotion "loving"—say, our devotion to our health? Indeed, why do we love at all?

To say, as the philosopher Robert Solomon does, that "Love is the concentration and the intensive focus of mutual definition on a single individual, subjecting virtually every personal aspect of one's self to this process"[1] is not to answer the question. For why concentrate on *that* individual? And doesn't the same definition apply to obsessive envy or hatred, in which case it tells us little or nothing about the specific nature of love?

The same is true of Robert Nozick when he says that what is common to all love is that another person's well-being becomes "tied up" with yours: indeed, that his or her well-being "is your own."[2] Which is very true—and a point made by many philosophers of love including, most powerfully perhaps, Aristotle and Montaigne; but why does just *that* other person's (or thing's) well-being become an extension of yours? So, too, when the sociologist Eva Illouz rightly says that "to love is to single out one person among other possibilities,"[3] or the psychoanalyst Erich Fromm equally validly sees love as striving for "the overcoming of human separateness,"[4] they both beg the question of why we love one person rather than another—whether the love in question is romantic, parental, filial, or that of friendship. And neither picks out love in particular: Illouz's conception of love is compatible with purely sexual attraction; while Fromm's applies just as well to a variety of personal attachments or social bonds structured by the desire for recognition, status, and companionship.

Nor is the question about love's specificity addressed by thinking of love as tantamount to compassion, as Schopenhauer does when he says that all genuine love *is* compassion—"*Alle Liebe . . . ist Mitleid.*"[5] For we can love those for whom we don't have compassion (for example, God), and we can have compassion for those we don't love (the injured stranger). Moreover, though we can of course be intensely compassionate to those we most love—romantic partners, close friends, our parents, our children—compassion hardly exhausts the nature, aim, and motivation of such relationships.

Nor, too, is love's specificity captured by David Hume's very different claim that "love and esteem are at the bottom the same passions";[6] for we surely love fewer people than we esteem. And, though we esteem everyone and everything we love, esteem is not the animating heart of the experience of love, any more than compassion is. It doesn't do justice to the richness and vitality of a great love, say for our children, our spouse, a life friend, or God.

Nor do we gain much insight into love's ground by seeking to characterize the virtues and behaviors that mark genuine love, or by asking why relationships succeed or fail. To say that the key to successful relationships is generosity and trust and patience and gratitude and admiration and respect and realistic expectations and everything that fosters them is surely true, but it doesn't explain what animates love in the first place; why we love, and so care for, just the people that we do; what motivates two people to make their relationship work; what induces each of them to listen, share, recognize, care, connect, give, empathize.

The degree to which couples evince such qualities might, as the psychologist John Gottman claims,[7] enable us to predict the longevity of their partnerships, but this sidesteps all those prior questions about love's ground and distinctiveness that I just raised. In particular: What is love's aim really, and so what should even count as "success"? And why do we love only some of those who are kind and generous to us, or toward whom we are kind and generous? Gottman tells us how to make "love" endure but he says nothing about *what it is* that we are trying to make endure. He is eloquent on the means but silent on the end.

Indeed, those same qualities are also crucial to relationships that are not centrally about love: relationships, for example, that are purely erotic, or companionate, or protective, or even professional and civic. Generosity and kindness, trust and listening, recognition and empathy, gratitude and admiration, sharing the joys and sadnesses of the other, exulting in their successes and consoling their failures—all such qualities can speak of love; but they can also express virtues or strengths of character, biologically determined altruism, respect for others' humanity, the desire, in accordance with the "dictates of reason," to form friendships with people that increase our power and theirs, which Spinoza calls *generositas*,[8] and, in a Kantian vein, actions motivated by moral duty alone.

Thus, the mother who happily gets up every hour in the night to care for her baby doesn't necessarily do so out of love—though if she does so out of ethical duty or out of a biological instinct to care and protect, her devotion is hardly worth less for that. The man who jumps off a bridge, at great risk to his own life, to save a drowning child doesn't necessarily do so out of love—altruism is also a virtue of character, or a desire to aid and support others, that can be extended to those we don't love, and is no less noble when it is. The colleague who delights in your promotion and consoles you for your professional failures doesn't necessarily love you.

Nor does the magic closeness of sexual intimacy, or the life-giving freedom that it inspires, always speak of love—though, to a dangerously misleading degree, we have come to assume that it does, or ought to. Nor is the respect or kindness we show a stranger—or anyone, simply in virtue of their humanity—a sure sign of love. Nor, too, do we necessarily love those values or projects we most deeply care about. All these magnificent qualities can also be found in relationships that aren't about love, and so they can neither describe what is unique to love nor explain why we love just the people and things that we do.

Moreover, powerful dispositions to altruism are to be found in animals, too, as well as in human infants too young to possess the self-conscious awareness of their own distinct selfhood and of the selfhood of others that belongs to self-giving love. Infants of only fourteen months can take palpable delight in helping strangers. They are clearly impelled by innate drives to empathy and altruism, long before they can be said to be socialized into such behavior, let alone to interpret or evaluate it, or to "know" differences between right and wrong, or to be seized by that complex directedness toward another person as a horizon of one's whole life which characterizes love as distinct from mere attachment. And chimpanzees can show remarkable dispositions to help others without any concrete reward to themselves;[9] yet we do not feel that we need to call this love.

Charles Darwin was clear that altruism as hard-wired behavior, rather than as special devotion to another person for their unique qualities, might have evolved because it enhances the survival and reproductive fitness of the group, even if, in the process, it destroys the self-sacrificing individual:

> [A]lthough a high standard of morality gives but a slight or no advantage to each individual man and his children over the other men of the same tribe, yet that an increase in the number of well-endowed men and an advancement in the standard of morality will certainly give an immense advantage to one tribe over another. A tribe including many members who, from possessing in a high degree the spirit of patriotism, fidelity, obedience, courage, and sympathy, were always ready to aid one another, and to sacrifice themselves for the common good, would be victorious over most other tribes; and this would be natural selection.[10]

Although the notion of group selection winning out over the selfish individual remains controversial, it is entirely plausible that dispositions to mutual aid and to limiting selfish behavior enhance the reproductive success of the communities in which they are found.

———

Why does it matter that, even in their most powerful forms, not all altruism, or generosity, or esteem, or attachment, or intimacy, or devotion, or sexual joy, or caring, or valuing are motivated by love? Or that love doesn't always express these virtues and dispositions? Why shouldn't we use the word "love" to denote, for example, every relationship marked by devoted altruism? Or by a powerful attachment? Or by sexual intimacy? What's the problem, in other words, with seeing all these things as love?

The problem is that in using the word so widely we miss something very particular about the character, ground, and inspiration of instances of, say, benevolence that are loving and those that manifest an excellence of character; or of sexual intimacy that is loving and sexual intimacy that isn't; or of life-long relationships that are grounded in love and those that are formed of a different bond, such as recognition of virtue or delight in shared ends and activities, though they might be just as durable. To the outside, and in terms of the actions that exemplify them, all these instances of benevolence or sexual intimacy or relationship might look the same (as, in a loose analogy, Andy Warhol's *Brillo Box* and the Brillo box on a supermarket shelf cannot be externally distinguished; and here, as Arthur Danto remarks, Wittgenstein's theory that instances can be picked out without the benefit of a definition fails when they appear to be entirely alike[11]). But those identical-looking instances frame, express, and embody very different experiences, needs, and meanings when they are loving and when they are not.

The more we use the word "love" to speak of, say, all instances of passionate benevolence or sexual intimacy, and the more we consequently lose sight of this experiential uniqueness of love, the more we will be confused about when we genuinely love and when we don't. By speaking of love as just another word for so many diverse emotions and virtues and attachments, none of which, alone or in combination, captures what, I will propose, really grounds and sustains and expresses it, we easily enter marriages, romances, friendships, and other relationships with those we don't love, and, conversely, spurn those whom we do love when they seem deficient in these qualities. The danger is that we forcibly deceive ourselves that we love merely because we strongly feel some of these emotions; and so end up, in the poet Fernando Pessoa's cruelly vivid words, just "cuckolding me with me."[12]

Moreover, the Babel of meanings that has become attached to love makes it hard to know what our expectations of it should be, why passion that we were certain was love can evaporate like smoke in the night, or whether relationships that we terminate were really lacking in love—a disorientation that perversely reinforces the widespread conviction that love's ground is ultimately too mysterious to understand: indeed, that makes this conviction self-fulfilling.

But love isn't inevitably a mystery. Nor does the fact that it is expressed in such diverse relationships—erotic, protective, altruistic, possessive, destructive, equal, and unequal—and has so many possible objects—from friends, to romantic lovers, to siblings, to parents, to one's children, to nature, to art, to God, to one's "neighbor"—entail that there can be nothing common to them all. (Hate can take as many objects as can love, and yet we don't have the same problem with, or resistance to, attempting to say what is common to all hate.)

Rather, there is so much confusion about the nature of love because, for all the prestige that we lavish on it, we have, in over two millennia of history in those cultures marked by the confluence of Greek and biblical heritages, seldom been as resistant to inquiring into its ground in a manner that can account for its great specificity. Though we assiduously cultivate and investigate it, we have, to that extent, willingly lost touch with what "love" really names, and so with love itself.

Why?

The explanation lies, I suggest, in a development, widespread in the Western world and dating from at least the late eighteenth century, to which I pointed in *Love: A History*[13] and that I will discuss here in detail: namely, that in direct response to the progressive decline of traditional religious faith—in the sense of faith in a god or realm transcending the material world of space and time, and taken to be the unifying locus of supreme value and power—human love has increasingly taken on the role and specific features of the Christian God, *as this God came to be conceived in the modern era.*

The key point here is not merely that love came to be a new god: a secular, earthly god—and so an ultimate source, or even *the* ultimate source, of value and meaning and the sacred. It is also that human love came to be ever more closely modeled on how God is said to love—indeed, on a strikingly recent picture of divine love. In particular, it is now widely taken to be intrinsically unconditional and disinterested—in other words, entirely unmotivated either by qualities of the loved one or by any benefit or good that loving him or her might bestow on the lover. On this conception, therefore, genuine love is seen as wholly spontaneous and wholly gratuitous. And in so mimicking the specific consolations promised by divine love, human love has become a good of such surpassing importance to us that we dare not radically question its inner nature, and especially its ground.

The divine characteristics on which human love has become so widely modeled are clearly not those of any old god—say one of those self-seeking, capricious, and frankly immoral Greek gods. Love, in this contemporary conception of it, is no Aphrodite, the Greek goddess of love: lustful, whimsical, vengeful, laughter-loving. Rather it is the spitting image of the Christian God—or, more precisely, of a sanitized version of the Christian God, designed, perhaps, to appeal to a post-Enlightenment world in which faith is a choice, not a given. This is a thoroughly decent God, who loves everyone without condition or exception, and who has been painstakingly cleansed of all that favoritism and punishment and wrath and cruel elusiveness that we read of in both Old *and* New Testaments, and on through the theories of predestination of theologians like Augustine and Thomas Aquinas, or Protestant Reformers such as Luther and Calvin, who hold that God mysteriously elects some people to be saved through no merit of their own, while others—according to the late Augustine and Calvin—will be selected for eternal damnation, through no fault of their own.

This updated Christian God—a God that took decisive shape only in the nineteenth century, with such thinkers as Kierkegaard, who insists (especially in his *Works of Love*) on the purely unconditional, disinterested, eternal, and benevolent nature of divine love—is one palatable to an era that, as Nietzsche rightly diagnosed, craves comfort and safety above all else: a one-sided God, forcibly stripped by his votaries of unruly desire, vindictiveness, and a capricious will; a God, always available and always ready to pardon, who no longer sends people to the eternal damnation of Hell promised by many of the greatest Christian authorities, such as Augustine and Aquinas, and set to poetry by such writers as Dante and Milton; a God who is deemed to love *only* in the unconditional, universal, all-giving, all-forgiving, all-affirming manner of "*agape*"; and so a God who offers salvation to everyone without exception, as twentieth-century theologians like Karl Barth, Karl Rahner, and Hans Urs von Balthasar insist is the case. Gone is the God who, in Franz Rosenzweig's words, is "simultaneously the God of retribution and the God of love."[14]

Human love has been widely called upon to mimic—to take the place of—*this* sanitized and very recent version of the Christian God: this late version of Christian love. (It is a fiction that there is a single thing called "Christian love.") And so to question the nature of love in any way that risks overturning such a secularization of this particular version of divine love meets the most tremendous resistance—not least on the part of those avowed atheists for whom love has become *the* religion. Indeed, the point of so much discussion about love is precisely to entrench this prevailing secularization of divine *agape* by exploring how it might be better explained, illustrated, justified, and achieved.

———

Even Nietzsche, the greatest diagnostician of modernity, missed this. "Almost two thousand years," he exclaimed in 1888, with obvious amazement, "and not a single new god!"[15]

But the new god—human love—was already everywhere around him: for no culture was more hospitable to this particular god than the Germany of his day. This was the period of late Romanticism, and Goethe's *Werther*, Novalis's *Hymns to the Night*, and Wagner's *Tristan und Isolde*, among numerous other paeans to love, had all been composed. The German thinker Friedrich Schlegel had written that through love "human nature returns to its original state of divinity," and he had declared the birth of the "religion of love."[16] Today, even more than when Nietzsche wrote, this faith in the divine qualities of human love is what ultimately stands between the contemporary West and despair.

The problem here isn't to see love as sacred and so as giving meaning and value to life that cannot be substituted by anything else. Nor is it to regard love as the virtue that must motivate all other virtues if they are to be most valuable (for example, to hold that generosity is most virtuous when motivated by love). Indeed, for reasons to which we will come in Part II, love *should* be ascribed supreme value as an ideal or as the yardstick of a life well led: the kind of yardstick by which we might assess our own life beyond all the accomplishments, recognition, status, self-confidence, security, and sundry good things we otherwise seek.

The problem is rather that to model genuine human love on the sanitized conception of how God is said to love is inevitably to generate expectations of love—and of those we love—that cannot be fulfilled, even in principle. As I just argued, this conception, perfected as late as the nineteenth century, is far from the rich—if, to our contemporary sensibility, often disturbing—model of divine love that we find in the Bible, with all its favoritism and jealousy and impulsiveness and vindictiveness; divine love that, in the New Testament, sits alongside condemnation of the wicked to the fires of destruction[17] as well as the predestination, as St. Paul tells us, of some whom God will save[18] and others who are "made for destruction."[19] Instead, the sanitized conception one-sidedly sees God's love as in no way a response to any special qualities or merits of the other, nor as capable of destructiveness or vengeance, but rather as a spontaneous outpouring and giving and affirmation and benevolence that is unconditionally and unalteringly available to the loved one.

The Protestant theologian Anders Nygren eloquently expresses this model of divine love, which human love is so widely expected to imitate. Divine *agape*, he says, is "spontaneous, unmotivated, *groundless*." "It has nothing to do with the kind of love that depends on the recognition of a valuable quality in its object; Agape does not recognize value, but creates it. . . . *Agape is a value-creating principle*."[20]

Similarly, for a deeply Christian thinker like Kierkegaard, divine love is "an absolute gift," which is "not conditional on any response from us."[21] All genuine human love has its origin in God, in this unconditional divine love, and so is "essentially indescribable."[22] Its source, being God, is ultimately mysterious; and so human love can be known only by its "works," only by how it is manifested in action:

> Love's hidden life is, in the innermost being, unfathomable . . . Just as the quiet lake originates darkly in the deep spring, so a human being's love originates mysteriously in God's love. Just as the quiet lake invites you to contemplate it but by the reflected image of darkness prevents you from seeing through it, so also the mysterious origin of love in God's love prevents you from seeing its ground.[23]

And in its workings such love is able to continue finding the loved one lovable, "*no matter how he is changed*."[24]

To a remarkable degree, we moderns have turned to this ideal of divine love as wholly unconditional and unfathomable in its ground and origin, whether or not we believe in God—indeed, *particularly* if we don't believe in God and so resort all the more forcefully to agapic love to fulfill an ancient religious need. It has become an ideal to which people can uncontroversially cleave, whatever their values, their ethnic or national loyalties, or indeed their other religious commitments.

2 }

Back to the Future: Secularizing Divine *Agape*

To the extent that our dominant assumptions about genuine or ideal love persist in being modeled on this sanitized and then secularized picture of divine love, they see human love as defined by four properties in particular. I have already mentioned two of these: unconditionality and disinterestedness. The other two properties of love, without which, on this view, it would not most fully be love, are to be necessarily enduring and all-affirming. As with all hubris that claims the powers of gods, such a grandiose conception of human love is doomed to confuse and to fail: for human beings and their intentions and actions cannot possibly be the sovereign bearers of any of these qualities.

So, let us now look in more depth at how each of these supposedly divine attributes is taken to determine our understanding and expectations of human love.

Love as Unconditional

Human love is deemed to be unconditional, on this prevailing picture, just as divine love is in the particular Christian tradition to which I am referring, in that it is not grounded in, and to that extent its origin and inspiration are not conditional upon, any qualities of the loved one. We value her, on this view, because we love her; but, emphatically, we do not love her because we value her. As Irving Singer puts it, genuine love is a gratuitous "bestowal" of value, *not* dependent on any "appraisal" of the qualities of the loved one.[1] Like divine *agape*, this bestowal of value is spontaneous and uncaused. Singer goes on to admonish any thinker, beginning with Plato and Aristotle, who fails to recognize this primacy of bestowal and who instead holds that love is fundamentally aroused by the value that the lover sees in the loved one—value such as beauty or virtue or goodness, or, more generally, that ethical-aesthetic fineness or nobility that is denoted by the Greek word "*kalon*."

11

The same distinction between bestowal and appraisal is repeated in different ways by many other prominent secular thinkers. Harry Frankfurt says:

> It is not necessarily as a *result* of recognizing their value . . . that we love things. Rather, what we love necessarily *acquires* value for us *because* we love it. The lover does invariably and necessarily perceive the beloved as valuable, but the value he sees it to possess is a value that derives from and that depends upon his love.[2]

In other words, even if the beloved is valuable to the lover, "perceiving that value is not at all an indispensable *formative* or *grounding* condition of the love."[3]

In support of this contention, Frankfurt cites his love for his own children, claiming, "my love for them is not at all a response to an evaluation either of them or of the consequences for me of loving them." Of course, he adds, "I do perceive them to have value; so far as I am concerned, indeed, their value is beyond measure. That, however, is not the basis of my love. It is really the other way around. The particular value that I attribute to my children is not inherent in them but depends upon my love for them."[4]

André Comte-Sponville repeats the same formula: "we do not love an object because it is valuable; rather, our love confers value upon what we love." Ironically Comte-Sponville says this in the same breath as he declares himself "an atheist and freed from God."[5] This is ironical only because the hard and fast distinction between, on the one hand, an inferior love aroused by value that the lover sees in the loved one and, on the other hand, a superior or genuine love that is indifferent to the loved one's value is just a restatement of the old Christian *erôs/agape* dichotomy, as articulated by Protestant theologians like Anders Nygren, or by C. S. Lewis in his famous distinction between "need-love" and "gift-love,"[6] or indeed by a Catholic philosopher like Max Scheler, who, going still further, claims not only that genuine love has nothing to do with apprehension of value but even that it "cannot be reckoned as [an act] of apprehension at all."[7]

The problem is that secular conceptions of love as entirely value-bestowing reject the theological framework from which such distinctions between *erôs* and *agape* derive and in which alone they can make sense. In doing so, this way of secularizing *agape* (or, more specifically, this way of secularizing the "sanitized" conception of divine love that I outlined in Chapter 1, which reduces that love to disinterested benevolence) dispenses, disastrously, with any doctrine of modesty about the human capacity to love, a modesty that is crucial to Christian accounts, from Augustine to Thomas Aquinas, to Luther, to Kierkegaard, and beyond.

For to greater or lesser degrees such Christian accounts see human love, in the sense of *agape*, as possible only with the help of God's grace—grace that cannot be "merited" but is gratuitously and mysteriously given, without any discernable conditions. By contrast, today human love, in this domi-nant conception of it, is itself attributed such power to be unconditional—in just this sense of being gratuitously bestowed; so that, as Frankfurt says, love need not be grounded, or founded, in *any* perception of the loved one's value. Indeed, though nothing human can be perfectly or intrinsically uncon-ditioned, such unconditionality is taken to be love's *defining* feature (as we see every day when people say to each other: "If you loved me unconditionally you wouldn't . . ."). And so what was once seen as a divine gift is now taken as our natural birthright; what was once seen as beyond our power is now taken to be our defining power.

Remarkably, even contemporary theologians like Jean-Luc Marion suc-cumb to this secular ideology of bestowal, somehow assuming, *without* any reliance on theological concepts such as grace, that human love is dignified by not being grounded in the loved one's qualities. "Why," Marion asks, "does the lover commit himself, first, without any assurance, to love this one and not that one?" And he answers, in line with the other thinkers we have cited, "there remains only one acceptable response: the other, become unique [through the bestowing gaze of the lover], herself occupies, by virtue of her role as focal point, the function of the reason that the lover has for loving her."[8] In other words, this person is our focal point because our love focuses on her.

Why this circular argument offers "the only acceptable response" to the question is not explained by Marion; but those words, "the only acceptable response," are of the greatest interest, for they are symptomatic of precisely the strange closing off of thinking about the ground of love that, I am suggesting, characterizes our age.

———

Now one supposed advantage of seeing love as not grounded in our appraisal of the loved one's value, but rather as bestowing value on her, and to that de-gree as unconditional rather than as conditional, is that it preserves her irre-placeable uniqueness for us as her lover. For, so the argument goes, if love were conditional on the loved one's qualities, then she could be substituted in our affections by anyone else in whom we see those same qualities; and she would be even more vulnerable to abandonment if we had the opportunity to "trade up" to someone in whom we discover greater value. And such substitutability is, in turn, deemed to be a problem for *any* "appraisal" theory of love.

But, one might reply, surely the loved one becomes replaceable only if the qualities that are taken to ground our love are general or widespread enough to be readily repeatable. A quality such as beauty or virtue or intelligence or humor or sexual attractiveness, on which appraisal theories of love have so often been based,[9] perhaps is, or can be, sufficiently repeatable—if broadly enough conceived (and especially if conceived in a way that takes it to be in some way quantifiable and instances of it as commensurable). But this doesn't defeat *any* appraisal theory if the sorts of qualities that are deemed to ground love are determined in highly specific ways for each lover—ways that are therefore hard if not impossible to repeat—as, I will claim, the four elements that make up a promise of ontological rootedness are.

In any case, can we really be so sure that bestowal ensures the irreplaceability of the loved one? Might the opposite not be the case? For if love unconditionally bestows value, then what is to stop us bestowing value on any number of people? And what is to prevent us from bestowing greater value on some than on others? Even if we bestow equal degrees but different qualities of value on different people, so that each of our loved ones is unsubstitutable, this still leaves love for, say, one's spouse or children vulnerable to being crowded out by other bestowed loves, which is precisely a promiscuity that the bestowal theory is supposed to insure against.

That bestowal might lead to a proliferation of great loves is hardly surprising. For the whole point of the alleged unconditionality of divine love (which, I just claimed, is the original and today usually unacknowledged template for seeing human loving as unconditional in its inspiration—and so as free of "appraisal") is precisely to explain how God could love countless human beings regardless of who they are and of what they have done.

So, too, the unconditionality of "neighbor love"—its noble indifference to the qualities of the loved one—ensures its *lack* of discrimination. Indeed, the whole point of neighbor love is that anyone can be a neighbor, and that today I can devote myself to one person and tomorrow to another.

Moreover, as I suggested in the Introduction, if love isn't grounded in any of the loved one's qualities—in anything that they do, say, believe, and so on—in other words, if our love for them isn't conditional at all on who *they* actually are, then if they were to ask us why we came to love them rather than any number of others, we would be forced to reply that nothing about them inspired our love. Even that, in a sense, our love for them is random. Which is a very odd compliment to their irreplaceable uniqueness: the very uniqueness that bestowal theories of love claim to safeguard.

Love as Disinterested

Allied to this belief that genuine love is—and must be—unconditional is a second, closely related, conviction: that love is intrinsically disinterested or selfless, seeking and expecting nothing for itself. Love is therefore never grounded in the joys that it might afford the lover, or in any deep needs of theirs that it might meet.

Though in one sense there is something noble in this, in another sense is it not strangely condescending to claim that, in loving someone, we bestow value on them disinterestedly?

Harry Frankfurt, again, speaks for this view, shared by many if not most philosophers of love today, when he writes that love "consists most basically in a disinterested concern for the well-being or flourishing of the person who is loved." Love, he goes on, "is not driven by any ulterior purpose but seeks the good of the beloved . . . for its own sake"[10]—and so in no way "for the sake of any benefit that [the lover] may derive either from the beloved or from loving [her]."[11] In other words, he says, an agent's "active love" aims at goods that "are *altogether* distinct from and independent of his own."[12]

Not surprisingly, this conception of love as disinterested and unconditional goes together with a throwing up of hands when challenged to say exactly what grounds love. Or why we love one person rather than another. As Frankfurt puts it, I love this woman in virtue of "her whole lovable nature . . . that inexplicable quality of which I cannot give an account." The obscurity of his account is not relieved when he adds: "The focus of a person's love . . . is the specific partic- ularity that makes his beloved nameable—something that is more mysterious than describability [note the similarity to Kierkegaard's description of genuine— i.e. Christian—love as "essentially indescribable," on account of its divine origin] and that is in any case manifestly impossible to define."[13] The causes of love, in other words, are "poorly understood." In the case of love for one's children, "the explanation presumably lies in the evolutionary pressures of natural selection."[14]

Such vague speculation leaves one none the wiser about the wellsprings of this disinterested love.[15]

———

Another philosopher, David Velleman, also insists that love is ultimately disin- terested, though for a different reason. For him love is, most fundamentally, a response to the rational nature that, following Kant, he takes to define our hu- manity: everyone's humanity, yours, mine, the criminal's, the saint's. In saying this he is guided by Kant's idea that this rational nature, with its intrinsic dignity, both grounds morality and demands our respect for all who possess it—requiring us to treat all those others as ends in themselves rather than as means to an end. But where Kantian respect is, Velleman says, the "required *minimum*" reaction to this rational nature, love is what it should ideally be calling forth: the "optimum *maximum* response to one and the same value."[16]

Velleman is careful to point out that this rational nature "is not the intel- lect, not even the practical intellect." Rather "it's a capacity of appreciation or valuation—a capacity to care about things in that reflective way which is dis- tinctive of self-conscious creatures like us." It is, he continues, a person's "core of reflective concern."[17]

Since our response to this rational nature is purely disinterested, Velleman is forced to the conclusion that "love can have an object but no aim."[18] Indeed, it is free of any "urge or impulse or inclination towards anything."[19] (Yet again, we should note the remarkable and unacknowledged parallel to divine *agape*, which is free of desire.) More than that, his theory of love leaves him, too, unable to explain satisfactorily why we love some and not others. For if this rational nature is the same for all human beings, why don't we love everybody? Or why don't we love this person and then that person and then yet another indiscriminately? For they all have a rational nature, which is equally worthy, on his theory, of our love.

Velleman addresses this question by proposing that although anybody and everybody is indeed "eligible" to be loved, the reason why, in practice, we love only some people is that, in our eyes, only *they* palpably manifest this rational nature in the actual living, flesh-and-blood person that they are. Or in his more technical language: "Whether someone is loveable depends on how well his value as a person [in other words his rational autonomy] is expressed or symbolized for us by his empirical persona."[20]

Let us leave aside the question of whether Velleman's claim that a person's rational autonomy—"his core of reflective concern"—can really be the ultimate ground of love: whether this claim corresponds more than partially, if at all, to our own personal experience of love; or whether it can account in any way for, say, Tristan's love for Isolde, or Dante's for Beatrice, or Paris's for Helen, or Montaigne's for Étienne de La Boétie, or Vronsky's for Anna. Aside from this question, Velleman doesn't tell us in any detail what it takes for someone to express or symbolize his rational nature in his "empirical persona"—and so what it is about him, "the manifest person embodied in flesh and blood and accessible to the senses"[21]—that makes us fall in love with just him.

Nor does he explain why you and not I will then fall in love with him; for it would seem on Velleman's theory that anyone will fall in love with him, assuming they are alert enough to notice this expression of his rational nature. On his theory of love, the reason we don't love everybody, in virtue of their being rational autonomous agents, is that either they fail to express their rational nature well enough for us to see it ("someone's persona may not speak very clearly of his value as a person, or may not speak in ways that are clear to us"[22]); or that we aren't attentive or perceptive enough to grasp this empirical expression of their rational nature ("we can see into only some of our observable fellow creatures"[23]); or, as he ends up saying, that we simply have a limited capacity for love. If we had sufficient stamina and ability to detect everyone's expression of their rational nature, we would indeed love them all.

Which is yet another example of how the extraordinary specificity of love's ground—and so the aim that it uniquely expresses—is denied by how we tend to think about it today. For this theory of love tells us that love has no aim at all; that it is free of any urge or inclination toward anything; that what we ultimately love in someone is nothing peculiar to him or her; and, moreover, that what is peculiar to her—those elements of her empirical persona that make her "lovable"—is not, it turns out, what we really love.

As bizarrely, on Velleman's theory of love it is impossible fully to love anything that plausibly lacks a rational nature, a "core of reflective concern," such as works of art or animals or landscapes or indeed newborn babies. Or severely handicapped human beings. If these lack self-conscious reflective concern, they must, for Velleman, all be unlovable.

Love as All-Affirming

If unconditionality and disinterestedness are the first two prevailing assumptions about the nature of love, the third is that, in Martha Nussbaum's words, to genuinely love others is somehow to love them "in all their full particularity," a standard against which she deems such thinkers of love as Plato's Diotima, Spinoza, and Proust to fail.[24]

Here again divine-like powers are uninhibitedly, if more subtly, attributed to natural human love, namely the omniscience of grasping the "full particularity" of another person—in other words, all their distinctness and uniqueness and specific qualities—and, over and above that conceit, the ability to affirm *everything* we see in them, notwithstanding the myriad narrownesses and prejudices by which human judgment is inevitably limited, even at its most generous and capacious, even given a lifetime to get to know the other, and even granted that love grows and develops. It sounds very fine to say that we wish, or are able, to see and rejoice in everything about our loved ones as individuals, but it is actually another manifestation of the hubris that imagines our love to be unconditional or disinterested or devoted to the loved one purely for their own sake. For, again, it is only God, defined as omniscient and omnipotent, who is capable of such love.

(It is, indeed, ironical that Nussbaum's emphasis on loving others' full particularity is of a piece with her magisterial rebuttal, throughout her writing, of an ancient tradition, exemplified by thinkers as enormously diverse as Plato, Epicurus, the Stoics, and Spinoza, that seeks "a godlike life" transcending luck, contingency, uncertainty, fear, loss, neediness, and other "constitutive conditions of our humanity": a self-sufficient life with no "hostages to fortune." It is ironical because in urging us to turn away from such yearnings to transcend the inescapable conditions of our humanity and instead to see ourselves as "deeply immersed in the messy world of human particularity"—in her tireless effort to redirect our attention, including our love, from a certain sort of transcendence, in particular of luck and contingency, back to the individual in all his or her mortal specificity—she ends up seeking an affirmation of that particularity which, in its comprehensiveness, is itself the prerogative of a divine being. How difficult it is, as Nietzsche said, to escape the shadows of God. . . .[25])

We humans, by contrast, who aspire to divine powers at the cost of corrupting or crippling our human ones, are glorious in love precisely when we are not tempted by the hope, let alone the expectation, that our loved one can be transparent to us in her full particularity, so that everything about her can be penetrated by our insight and by our Yes-saying. The ambition to love the other in her full particularity is not healthy, even just as an ideal that motivates us to exceed our habitual limits, because we honor our loved one—and our love—by recognizing her fundamental inaccessibility: by not demanding to see more than she discloses to us in our ongoing encounter; by deeply identifying and empathizing with what she reveals, whether we can love it all or not; and by understanding that love of the individual person is not the same as—and nor does it entail—affirmation of all her particularity.

Indeed, our love is most genuine when our loved one is free from any such comprehensive subjection to our insights and valuings, and so from the oppressive expectation that she is to yield to our inspection—just as our love is most genuine when she feels free to be let go by us, though we desire her presence more than anything else. To love is maximally to crave the other's existence—not maximally to affirm her essence. It is not to say to her, "I hereby love you in your full particularity," but rather to say, in the words attributed by Hannah Arendt to Augustine, "*Amo, Volo ut sis*," which means "I love you; I want you to be."[26]

Love as Enduring

Finally, the fourth assumption of secularized *agape* is that genuine love necessarily endures—so that if love doesn't last it couldn't have been true in the first place.[27]

But is this so? Aristotle, for example, rightly saw that love could die if those qualities of the loved one that ground our love for her—such as, in his view, similar virtues of character—themselves decline in some crucial way, say through a moral deterioration that isn't reversed or through anything that seriously undermines trust. More than that: Aristotle thought that love *shouldn't*, under those circumstances, remain constant. For, he says, "[w]hat is evil neither can nor should be loved."[28] In a similar vein, the twentieth-century philosopher Robert Nozick holds that love's resilience "*can* be overcome over time by new and sufficiently negative other characteristics."[29] So, too, Troy Jollimore argues eloquently that though genuine love is resilient, it need not endure.[30]

But to oppose the view that love is genuine only when it endures—or to regard it as deeply wrong to say, as we read in Shakespeare's 116th Sonnet, that "Love is not love / Which alters when it alteration finds"—is in no way to say that love *cannot* last. Of course love can last. But it will last not because it is unconditional in the sense I have been arguing against—in other words, in the sense that love can spontaneously come into being, without being inspired by any qualities or value It sees in the loved one—or because it is for some other reason impervious to changes in him or her, but precisely because the specific conditions that grounded it in the first place have themselves endured, even if much else about our loved one has changed. Or because our memory of those grounding conditions—and the living reminders of them that, filled with gratitude, we see in our loved one today, such as her glance, her habits, her gait, her character—are able to sustain deep love even when some of the qualities by which it was originally motivated have disappeared.

Memory, history, gratitude—these are potent in sustaining love, as of course they are in our love for the dead. For memory—like gratitude and commemoration—is how the dead and the past become eternally present (though, by contrast, memory, like gratitude, can also banish the dead and the past to the eternally absent), just as the pious Jew recalls the exodus from Egypt not only as a distant event to be celebrated but, crucially, "as if he himself had been one of those to go."[31] As if he were now living what he is recalling. Indeed, love for the dead is perhaps the purest of all expressions of love insofar as we expect nothing in return. And, as Kierkegaard says, it might also be the freest.[32]

So to sum up where we have got to: I am suggesting that today our expectations of love have become hostage to a dominant model that holds it to be intrinsically unconditional, enduring, and disinterestedly devoted to the loved one for their own sake—a devotion that is moreover assumed to be capable of seeing and loving the other in all their particularity. Whether love speaks the sometimes unruly language of *erôs*, as in romantic or mystical love, or expresses itself primarily as protective care, as in parental love, whether it is passionately submissive, like love for God, or characterized by a more sober, though equally intense, devotion, like the best friendship, these four qualities are seen as the heart of love—as marking out true love from all its counterfeits.

The problem, however, is that this model of love makes sense only given certain theological doctrines, especially of divine grace. So that to the extent that we seek to love like God, to the extent that we take ourselves to strive for *imitatio Dei*, we succeed at all in doing so only because God is infusing us with the necessary power; and because to be in relation to God is to strive to be close to God, and to strive to be close to God is to follow in God's ways—though we recognize that ultimately it is impossible for us to be like God.

Yet once we step outside this religious form of life, things become very different. Loving in the manner of divine *agape* is unintelligible if espoused by those who have abandoned this theology and think that unconditional, disinterested, all-affirming love is a sovereign power of human beings—indeed, a sovereign power that can be widely, even universally, attributed to us; and that generates very specific expectations of those who love us, to which we are going to hold them.

Moreover, it should be underlined, to model human love on the sanitized version of divine love is unintelligible not just for atheists, agnostics, and other secularists but also for those religious believers who, though their faith might otherwise be deeply committed, no longer see all genuine love as flowing from, or empowered by, God. That great parts of the West, and notably of the United States, remain devout—that the "death of God" is far from complete and, indeed, is in some respects reversible—does not, of itself, make it coherent to think of genuine human love as intrinsically unconditional, disinterested, enduring, and all-affirming.

———

Of course, one might ask: Wouldn't such a hubristic conception of love, in which human love is ascribed characteristics that only God can coherently possess, eventually collapse under the weight of disappointment that it must generate? (And that it, indeed, does generate, judging at least by the number of relationships that end in conflict, separation, and divorce.)

To which I think the answer is No. An ideology rarely collapses merely because it disappoints. Few of our most cherished ideals crumble because they fail, or encourage false expectations. Our highest values are abandoned less because they engender terrible suffering, or because their value is somehow disproved, than because of a deep change of taste that renders them no longer palatable—and that makes us receptive to reasons and evidence against them. As Nietzsche remarks: "An article of faith could be refuted before [a person] a thousand times; if he still needed it, he would consider it 'true' again and again."[33] And this particular conception of love is so entrenched, the hopes for salvation and redemption from life's suffering that rest on it remain so powerful, and the need for a supreme ideal that mimics the old God is so deep (especially, perhaps, among atheists, agnostics, and others who believe weakly or not at all in that God) that disappointment in love, failure to reap the blessings promised by the ideal, leads us not to question our model of love and the expectations it generates, but—on the contrary—to keep "moving on" to new relationships in the undying hope that with *them* the ideal will be finally achieved.

But, one might persist, isn't our tendency to "move on" nothing to do with a restless search for ideal love—but, rather, evidence that love, like much of contemporary life, is governed by the spirit of the marketplace? In other words, isn't love—or what we take love to be on this dominant model—becoming merely another commodity for the quick satisfaction of passing desires, with lovers valued according to the pleasures they can deliver, cast aside when they fail to meet a checklist of expectations within whatever time frame our patience stipulates, and "loved" as long as they succeed in doing so?

This might be widely true of the search for purely sexual satisfaction, or of the pleasures of novelty and affirmation and a hoped-for end to life's uncertainties and loneliness that are to be found in successions of quick romances; but it is far less true of love. Rather than being enslaved by the spirit of the market, love is where we *resist* the spirit of the market and a life coldly dedicated to maximizing preference-satisfaction. "Moving on" is less a result of the commoditization of love[34] than it is of our deep commitment to the prevailing religion of love. It is evidence less of a casually hedonistic approach to love than it is a way of repeatedly refreshing our hope that we will finally attain the ideal of an enduring, unconditional love—and, through it, a sense of absolute meaning and value in our lives.

Indeed, so great is our need for this hubristic ideal of love—modeled, I have suggested, on a conception of divine *agape* that is itself questionable, because untrue to the rich accounts of divine love in the scriptures and theologies from which it is descended—that none of the revolutions in love of the past century has succeeded in freeing us of it. On the contrary, the extraordinary liberations of sex and marriage and of romantic-erotic relationships more generally— thanks in part to the ever-growing acceptance of divorce and contraception; parity between the genders; equal rights for gay love; polyamory; and love's independence from social, familial, or religious supervision—have so far been exploited mainly as opportunities to pursue and entrench precisely this ideal of secularized *agape*.

With one crucial proviso: romantic or marital love is inexorably being supplanted by parental love as the highest—the most sacred—expression of love as so conceived. The child, rather than the romantic lover or the spouse, is increasingly taken to be the privileged object[35] of love pictured on exactly this divine model: love as quintessentially unconditional, disinterested, unchanging, and affirming of the loved one in all their particularity.

Again, Harry Frankfurt expresses this gathering consensus eloquently: "the love of parents for their infants or small children," he says, "is the species of caring that comes closest to offering recognizably pure instances of love."[36] Echoing him, the movie star Brad Pitt says that he felt like "the richest man alive" on becoming a father.[37]

Though romantic love is far from dead, it is no longer going to be the supreme instance of love, that touchstone of the highest, freest, most unconditional love, without which one's life cannot be deemed to be complete or truly flourishing. Instead, public avowals of unconditional love for one's children— along with declarations that nothing in life is or could be more important, including any other love; that one's child is "the greatest gift of life" or "the love of one's life" (accompanied by an often quite explicit sense that one's romantic or marital love is second in both intensity and significance)—are becoming as central to one's sense of living a full and flourishing life—and, crucially, of being seen to do so—as public demonstrations of undying commitment to romantic unions have been for over two centuries, and as, before that, such demonstrations of fidelity to God and Church had been. And to that extent the modern Romantic era, which began in the late eighteenth century, and which Isaiah Berlin calls "the largest recent movement to transform the lives and the thought of the Western world,"[38] is slowly coming to an end.

3 }

The Six Major Conceptions of Love in Western History: A Summary

As we have seen, one key consequence, or correlate, of seeing love as unconditional is that no answer can be given to the question "Why do we love this particular person (or work of art or landscape)?" If human love isn't grounded in any specific qualities of the loved one, but is gratuitous, or if all we can say is, with Montaigne, "If you press me to tell you why I loved him, I feel this cannot be expressed, except by answering: 'Because it was he, because it was I,'"[1] then this question must be deemed unanswerable and even nonsensical. And, as I have suggested, many contemporary philosophers of love, and along with them countless lovers, seem entirely satisfied with this state of affairs. Alexander Nehamas, for one, declares that Montaigne's famous non-explanation contains "the full truth" about why we love.[2]

Indeed, they might find love dignified by the absence of any answers to questions about the ground of love, and so about why we love. To seek answers, so a popular view goes, is an affront to love, whose spontaneity and mystery cannot be fathomed. Once again Harry Frankfurt expresses prevailing opinion vividly: "[I]f I ask myself whether my children [the new paradigm of a loved one] are worthy of my love, my emphatic inclination is to reject the question as misguided."[3] On this view, the very attempt to analyze or specify the ground of love invalidates itself; for it shows that we don't understand what love is and so it can result only in falsehood.

But we should remember that for most of Western history—or rather the history of those parts of the world marked by the confluence of ancient Greek and biblical heritages, the former crucially preserved by Muslim scholars throughout Europe's "Dark Ages" before the Italian Renaissance—answers *were* given to this question, by the most canonical thinkers and texts, without any sense that to seek an answer is to detract from the sovereignty and majesty of love. Indeed, six main ways of conceiving love have emerged since Hebrew scripture and Greek thought, the principal origins of Western love, all of which very much address the question: "What exactly grounds love?"

And in their essentials they all came on the scene before Jesus. Though the New Testament broadens the scope of love for neighbor very considerably, indeed in some of its utterances appearing to universalize it with a clarity not seen anywhere in Hebrew scripture, it does not develop a single new conception of love's *nature*.

1. Love as Responsibility for Our "Neighbor"

The first way of conceiving love originates in the Old Testament, where we get the idea that to love is to make ourselves available to anyone else in our community, including the foreigner or the stranger living in our land, and even enemies, based on their needs. In Leviticus we find the command to "love your neighbor as yourself,"[4] which is still at the heart of Western morality, whatever foundations it now seeks for its norms, whether eudaimonistic, rational, utilitarian, or otherwise. It is this command, stipulated a few verses later to include the foreigner—"you shall love the alien as yourself"[5]—that the great first-century sage Hillel reformulates as the "Golden Rule," which, he says, is the essence of the first five books of the Bible: "What is hateful to you do not do to your neighbor."[6] And it is this command, too, that Jesus cites, when asked by a passerby to name the supreme commandments of the Old Testament; and that he extends so dramatically in scope in the Sermon on the Mount, where he demands that you are to "love your enemies, do good to those who hate you, bless those who curse you, pray for those who abuse you"[7]—though it is arguably only with St. Jerome (ca. 347–420 CE), and even more emphatically with Augustine, that the "neighbor" is explicitly defined as every human being. (Thus Augustine says: "Because a man, therefore a neighbor" and "Every man is a neighbor to every man."[8] By contrast, in the New Testament itself the scope of the command to love one's fellow human beings is *not* clearly universal, even through the four gospels: in John's gospel the principal arena of love is the community of fellow believers, and not humanity as a whole; while in Luke's gospel love's range is far wider, and arguably universal, as in the story of the Good Samaritan.[9])

To the further question "why love our neighbor?" the predominant answer is "for the sake of God"—in other words, because we love God and because God commands it; because we are to imitate the ways of God; because our neighbor is, like us, made in the image of God—a mark of his or her creator—or belongs with us to a community of faith in God. For Augustine, paradigmatically, love for God—who is the single absolute end of all human striving and the single absolute source of all value—must order and motivate every other love.

In short, Hebrew scripture is the indisputable foundation of the ethics of love, conceived as benevolence and owed to everyone in virtue of their humanity, that is central to Western morality to the present day. When, in the fifth century CE, Augustine says that love is the root of all true virtue and proclaims that everyone is a "neighbor" to everyone else; when, in the nineteenth century, Kierkegaard says that we are to love all people unconditionally;[10] when, in the twentieth, Levinas tells us that our fundamental obligation is to the "Other"—they are, each in their own way, interpreters of these Old Testament commands.

2. Love as the Desire for Ultimate Goodness or Beauty

The second answer to the question "What is love?" we get, again, from Hebrew scripture, but also and even more explicitly from Plato. This is the idea that love is grounded in and yearns for the supreme, absolute good—seen as pure, unchanging perfection.

In scripture the supreme good is, of course, God—and, though an insuperable distance remains between the human being and God, the well-lived life is structured by desire to be oriented toward God. As Deuteronomy says: "You shall love the Lord your God with all your heart, and with all your soul, and with all your might";[11] and this is, of course, the other supreme commandment, in addition to love for neighbor, named by Jesus in answer to the passerby.[12] Nor are we left in any doubt that perfection is the goal: "Be perfect, therefore, as your heavenly Father is perfect."[13]

In Plato we read that the supreme good is absolute beauty—the eternal, pure essence of beauty: beauty itself. Love's desire is to perpetually possess what is beautiful, and so to give birth in, and to, beauty.[14] And, in particular, to give birth to genuine virtue, which will outlive its creator and thus be a form of immortality. Love's ultimate desire, Socrates reports in the *Symposium*, is to be in constant union with absolute beauty or goodness.[15] To be in constant union with absolute beauty is not to possess this or that beautiful body, or soul, or thing, or law, or idea, but to contemplate beauty itself: what all beautiful things participate in, what is common to them, and yet what is beyond them. This ultimate reality is immortal and unchanging. And so, on this conception of it, love ultimately becomes desire for a realm beyond the mortal and the changeable.

Since such a realm is of course beyond life and the very conditions of life, such as space, time, causality, and individuation, love that desires it can morph into a death drive, seeking a consummation for love that is not of this world and in which all individuality has been subsumed into oneness—into the absolute. When this happens, love, the primal life force—creator of fine children, ideas, laws, and virtuous deeds worthy of immortality—ends up craving nothing more fervently than death. Which is exactly what we see in nineteenth-century *Liebestod*: death as the gateway to love's union.

3. Love as Yearning for Wholeness—for Our (Unique?) Other Half

The third sort of conception of love, which once again we find articulated by Plato, but also by modern writers from Hegel to Proust and Freud, is that love is, or involves, a search for wholeness, which is often characterized as a search for our unique other half. Here the reason why we love someone isn't because they are beautiful or good, let alone because they are a neighbor, but rather because we in some sense find completion with them. And so love is now not an aesthetic or moral journey, but rather the yearning to end the agony of separateness by finding and securing, if necessary by foul means as well as fair, one with whom we feel a predetermined "fit." Hegel sees lovers becoming "one organ in a living whole."[16] As Proust's Narrator puts it: "Love, in the pain of anxiety as in the bliss of desire, is a demand for a whole."[17] In a similar vein, Baudelaire sees in love "the need to lose one's *self* in the external flesh" of another, a need motivated by horror of solitude.[18]

Such narratives of love as a search for wholeness in which individuality, with its loneliness, can be overcome or even dissolved are often marked by a powerful sense that the lovers are discovering or recovering an original state in which together they can be complete. Indeed, this experience of love as *return* to a state of unity is a recurring motif in the history of love. We find it already in Plato's account (attributed to the comic poet Aristophanes) of those original human beings who, bisected by Zeus as punishment for challenging the gods, spend their lives searching for their lost other halves.[19] And we find the same motif in our own age, now expressed in the new language of psychoanalysis, when Freud describes the experience of the lovers' union and the melting of boundaries between them as a regression to a primitive state when the infant was united with its mother. Love (*erôs*), says Freud, "strives to make the ego and the loved object one, to abolish all spatial barriers between them."[20]

4. Love as Friendship

The fourth and very different idea of love is as dedication to the well-being of a specific person, grounded in a sense that they are just like us in those respects that we take to be most fundamental to who we are, and whose flourishing matters so much to us that we experience them as a second self with whom we wish to entwine our life. Although we already find this sort of love in scripture—for example, between Jonathan and David, or Ruth and

Naomi—and praised by thinkers in a rich tradition from Epicurus to Cicero, Montaigne, Nietzsche, and Emerson, it is most fully and canonically articulated by Aristotle, who calls it "*philia*" (usually translated as "friendship"). And he sees such friendship love as genuine only between two people who possess similar virtues and character traits, and to that degree a deep oneness of mind.[21]

As a result, says Aristotle, your friend becomes a mirror to yourself. He enables you better to love and know yourself—to understand and enjoy and endorse what you most deeply care about: what really guides your life and provides its ultimate ends. In more contemporary parlance, which of course is utterly alien to Aristotle, your friendship encourages you to become and affirm who you authentically are; to discover and shape an identity, a narrative of your life, that is true to your potential and through which you can flourish to the full.

At the heart of Aristotelian friendship is reciprocal goodwill, rooted in shared virtues of character. Such goodwill takes time to mature: two lives and their myriad activities must be mutually intertwined for long enough, and embrace a sufficiently broad range of both friends' projects and interests, to enable them to get to know and love each other's characters well, to discover their thrilling oneness of mind, and to experience that enlargement of each of their existences that a shared life can bestow. And since such friendship is essentially an ethical bond, a dialogue between ethical equals, a "sharing in discussion and thought,"[22] inspired by virtue and geared toward living a virtuous life, it is durable only to the extent that good qualities of character—the ground of this sort of love—are stable and similar. As we saw earlier, Aristotle allows something that might seem to us quite radical: that love can decline, that it isn't necessarily enduring. Indeed that it *should* decline if the virtues that aroused it in the first place and that are its bond themselves decay.

5. Love as Idealizing Those We Sexually Desire or Regard as Reproductively Suitable

The fifth idea of love is that it is grounded in nothing more than our sexual drive seeking satisfaction or procreation. Love, or at least romantic-erotic love, is how we idealize those whom we sexually desire, or whom we regard as appropriate mates for producing and raising children. Virtue and goodness neither inspire it nor are necessarily fostered by it; and it is certainly no privileged route either to spiritual achievement or to redemption from suffering and evil. Its purpose is sexual pleasure or to produce the next generation—not to overcome the pain of separateness, cultivate the lovers' characters, enable them to discover their identities, or launch them on a journey toward oneness or the absolute.

We might think that this view is developed only in our time by a psycho-analytic conception of human nature, such as that of the early Freud, which sees "libido" as the driving force behind *all* love, even that which isn't phys-ically sexual, and indeed behind all human activity of whatever kind. Or by evolutionary conceptions of love that regard its idealizations as crucial to motivating us to find and keep the right mate and to invest the neces-sary effort in rearing offspring. Or else by theories of the "chemistry of love," which ascribe our sexual choices to pheromones or smells that identify mates with compatible genes and immune systems. But though such psychoana-lytic, evolutionary, and chemical accounts use modern jargon—such as "li-bido," "ego ideals," and "introjection"; or "genes," "reproductive fitness," and "pheromones"—they are, in their basic form, not new.

Like all six of the major conceptions of love that have existed in Western history, this one goes back to the ancients. For example, we encounter elements of this view in the Roman poet Lucretius, a contemporary of Julius Caesar writing in the first century BCE. For Lucretius, as for Schopenhauer's conception of "the Will to Life" and the early Freud's idea of libido, love is an erotic drive relentlessly seeking satisfaction, a drive that is egoistic, even violent, and that almost always issues in unhappiness, illusion, and dissatis-faction. The art of love, says Lucretius, is to enjoy this unscrupulous, manipu-lative instinct without getting hurt by it. Far from setting lovers on a spiritual journey that perfects their virtue and issues in higher achievements such as law, letters, and philosophy, love easily incites them to selfishness, stupidity, and sadism. He doesn't mince his words:

> They squash the body they sought until it squeals
> And often their teeth make a gash on the lips
> In the course of affixing a kiss, which is hardly pure pleasure.
> They are indeed rather provoked to injure the object,
> Whatever it is, which causes this onset of lunacy.[23]

In a similar spirit, Schopenhauer sees sexual love as just expressing the "Will to Life" (*Wille zum Leben*) of the species: the drive to perpetuate itself by producing the fittest possible offspring. In other words, passionate lovers, so sure that their craving for just each other is the paradigm of a personal and private choice, a choice with no ulterior aim beyond their own intimacy and joy, are in reality playthings of the Will to Life, which is entirely indifferent to whether it benefits or harms them and which induces their mad desire for each other only in order to ensure the next generation. Their paeans to each other's virtue and beauty and uniqueness, and their search for pleasure and fulfillment, are merely tools of this inborn instinct to reproduce with a biolog-ically suitable mate. So much so, Schopenhauer says, that the lover "no longer belongs to himself."[24]

We are obviously a long way here from love as a refined striving for heavenly beauty and goodness.

Nonetheless, in practice if not in theory, these five definitions of love are not mutually exclusive. You can see love as a search for ideal beauty or goodness; and as friendship's devotion to the other as a second self; and as the yearning for an otherworldly perfection; and as the desire for our lost other half; and as expressing the motives and virtues of neighbor love; and also as the idealizations of sexual desire. These forms of relating might be in tension with each other, but this doesn't mean that they cannot coexist in one relationship.

6. Love as (Divine and Then Secularized) *Agape*

Finally—and to return to my opening theme—there has been a sixth approach to love, which we owe to religious tradition, Jewish and Christian, and which concerns how God is said to love. This conception, or family of conceptions, often denoted by the Greek word *agape* or the Latin word *caritas*, has historically been far richer than the sanitized picture of a divine love that is unconditional, unchanging, disinterested, impartial, and capable of affirming everything about the loved one. The least that can be said is that the sanitized picture faces stiff competition from another understanding of God's love as deeply conditional on "merit," or behavior pleasing to God; as capable of being destroyed or overridden by divine "hate," which, so we are told by such an authority as Thomas Aquinas, can consign people to eternal damnation without hope of reprieve; as inscrutably partial in how it dispenses grace, mercy, and salvation; and therefore as neither all-affirming, nor all-forgiving, nor straightforwardly unconditional. (To cite an aphorism that Samuel Beckett attributes to Augustine: "Do not despair; one of the thieves [crucified with Jesus] was saved. Do not presume; one of the thieves was damned."[25])

Troubling though they might be, these intensely contradictory images of divine love in scripture and theology present, I suggest, a more complete, and therefore a more accurate, description of the nature of love, as manifested in divine favoritism, hate, vengeance, and destructiveness, and the terror they evoke in those who love God, than do the pieties of today's received view of human love. Indeed, as I will argue in Chapter 16, we might learn something about the real nature of human love by attending to these complexities and contradictions in how God is said to love.

But even if we insist on the sanitized version of divine *agape*, one thing is clear: nothing licenses the view that purely human love can exhibit its defining features. This is a model of love that, if it makes any sense at all, can do so only if we accept the theology that deems genuine human love to be inspired by, and dependent on, the grace of a God who is taken to possess precisely such features: to be entirely self-caused and thus unconditioned by anything beyond the divine being; to be capable of unchanging commitments; to be so free of (involuntary) neediness and of partial perspectives that truly disinterested devotion to others is possible; and, of course, to possess both the omniscience to see everything about loved ones and the omnipotence to affirm them in their full particularity.

Much religious tradition has told us that, through the gratuitous gift of God's grace, this divine manner of loving could be infused into human beings, so that they could love like gods. In this way genuine human love gets modeled on how God is said to love us—a model epitomized by Pope Benedict XVI in his first encyclical, where he says, "God's way of loving becomes the measure of human love."[26] But religious tradition never held that humans have it within their sovereign power to love in this full sense. To the question "why can human beings love in a divine way?" the answer is clear: if they can do so at all, it is thanks to grace; it is because they are enabled by God.

The great theologians of love are absolutely clear about this necessary modesty, which is a major theme in thinking about human love from the Bible onward. St. Paul speaks of "the love of God . . . poured into our hearts through the Holy Spirit that has been given to us."[27] Augustine holds that the love of God is "the love by which *he makes us* his lovers."[28] Thomas Aquinas insists that the highest love is beyond human nature and can be attained only with the aid of divine power.[29] Spinoza, deeply religious thinker that he is, says, "The mind's intellectual love of God is the very love of God with which God loves himself."[30] Kierkegaard, as we have seen, holds that the origin of all genuine human love is in God's love,[31] asserting that God "has *placed love* in the human being."[32]

And so the extraordinary conceit that in loving "we can be like God," as Kierkegaard says,[33] or that "we are gods through love," as Luther puts it—that someone who loves is no longer "a mere man, but a god"—necessarily goes hand in hand with a severe doctrine of modesty, which reminds us that this happens *only* because God chooses to use human beings as a channel for divine love—a choice that human beings cannot influence or merit, no matter how many good works they perform or how pleasing they are to God. "God Himself is in him [who loves]," Luther tells us, "and does such things as no man nor creature can do."[34] Human nature, he insists, is radically corrupt and, unless aided by the blessing of divine grace, is totally incapable of loving in the manner of unconditional, disinterested *agape*.

Protected by such a doctrine of modesty, a great ideal—in this case to love unconditionally; to seek to walk in God's ways; *imitatio Dei*—can be an inexhaustible source of motivation without at the same time becoming a source of hubris. It offers an end that structures all our strivings, while remaining clear that to attain such an end is beyond human power.

Whereas the disaster that love has suffered in the West for roughly the last two centuries is that, as belief in Christianity has declined—as God has "died," to use Nietzsche's phrase—this conception of how God loves has increasingly come to be applied to sovereign human love, not least by atheists. As a result, we have been dominated by a conception of love whose intelligibility depends on the very notions of God and of grace that have been so widely rejected—a conception of love that cannot therefore either make sense or offer a coherent ideal.

And in doing so we have also, as I suggested at the beginning of this chapter, turned love into a new secular god to which we are all regarded as having access, analogous to the way in which the old God of love was regarded as open to anyone of sufficient faith. So that love that is unconditional and unchanging and disinterested and all-affirming has come to be seen not just as the preserve of a handful of saintly figures who are privileged recipients of divine grace, but as within almost everyone's power, unless they actively "resist" it, or unless reality or pathology otherwise gets in the way.

4 }

Why We Need a New Conception of Love

Unlike the contemporary conception of love that I am questioning, each of these six basic ways in which love has been understood in the Western world very much supplies an answer to the question: "What is the ground and aim of love?" None of them holds with Velleman that love has no aim at all, or with Frankfurt that what we love in someone is "impossible to define,"[1] or with Singer that love is not the result of recognizing any value in the loved one.

Nonetheless, none of these six ways of understanding love sufficiently accounts for the selectivity of almost all passionate love, whether for friends, children, spouses, siblings, works of art, landscapes, God, or any of its many other possible objects and expressions. None of them, I suggest, gives us a ground for love that is specific enough to explain this selectivity, as we can quickly see:

Love for neighbor might be grounded in love for God, or in love for humanity as an end in itself; but what motivates *those* loves? The theological answer is: God does. We are commanded to love God with all our heart and soul and might, "to walk in all his ways,"[2] and so to love our neighbor as God does and for God's sake. But this merely pushes the question one stage back: Why might we love God and so obey the divine command? (This is a question that I briefly address in *Love: A History* and to which I will return in Chapter 7.)

Beauty or goodness cannot be the ultimate ground of love, as we do not love everyone and everything we find beautiful or good or otherwise "fine." If love is, as Plato's Socrates reports in the *Symposium*, inspired by beauty, by the loved one's participation in the "Form" of beauty, how is it that we love far fewer people (or things) than we find beautiful, and, moreover, that we fail to love them in proportion to their beauty? (This is at least as much a problem for Diotima's ascent story as is the frequently cited "fungibility" problem—in other words, that to love another simply for her beauty and its value to our creativity is necessarily to regard her as substitutable by anyone of equal beauty; indeed, it is to justify our abandoning her for anyone of greater beauty. And, the criticism goes, it is therefore to be indifferent to her individuality and particularity, and so to fail genuinely to love her for the person she is.[3])

Conversely and more controversially: as writers from Shakespeare, in his "Dark Lady" sonnets, to Dostoevsky have shown, and as we will discuss in Chapters 31 and 32, we can love those whom we experience as ugly or evil. Not in spite of their ugliness or evil, or because we deludedly see them as beautiful or good, but rather *because* they are ugly or evil.

Yearning for our (unique?) other half is indeed how we often experience love, but this explains little. For it begs the question: Why does only one, or, over a lifetime, at most a few, out of the innumerable people we meet feel like our other half? And anyway, what is this yearning for another half symptomatic of? What is it really about? Why in the myth recounted by Aristophanes in Plato's *Symposium*[4] do all human beings—and not just those in the first generation, who were in fact the only ones to be bisected by Zeus—take themselves to be seeking, through love, a *lost* half in order to feel whole again? Why, as thinkers from Plato to Freud have claimed, do we crave this state of wholeness, this abolition of all barriers between us and one other, or a select few others, whom we love?

"Attachment" theories succeed even less well in explaining love's real nature. If love were merely the striving to overcome separateness, as psychoanalysts such as Erich Fromm claim, or were merely another name for powerful attachment, then we would have to say that animals love in the way that human beings do. After all, animals, too, especially mammals, fear separateness, and need closeness to their parents and communities. They too crave warmth and intimacy. They too can be bereft or die if they lose the object of their attachment. Even the proud lion lives in his pride, thriving not alone but only among a group of kindred lionesses and their offspring. Yet do we want to say that the attachments of animals show the bizarre specificity of human love: its focus on one stranger out of a thousand, its capacity to prefer someone who offers the lover little recognition or care or intimacy over another person who showers her with these things, and its drawing of world-creating meaning from its loved one?

Friendship love as dedication to the well-being of another who is alike in virtue: Aristotle's wonderful conception of *philia* reminds us how central a shared ethical world is as both the inspiration and the goal of any deep relationship of love: how powerful a bond can be created when two people recognize similar virtues of character in each other—indeed share an entire conception of the best way to live life and of the right ends of life, and give voice to that shared conception in a rich dialogue of their lives. And it teaches us that to build and cohabit such a shared ethical world with one we love can inspire us to explore, understand, and become that world in a way that we could never do alone.

But though such friends are rare, and though the great philosophers of friendship, from Aristotle to Montaigne to Emerson, insist on its rarity, even here love's tremendous specificity is not done justice. For like beauty and goodness and perfection, the reality is that similar virtues of character do *not* necessarily inspire us to devote ourselves in love to the welfare of others; and many people will possess them whom we don't love. Nor, conversely again, do we love only those who are virtuous, or virtuous in similar ways to us; for the shared ethical world that love seeks might be one of vice rather than virtue, as in the devotedly caring friendship that criminals can form.

Aristotle himself doesn't tell us why of three people in whom we recognize similar virtues of character we might intensely love only one. Montaigne, as we have already seen, invokes a non-explanation for why he so loves his friend Étienne de La Boétie: "Because it was he, because it was I."[5] Nor does the Bible say why Jonathan is smitten with David to the point where he wishes to surrender his kingdom to him, which as far as we know he wasn't motivated to do for anyone else: "When David had finished speaking to Saul, the soul of Jonathan was bound to the soul of David, and Jonathan loved him as his own soul"[6]—language remarkably similar to Aristotle's conception of a second self.

Love as sexual intimacy or as idealizing a suitable mate: Here we encounter the problem of love's specificity to, perhaps, the greatest degree. Few of us need reminding about what a perilous guide to love sexual intoxication can be: about how we can be unable to love those who sexually inebriate us, but might deeply love others who don't do so at all. To be erotically obsessed by someone; to be transported by them out of the banality of our everyday selves and lives—we do not need the dire fates of Anna Karenina or Emma Bovary to teach us that, though sexual desire can open the door to love or thrillingly express it, it is neither necessary for love, nor sufficient for love, nor what ultimately sustains it. As with seeing beauty or goodness in one we love, so too with the desire for sex, or to create offspring, with them: these can all be consequences of love, but they are not its fundamental ground.

Love as secularized agape: We have already said why this now-dominant conception of ideal love, modeled on a sanitized picture of divine love as unconditional, unchanging, disinterested, impartial, and capable of affirming everything about the loved one, is hubristic, incoherent, and fails the specificity test altogether. It fails the specificity test because, on its own admission, it cannot account at all for why we love one person and not another. It is incoherent because once we have repudiated a theology of divine grace that can be understood as imbuing human activities such as loving with divine qualities like unconditionality, and once we instead see ourselves as purely natural creatures, driven by needs and desires and purposes that have conditions for their fulfillment—conditions imposed in part by the particular world into which we have been cast, and in relation to which things show up as significant for us—no human activity can coherently be regarded as intrinsically unconditional, unchanging, or disinterested, even if its significance for us is so great that we yearn to think of it as such, and no human perceptiveness is powerful enough to see and affirm everything about another person.

To conceive love in these terms is hubristic and thus doomed to fail—as is all ambition, conscious or unconscious, to transcend the limits of our nature, from Adam and Eve eating from the tree of the knowledge of good and evil, to Prometheus's theft of divine fire, to the people of Shinar's attempt to build a tower, the "Tower of Babel," mighty enough to repel divine attack, to Icarus's denial that the sun could melt his wax wings, to the original human beings described by Aristophanes in Plato's *Symposium*, who were bisected by Zeus for challenging the gods, to modern nations and leaders who believe they can remake the entire world in their image. "Remember that you are not a god," the wise men of Greece were fond of warning.[7] Or as, in the *Iliad*, the Greek god Apollo bluntly says to Diomede, the man who attacks two gods: "Reflect, son of Tydeus, and fall back; do not try to make your spirit equal to the gods."[8]

In short: if we hold—rightly—that love is central to a flourishing human life (and, as I will suggest later, to "re-enchanting," in a contemporary idiom of autonomy, a disenchanted world), we must take particular care not to turn it into a source of omnipotence and all-purpose salvation. Indeed, the more we hold something sacred, the more careful we must be not to press it into the service of pride or vanity.

———

And so we need to ask: Is there an alternative way of understanding love; a way of characterizing the experience—the structure of experience—unique to love in its many expressions; a way that, unlike these six dominant conceptions in Western history, might do justice to love's specificity—and rarity? That is, might do justice both to what grounds it and to what it most primordially seeks? As I indicated in my Introduction, I think there is; and it is to this alternative understanding of love that we now turn.

PART } II

Love

TOWARD A NEW UNDERSTANDING

5 }

Love and the Promise of Rootedness

Suppose that love—all love—is joy inspired by whomever or whatever we experience as promising us a home in the world.

More precisely, suppose that we love only those we experience as offering us a promise of home in that *particular* world in which we yearn to be grounded—that very particular world in which we feel we can most vividly exist: in which we see the real field of possibilities for our flourishing.

This is a world that we supremely value, that feels as if it can be truly ours, and that *only* love can open up for us. It might be another world, real or fictional, to the one we now inhabit; it might, for example, be another epoch or perhaps a world altogether beyond this one, like the kingdom of Heaven, or, in a certain conception of romantic love, death.

Likewise, the loved one, whom we take to embody a promise of home, might be real or fictional. They might exist actually—our newborn child—or potentially—our still unconceived child. Or they might be an impossible construct of fantasy.

But it is always their *presence to us* that seems deeply to ground us in whatever world we supremely value, to intensify our sense of existing, to endorse the "quiddity" of our lives, and to lead us out of our repeated—and, I will suggest, inevitable—pain of alienation or exile, from others and from ourselves, into a sense of home.

Indeed, there are moments when we might feel that only in and through the loved one can the world in which we yearn to be rooted come into clear view at all. Only in and through them can we hope to approach it and to grasp it. As, for example, in *La Vita Nuova* Beatrice is Dante's guide and traveling companion in his striving for the heavenly realm—the indispensable guide to a realm by which she is herself surpassed.[1] So that to lose the loved one would be no longer to have access to that world or to be able to orient ourselves within it. As a result, any possibility of being grounded there would disappear.

Perhaps this is what Rainer Maria Rilke points to when he writes:

World was there in my beloved's face—
then in an instant it had poured and emptied.
World on the outside, world not now for grasping.[2]

Perhaps, too, Walter Benjamin suggests something similar in his aphorism "First aid" (*erste Hilfe*), where he describes how someone we love can instantly give us orientation in a place that has long remained strange to us—often, even usually, without them realizing that they are doing so. Their mere presence suffices:

A highly confusing neighborhood, a network of streets that I had avoided for years, was clarified for me at a stroke, when one day a beloved person moved in there. It was as if a searchlight was set up in his window and dissected the area with clusters of light.[3]

Here we must bear in mind how important mapping a city is to Benjamin as a way to speak about establishing orientation in life. "I have long, indeed for years, played with the idea of setting out the sphere of life—bios—graphically on a map," he tells us. "First I envisaged an ordinary map, but now I would incline to a general staff's map of a city center, if such a thing existed."[4]

So the loved one, in Benjamin's aphorism, might be not merely providing orientation in an actual city; rather he is "at a stroke" orienting the lover in "the sphere of life" as such. He is illuminating neighborhoods in which his lover feels called to live—neighborhoods that, until the moment he appeared, she had "avoided," finding them "confusing," unclear, and shrouded in darkness. As with Augustine, the city is also a metaphor for, or an allegory of, life itself. And, like Rilke, Benjamin speaks through a "spatial imagination," a "topographical consciousness."[5] The fragments, just quoted, from both these writers suggest that the world in which we must live and find our bearings comes into view, and our relationship to it comes to be mapped, only in and through the presence of the beloved.

———

Such a promise of rootedness—of finding a home, or grounding for our life, in relation to a world that we supremely value—always seems directed specifically at us, even when the loved one is unaware of offering it or cannot requite our love. After food, water, shelter, and community, it belongs, I suggest, to the most fundamental of all needs; and, those first four needs being shared by other animals, it is a quintessentially human need. Indeed, Simone Weil claims that "[t]o be rooted is perhaps the most important and *least recognized* need of the human soul."[6] (And one might add that lovelessness is not the same as loneliness or failure to recognize or be recognized, but is rather a condition where we feel ontologically ungrounded, unanchored, detached. Which we can feel even when we are amply embedded in relationships of mutual recognition and esteem.)

Though the urgency with which this need for a promise of rootedness is experienced, the meanings attached to it, and the diverse objects of love that are taken to offer its ultimate fulfillment—from God to the romantic couple; from art to one's children; from a country to a soul-friend; from parents to possessions that buttress identity and status—vary greatly from one culture and epoch and individual to another, it is, I propose, a universal human need.

It is a universal need because we are all cast at birth into a world not of our making, a world in which we are necessarily strangers and in which we can never entirely cease to be solitary, a world in which genuine grounding cannot be wholly given but must be discovered or created for ourselves—no matter how robust are the social networks, status, and power that we inherit, and no matter how completely we feel part of a familial, communitarian, or cosmic whole.

My proposal is, therefore, that "love" names our joyful response to a promise we glimpse in another to meet this need for rootedness or groundedness or home in a world that we supremely value; and that, by contrast, ways of considering love in terms of, for example, self-giving, benevolence, sexual desire, intimacy, attachment, recognition, esteem, and bestowal of value, or as grounded in the beauty or virtue of the loved one, fail to name what is *specific* to love. For all these things can motivate and structure relationships that have nothing to do with love. Indeed, if love were reducible to any of them we could just as well call it by those names; we wouldn't have any need for the word "love."

The joy evoked by such a promise of groundedness might be quiet or rapturous (rapture here understood as akin to the "feeling of increased strength and fullness," of overflowing vitality, that Nietzsche calls *Rausch*[7]); unqualified or admixed with pain, hate, and even revulsion. It is the source of the greatest devotion of which humans are capable as well as of a trajectory of relationship and giving to the loved one, in and through whom we seek to attain such home in the world.

In responding to the loved one's promise, as the lover sees it, love reveals a trajectory toward a new sense of home—a trajectory that is a source of powerful hope. However fulfilled love is in the present, it is always directed to a future created by that promise. This is a future whose contours and demands might yet be barely visible or understandable; but we sense that our true home is to be found within its horizons—horizons that a loved one's presence delineates or points toward. Indeed, though love feels intensely in the now, the very intensity of this "now" is a child of the future that is opened up by all love, including for the dead or for the past.

And so if "time stands still" this is because the promise—in other words, this future, and the hope that we have of attaining it—stands before us right now, concentrated in the loved one's presence to us, though at the same time the precise ends and demands that this future will bring remain uncertain.

Time does not stand still because the promise has fully revealed itself, let alone because we have fully attained it. And if this seems to be the case that is because we are too overwhelmed by the magic of the moment to realize that it is only a stage on a journey that can never be completed because there can be no state in this life in which all the conditions of groundedness in a world that we supremely value have been perfectly and stably satisfied, and all possibility of loss or alienation overcome. To that extent the expectation that in love there is a culmination where we feel "complete" is a dangerous illusion.

———

Since love thrusts into view such a trajectory toward a new sense of home, it uproots us from where we are, from how we now live, in order to root us more fully in the place to which the promise beckons. In order to (re-)discover our true home we must lose our accustomed habitat—our habitual mode of living. We must, in a certain sense, experience ourselves as being displaced, and even in exile.[8]

This new world opened up by love is not merely a consoling shelter; it is a home, which we *learn* to inhabit, and which impatience or complacency (itself often a result of impatience: what is difficult takes too much time and effort, so we convince ourselves that things will sort themselves out or are fine as they are) can easily cause us to lose. And what we find in this new world—in this home—is not stasis but the dynamism of roots. For roots involve continual growth, both probing down into the soil from which they draw life-giving nutrients and also driving the transformation of the organism.

Moreover, the promised home is necessarily one that we haven't fully attained: a realm, beyond the confines of our usual habitat, that is so far unknown to us in its form and possibilities—though it might also feel uncannily familiar. Indeed, we wouldn't fall in love with the other, or at least not for long, if we saw in her a home that we had already made our own, all of whose possibilities we felt able to master. And so the loved one—and the home that her presence promises—always evokes in us an unsettling and yet exhilarating juxtaposition of the deeply unfamiliar and the deeply familiar (a juxtaposition that resembles what Freud calls "the uncanny"). And of the unfamiliar and familiar haunting each other, in unspoken collusion, so that intensely to experience one is also to come to experience the other.

This home might be an entirely new territory, radically removed, perhaps inconceivably distant, from one's actual origin and so at the outset uncharted—like the Promised Land toward which God commands Abraham to journey in the Bible.[9] Or like the fledgling city of Rome to which, Virgil tells us, Aeneas, son of Aphrodite, the goddess of love, is commanded by the gods to travel—a city that he calls his "love," his "homeland," even before he has set foot in it.[10]

Or the journey might lead us to a fresh encounter with the place from which we set out—a return that enables us to discover a new relationship to a traditional home that, perhaps, we never genuinely made our own, or the possibilities of which we never fully lived. Which is what happens in Homer's *Odyssey*, where we read that for all the temptations of love and sex and immortality that Odysseus encounters in his long voyage home from Troy (to some of which he briefly succumbs), he yearns to return to his family and to the land of his lineage and kingship, Ithaca—and in the process of returning, I will suggest, finds himself and so his relationship to his loved ones ethically transformed.

Both these foundational myths of the Western world—Abraham's journey to the Promised Land in the Bible and Odysseus's return to Ithaca in the *Odyssey*—can be interpreted, I propose in Part III, as connecting love with the promise of, and the search for, ontological rootedness in a world that the lover supremely values.

———

Or else the realm glimpsed by love might be experienced as both new and old, to be reached by going forward to an unknown world *and* by affirming, or returning afresh to, an origin. As it quite explicitly is in many mystical encounters with the divine, from those of Origen in the third century CE to St. Teresa of Avila and St. John of the Cross in the sixteenth—encounters in which, as John writes, "a soul journeys *toward* that divine light of perfect union with God which is achieved, insofar as possible in this life, through love," a union that is also experienced as a *return*—a going down, or above, or within—to God as the original source.[11] As it arguably is for Augustine, who speaks of love both as return to our spiritual roots and as striving for what he calls our "sufficiency," by which he means striving for maximum being. As it is, too, in some images of erotic love, portrayed by thinkers as diverse as Plato and Freud, which centrally involve the drive to recover, or regress to, a primitive source of life—to reclaim an original union that was once lost—but which at the same time evoke a movement or development toward a future consummation or unity or integration.[12] As it is for Nietzsche's ideal of *amor fati*, love of fate, which affirms or wills both the past that has made us exactly what we are now and the future to which that past will give rise—and which sees beauty in the necessity that determines both what has been and what will be. And as it is in today's emerging successor to romantic love as the supreme expression of love: namely parental love.

In terms of the structure of its experience, love often comprises such a dual trajectory: a going forward and a return, which are actually one movement. It is as if love's yearning were Janus-faced: as if it looks in two directions, to the past as well as to the future, or to the past in order to look to the future; so that, at the limit, it nostalgically seeks to retrieve a lost paradise, which is to form the kernel of a hoped-for utopia. Thus pictured, love is directed at a recovery as well as a discovery of one's relation to the ground of one's being; indeed it is one of the most powerful ways in which we advance and create a future by revisiting, repeating, and so renewing what is past.

6 }

What Is Ontological Rootedness?

Hic amor haec patria est. (That is my love and that my homeland.)
—VIRGIL, *THE AENEID*[1]

My proposal that all love is grounded in a promise of home finds scattered echoes in the history of Western thought. Virgil, as we have seen, connects love and homeland. Plotinus speaks of the "One"—in other words the ineffable foundation, or possibility, of all being toward which love strives—as "homeland" or "fatherland" (πατρίς).[2] Augustine talks of lovers dwelling inside one another in *caritas*.[3] Thomas Aquinas refers to Heaven, the place in which love finds its fulfillment, as "home" or "homeland" (*patria*),[4] and to "dwelling in the lover" or "mutual indwelling" (*mutua inhaesio*)[5] as "both a cognitive and orectic effect of love."[6] Walter Benjamin alludes to how the loved one illuminates—orients us in—a hitherto unfamiliar place. Rilke finds the world in the face of the beloved.

But the connection of love to home, or rootedness, or groundedness, has nowhere been systematically developed.

And so we must now ask: What, more specifically, is the nature of this home, this ontological rootedness, that, I suggest, is promised in all love?

In particular, when we glimpse such a promise in another what does our gaze—the famous "gaze of love"—really see?

Surprisingly, this latter question has seldom been addressed in the history of love. Innumerable poets, novelists, and thinkers have spoken of the gaze, or "the look," of love—its rapture, its awe, its idealizations—but few have attempted to say what exactly evokes it. Shakespeare, for example, gives us no clue why Romeo and Juliet fall so fatally in love.

Our first impression will be that "rootedness"—or a similar term like "home" or "groundedness"—sounds horribly vague, if no more vague than many of the dominant explanations for what grounds human love that have been advanced historically, notably beauty, God, the good, divine grace, truth, or today's widespread explanation: the question mark, or blank, that theories of love as spontaneous or mysterious bestowal of value substitute for any attempt to answer the question about the ground of love.

44

Words such as "beauty," "goodness," and "truth" are notoriously hard to define, and after centuries of effort to do so remain mysterious. We can be sure that ontological rootedness won't be much less elusive. We must speak allusively.

Yet if we contemplate this word "rootedness"—or "home" or "groundedness"— in the context of love, we can indeed venture to say a lot about it. If, in that mode of reflection or inwardness that Plato calls a silent dialogue with oneself,[7] we ask ourselves the question "what do we feel when we indubitably love?"—what, for example, distinguishes devotion to the well-being of one we love from devotion to the well-being of someone out of moral duty, or benevolence, or social solidarity, or other virtues of character?; or why does kindness or strength of character or beauty arouse love in one case but only gratitude or admiration or habitual attachment in another?—or if, persisting with this self-questioning, we ask, "what do we feel when sex leads to sustained love rather than just to the fleeting sensation of love that accompanies its most intense moments, followed by confused indifference?," we will, I suggest, come to see that the promise of groundedness, to which love is such a joyful response, involves four closely related ways of experiencing another, all of them found in love at its richest.

First, we see in our loved one a powerful and very specific lineage or heritage (or perhaps more than one), and so a source of life, with whose sensibility we deeply identify. This lineage needn't be ours, but we feel immediate kinship with it. In it, and in relation to it, we experience the supreme possibility of our existence, in which we can be most luminously present to ourselves and to others, and in which we have discovered a world that implicitly understands and welcomes us, and we it. Indeed, in the most intense love what seems to be at stake is the possibility of *any* existence we can have; of any real presence to ourselves and to others; of any world or life that is truly available for us to inhabit.

Second, we have the sense that the loved one offers us an ethical home: that they embody, or potentially embody, those ultimate values and virtues that are most vital to our sense of being stably grounded in the world and—crucially— that, of all our ethical commitments, we feel least able to live out on our own.

The ethical home that we discover in and through a loved one isn't, therefore, an echo or projection of *all* those ends for which we most care. To glimpse an ethical home is not to see the full panoply of our own values or virtues embodied or idealized in the loved one. Nor is it to love them on account of their whole set of virtues or of everything about them that we value. Rather an ethical home comprises just those few ends, values, and virtues that we experience as most decisive to being the kind of person we authentically are or hope to be—*and* that we feel are truly achievable or dependable only if we see them thriving in another person as their first nature.

Importantly, these values feel fated, not autonomously chosen: built into us and built into the loved one. They are building blocks not merely of a narrative in terms of which we constitute and value ourselves—our "practical identity"[8]—and in which we might take aesthetic pleasure, but also of a description under which we constitute and value the world as a place to which we inextricably belong and of which we are a life member.

Third, we feel that the loved one possesses decisive power to deepen our sense of existing: to intensify the reality and vitality, and therefore the validity, of our existence. We see in them—rightly or wrongly, we will eventually discover—special power to give us, or to inspire in us, something that we crave as fundamental to our preservation and flourishing, and that we cannot otherwise secure for ourselves. This "something" might be a feeling of being deeply understood, of safety from a paralyzing source of insecurity, of freedom from a dead-end way of living—among other possibilities; and for some, perhaps many, people it might also include money and social status (pleasant though it would be to deny this fact). Whichever it is, we experience such a gift of the loved one as blessing us with new vitality, new horizons, new possibilities of being, all of them experienced in terms of a more vivid sense of existing.

Love is unfailingly aroused by and attracted to such existential power of another over us—not only of another person but also, potentially, of a work of art, a vocation, a god, a new country, even a landscape—and the worlds that they open up to us. All other gifts that we might hope for, including being valued and praised and respected and cared for, will arouse gratitude and joy—but, unless they have this existential import, they will not arouse love. Conversely, a loved one might scorn us or attack our self-esteem; and yet, because we experience them as intensifying and to that extent as validating our existence, we will nonetheless love them. (Let us therefore not confuse esteem with such existential recognition. Someone can recognize us in this way—who we are, what we need to flourish, our taste, our style—and yet not esteem us. And conversely, they can esteem us but fail to recognize us existentially.)

This power of another to bestow—or deny—something we crave as indispensable to the preservation and flourishing of our life in a manner that enhances the density and vitality of our existence, inevitably turns us, as lovers, into hostages. In particular, a lover is the sort of hostage who comes, under pressure of the loved one's existential power over her, to identify intensely with his values (and perhaps with his lineage too, discovering in him a world, a source of being, and, as we will see in Chapter 8, an associated "taste" that she experiences as, potentially at least, understanding and welcoming her). These values—and that lineage—might once have been alien to her; but, through such identification, they can join those to which she was already committed. And so they can in turn become building blocks of an ethical home, in that the lover sees them as attainable not on her own but only in and through the loved one by whom she is captivated—an ethical home to which she then even experiences herself as called by him.

In the extreme case, however, the loved one's power—the power for the sake of which he is loved—extends to total control over the lover's freedom and even over whether she lives or dies; and his means of exercising power over her is the implicit or explicit threat of brute force, devoid of all kindness and care. We can truly call this "pathological" insofar as the lover is, in reality, admitted by the loved one only to zombie status—to mental and ethical servility—in the world in which she is putatively being grounded, and never to any richly active membership in it. And yet, as long as the loved one keeps open the *possibility*, or indeed offers an explicit or implicit promise, that his power will be used to preserve and even enhance the life of the lover—and as long as the lover sees in him, or comes to see in him, an ethical home to which she aspires (even if this ethic is violent or otherwise warped)—it can nonetheless be a case, albeit a disturbing case, of genuine love.

Indeed, it is not so rare for people to fall in love with another having come to identify with his values under pressure of his existential power over them (though they might previously have found those values abhorrent), and thus having come to see an ethical home in him. For this is surely to be found not only in instances of "Stockholm Syndrome" but also in the adulatory love—genuine, I think—of millions for Hitler, Stalin, and other murderous dictators.[9]

As a result of their existential power over us, separation from someone whom we deeply love involves more than catastrophic loneliness or loss of intimacy; it doesn't just tear us from the familiar moorings of an "attachment" or undermine our self-esteem. Rather it is a fundamental attack on our sense of existing, in which our self feels hollowed out and our existence loses definition, reality, and force. So that we are less present in the world—less *able* to be present in the world, or in any world where we can feel deeply at home. This is why love is aroused by a promise of *ontological* rootedness: rootedness in which what is at stake is our experience of existing—an experience which, even when it seems wholly in the now, is always structured by the promise and its trajectory.

Fourth, we experience the presence of the loved one as calling us to new life, to our unlived destiny, to our individual "I am" or "I will be." This call doesn't necessarily show us in a direct or exhaustive way who we are; for that is something that we have to discover ourselves through often-prolonged trial and error, doing and experimenting, some of it in relationship with the loved one, some of it unavoidably solitary. Rather the call opens up a space for us to become who we are. It can be experienced as a call to be reborn.

To love another is to welcome, indeed to feel blessed by, this call that their very presence-to-us seems to issue, even if we also fear it or are tempted to repudiate it. At its heart is a powerful summons to responsibility: the responsibility of willing—of taking the most active ownership possible of—our fatedness; the responsibility wholeheartedly to devote ourselves to those ends, to do those deeds, to engage in those projects, to draw vitality from those inheritances, including the most difficult and painful, which remain unlived and which define and express who we are—ends and deeds and projects and inheritances that since the end of the eighteenth century have been called "authentic" and that are inseparable from an inner pathos of existing.

This is a responsibility that we feel simultaneously to ourselves and to the loved one. For if we can sustain the first three elements of a promise of ontological rootedness—our powerful identification with the loved one's lineage, with the ethical home they offer us, and with their power over our sense of existing—then we will be prepared to be called into an authentic relationship with both them and ourselves: commanded to become not only who we are but also who *they are*.

Taken together, these four conditions of love, all of them necessary to its fullest expressions, are so specific that we, as lovers, will find few people, or works of art, or landscapes, or any other objects of love, that meet them. Precisely because of that specificity, the greatest love for other people will always be for individuals, though communities too can be experienced as ultimate sources of life and lineage, of an ethical home, of power over our sense of existing, and of a call to our destiny—and to that extent can powerfully ground love. (Yet, as I will suggest in Chapter 24, since love cannot be grounded indiscriminately, there can be no "love for neighbor," in the sense of love for anyone regardless of their qualities. As a *virtue of character* benevolence can indeed be extended to anybody, but as the product of *love* it can be extended to the world beyond our particular loved ones only as part and parcel of the "overshooting" that I describe in that chapter.)

There will therefore be no ready substitute for those we genuinely love; indeed we can count ourselves fortunate if, throughout our life, we meet just one or a few people in whom we glimpse a powerful promise of ontological rootedness. When we add to this rarity the necessarily unique history of relationship that we go on to have with such loved ones—relationship that, if marked by sufficient attentiveness, fosters the deepest attachment—we can see why those we love occupy such unrepeatable places in our lives. Indeed, when we abandon one we love it is all too often not for another whom we love more but for one whom we love less—so as to be relieved of the effort and vulnerability and, as we will see, the fear intrinsic to all great love.

God as Paradigm of a Loved One—But Not of a Lover

It is in no way necessary to believe in the monotheistic God—shared to a great degree by the Abrahamic religions: Judaism, Christianity, and Islam—in order to see that this God is the paradigm of a loved one on the model I have just proposed, a limit case that can teach us much about the ground and aim of love.

First, God is conceived as the ultimate source of life and lineage. Indeed, as Genesis narrates it, God is the source of at least a twofold lineage. One is a divine lineage, which stems from God making human beings in the divine "image,"[1] so that humanity has, to that extent, a divine genealogy. And the other is a specifically human lineage, governed by covenant and embracing an identifiable people and its descendants.

This human lineage begins with Abraham and, similarly, originates in God. Like the divine lineage, it is directly caused by God: "I will *make of you* a great nation,"[2] God promises Abraham when he is commanded to leave his ancestral country for the new and at first unnamed homeland that will turn out to be Canaan. (And since Abraham's wife, Sarah, is unable to conceive, even their son, Isaac, is born of divine intervention.[3])

Second, God is the source of an ethical home, constituted by divine law, the ultimate point of which, I suggest, isn't to provide tests of obedience and merit, or a set of rules and responsibilities for a well-ordered society, but rather to offer those who love God ways to hear, understand, and reach the divine, and so for their lives to become grounded in it.

Third, God is ascribed absolute power to give or take away life—to deepen or weaken our sense of existing. And in a hugely prominent strand of the Christian narrative God is the arbiter not only of whether one lives and dies in the conventional sense of a natural life and death but also of what Augustine calls the "second death":[4] the eternal death that is God's punishment for sin, to be contrasted with the eternal life that only divine grace can vouchsafe.

Finally, the monotheistic God is the epitome of the loved one who calls us to our destiny, always conceived as a destiny of relationship with the divine being—whether individually or intersubjectively as a community. Indeed, "the call"—necessarily heard, of course, in human language—is one of scripture's great motifs: God's call to Abraham to leave his home and journey to Canaan;[5] his call to Moses to receive the law at Sinai and convey it to the people;[6] his call to Israel to be a holy people;[7] his call to Paul on the road to Damascus;[8] and, as Paul reports again and again, his call to those who love him.[9]

This is why the greatest of the biblical commands is to "love the Lord your God with all your heart, and with all your soul, and with all your might."[10] For here, in love for God, this human need for ontological rootedness finds its most extreme articulation. Indeed, every other case of love—for our romantic partner, for our parents, for our children, for our country, for nature, for art— is, in its motivation, aim, and form, a special and partial case of love for God.

———

That the monotheistic God is the paradigm of a loved one on this model of love does not, however, entail that devotion to God (or to any supreme object of love) must crowd out, or otherwise be at the expense of, other great loves; or that all other great loves will be experienced by the person of faith as being for the sake of God. We are earthly creatures who need a web of human relationships of love as well as love for music and art and nature and history and whatever speaks most poignantly to us of the times and places in which we live, or of those other times and places that feel like our true home. And even if God were taken to be so perfect a source of ontological rootedness that believers would not be motivated to seek any further relationships of love, love for God is, in practice, vulnerable to doubt—doubt that the greatest heroes of faith have repeatedly suffered—as well as to God's much-recorded disappearances and capriciousness; so that we will be moved to seek earthly loves as well.

Moreover, a fully realized home in God is, by definition, an ideal end that is impossible to attain in this life of space and time and error—thus leaving a residual craving for home that a believer might seek to fulfill in and through other loved ones. (Like many supreme ends, such as achieving excellence as an artist or pianist or sportsperson, a fully realized home in God cannot, of course, be exhaustively specified, and so we could never say for sure that we have attained it.)

And there is a more general point here: namely that we can, in principle, see a promise of ontological rootedness in many loved ones at the same time, just as we can love more than one work of art or nation or ancestor, and just as we can claim a mosaic of identities. Such tension as arises between these loves is likely to flow from the competing demands on us that they make, or from conflicts and jealousies between these loved ones themselves—say between our child and his or her stepparent, or between two of our friends who dislike each other.

———

In any event, to say that the God of monotheism is the paradigmatic loved one on the model of love I am proposing does not entail that this model is *itself* religious in the sense that it depends on faith in a realm that transcends space and time and that is taken to be the unifying locus of supreme value and power. Indeed, as I suggested at the beginning of this chapter, we don't need to believe in this God to see that in the stories or "myths" that speak of love for God all four elements of love as a promise of ontological rootedness are represented with extraordinary power and precision.

Nor, clearly, is my model of love religious in the sense that, for example, love conceived as secularized *agape* follows a religious template. For it doesn't mimic any of the ways in which the monotheistic God is said to love according to what I called the "sanitized" conception of divine love. Which is, I argued in Part I, a conception of love that reaches its height in the late Protestantism of the nineteenth century with such thinkers as Kierkegaard: a conception that sees love at its most genuine as unconditional, disinterested, enduring, and all-affirming;[11] and that, when attributed to sovereign human agency, becomes that prevailing theory of love against which I take aim. If, by contrast, we think of love as grounded in a need for, and promise of, ontological rootedness, none of those four elements of secularized *agape* could be constitutive of it.

In fact, if love is necessarily grounded in a need, whatever it is, then God cannot be said to love at all. For insofar as God is taken to lack nothing, and so to need nothing, including ontological rootedness, the motivations that structure human loving—and to that extent the experience of human loving—cannot be shared by, and so cannot coherently find their ideal in, such a divine being.

By contrast, a self-creating, self-sufficient god *can* intelligibly be thought to emanate—in the most perfect and abundant possible way—devotion, benevolence, compassion, mercy, empathy, and care for the flourishing of others: in other words, those related virtues that human love can foster in the highest degree, once it has got going. And, moreover, to emanate such virtues in a manner that is spontaneous, disinterested, unconditioned by any qualities of the loved one, and free of all striving or yearning. It *is* coherent to consider God the supreme font of compassionate kindness—and for a person of faith to see interventions such as saving the Israelites from slavery in Egypt, sending Jesus to redeem humankind, and indeed creating the world itself as expressions of supreme benevolence.

But there is no meaningful sense in which *love* can be said to motivate and structure such divine self-giving. For if God's existence is entirely self-caused and self-sufficient, and depends on nothing beyond it, then God's exemplification of the benevolent virtues, including self-giving, cannot be animated by that whole world of disorientation and existential fragility and tenuous ontological grounding from which the rich intentionality of human loving emerges. (And although there are theologians who argue that God has needs, or can decide to have needs, including to be loved[12]—a position that almost all ancient philosophers rightly opposed—it is hard to see how the origin and experience of such needs can in any way resemble, for example in their vulnerability, those that I, or those that others, ascribe to human loving.)

Which doesn't entail that there is no value or meaning in the idea of love *for* God. On the contrary: to hold up the virtues of divine self-giving as the standard to emulate can be a tremendously powerful source of motivation to self-giving for distracted, destructive, and self-absorbed human beings. *Imitatio Dei* is best thought of not as encouraging us to imagine, hubristically, that our love can be ungrounded and disinterested in the divine manner, but rather as enjoining us to pattern our love—grounded and motivated as it is in its own needy, conditional way—on the highest possible ideal of self-giving. ("As God is merciful and compassionate, so too must you be merciful and compassionate," it is said in the Babylonian Talmud.[13])

Moreover, to espouse the ideal of love for God does not just encourage us to emulate divine self-giving; it also places front and center the idea that, unlike say the Homeric gods, the monotheistic God is *available to be loved*—a theme I will take up in Chapter 21. Such availability to be loved, and so to ground human lives, is perhaps more valuable to our flourishing than any putative love that God has for us. Indeed, by being posited as the maximum source of ontological rootedness, and so as the maximum object of love, God—as loved one, rather than as lover—becomes the model for all human love: the limit case that shows us why and to what end we love.

Love as Recognition of Lineage

Everything completed falls back home to the ancient.

—RAINER MARIA RILKE, *SONNETS TO ORPHEUS*, XIX

All things, according to their kind, will veer towards their origin.

—DANTE ALIGHIERI, *PARADISO*

The beginning is like a god, which as long as it dwells among men saves all things.

—PLATO, *LAWS*[1]

Let us now delve a little further into each of the four ways in which, I have suggested, love's gaze sees the loved one—sometimes, of course, uncertain if it is really seeing what it thinks it sees; fearful that it is seeing merely what it wishes to see; anxious that its love isn't true.

First and foremost, we said, the gaze sees a lineage: an origin, a source of life, with which we, the lover, thrillingly identify, either because this lineage closely resembles and reanimates our own, or because we stumble across one that, though very different to ours, feels as if it is or should be—should always have been—ours. So that our loved one feels like family even if we have nothing in common with her actual social and ethnic background. (This identification with a different lineage is exemplified by the love of Ruth, the Moabite, for Naomi, the Israelite, in the Bible, to which we will come in a moment.)

In either case, we feel as if we are recovering or discovering—the two are not so distinct—a deep truth about ourselves, a truth that lay dormant until we encountered the loved one, or that we had forgotten or repudiated. This is the truth about our own taste—what we find clean and unclean, palatable and unpalatable, magnificent and repellent—and the all-encompassing way in which it reveals, and relates us to, the world around us: the way taste opens the world to us (and us to the world), determines how people and things show up or matter to us, and governs what we can—and what we cannot or refuse to—seek and find there.

Taste—that total sensibility of our being, that ordering of the soul, which governs all our decisive choices and responses—is the background of any action and thought that is genuinely ours. From taste flow those ultimate ends and values that speak most distinctively of us—of how, like everything we feel, fear, desire, do, and value, we have been forged by our heritage, our character, our choices, our life circumstances, and a myriad of external influences. From it flows what we affirm, reject, fasten onto, and fail to fasten onto, in all we encounter, which is perhaps related to what Thomas Mann means when he speaks of "style" as the "mysterious assimilation of the personal to the objective."[2] And from it too flows a sense of its own lineage: for such deep commitments cannot be forged in a single generation—in just you or me—but have a history, an archaeology, a cosmogony, a relationship, pious but also critical and questioning, to ancestors or gods or peoples that are in every sense prior to us. (There is a sense in which taste does not just have a lineage but is a lineage: a lineage of ethical-aesthetic sensibility, which education can develop, refine, make more nimble, more receptive.)

A loved one, therefore, never exists for us, the lover, just in the present in the sense of a static "now." As well as opening up a future in her promise of ontological rootedness, we always experience her as history, as *coming from* somewhere. Indeed, the power of her presence to us in the moment, when time seems to stand still, is a product of precisely this intensely time-bounded way in which we encounter her as embodying both a promised future and a distant past—a future and a past that constitute the now in which she is present to us.

Though we have so little access to this past, to her specific history—one reason why the loved one will always remain mysterious—it is central to the power she wields over us. To love her—to identify with her lineage as it has culminated in this singular human being in front of us—is a privileged way of slowly discovering our own taste through glimpsing it, in kindred form, in another whose very existence then becomes a blessing or endorsement of our own life at the level of its deepest commitments.

(Such a discovery is akin to the way in which, according to an idea articulated by Plato, we "recollect" truths that lie buried within our immortal souls—so that, for him, ignorance is forgetfulness: forgetting the true beliefs within us, failing to recognize them when circumstances prompt us to do so. And it finds echoes in the way in which, according to Nietzsche, we slowly discover the granite-hard "spiritual *fatum*" that we, deep down, are; which sets for us certain "predetermined" questions that guide our thoughts and actions; which disposes us to predetermined answers and decisions; and to which all our values and convictions and faiths are merely "signposts."[3])

The Motif of Return

Lineage, and the rootedness it affords, is nowhere more vividly exemplified than in talk of love as involving a craving to return to an origin. Though this motif of return is merely one possible manifestation of one property of love, namely identification with a lineage (and so should not be thought of as its *whole* nature), it recurs again and again in the history of love.

We see it in Plato's *Symposium* when the comic poet Aristophanes speaks of love as a search not just for our other half, but for our *lost* other half, and so as a desire to return to a primal wholeness. And in a very different metaphor offered by Plato, we see it in the *Phaedrus*'s picture of love as the desire for a vision of absolute beauty; for this desire, we are told, is actually to recover, or "recollect," a vision enjoyed by the soul in its antenatal state—before it was incarnated: before it was born into a body. In going forward, in striving for a supreme vision of absolute beauty, love actually takes itself to be regaining, and in that sense going back to, an original condition. Indeed, the "madness" of love, Plato writes, is induced precisely when, in encountering a beautiful object, we are *"remembering the true beauty"* that our soul had once seen and known.[4]

We see it in Augustine, for whom to love genuinely is to seek to return to our spiritual origin in God. Indeed, says Augustine, to "return to God" through love is the only way in which a being can "return to itself"[5] and so truly love itself.

We see it in the eighteenth- and nineteenth-century Romantic sentiment, perfectly expressed by Friedrich Schlegel, that through erotic love "human nature returns to its original state of divinity."[6]

We see it in Schopenhauer's idea that genuine love—compassionate love—is attuned to that ultimate reality beyond our illusory state of individuality: the reality of the impersonal Will behind all things; that single, timeless essence of which each of us is a manifestation, and to which each of us must await a kind of return—through the self-negation of our will to life as individuals—if we are to find salvation.

We see it in Kierkegaard's insistence that God is the necessary "middle term" or "the third party" in all genuine relationships of love (which, for him, are structured by neighborly love).[7] In other words, God, the origin of life and the source of love, by whom we are all created, is implicit in love as its real inspiration, aim, and ground. God is the ultimate ground of being to which, in every genuine relationship of love, we, as lovers, wish to relate and return.

We see it, in very different guise, in Freud's description of the lovers' union, and their "oceanic" sense of being at one with the universe, in terms of regression to a primitive stage of development when the infant was united with its mother. So that, to this extent, our adult loves recapitulate, and are animated by, our early libidinal attachments to our primary caregiver.[8]

We see the motif of return in Simone Weil's seemingly nihilistic conviction that the highest goal of a human life is to will to "de-create" oneself: to refuse to exist outside God. Indeed, she says, in one of her customarily extreme formulations: "God gave me being *in order that* I should give it back to him."[9]

And, reverting to scripture, we see it, too, in the marvelous poetry of Solomon's Song of Songs when the young girl, having desperately sought her lover in the city's dusky alleys and fruitlessly asked the night watchmen for his whereabouts, finally finds him, and, in doing so, discovers that her love impels her to take him to only one place: her mother's house. And not just to her mother's house, but specifically to the room where her mother had conceived her. In other words, her love drives her right back to the origin of her being: to her family home, to her mother, to the very place of her conception. "Scarcely had I passed" the unhelpful night patrol, she tells us, "when I found him whom my soul loves."

> I held him, and would not let him go,
> until I brought him into my mother's house,
> and into the chamber of her that conceived me.[10]

Beyond the shores of Western thought, we find in the early Confucian conception of *jen*, as developed by the Chinese fourth-century BCE philosopher Mencius, a close link between love and lineage. For Mencius, *jen* begins as the natural emotion of love felt toward one's parents, an emotion characterized by pious sympathy or compassion for elders—which, once cultivated within this orienting primacy of lineage, can be extended outward to become the basis of the social virtue of benevolence, a virtue not unlike Humean sympathy. In other words, love, which, on Mencius's conception, is naturally oriented to lineage, indeed which, in its origin, is grounded in lineage, becomes transformed into a wider benevolence when it is extended beyond the family—albeit a benevolence that remains strictly a this-worldly virtue, not yet seen as the origin and cause of the universe, or as the innate nature of Heaven, or in other such metaphysical and cosmological terms, as much later and highly diverse neo-Confucians, from Zhu Xi in the twelfth century CE to Wang Yangming in the fifteenth to sixteenth, would come to conceive *jen*.

Mencius bases his idea that *jen*'s specific origin is within the family in the prominence given by his master, Confucius, to *jen* and to its associated humanity and nobility of feeling, which he, Confucius, sees as rooted in filial piety and respect for elders.[11] Thus Mencius says:

> There are no young children who do not naturally love their parents, and when they grow up will not respect their elder brothers. Loving one's parents is benevolence [*jen*]; respecting one's elders is rightness [*yi*, another Confucian virtue, akin to justice, and which grows out of love].

What is left to be done is simply the extension of these to the whole Empire.[12]

In its very structure, therefore, love identifies with a source of being, for which the lover feels the deepest affinity, in order to move forward to a condition of bliss that can never be perfectly attained: secure rootedness in the world, or, more precisely, in that world which we supremely value.

But, as we said earlier, the source of being, and the lineage that expresses it, need not, in fact, be close to our own. Instead we might feel drawn to a very different lineage because the taste that speaks of it is already latent and undiscovered in us, awaiting its call. To align oneself with this new lineage, to take its law into one's soul and there to pledge allegiance to it, can ground us more powerfully than a direct return to our own acknowledged origin.

So when Ruth, the Moabite, after being widowed, renounces a return home to her mother and her gods and her land of Moab, where she might have found a new husband drawn from her people, and instead demands to follow Naomi, the Israelite, back to her very different land and people and god, does she not do so because she has discovered within herself precisely this overpowering affinity for a new lineage: for the people, land, and God of Israel? And so for a taste that speaks to her, and of her, more powerfully than can the world from which she comes? Doesn't she love Naomi not in spite of the Israelite's different lineage but because of it, breaking with what is familiar to her in order to find a more vibrant rootedness in the world, a fresh and vaster field of possibilities for life? Though she has as yet no practical knowledge of this land and people, for she hasn't ever left her own, she nonetheless swears allegiance to them in her moving words to Naomi:

> where you lodge, I will lodge;
> your people shall be my people,
> and your God my God.
> Where you die, I will die—
> there I will be buried.
> May the LORD do thus and so to me,
> and more as well,
> if even death parts me from you![13]

So, too, when Proust's Narrator, Marcel, thinks he is falling in love with Albertine because she offers a new and mysterious world, a life hitherto unlived by him, is he not also identifying a new, mysterious, and hitherto unknown dimension of himself—of his own taste? After all, as Marcel says, one desires precisely those who afford one "that prolongation, that possible multiplication of *oneself*, which is happiness."[14] These new dimensions and worlds might turn out to be mirages; the lover might, as Marcel suggests, see and value them only for as long as the loved one remains inaccessibly distant; but it is precisely their novelty and its mysteriousness that arouses his love.

And perhaps we find this same archetype—of love as identifying with, and inspired by, a new source of life—in Virgil's *Aeneid* when the Trojan prince Aeneas is commanded by the gods to leave Dido, queen and founder of Carthage, and voyage to an unknown homeland, Italy, where he is destined to found a new city—Rome—and so a new lineage. Italy: the enigmatic place to which he is called, despite yearning to go back to his original home of Troy and restore it after the ravages of war. *Hic amor haec patria est*: "That is my love and that my homeland," he says of Italy. Like Ruth, he pledges himself to the home to which love calls him before he has any real familiarity with it.

The seeming paradox that to move forward toward our greatest ideals—in the case of love, secure rootedness in the world—is also to return to who we are, or to those with whom we feel the closest affinity, is echoed in the words of Rilke at the head of this chapter: "Everything completed falls back home to the ancient." It is beautifully expressed, too, by a very different prophet, Isaiah, when he says to the Israelites of his day:

> Listen to me . . . you that seek the LORD. Look to the rock from which you were hewn, and to the quarry from which you were dug. Look to Abraham your father and to Sarah who bore you![15]

"Rock" here, the philosopher Maimonides writes, means the source or basis of something[16]—its most fundamental and archaic principle.

These words of Isaiah and Maimonides confirm that to fall back to our source, or to identify with a lineage, is not at the expense of the future. On the contrary: it confronts us with the future, with a trajectory forward—a trajectory without a terminus, which we experience as a destiny: as who we are fated to be. Lineage necessarily refers both backward *and* forward. In identifying with it, we recover ourselves in order better to discover our future.

Just as we need our past to claim a future, so we need a future to claim our past.

———

Indeed, we need to be clear that return can never be to the *status quo ante*: to precisely the form of life or way of being that we, or our ancestors, once inhabited.

To believe that it can be is the error of all nostalgic ideologies that see salvation in reclaiming, in its wholeness and wholesomeness, a past in which all was innocent and pristine. For by the time we have developed the desire to return, the place from which we come and the person who we are have both altered irrevocably.

To ignore this is to court terrible danger, of which many writers have spoken.

Proust's Narrator yearns to find in Albertine just the reassuring quality of his mother's goodnight kiss—the kiss that she would come to his childhood bedroom to give him at the end of each day; but this deluded expectation only leads him—and them—to grief.

Freud sees in the "oceanic feeling" of lovers who crave to merge with one another the same dangerous desire to regress to a primitive stage of development when the infant was united with its mother. This is a stage before an "I" has developed, before other selves can be recognized as distinct individuals, and so before we are capable of caring about, or even noticing, the harm that we inflict on others. Lovers who regress to this stage therefore only *appear* devoted to one another's welfare. In reality, they are incapable of doing more than seek their own narcissistic satisfaction.

And the desire to regress is, of course, not just dangerous but deluded. Love's ambition to find its other half, to *actually* return to the beginning, as recounted by the comic poet Aristophanes in Plato's *Symposium*, will get nowhere. For if we read this story carefully, we see that after the primordial humans were bisected by Zeus none of their descendants, in all the generations since then, has had an actual other half to recover, for they all stem from already bisected creatures. The search is in vain.

And even if it weren't in vain, even if an original condition could be restored, would it provide contentment once we have tasted the fruits of individuality? Wouldn't a perfect union of two individuals be sterile: a frozen life emptied of desire or change, hope or ambition, culminating only in a common death? This is the nightmare scenario that Plato forces us to contemplate, when he imagines the god of fire, Hephaestus (who is married to Aphrodite, the goddess of love), offering to weld a pair of lovers into just such a union.[17]

In reality, the only possible and fruitful way of recovering an origin is not literally to return to it—not to try to relive a primal experience—but rather to discover the possibilities of existence that the origin confers on us *now*, the taste and practices that it shapes today; and, thus inspired, to move forward into a future of new possibilities. In short: we retrieve the past only by letting it guide and energize the present, in order to prepare an unpredictable future.

Differently put: the only genuine return is as a different person to the one who departed from the origin, our life enriched by overcoming separation from where we belong, liberated by the pain of displacement or exile, and thus seeking the past only in the future. This fresh encounter with an original home, as a different person, means that return is never to the same life. Which, I will suggest in my interpretation of Homer's *Odyssey*, is exemplified by Odysseus's recovery of his homeland, Ithaca, and his wife Penelope.

"The again-recovered heart is the most lived in," says Rilke in his last known German poem; it is "freer through withdrawal":

> Oh the thrown, oh the risked, ball,
> Does it not fill the hands differently on its return,
> By the pure weight of its homecoming it has become more.[18]

Or in T. S. Eliot's famous lines from the *Four Quartets*:

> With the drawing of this Love and the voice of this Calling
> We shall not cease from exploration
> And the end of all our exploring
> Will be to arrive where we started
> And know the place for the first time.[19]

9 }

Love as Recognition of an Ethical Home

If lineage is the first thing that the "look" *recognizes* in the loved one, the second is an ethical home that you, the lover, want to make your own.

By "ethical home" I mean those very few ultimate ends that are built into you by all the power that character, heritage, and experience can muster; that ground your life with intoxicating purpose; *and* that feel genuinely achievable or dependable only if you see them alive in another as his first nature. (Even a parent's love for his or her children involves, at least often, the sense or hope that they will develop, each in their own way and perhaps transformatively, that parent's own ethical world; and infants need not yet have developed their own ethical world in order for this hope to pervade and structure parental love from its earliest stages.)

Such ultimate ends are more than merely signposts to what you find good and bad. They are the ideals and virtues and moral insights through which you believe you can find a reliable place in the world, and through which it comes alive to you as a home. They enable you to feel that the world is hospitable to you; and at the same time they disclose—or seem to you to disclose—thrilling new possibilities for your flourishing and freedom.

To find them in another who, you feel, cannot help giving life to them can inspire immediate and lasting love for him or her, and a sense of wonder, as if you didn't believe it possible. So that their very presence promises you the safety and excitement of a world that you hope—and perhaps have long hoped—exists, but that has so far eluded you. As, perhaps, when Lizzie, in Jane Austen's *Pride and Prejudice*, who is in love with Mr. Darcy, "could do nothing but think, and think with wonder, of Mr. Darcy's civility."

Indeed, the strange and involuntary humility of love is that the loved one so often appears to us, the lover, more vibrantly to articulate and live out these decisive ends and values than we ourselves do—and therefore to offer us an ethical home more robust and developed than any we can construct on our own. Though the risk of this humility is that we become parasitic on our loved one, delegating our life to them and loving them only for as long as we can live through them, in the healthy situation the opposite is the case: namely, that in beckoning us to an ethical home in which we feel we belong, they—in and through our love for them—seem to issue a radical command to us to become ethically who we are. In modern terms, the terms that began to be formulated around 1800, we would say that this is a call to selfhood or personhood in the sense of a fully authentic and creative subjectivity.

———

The values that we see in the loved one need not, however, be commonly regarded as good. Criminals are often attracted to other criminals. Liquid, un-structured, unscrupulous characters might feel freest, safest, most intoxicated, with those of similar character. So, too, might weak individuals for whom crime is an escape from responsibility, a shortcut to riches that they lack the patience to create for themselves. (Not all impatience is a vice, but all vices might be forms of impatience.[1])

And there are lovers who can be united *only* by their mutual betrayal or ex-ploitation of others who love them. Their erotic energy is fueled precisely by the cruelty—especially the mocking rejection—they inflict on their spouses, siblings, friends, or parents. They palpably relish the power they discover in such betrayals; and love is sweetest for them when its delights are paid for by the misery of others. Indeed, their betrayals not only energize their love for each other but also seem to vindicate and bless it.

But whether the ethical home that love seeks is made of virtue or of vice, we cannot love without craving such a home wholeheartedly. Indeed, in those phases of our lives when we are ethically diffident, when we don't know what we care about, and don't care that we don't know what we care about, we might lack even the motivation to love. For the ultimate ends that make an eth-ical home—ends that if violated deeply unsettle us, and can make life itself offensive—belong to the very rootedness in the world that love seeks.

10 }

Love as Recognition of Power

When we experience someone as offering us a promise of ontological root-edness, we also see in them decisive power over our sense of existing: over its depth, its density, its weight, its vitality. In particular, this means power to confer on us those conditions that we regard as fundamental to our preserva-tion and flourishing—yet that we most painfully lack because we cannot oth-erwise secure them for ourselves: for example, freedom, peace, frivolity, youth, career, recognition, children, vitality, homeland, safety from a paralyzing source of insecurity. It might also mean the power to remind us of other great anchoring loves, such as our parents or grandparents. And when our life itself feels physically or spiritually endangered, we will readily love those whom we take to have the power to save it.

This is why the captive can fall in love with their captor—as long as the captor keeps open the possibility that his power will be used to preserve and even enhance their life, *and* as long as they see in him, or come to see in him, an ethical home to which they aspire. For the captor's power over the captive's freedom is also power over their inner feelings of vitality and deadness, and, at the limit, over whether they actually live or die. It is also reflected in the way theologians like Augustine and Thomas Aquinas insist that love for God, who is taken to possess such power to the maximum degree, can be, quite properly, motivated by self-interest in eternal life and fear of what Augustine calls the "second death" of eternal damnation (the death that is the punishment for sin and that would follow our first, natural or biological, death).

And—unsavory though this reality is—the sources of power on account of which people can fall in love very much include fame and wealth. Indeed, we misrepresent the nature of love if we primly deny that fame and wealth and other markers of status can be genuine objects of it, albeit among the least noble. Lizzie, who is one of Jane Austen's most attractive characters, falls in love with Mr. Darcy precisely when she sees the magnificence of his country estate. Asked by her sister Jane to name the moment her love was born, Lizzie replies: "I believe I must date it from my first seeing his beautiful grounds at

Pemberley." (And as great a philosopher of love as Aristotle acknowledges that love, although not the highest love, can be based on such self-interest in the pleasure or utility afforded by the loved one.)

Indeed, for many people, status and whatever goods bestow it, of which money and fame are just two, are the supreme arbiter of social life and death, and more widely of their security and insecurity. Although they might deny that this is so, the loss of nothing else, save a parent or spouse or child, will leave them as bereft. Everywhere we look, people fall in love on account of wealth or position or power and find themselves falling out of love when it disappears. Even for the medieval troubadour, one of the great sources of modern romantic love, love for a woman's virtue and refinement and taste cannot be separated from the prestige that these qualities command at court; and his devotion, as her suitor, is not merely a personal but also a political act. And yet today that brute reality seems strictly inadmissible in our courts of love.

All our great loves are sustained by this power we see in the loved one to give, and so to destroy, vitality. One we love erotically can do this, our children can, a work of art can, a homeland can, even a landscape can. As a result, to love is often to feel that we exist for the first time.

And all of these objects of love, when lost, can plunge us into a living death. The terrible vacuum into which we are thrown when the loved one withdraws or, perhaps worse, when we cease to love her is a loss of the experience of being: a loss of something akin to what Jean-Jacques Rousseau called "le sentiment de l'existence," the primitive "sentiment of being," the awareness that *I am*, on which Wordsworth also places such emphasis and that Walt Whitman declares to be the "hardest basic fact and *only* entrance to all facts."[1]

Spinoza is sensitive to this reality of love when, speaking of the passive affects, he says that we love others whom we experience as empowering us and we hate them if we experience them as disempowering. But he conceives of power's relation to love in too general a way; for we do not love others on account of any form of power that they bestow. We love them, specifically, for bestowing on us those sources of existential security that we most crave, most painfully lack, and otherwise most stubbornly fail to attain.

———

By contrast, anyone who lacks the power to imbue us with such a feeling of our own existence will be unable to inspire our love. Worse: if they evince vulnerabilities that we experience as contagiously weakening our feeling of existing, or threatening those sources of security that we most crave and lack—or if they otherwise seem to sabotage the four conditions of ontological rootedness—we might actually be repelled by them.

Indeed, we will be especially repelled if we also love them—in other words, if, under a different aspect of their person, they also offer us a promise of home: a conflict of emotions that is quite possible given the opposing feelings that can coexist in a single heart at the same time. Moreover, insofar as they undermine us ontologically, we will refuse even the pleasure of being seen and understood by them, and will never feel at ease in their company; yet insofar as they can also ground us ontologically, we will love and desire them, and yearn to be recognized by them. (Were we not to love them at all, we might find it easier to straightforwardly respect, and be respected by, them.)

The inconsistency at play here is not between love and hate. Rather it is between love and what is love's true opposite: not indifference, let alone hate, but rather disgust.

Love can give rise to hate, but not to disgust. Hatred can still crave the other person, but disgust cannot. Indeed, hatred, along with its associated violence, can be the product of craving them. As Freud, Winnicott, and many others have pointed out, hate is latent within all love to the extent that the possibility of loss, absence, or unreliability of the loved one is intrinsic to love; so that the greater our love for another, the greater can be the potential to hate them. Whereas disgust experiences the other in exactly the opposite way to love: namely, as dissolving the possibility of ontological rootedness.

And so, far from offering a lineage or ethical home that we yearn to inhabit, such a person seems to endanger the integrity of what already grounds us, threatening to corrupt it and to make it amorphous, unclean, unmoored, fragile. Far from being a source of existential power over us, they are a source of existential fragility. Far from promising us a home in the world, they threaten to degrade any possible home in the world. They invade our life, so we feel, with an alien sensibility and way of being that can violently disorient us and from which our taste recoils. There is nothing they can do to make themselves harmless to us—least of all by loving us, or accommodating themselves to us: for the closer they approach us the more we will viscerally turn away.

These are terrible feelings, and they often add up to a powerful indictment of the cramped, crabbed, fearful spirit of the one experiencing them. But they show how disgust is the antithesis of love, refusing not just intimacy with the other but also all desire and receptivity, and all listening and patience (which is why it is so unrelentingly stubborn). As I suggested in *Love: A History*,[2] disgust is an "ontological fight-and-flight reaction" that escapes—and if it can't escape, purges—all vivid awareness of the other, until they exist for us "neither as subject nor even as object, but only as a shudder banished to the past."

Which is all the worse when, on account of their other qualities, we also love that same person.

Love and the Call to Existence

Finally, the gaze sees the loved one as calling us to our individual "I am": to our unlived destiny, to become genuinely who we are. They call us not necessarily through anything they say or do, or even knowingly, but just through who they are for us: through our identification with their lineage and taste, with the ethical home we glimpse in them, with their power over our sense of existing—and through the authority over us that such identification bestows on them.

This "I am" is necessarily an "I will be." The loved one's call is always to a life, a responsibility that we are not yet living—though the desire for it might lie powerfully latent within us: parenthood, vocation, new ends and values, devotion to a god. Like Heidegger's call of conscience, or the call to be reborn experienced by many a religious convert, the call that we hear from our loved one "is precisely something which we ourselves have neither planned nor prepared for nor voluntarily performed." Indeed, we can be called "against our expectations and even against our will."[1]

But their call doesn't show or tell us who precisely we should become, or how we are to become it. Rather they—in their very presence to us—open up a space in which we can discover for ourselves the precise contours of who we are; a space in which, moreover, dialogical relationship with them enables us to excavate and create and guide and refine our ends and motivations.

To respond to this call is more than to live out our preexisting potential, with its already established taste and ideals. It is also to live the lineage and the ethical ends that we identify in our loved one; to be revitalized by their existential power over us; and to this extent to become not only who we are, but also who they are.

As a result, to love is also more than for an "I" to relate to a "You" in a manner of ultimate respect and responsibility for their "Otherness," magnificent though that is. If a loving relationship were just that, if lovers were to experience one another as ultimately unreachable in the fortresses of their Otherness, no genuine We would be possible: a We in which we become who we each are, creating two different collective identities through seeing in the other a lineage and an ethical home that we crave to inhabit and to make our own.

Nor, at the other extreme, is to love to merge into a single unity, as the cliché of love's union has it, from the myth of Aristophanes in Plato's *Symposium* to Gottfried von Strassburg's *Tristan und Isot*, written in the early thirteenth century, where, in their indissoluble union, Isot becomes Tristan and Tristan becomes Isot as their names and persons are mingled and their separate identities disappear;[2] from Rousseau's *Julie, ou La Nouvelle Héloïse*, where "*you* and *I* are words banished from [lovers'] language: there are no longer two, they are one,"[3] to Catherine in *Wuthering Heights*, who proclaims, "I *am* Heathcliff—he's always, always in my mind . . . as my own being."

Rather, to love is for each of us to become *two* people, two selves—not interchangeable, like the names of Tristan and Isot, but two utterly different composites of each other.

And because lovers become composites of each other, rather than a single fused existence, the identity that each of us discovers through love is always an identity enriched by the lineage, ethical home, and existential power of the other, which, when lived in by us, takes us to a very different life to the one we have led up to now.

As a result of becoming these two distinct composites, we become more mysterious to each other through love—at the same time as love's clarity of vision *also* reveals each of us to the other with unsurpassed immediacy. (As Gottfried von Strassburg writes: "Love *should* be of crystal—transparent and translucent!"[4])

In addition, in fostering this newly enriched identity, love makes us more mysterious to *ourselves* as lovers—again, at the same time as it thrusts into view needs, powers, and limitations that we hadn't known ourselves to have. "Is this really me?" is the silent question that sooner or later confronts almost every lover, precisely when her love is genuine, precisely when the loved one comes to inhabit her and she him.

The home that is promised in love is, therefore, not one of mere domesticity: a protective stronghold aimed at securing the *status quo* and enabling seclusion or escape from the world. It does not picture the loved one as offering mute support and safety, or passive comfort and mirroring. It is not a place of stasis where lovers can readily become a union of merged selves—thus forging one where there were two, the same where there was difference.

Rather, on my conception of love, home is an evolving psychic space in relation to which the trajectory of a lover's life—its law, its language, its selfhood, its cluster of ends, its symbolic structure—is forged, often disruptively. Home is *the* place where, in and through relationship with another, the world, as a horizon of unfolding possibilities for our particular life, opens to us; where we are challenged to become ethically who we are; where our life gradually acquires a new orientation, experienced as a being-toward-home (exemplified, as we will see, by Odysseus's homecoming—his "*nostos*"—and by Abraham's call to Canaan); where we encounter—are confronted by—fresh sources of vitality as well as decisive power to deepen our sense of existing; where, in short, we hear the call to our destiny, or, differently experienced, to our birth, and are challenged to new ways of self-understanding and self-expression.

On this picture, home—being at home—is no fixed terminus, let alone one that can be specified in advance, but is a place that is progressively revealed; an opening for groundedness in the world that, like Moses on the way to the Promised Land (which he glimpses only just before he dies and never actually reaches), we might spend our whole life searching for and attempting to inhabit; a destiny that, instead of being securely attained once and for all, is, like Canaan for the Israelites and Ithaca for Odysseus, to be earned anew, perhaps repeatedly.

In short, this understanding of home is radically opposed to the conventional idea of a domestic cocoon that shuts out the world—a cocoon of stability, to be left as soon as one embarks on adulthood. Instead it sees home as a potentially unsettling realm, embodied or pointed to by the loved one, where the lover is called to their destiny; a realm that structures the trajectory of a whole life, including its evolving ends (which in modernity would include the achievement of autonomous subjectivity); a realm not to be abandoned but to be discovered. And it goes together with conceiving relationships of love in terms of *inhabiting* rather than, more traditionally, in terms of possessing—an inhabiting that does not assume sovereignty over the home, just as Abraham's descendants do not own the land to which they have been called by God but must continually strive for a future within it. Moreover, such a home, and the horizon of possibilities for our life that it opens up, is promised by *all* those we love and in all expressions of love: for romantic partners, for siblings, for friends, for God. And its embodiment by our loved ones is entirely consistent with their seeking prominence and ultimate satisfactions in the public sphere.[5]

Yet to be thus displaced to a new life—to be uprooted from our accustomed identities and habitats in order to attain love's promise of home—can make the call as frightening to heed as it is thrilling to hear. So that we often demand from love exactly the opposite of what it naturally offers: we demand that, far from upending the *status quo*, the loved one protect and entrench and celebrate precisely who we now are; even that they offer us a way back to being a happy child who doesn't need to secure their own grounding in the world. We see one whom we genuinely love, but we say to ourselves in advance, "this is not going to work" precisely because we refuse to be called to anything that we do not already want to be or do—so destining our love to be stillborn.

To feel called in this way by one we love is not, however, an onerous duty but the greatest of all privileges. For we go out into the world inspired by what the other's very existence gives us: vitality; the gift of new life.

12 }

Relationship

The tremendous expansion of the borders of our life that the loved one inspires; the multiplication of the possibilities of our being to which they draw us; the sense of being powerfully grounded in, indeed a hostage to, their promise of rootedness and yet, or rather as a result, dizzyingly free—all this evokes that ecstasy of existing typical of love. Ecstasy that, as so many poets and thinkers have remarked, will cause the lover extravagantly to idealize the loved one, seeing in them goodness and beauty that might be invisible to anyone else.

Love is literally an ec-stasy, from the Greek word "*ekstasis*" (ἔκστᾰσις): "a being put out of its place."[1] For when we love, we experience ourselves as displaced from our customary life: as standing outside or beyond the place where history and habit have so far tethered us—though in fact we are, of course, always an incarnation of our individual history; and we feel the promise of coming-to-be-rooted-in, or the hope of being oriented toward, a new world, much more authentically ours, in which our life feels indestructibly real, our belonging inviolable, and our existence luminous, undeniable, dense. It is a promise that gives rise to the greatest gratitude of which we are capable: our gratitude to our loved ones for the fact that, through them, our existence acquires this tremendous facticity.

But if the promise of home that we glimpse in the loved one is to be richly developed, this ecstasy that they inspire in us must animate relationship—whether or not it is reciprocated, and so *even if it is a one-way relationship*. (In case we are inclined to dismiss the idea of a one-way relationship as absurd, we should recall the intense relationship we can have to our ancestors, even those we have never met, or to fictional figures, or to works of art and landscapes and other objects of love that cannot reciprocate.) And it is worth saying, even if obvious, that though we can love in a second, "at first sight," on glimpsing a promise of home, love—like any virtue—will not develop unless it is cultivated, cared for, practiced, learned.

To be in "relationship" to, or with, another is, of course, no mere stance but centrally involves action: the ongoing goodwill and benevolence, the practical concern for the other's needs and flourishing, the recognition and fostering of their ends and values and achievements, the self-giving grounded in a pure will—about all of which, in their diverse ways, philosophers of love from Aristotle to Kant to Kierkegaard to Frankfurt speak. And all mutual relationship of love, all home that is jointly constructed, is marked by the intertwining of two lives: the activities undertaken together, on which Aristotle places such emphasis; the shared memories that are formed and lived as a result; the profound commitment to the other's future, which has now become a joint future; and the hope of being born together.

For loved ones who are dead, or have disappeared, or do not requite our love, we are no less focused on the intimate texture of their lives, though that focus must feed largely on conjecture, imagination, hope, and memory. We feel ourselves to be in unceasing dialogue with their sensibility and ends and experiences and joys and sadnesses. We wait for them, as we do for one who is present, hoping that they will still reveal themselves to us, questioning them, yearning for our life to become ever more enmeshed with their own, as it lives on in us—indeed even if, like with a long-departed ancestor, we know little or nothing about them. Just as, in one of the greatest of all loves, Dante waits and yearns for Beatrice, who is deceased and in Heaven, as the crucial condition of his salvation and as the guide to his love's ultimate end: attaining the divine presence.

———

For any of these virtues of devotion to be truly loving, however, they must be animated by love's *primary* virtue: attentiveness. Attentiveness is a resolute and unequivocating openness to the loved one that leads to us becoming a "We" in addition to being an "I" and a "You"—a "We" that doesn't just have a panoply of feelings and activities in common, but becomes itself a grounding for each of us as individuals.

Such attentiveness to the other is the quintessence of humility in its capacity to wait and listen, in its passionate submission to what is knowable and also to what is mysterious in the loved one, in its suspension, its forgetting, its unawareness, of all self-interest, as well as in its resolute preparedness for them to leave us if that is what they wish to do. (For only if we are willing to lose loved ones are we ready to come close to them. Only if we are prepared to let them go has our love truly matured.)

In particular, attentiveness is a focus of our whole will on what we might call the "law of the loved one's being": the law to which we must become attuned, to the point where it saturates and structures our own being as lover, if they are to root us in the world; the law to which we must be uncompromisingly responsive and responsible if love's rapture or joy is to become embedded in relationship. (This is the law, I suggest, that divine commands are most fundamentally concerned with. For such commands are, ultimately, signposts to God as loved one, beacons of divine presence that enable human love for

God to progress from initial rapture to ongoing relationship. Their role is not merely to impose a morality on human beings, to test human obedience, and to forge community. Indeed, these last three functions of divine command draw their full meaning only from the prior attentiveness to God that law—the very form of law, regardless of its specific content—makes possible.[2])

By the "law of the loved one's being" I mean that very particular world of lineage, ethics, and power embodied by them: that cluster of principles, or ordering of the soul, whether harmonious or not, expressed in the elusive quality we call "taste," which most authentically governs and speaks of their life—including how things show up and make sense for them—and to which their lover must be receptive with all his or her being, hard though it is to comprehend that law or taste even very partially. For attunement of taste between lover and loved one—alignment of the intrinsic laws of their beings, over which neither of them has any control—is the indispensable animating heart of all flourishing relationships. Between them everything else can be different, but on the fundamentals of taste they must be at one. Love is, therefore, not only compatible with law in this intrinsic sense; it is centrally a *search* for law.

By contrast, what one might call the "extrinsic" relation between love and law—in other words, the law by which a society guarantees the right and freedom of lovers to choose whom they will—is less fundamental to love's flourishing than such an intrinsic relation. Extrinsic laws, which protect our freedom to choose our loved ones regardless of who they are—laws as "fall-backs to underpin social relations that are constituted on other terms," as Jeremy Waldron puts it;[3] laws that would have underpinned the love between Romeo and Juliet—are only necessary to the development of love and its relationships insofar as the world (family, community, religion) opposes the lovers' choices. Moreover, it isn't clear that a guarantee of love's rights and freedoms to transgress established social boundaries and their norms is "a *condition* of being able to identify intensely with one's attachments," as Waldron suggests it is.[4] For, as poets down the ages have insisted, the relation between love, or at least romantic love, and freedom is often exactly the reverse: attempts to *deprive* lovers of rights and freedoms to choose their loved ones, obstructions thrown in the way of love's consummation, are what intensify lovers' identification with their attachments. "The last and best Cure of Love-Melancholy," says The Reverend Robert Burton in his classic book *The Anatomy of Melancholy*, published in 1621, is "to let them [lovers] have their Desire."[5] Indeed, impediments arguably cause not just love but all human desire to burn brighter. (Denis de Rougemont, in his fascinating analysis of the Tristan myth, goes further, suggesting not only that obstruction intensifies love but, I think, tendentiously, that obstruction is "what passion really *wants*—its true object" . . . "the goal and end wished for *for its own sake*."[6])

The freedoms underpinned by extrinsic law aren't, therefore, as central to love's development from initial rapture to ongoing relationship as is attunement to the intrinsic law of the loved one. For even if lovers are free from all external impediments to their love, the need to discern, grasp, and scrupulously align themselves with the intrinsic law of the other—the world of lineage, ethics, and power of their loved one; that cluster of principles definitive of his or her taste—remains absolute. Only through such attunement can a lover become intertwined with the reality of the other's life. And only then can he or she hear who their loved one, perhaps unawarely, is calling on them to become.

This is true not only for relationships with the living, but also, as I just suggested, for that ancient and noble love for the dead; for ancestors; for those on whose shoulders we stand, whose question marks are built into us, whose lives and ends we feel compelled to interrogate, critically as well as reverentially, whose destinies—explored and unexplored—it falls on us to continue living out, and whose experiences might bear fruit only in our own lifetimes. Though they are dead, we feel that our life is in dialogue with theirs at every important moment; indeed, that we love *each other*—as, in a poem by Fernando Pessoa, the speaker-poet loves his great predecessor Walt Whitman:

> I am with you, as you well know, and understand you and love you,
> And though I never met you, born in the same year you died,
> I know you loved me too, you knew me.[7]

And as the Book of Job exhorts:

> inquire now of bygone generations,
> and consider what *their* ancestors have found;
> for we are but of yesterday, and we know nothing,
> for our days on earth are but a shadow.
> Will they not teach you and tell you
> and utter words out of their understanding?[8]

Again, however, we should not lose sight of love's specificity. Attentiveness—or the attentive gaze—is not the *same* as love, as Iris Murdoch and Simone Weil hold it to be. Love is joy at glimpsing a promise of ontological rootedness; whereas attentiveness is the supreme virtue that the lover must perfect if she is to seize this promise—if she is to be able to inhabit the new home to which the loved one points. Ontological rootedness, or its promise, is the goal and ground of love; attentiveness is the means to that goal, the virtue without which love cannot mature from initial rapture to ongoing relationship. Attentiveness can be commanded and cultivated; love cannot.

By the same token we mustn't conflate love and mutual relationship. Love can exist without triggering a mutual relationship; and a mutual, indeed deep, relationship can exist without triggering, or being animated by, love. We can love people (or things) in a passionate if truncated way without entering into a relationship with them—be it a healthy relationship of benevolence, devotion, joint feelings and activities, and respect for their knowable and unknowable otherness; or an unhealthy one of crude possessiveness, wanton destructiveness, lazy inattentiveness, and cold exploitation, pervaded by the will *not* to see the other—a will readily fostered by the fear that, as we will see, is constitutive of all love.

Though love is sometimes equated or reduced to a mutual relationship in which two lives are shared and intertwined—whether conceived as an "I" to a "Thou," where love is seen as a reciprocal and equal "responsibility of an I for a You [Thou]" (Martin Buber[9]); as a "common venture" embracing joint feelings and actions and other "emotional and practical sharing," which can in turn be understood only as contributions to ends or principles that are shared (Angelika Krebs[10]); as an "ongoing history" of two people (Niko Kolodny[11]); or in other "dialogical" ways—this is inadequate as an understanding of love because, unlike Aristotle, who also sees joint feeling and action and mutual responsibility as central to love in the sense of perfect *philia*, these models do not explain the specificity of love in precisely the sense that I outlined in Part I. Though, like Buber and Krebs, they can beautifully describe certain elements of a relationship of love *once* it has got going, in particular its between-ness—the sense in which both lovers dwell in the We—they do not tell us what grounds and inspires it, and so why we seek such a relationship with some and not with others. (Buber, for example, resorts to the miraculous to explain selective love: "exclusiveness comes into being miraculously again and again," he says[12]—an explanation similar to the invocation of "something that is more mysterious than describability" by a secular philosopher like Frankfurt.)

Nor do they offer a picture—a phenomenological picture—of how such sharing, between-ness, intimacy, and ongoing history between two people is *experienced* when it is loving and when, by contrast, it is motivated by duty or virtue alone; or by a biologically determined disposition to altruism and community; or by professional or vocational bonds; or, on occasion, by bonds of masters and servants, such as between a political leader and his closest advisers.

Mourners at a funeral, for example, even if they know nothing of each other, can constitute a powerful We in sharing their grief, in comforting one another, in keeping alive rich memories of the deceased—from which intense and life-long attachments might develop. Any great shared experience—of joy, of success, and especially of tragedy—can bring strangers together into a We, which, for all its power, isn't necessarily a We of love. Hurricanes, tsunamis, and airplane crashes can forge a solidarity among their survivors that has much of the sense of uniquely defined We-ness and many of the other-regarding elements of the relationship fostered by love.

But a "We"—however extensive its joint activities and feelings, or its mutual benevolence; however many are the common ends and values that it embraces; however rich is the shared world that it encompasses, or the dialogue that characterizes it—is, I am proposing, a "We" of *love* only if it is inspired by and oriented toward a promise of ontological rootedness offered by the participants to each other.

13 }

Fear: The Price of Love

Love and life together first take something away from a person before
they give.

—SØREN KIERKEGAARD[1]

We can quickly see why love is simultaneously consoling and alarming; why,
however joyful, it is never far from fear, even despair—and therefore from
hate. For to respond to a promise of true home in a loved one is also to be
uprooted from where we are now—and from how we are now. The very same
vision of being rooted in a world of new possibilities renders banal the habitual ground of our life, which no longer compels us. We are thrust toward
unknown territories or unknown ways of relating to familiar territories, inspired by a loved one whom knowledge makes ever more mysterious—who
becomes more unfamiliar the more we come to know her. We lose the present
with no guarantee of securing the future.

In *Love: A History* I introduced the idea, which now needs to be developed,
that fear is not an occasional or contingent accompaniment to love, but rather
belongs to its very nature.[2] In the child this is principally because of the terror
of losing the vital caregiver and perhaps, too, because he or she gradually
comes to feel how ungraspable that caregiver is: how there is no point at which
a loved one is securely possessed. But in the adult love necessarily incubates
fear not only because we dread the loved one's absence and inscrutability; not
only because the possibility of loss is intrinsic to anything we deeply desire;
not only because in reality love has no final terminus where it attains "completion," such as the perfect union of romantic dreams—and so, to that extent, the
beloved is always "lost in advance," as Rilke puts it, and even experienced as
"never-arrived";[3] but also, and far more so, because we fear their *presence* and
what it calls on us to become.

This is a presence that, whether our loved one is aware of it or not, forces
light into our soul with all its locked doors, and displaces us to a new world
where we are called to our "I am" or "I will be"; to creatively discover and
risk ourselves, regardless of the costs to our comfort. A world where love
compels us to abandon the homely in search of home. Yet only in the mode of

terror—only in the extreme alertness nurtured by terror—can we begin to see the full ontological possibilities opened up by love.

For genuinely to inhabit the new home promised by love is to see it as far more than a refuge. It is also to be struck by a piercingly fresh awareness of our existence, an existence thrilling in its power and frightening in its as yet unlived possibilities. Frightening, too, in the spotlight it throws on our inner void of nonbeing: on the life within us that is dying and lying and unrelated to anything beyond it, and that doesn't know or doesn't care that it is; a void of nonbeing with which we have so far lived more or less comfortably.

Frightening *and* thrilling: unlike the more primitive fear of losing the loved one, which triggers the equally primitive emotion of possessiveness, the terror of being called in love to new homes, and so of being uprooted from old ones, is accompanied by hope and so by bliss.

We are speaking here of a terror close to awe: the exhilarating combination of euphoria, anticipation, wonder, and fear that we feel in the presence of tremendous power when we are able to contemplate it from a position of safety, rather than when it is about to destroy us. This is a feeling akin to that described by Kant in his evocation of the "sublime," which arises from our superiority, as rational beings, to nature's grandiose might,[4] despite the failure of our imagination to comprehend its absolute greatness—the greatness, to cite Kant's own examples, of "threatening rocks, thunderclouds piled up [in] the vault of heaven, borne along with flashes and peals, volcanoes in all their violence of destruction, hurricanes leaving desolation in their track, the boundless ocean rising with rebellious force."[5] Such moments of the sublime, says Kant's near-predecessor, Edmund Burke, writing in 1757, arouse "the strongest emotion which the mind is capable of feeling."[6]

The point about such awe or fearfulness is not that it is *merely* overwhelming. A murderer approaching you in an alleyway with a gleaming knife doesn't evoke awe of this kind; a tsunami from which you cannot escape, or the "boundless ocean" in which you are stranded without help, doesn't either. It is that to be confronted by such unmasterable immensity from a position where safety is possible, if not certain, fills you with an ecstatic sense of your own vitality and reality, precisely by diminishing you to the irreducible core of life and existence that you are, when all your own ambitions, social roles, and even ethical ends become irrelevant in the face of the other's indomitable independence of us. In spotlighting our puny limitations, the awesome also throws into relief our power to perceive, think, imagine, and endure. Thus in being humbled we also feel exalted.

Awe, in other words, isn't just about being dwarfed by invincible, unimaginable power; it is also about feeling rejuvenated by a privileged relationship to it. It is about the intoxication of being witness to power that could, but doesn't, destroy us; indeed, that even saves us as it overwhelms us. In awe, terror, wonder, and bliss become one.

Love therefore forces on us the uncanny feeling both of existing more intensely and alertly than ever and also of being more confronted than ever by the nonexistence or unreality at our core—nonexistence whose horizon, as we will note in Chapter 23, is death. The feeling is uncanny because existence and nonexistence seem in such close dialogue; because, as rapture fosters relationship, each throws the other into ever-sharper relief—and so, as we experience it more immediately, into ever-greater mystery. As in the feeling of awe, our relation to a loved one both empowers us by intensifying our sense of existence and also humbles us by bringing to light our ontological smallness. We are humbled because we are empowered. (Just as freshly elected leaders so often speak of being humbled by contemplation of their new power.)

Yet the loved one cannot rescue us from this inner torment of nonexistence that they inspire. They cannot fill the void to which their presence draws our attention; they cannot heal the self into which they cast such generous and cruel light. And they must under no circumstances be asked to do so, or we risk eviscerating their ontological power over us—and so eviscerating our love itself.

What they can do is to be there as an orienting pole star that guides us to become who we genuinely are—provided we submit to the intrinsic law of their being, just as, at the limit, a hostage submits to his or her captor, internalizing the captor's law to the point where it becomes the hostage's own; provided we accept that we can belong to ourselves only in belonging to the loved one.

And so the greater our love, the more powerfully our loved one will evoke ambivalence. Since their very presence both promises us rootedness in a home that is authentically ours *and* in doing so tears us from our existing habitat and habits, we easily experience them, simultaneously, as our only possibility of home and as deeply alien; as creating a new world for us and as destroying who and where we have so far been.

Destructiveness

Fear would be at the heart of love even if relationships were entirely free of destructiveness. For none of the lover's four intrinsic fears—of losing the loved one, of never truly winning them in the first place, of their calling us to our destiny, and of being uprooted from our habitual life—is necessarily of destruction or is necessarily destructive. Whereas fear is constitutive of love, destructiveness isn't.

Nonetheless, in love, destructiveness is seldom far away. Not only in romantic-erotic love, which by no means has a monopoly on hurt, jealousy, and the will to destroy, but also, and perhaps above all, in the various bonds of family love: parental, filial, sibling. Why else are so many tragedies—Greek, biblical, and modern—about families and the murderous impulses they can incubate: from Euripides's *Medea* to Shakespeare's *King Lear*; from Sophocles's *Antigone* to Pinter's *The Homecoming*; from the Bible's Cain and Abel to Lorca's *The House of Bernarda Alba*? For families can be closed societies, pervaded by the unsaid, whose members love each other to vastly different degrees, are irreplaceable sources of recognition and groundedness for each other, and so become lifelong hostages to the often-perilous hope of being seen and understood by each other.

Love's destructiveness has many causes: the lover's impatience for the fruits of love, including union with the loved one insofar as that is always an aim of love; the lover's jealousy of any life and talents of the loved one that he cannot master and if possible exceed; his fury at her other loyalties, real or perceived; his frustration when she turns out not to be the person who he thought she was and who he imagines he *really* loves; his pride, fearful and haughty, that refuses to countenance any possibility of her absence, however fleeting or partial, and so tries to preempt it with futile and often brutal possessiveness; his vanity that demands her perfection and sees her flaws as making her unworthy of his love and, worse, as threatening his understanding and so his control of her; his anger (sometimes justified but often stoked by nothing more than love's four intrinsic fears) at her alleged mistreatment of him: her betrayals, indifference, coldness, and unscrupulous use of him to support her emotional needs, career, social advancement, and material comfort.

And finally there is that most distasteful emotion, resentment, which can be fed by all these other sources of destructiveness and which ends up stifling our love in airless confinement, where it cannot enjoy, forgive, or even address the loved one. Resentment bars love from all development, condemns it to remain eternally unlived, isolates the lover, and casts the loved one into a purgatory of repudiation or accusation, from which she could be liberated only by being someone whom she is not. (Someone whose qualities the resentful lover probably couldn't even define.)

The idea, so prominently articulated by Plato, that love, if genuine, will necessarily foster "true goodness" or virtue[1] and in particular justice and wisdom—that to love is to love beauty, and to love beauty is not only to desire what is good but also to be *made virtuous* by doing so—does not survive the briefest contact with reality. We do not need to invoke the famous instances of concentration camp guards who are loving fathers or moved to tears by the beauty of music to see that there is no way in which love—whether it is taken to be grounded in beauty or not—entails a commitment to a benevolent morality or can be assumed to cultivate a fine moral character.

Nor is love necessarily killed by being on the receiving end of such destructiveness. Perhaps it is almost never killed by such means. For as long as the lover sees in the loved one a promise of ontological rootedness love cannot die, no matter how loathsome, indifferent, treacherous, ugly, or evil he finds her.

Nonetheless, any of these types of destructiveness can slowly kill the loved one. And of all of them the most terrible is jealousy—jealousy not only of rivals, or imagined rivals, but, still worse, of precisely the loved one herself, who, the lover demands (usually implicitly), must never equal, let alone excel, him in vitality and ability and achievement, or in anything else to which he aspires.

Such jealousy of the loved one, which needs no thought of a third party to inflame it, can infect *any* relationship of love between two people. Though the power of jealousy to decimate the lover's world, his bond with the loved one, and ultimately the loved one herself, is most conspicuous and—ever since Homer, Lucretius, Ovid, and other classical authors—best documented in relation to romantic-erotic love, perhaps because it is regarded there as most acceptable and, on occasion, even as called for, it can be equally intense, if more subterranean, in friendship love, parental love, filial love, and, perhaps above all, sibling love. In all cases, it begins as the lover's narcissism: as his inability or refusal to imagine someone different from himself, which turns to fury when he realizes that the loved one *is* different—and perhaps unknowably, triumphantly so.

This jealous fury quickly intensifies as it increasingly dawns on the lover not only how great is his need for the loved one but also how elusive she is, especially if he has given up on the illusion that people possess a fixed essence or core that can be "grasped," and realizes instead that they have a fluid nature, without fixed or even definable dimensions, which cannot be possessed. What if, in Proust's wonderful image, he comes to think of his loved one as a being "scattered in space and time, . . . a series of events on which we can throw no light, a series of insoluble problems, a sea which, like Xerxes, we scourge with rods in an absurd attempt to punish it for what it has engulfed"?[2] How can a flux of events scattered in space and time be possessed at all, let alone stably?

And beyond this, in the extreme case of jealousy, which is more common than we might imagine, the lover finds the very existence of the loved one a mortal threat to his own. He feels most endangered by the person he most needs, no matter how benevolent and indeed faithful she is to him. Indeed he is angered by her kindnesses, which he experiences as mockery, or as threatening expressions of her independence, or even as cunning distractions from the existential threat she poses.

And so he searches for ways to undermine her vitality and legitimacy, meticulously denying all praise even for what he admires and extinguishing any joy he takes in her with all the antipathy he can summon. And if he can't undermine her existence by boycotting her and everything she most cares about—by seeking to starve her out of her own life by refusing to recognize or trust it—he will attack it directly by condemning her ends and values and projects and motives as frauds, failures, and ethically suspect, so assaulting the foundations of her life one by one until none retains legitimacy in her eyes; until, with a thousand humiliations and accusations, few of them too trivial to become obsessive, he succeeds in destroying her spirit.

Ultimately, this jealousy isn't so different in kind from Othello's—though unlike Othello this lover doesn't need any suspicion of infidelity to arouse his jealousy to the point where he seeks to destroy not only the bond but also the loved one. For what starts as narcissism ends in the will to murder. And what fuels the lover's jealousy is, in part, the loved one's mere *possibilities* of belonging to a world beyond the lover, and so of being unavailable, even if only potentially, to ground his life—jealousy that is likely to be as intense as the void that the lover feels within himself. (An inner void palpable in Othello, for all his braggadocio.) "Wrath is cruel, anger is overwhelming," says the Book of Proverbs, "but who is able to stand before jealousy?"[3]

Such a lover therefore traps himself in an excruciating dilemma where the loved one's existence, which he craves in order to feel grounded, seems to threaten his own existence, and so feeds his destructive hostility toward her— hostility that, even when it provokes the complete breakdown of the loved one's life, is insatiable. It is a dilemma between affirming and denying his loved one's being from which the lover's jealousy permits no escape. He annihilates her reality in his own mind; yet he has then caused himself to lose the very person that he most needs, so casting himself into "that desert of loneliness and recrimination that men call love" of which Samuel Beckett speaks.[4] Though he sees a promise of ontological rootedness in the loved one, he strives unceasingly to vitiate this vision by construing her as the precise opposite: as an ontological thief,[5] as someone who steals from him the world and his relation to it.

But to see another as an ontological thief—as leaving us without our world; as undermining any possibility of groundedness in it—is, I suggested in Chapter 10, central to the emotion of disgust. For this is what extreme jealousy does: it brings love and disgust—which are each other's true opposites—into the closest proximity, so that we experience the very same person both as promising to ground us in that world we most value and as threatening to expel us from it.

Why Love Isn't the Same as Benevolence

So is it "pathological" to love one who tries to destroy us?

I do not think it necessarily is. Our need to be grounded in a world that we supremely value is so great that if we glimpse a sufficiently powerful promise of such grounding in another—be they a romantic partner, a child, a parent, God—we might love them and crave them regardless of how they behave toward us. The promise they embody, and the grounding they inspire, will then evoke joy at the same time as their cruelty or betrayal brings misery. If so, we will love them whether or not they reject us. We might love them even if we recognize that relationship with them is impossible, or intolerably destructive—even if we discover that they are a mass murderer. Just as the mother of Charlie Roberts, the man who shot ten children in cold blood in 2006, says that she loves her son no less after his crimes; or as the mother of Dylan Klebold, one of the two killers at Columbine High School, insists that her love for him "has been the single greatest joy of my life."[1]

Such tolerance of destructiveness does not, however, prove that love is unconditional. All it shows is that love isn't conditional on the loved one's benevolence—nor even on forgiving or understanding their iniquity. Equally, to claim that love for those who are cruel to us is a masochistic perversion, or isn't love at all, is to make the category error of seeing love as intrinsically inspired by or searching for benevolence—an error that gives rise to tremendous confusion about when we love and are loved.

If love's real ground is the promise of home, it will be aroused by benevolence only to the extent that we see benevolence as indispensable to any promise of home—to the extent that, without it, or without its consistent presence, everything else that makes up a loved one's promise of home would lose its power to move us. And although love can give rise to the greatest benevolence of which humans are capable—to kindness that goes far beyond the bounds of duty or law—it does not *necessarily* give rise to any.

No matter, therefore, how kind or self-giving two people are to one another, theirs will not be a relationship of love if it isn't grounded in a mutual promise of ontological rootedness in whichever world they each supremely value. You can be devoted with all your heart and soul to another person; do everything in your power to inspire joy and peace and trust in them; evince every virtue or beauty they admire; listen, share, recognize, and empathize to a fault; but they will never love you unless they see in you a promise of groundedness for their life. Your virtues can make them like you, but they can never make them love you. Far from being unconditional, the conditions for love are terrifyingly exacting, and no one can love because they have decided to. W. H. Auden is surely right to say, "We cannot choose what we are free to love."[2]

Indeed, two people who hope or think that they are in a relationship of love but are actually in one of benevolence can come to despise each other precisely for their goodness, which strikes them as false coinage, promising love but never inspiring it. And such resentment is, in turn, a potent source of guilt; for how can we fail to love, or at least be grateful to, those rare people whose devotion to us is wholeheartedly kind? How, instead, can we resent and repudiate them?

Kierkegaard might be expressing just such a point—that love's indispensable ground is a promise of ontological rootedness in a world that we supremely value—when he says that love is genuine only if a relationship to God is its true aim. In other words, lovers always seek to achieve, for themselves and for their loved ones, a relationship to what they take to be the ultimate ground of their being, in which they might anchor themselves and each other. If this relationship to the ground of their being—which, for Kierkegaard, is God—is lacking, then their "love" is a fraud, no matter how benevolent or self-sacrificing it is:

> However beautiful a relationship of love has been between two people, or among many, however complete all their desire and all their bliss have been for themselves in mutual sacrifice and devotion, even though everyone has praised this relationship—if God and the relationship with God have been omitted, then this . . . has not been love but a mutually enchanting defraudation of love.[3]

And, as if to leave no doubt that the supreme aim of all genuine love is God, whom Kierkegaard calls the "middle term" or "third party" in love between people, he reformulates this same point as follows:

> The God-relationship is the mark by which the love for people is recognized as genuine. As soon as a love relationship does not lead me to God, and as soon as I in the love-relationship do not lead the other to God, then the love, even if it were the highest bliss and delight of affection, even if it were the supreme good of the lovers' earthly life, is still not true love.[4]

In short, love isn't merely another word for benevolence—or the search for benevolence. And the mistaken belief that it is underlies not only the incoherence into which Christian concepts like *caritas* and *agape* have been mangled, especially by post-Reformation theology such as that of Anders Nygren, but also by such clearly secular adaptations of *agape* as Harry Frankfurt's, which conceives love as nothing but "disinterested concern for the well-being or flourishing of the person who is loved,"[5] a concern of spontaneous or mysterious origin. For one who is benevolent might not offer us a promise of such ultimate grounding; while another who does offer us that promise might be in no way benevolent.

———

This is why we should be careful about condemning as counterfeit love for a God who reportedly ordains massacres, child sacrifice, slavery, eternal damnation, and other extreme cruelties. For if we ask, "Is it possible genuinely to love such a destructive God?" the answer, as in love for destructive or vengeful human beings, is "Of course it is!" If we love God we do so, most fundamentally, because we believe God grounds our life in precisely the four senses I mentioned earlier: as the origin of our being; as the ultimate source of an ethical home in the form of divine self-revelation in general and divine law in particular (even if God occasionally flouts his or her own norms); as the supreme power over our sense of existing; and of course as the one who calls us to our destiny. It is dire need for these goods that inspires love for God, not God's generosity, kindness, and protection, in and of themselves—all of which evoke gratitude and joy, but not necessarily love.[6]

Indeed the gods of Homeric Greece can *also* protect mortals, shower men and women with gifts and concern, and, on occasion, exhibit loving-kindness—but they are not loved on this account. Odysseus, Homer tells us, is rescued from the clutches of the beautiful Calypso by the gods. He is saved from drowning by the goddess Leucothea. He is forewarned of the dangers awaiting his return to Ithaca by Athena, who intercedes with Zeus on his behalf and watches over him like a guardian angel throughout his perilous journey home. Divine intervention assures his return to Ithaca from the battlefield of Troy, just as divine intervention assures the Israelites' passage to Canaan from their enslavement in Egypt.

Yet none of these Greek gods offers mortals a promise of ontological rootedness.

The gods of Olympus are not, either individually or collectively, the ultimate source of all human life and lineage. Even Zeus, their king, only has a minor role in world creation, as the foundational text of Greek cosmology, Hesiod's *Theogony*, makes clear.

Nor do they in any sense offer an ethical home. On the contrary, as Plato himself laments, in line with a whole tradition of criticism going back to Xenophanes in the sixth century BCE, the gods of Homeric epic are utterly indifferent to ethics and devoid of ethical qualities.[7] They neither define themselves by their ethical ambitions, nor place ethics at the heart of their relationships with human beings. And even when they come to be more concerned with justice, they remain subordinate to the supreme law of Fate, rather than being its creators.

Nor, too, do any of them have anything remotely like the existential power over human lives of the monotheistic God. A Greek hero like Achilles doesn't experience the meaning, value, and depth of his existence as hostage to his relationship to the divine to anything approaching the extent that a biblical hero like Abraham does.

And so the Homeric gods fail to inspire the reverential fear or awe commanded by the God of Abraham[8]—indeed no word for "god-fearing" ever appears in the *Iliad* or any other epic.[9] "The strongest moral force which Homeric man knows is not the fear of god, but respect for public opinion."[10]

So, too, none of them calls humans, individually or as a community, to their selfhood or destiny in the all-encompassing, eschatological manner of the biblical God. An Achilles might be a plaything of the Fates or be filled with piety toward Zeus; an Odysseus might appeal to Zeus for protection; but neither of their lives is for a moment oriented in its totality toward the divine call, or entirely structured by faith in God or obedience to divine law, as is the case for an Abraham. Rather what drives Achilles is hunger for immortal glory: to be celebrated eternally in the tales of the singers.

In short: we cannot find in the Homeric gods any of the four elements that make up a promise of ontological rootedness. There are no grounds for a Homeric hero to love the gods of Olympus with all his "heart and soul and might," never mind to find a salvific or redemptive promise in such love. And nor is there any evidence in the *Iliad* or the *Odyssey* that he does.

Aristotle was surely correct to write that it would be strange, out of place—*atopon*—to love, or to say that one loves, even Zeus, their king. In fact, the word *philotheos*, "god-loving," is not found at all in Greek texts, whether in poetry, philosophy, or plays, until the end of the fourth century BCE, when it appears, for the first time, in Aristotle—who dismisses it as impossible.[11]

Not all wholehearted devotion is, therefore, loving (one constant theme of this book; just as not all powerful benevolence or altruism is loving). Humans can be devoted to gods in fervent piety, as, Homer tells us, Odysseus is to the goddess Athena, and bound up with them in absolute trust, without love coming into it. And without the relationship being defined by ethical strivings or structured by ethical concerns. The Abrahamic religions—Judaism, Christianity, and Islam—are not the norm, but the bizarre exception, in seeing love as central to mutual relations between the human and the divine. Humans need not love gods, nor gods humans, for a religion to thrive and for its ethics, its rituals, and their inner meaning for its votaries all to find enduring foundations—though perhaps not the most enduring.

16 }

What Divine Violence Teaches Us about Love

The facts are brutal, though they are purged from the sanitized version of God, and of divine *agape*, that is the model for the dominant contemporary account of human love against which I am taking aim: God's destruction—by drowning—of his entire creation (save Noah, his family, and two of every species of animal); his intent to annihilate the cities of Sodom and Gomorrah and all their inhabitants; the killing of twenty-four thousand people in revenge for some Israelites worshipping a foreign deity called Ba'al;[1] his cursing Moses's sister Miriam with leprosy merely because she disapproves of her brother's choice of bride;[2] the massacre of the people of Jericho by the armies of the Lord;[3] not to mention the genocide of whole peoples, such as the Amalekites, who imperiled the Israelites—genocide not just condoned by God but *commanded* by him:[4]

> Now go and attack Amalek, and utterly destroy all that they have; do not spare them, but kill both man and woman, child and infant, ox and sheep, camel and donkey.[5]

When we come to the New Testament, as some of the greatest Church Fathers, such as Augustine, have taught us to understand it, we find cruelty elevated into an entirely different dimension: eternity. An eternity co-sponsored by God's enemy and rival, Satan. For here God doesn't just exact vengeance against people in this world, which is the main arena for punishment in the Old Testament and especially in the first five books of the Bible; he also damns people beyond this world. Where Adam and Eve are given only a life sentence, those unrepentants who displease God in the New Testament are doomed to "eternal punishment." On the Day of Judgment the heavenly judge will not mince his words: "You that are accursed, depart from me into the eternal fire prepared for the devil and his angels."[6] This is damnation from which, as this biblical passage makes clear, no divine forgiveness will offer rescue: there will be no redemption, no last chance, no restored relationship.

On whose authority do such figures as Augustine and Thomas Aquinas tell us about God's infliction of unending cruelty? None other than Jesus's. In the Bible it is the New Testament that speaks most vigorously of the realm of torture and destruction that the Church later calls "Hell,"[7] and it is Jesus who most vividly depicts it—warning, according to the Gospel of Matthew, that there will be damnation without hope of forgiveness: "The Son of Man will send his angels, and they will collect out of his kingdom all causes of sin and all evildoers, and they will throw them into the furnace of fire."[8] Fire that is never extinguished and that destroys absolutely; so that those thrown into it cease to be. Fire, moreover, to which it is remarkably easy to be consigned. For, as Jesus warns in the Sermon on the Mount, merely saying "You fool" to your brother or sister is enough for you to be "liable to the hell of fire."[9] That is all it takes.[10]

These Church Fathers do not, however, develop their understanding of Hell solely from out of Jesus's own words. It is Augustine who most prominently turns the life sentence of Adam and Eve into hereditary crime ("original sin"), on account of which the whole of humanity—every subsequent human being—is born guilty, without statute of limitation; and, by that token alone, is liable to eternal damnation but for the redeeming grace of God. Chillingly, it is the same Augustine, arguably Christianity's most important theologian, who decrees that God mysteriously elects some people to be saved and, in his later thought, maintains that others are chosen for damnation—including those not yet born, or who die in infancy before they have had a chance to do good or bad:

> From two little ones equally bound by original sin, why is the one adopted [for salvation] and the other left? And from two non-believers who are already adults, why is this one called so that he follows the one who calls him, but that one is either not called or not called in that way? These are God's inscrutable judgments.[11]

Thus no "merit"—no love for God or for neighbor; no good works; no obedience to divine law—can be counted on to earn salvation or to be spared the fires of everlasting torment. In this way, Augustine adds, even twins with identical merits can meet very different fates, one of them taken to paradise and the other consigned to damnation:

> [T]he outcome is different for two twins, of which the one is taken and the other left, but they have their merits in common. And yet one of them is set free by the great goodness of God, while the other is condemned with no injustice on his part.[12]

Thomas Aquinas, for his part, is blunt about God's partiality and vindictiveness—which coexist, of course, in mysterious relation to the vastness of divine forgiveness and mercy and self-giving. Again we are talking not only about temporary punishments, such as plagues and damage to crops, but the maximum possible punishment: to deprive people of eternal life with God, and so of salvation. God, he says, "does not wish every good to [all human beings equally]. In that He does not will to some the blessing of eternal life He is said to hold them in hate or to reprobate them."[13]

God's reprobation or "hate," Thomas asserts, "includes the will to permit a person to fall into fault [sin], and to inflict the penalty of damnation in consequence."[14]

To be clear about what Thomas is saying here: God is pleased to withhold the indispensable grace that gives human beings the will and the knowledge to avoid sin. And yet this same God, he tells us, will then punish such people with eternal damnation for committing sins that they could have avoided only with the help of divine intervention.

St. Paul speaks in similar terms of human beings who are destined by God for damnation:

> What if God, desiring to show his wrath and to make known his power, has endured with much patience the objects of wrath that are *made for destruction?*[15]

Paul's words remind us that divine partiality and punishment and "hate," far from being a later invention of theologians such as Thomas, go right back to the Bible itself. In both Hebrew and Christian scriptures we learn how God is prone to punish those who displease him; how he is willing to bestow blessings on some and destruction on others; how divine justice contemplates harsh trials for a virtuous few such as Job, whom God grievously afflicts merely in order to test his loyalty, while letting many evildoers go free; and, perhaps above all, how a profound favoritism permeates the way God is said to love humans in both the Old and the New Testaments ("I have loved Jacob, but I have hated Esau," cited by St. Paul,[16] while in the parable of the wedding banquet Jesus says that "many are called, but few are chosen";[17] and there is his one "beloved disciple," spoken of in the Gospel of John[18]).

All this being the case, God's own love—contrary to the "sanitized" conception of it—cannot be assumed to be unconditional or equal. Nor is it necessarily enduring for all if some are consigned to eternal damnation on account of their misdemeanors. Nor, too, can it be, in its very nature, disinterested if human goodness and sin can determine whether people are saved or not. And nor, for these same reasons, can it be all-affirming of loved ones, regardless of who they are or what they do.[19]

Here in scripture—in the unsanitized version of how God is said to love; and in the human willingness to love such a God with *all* one's heart and soul and might—we see as true a picture of the nature of love, of its brute reality, as is to be found in any philosophy, literature, or mythology. A picture that, precisely because it describes the truth about love's capacity to tolerate violence and favoritism at the hands of the loved one, need not and must not be whitewashed either by reinterpreting its offending narratives as allegories or parables that shouldn't be taken literally; or by claiming that they (unlike more acceptable passages) fail to report accurately the word of God, who didn't in fact issue the violent commands attributed to him; or by excusing their savagery as merely an outmoded way of speaking to people in their own moral language back in the days when the Bible was composed; or, least acceptably of all, by seeing, say, divinely mandated suffering, such as God's order to kill the entire Amalekite people, as serving a greater, morally acceptable, good ordained by God.[20] Nor, of course, should we simply edit out of our account of God whichever divine commands or doings our contemporary morality deems unacceptable—which is exactly what the sanitized version of divine love does. Rather we should see that, as the paradigm object of love, we find in God destructiveness as well as the highest call to life ("for as all die in Adam, so all will be made alive in Christ"[21]), eternal damnation as well as ultimate forgiveness—"contradictions" that we should neither ignore nor seek to dissolve. As Job says, after his nightmarish trials in which he loses almost everything he cherishes, including his seven sons and three daughters, "Shall we receive the good at the hand of God, and not receive the bad?"[22]

———

Again we should ask: Isn't it perverse to love a God who destroys, or orders destruction, in this ultimate way? Indeed, not merely to love this God but to make him the *greatest possible* object and ground of love, as he is in both Old and New Testaments? Surely this speaks only of a repugnant extreme of love, and bears no relation to normal expressions of it? Surely the moral horror stories of the Bible or of Christian tradition are a trump card against faith in, and love for, such a God?

To which once again we must answer No. For, as we have already seen, love seeks something extraordinarily specific—and difficult to attain: grounding in a world that we supremely value. That is love's whole raison d'être; it is what distinguishes love from other emotions of attachment and esteem and desire and self-giving. As lovers we do not, in the first instance, seek to be shown kindness and respect by our loved ones, no matter the pain when they are withheld. Nor is our love conditional on being valued and recognized, essential though esteem, recognition, and "mirroring" by loved ones, beginning with our parents, are for the development of selfhood that is rich and robust. If our loved ones ground us, but also turn away scornfully and cruelly, or are unjust, ungrateful, destructive, and resentful toward us, we will, as often as not, still love them, as we see every day in enduring romantic relationships as well as in parents' love for their children. Recognition and respect are crucial to a rich and harmonious relationship; but they are not necessary, let alone sufficient, conditions for either inspiring or sustaining love. We can intensely love someone who fails to recognize or even value us.

Of course, it is profoundly to be desired that our loved ones should harbor no impulses to hate or destroy us, or to possess or deny our freedom; and that they should properly recognize and value us. That is uncontroversial—at least to our contemporary moral sensibility (though hardly self-evident to some of the greatest thinkers on love, from Thomas Aquinas to Sartre). But that doesn't mean that to love those who are destructive toward us should automatically be deemed pathological. Nor does it mean that any lover who tolerates such treatment should be castigated as masochistic or ethically deficient, let alone that we should accept only conceptions of love—of its ground and aim—that hold it to be valuable to the degree that it refuses to tolerate malice from a loved one.

If love reflects a highly particular need (for, I claim, a promise of onto-logical rootedness) whose satisfaction can be more fundamental to a lover's flourishing than being treated respectfully or benevolently, then our under-standing of it must accommodate this reality and not succumb to a moralism that has no truck with it. Again: of course it is vastly preferable that we should love only those who are kind to us. Of course it would be preposterous, at least to our contemporary moral sensibility, to say that we *ought* to love those who are cruel to us, despite their cruelty (though Jesus's talk, in the Sermon on the Mount, of turning the other cheek can be interpreted as coming close). And, of course, it would be even more absurd to say that we ought to seek out abusers to love. But the problem with a morality that dismisses as pathological all love for those who are malevolent to us is that we can miss the point that there are times when the blessings of our loving such people—or indeed such a God—can vastly outweigh the ordeals we endure at their hands: times when it feels as if our life hangs on their availability to be loved, and so on their prox-imity; when, to put it crudely, our flourishing really is helped more than it is hindered by our loving them; or when our love for them inspires in us a loyalty and a devotion that are unimpaired by their mistreatment of us, or indeed of others—as, for example, in parental love for a violent adult son or daughter.

Under such circumstances it is just not true that it is either wiser or ethically imperative to repudiate such a loved one and to seek to extirpate our love for them (if that were possible). Nor is it true that it would always be preferable to be in relationship to someone who treated us kindly and respectfully but whom we did not love. This, as I suggested earlier, is why the reported cruelty and vindictiveness of the Judeo-Christian God is not sufficient reason, as "The New Atheists" tend to assume it is, to conclude that we are necessarily better off not believing in him or her, or that any love for him or her should, *ipso facto*, be deemed repugnant, pathological, and ethically undeveloped.

To a contemporary readership, which will readily identify with the child, but not necessarily with God, as the supreme object of love, we can say, in rough analogy: the cruelty of an adult child, vis-à-vis its parents or others, does not entail that his parents are better off not loving him; or that their continuing love for him should be deemed repugnant, pathological, and ethically unde-veloped; or that he is otherwise an inappropriate object of their love. Because the child is becoming the supreme object of love, such parental tolerance will today seem acceptable, even touching, and possibly noble, just as in previous eras fidelity to a vindictive God might have been so regarded. It is a reflec-tion of the historic change in the archetypal object of love that unwavering devotion to a loved one who is destructive and even murderous will now be despised when that loved one is God but attract a measure of admiration when it is revealed to be offspring. And that these divergent judgments will seem, ethically, self-evidently right.

Indeed, it is here, I think, that we find the distinction between liking and loving. The necessary condition for liking someone is that they show us kind-ness and respect. The necessary condition for loving someone is, by contrast, that we see in them a promise of ontological rootedness. So that if we fail to see a promise of rootedness in those who value and cherish us we will not love them, though we might greatly like them. And, by contrast, if we do see that promise in others who despise us, we will love them, even if we dislike them. Liking and loving, in short, are almost entirely different emotions, with almost entirely different grounds and aims. We do neither of them justice by simply placing them, as C. S. Lewis does, at two ends of a single scale, with loving at the higher end and liking at the lower.[23]

Unrequited Love

If love's necessary condition is to see a promise of ontological rootedness in another, this also means that unrequited love can be genuinely love in its mo-tivation, in its relation of attentiveness to the other, and, indeed, in finding grounding in and through them—a fact to which innumerable poets have testified and that would be too obvious to state if so many didn't continue to hold with Karl Marx that "If you love without calling forth love, that is, if your love as such does not produce love, if . . . as a loving person you do not make yourself a *loved person* . . . then your love is impotent."[24] Or if a thinker like Martin Buber didn't insist that the "I–Thou" encounter of love is funda-mentally reciprocal. Or if a philosopher like Niko Kolodny didn't define love as a *two-way* relationship of shared concern, going so far as to say that "one's reason for loving a person *is* one's relationship to her: the ongoing history that one shares with her,"[25] as say lover or friend or spouse or daughter; so that, for Kolodny, one's relationship is the "single ground"[26] of love. And from this he draws the somewhat prim assertion that "unrequited non-instrumental con-cern for another person is . . . *inappropriate*."[27]

But to define love in this way is not only to beg the all-important ques-tion of why one is in a relationship of love, as opposed to any other kind of relationship, with just this friend or that lover. It is not just to sidestep the question of whether all who are born into relationships with an "ongoing history," such as siblings, really love each other. It is not just to rule out of court the possibility of love at first sight for a stranger who fleetingly appears and then vanishes, but ignites a passion that never leaves us. It is also, against all the evidence, to insist that unrequited love is not genuine love. And it must also rule out of court all unrequit*able* love, such as love for the dead as it is generally conceived today, and, if they really cannot reciprocate, for the most severely handicapped. Dante's love for Beatrice as well as a geriatric nurse's love for her seriously demented charge would both be dismissed, on this relational account, as not fully loving. As would much, if not most, courtly love. Yet we do not need to go as far as Jesus in the Sermon on the Mount—"If you love those who love you, what credit is that to you? For even sinners love those who love them"[28]—to see that some of these unrequited or unrequitable expressions of love, such as for the dead or the handicapped, can be among the purest of all.

Indeed, love's genuineness might be tested precisely by its willingness to expect nothing from others, including requital: to let them go, have their freedom from us, disappear.

Self-Interest as a Source of Self-Giving

One thing naturally loves another only as good for itself.

—THOMAS AQUINAS[1]

If love is joy at glimpsing a promise of ontological rootedness in another, then it is necessarily self-interested (though not selfish). It is one of the most needy and conditional of all emotions. Albeit one of the most farsightedly and complexly needy, for the stable groundedness it seeks is enormously ambitious, often hard to recognize even when a promise of it stares us in the face, and never finally achievable.

We might not notice this neediness of love if we catch it just in its greatest moments of giving, when the lover is willing to sacrifice anything, even his or her life, for the loved one. But ultimately the inspiration for love's self-giving is always self-interest, in the sense of being grounded in the need or desire for such a promise of rootedness.

Thus our rapture for another whose mere presence—in face-to-face reality; in imagination; in our memory—offers us a promise of rootedness might not only lead us to tolerate their destructiveness toward us (and at times even to regard it as a sign of engagement with us). It might not only lead us into the desert of loneliness where unrequited love strands us. In addition, and despite all this, it can also motivate us to passionate self-giving, self-forgetting, and even self-sacrifice. For in the healthy situation, where love's rapture develops into a relationship, this ongoing engagement with the other, this focus on their particular needs and individuality, is what love, once inspired, naturally seeks.

In other words: though love's indispensable condition is a promise of ontological rootedness, this is its only condition. As long as we have glimpsed such a promise in another our love will, beyond that, be unconditional to the extent that no other condition need be satisfied to continue loving them, and nothing they say or do could undermine our love. We will be dedicated to them without thought to our self-interest or to the benefits that our devotion will bring; for no great devotion, to a loved one just as to a vocation or a country, is dominated by awareness of its motivating conditions once it gets underway (which, again, does not entail that those conditions—and the needs they express—won't still be at work). Indeed, we will likely love them—or an idealization of them confected by our gratitude for their existence—even if relationship with them is intolerable or impossible. And in the case of, for example, an ancestor or a stranger we see on a bus, even if we have never met them.

Love can die, I am suggesting, only if we come to see the loved one as no longer offering, or as somehow refusing, a promise of ontological rootedness; for this is the single condition that, whether it remains in the forefront of our consciousness or not, never stops grounding our love.

———

To say that our love is grounded in need or self-interest is, therefore, in no way to say that we experience the loved one as a means to an end, a stepping stone to self-satisfaction. Nor, as I just emphasized, that we are continuously aware of the promise of home in the world that they embody for us—always, as it were, conscious that it is this that grounds our love; always checking that the promise is still there. On the contrary, our need for the loved one bestows such immense significance and presence and, as we have seen, *power* on them, it allows their life to break so decisively into ours, and it makes them such a singular focus of our attention and responsibility that we lack anything close to the detachment that would be needed to see them in instrumental or calculating terms. Indeed, at the limit our existential need for the loved one's promise of ontological rootedness turns them into a sacred being for us, and our relationship with them into a sacred space.

And so from profound, even violent, need arises the greatest devotion of which we are capable: devotion to another whose existence and ends and welfare can become more important to us than our own; indeed, can easily come to command our own. To the one whom we experience as offering us this promise of a home in the world we at once say "*hineni*"—"here I am"— which, as Hilary Putnam reminds us, is what Abraham says to God when he is summoned to sacrifice his son Isaac.[2] As it is how Moses replies to God's call from the burning bush and how Jacob, on his way to Egypt, answers God's summons.[3]

In genuine love there is, therefore, no necessary conflict between self-interest and self-giving, between care of our self and care of others. Far from demanding that we "transcend" or "annihilate" our self, devotion to another— our romantic partner, our child, nature, art, ancestors—cannot be achieved unless it engages all the resources of that very self, resources that we can then devote to the loved one: in other words, place at their disposal. And far from being an inevitable prison of narcissism that renders us unable to see beyond our self, or that treats the loved one as an object to be used, love's self-interest is precisely what prizes open our eyes and ears and attention to them and what makes us so relentlessly focused on addressing and giving to them—whose existence and flourishing we experience as inseparable from our own, and who in some ways feels closer to us than we do to ourselves.

In short: if we ask about the "why" of love—why we love this particular person; why we love at all—the answer will be that love is in its essence needy or self-interested: that it seeks a promise of ontological rootedness, and that its arousal is grounded in the belief that we have glimpsed such a promise. And if we then ask about the "what" of love, and in particular about what a flourishing relationship of love looks like, the answer will be that love is in its essence self-giving: that, once aroused, its orientation is fundamentally other-regarding.

———

It follows that to see love as intrinsically "disinterested" or "selfless" is deeply misleading because its unsurpassable generosity proceeds out of the most powerful self-interest there can be: the will to exist. For the dialogue of love is most fundamentally about existence: it is always ontological in its character and concerns. Our loved one's very presence deepens our own sense of existing; it makes vivid the "there-ness" of our own life; and it promises to ground us in a world that we supremely value and that is hospitable to our existence— a promise through which our life finds, and is structured by, a trajectory of meaning.

And we, as the lover, naturally say to the loved one not only *hineni*—here I am—but, in the same breath, "*Amo, Volo ut sis*," the maxim attributed by Hannah Arendt to Augustine, which means "I love you; I want you to be."[4] We say this not out of a duty to reciprocate, or out of any impartial moral considerations, or motivated by an innate altruism, but because to glimpse a promise of rootedness in another *is* to experience them as maximally being—and to will that this be so. Indeed, the closer love's neediness propels us toward them, the more overwhelming, ungraspable, and autonomous their being becomes for us. Perhaps this is what Simone Weil is gesturing at when she says that "only the existence of those we love is fully recognized"—though we might add that this is true too of those we fear; and that "to love and to be loved only serves mutually to render this existence more concrete, more constantly present to the mind."[5]

To love our "neighbor" impartially is, I suggest, also to be overwhelmed by their singular existence as a place for our own rootedness, *prior* to understanding their particular needs—and at the same moment, to offer one's own singular existence as a place for their rootedness. This existential focus colors the entire way in which we are present to them and give to them, and so makes our every act of generosity to them different in its motivation and in our experience of it from an act of generosity motivated by character, or duty, or the instinct of altruism—though, *outwardly*, giving to our neighbor out of love and out of these other motives might look exactly the same.

———

The self-giving devotion expressed by this "here I am" and "I want you to be" is characterized by what we can call *the four cardinal virtues of love*: care, empathy, gratitude, and—the precondition of all of these—attentiveness, which, as I will discuss in Chapter 22, is love's primary virtue. (Patience, we might think, is a fifth virtue, but it is contained within, indeed is constitutive of, attentiveness and its capacity to wait.)

Love's self-giving to the loved one, its deep identification with their life, including their ends and needs, its gratitude for their existence, and its attentiveness to their presence, are the tribute that the lover pays to the loved one's being—once, thanks to their promise of groundedness, we have their existence clearly in view.

Indeed, if our love for them trumps our love for others our devotion to them might involve terrible immorality to these others; like Abraham's devotion to God clearly trumps his love for (and the *hineni* he also says to) his own son, Isaac, whose life he is prepared to sacrifice at God's command. Though we can deeply love many people if we see a promise of ontological rootedness in each of them (just as there is more than one nation that we can love or more than one identity that can powerfully ground us), nonetheless love's tendency, when it discovers another in whom it sees a hitherto unprecedented such promise, is to relegate, or, at the limit, even obliterate, all other possibilities to love so as to exist with *all* one's heart and soul and might in and through this loved one.

This wholeheartedness sometimes shows up as patient devotion to one beloved, who becomes the center and ground of our life, structuring, as we have seen, a trajectory of hope; and at other times it can be manifested as treachery to all others who are sidelined by this fundamental choice. Either way, only thus can the lover identify totally with this single loved one's existence.

We, as lovers, therefore extend care, empathy, gratitude, and attentiveness to our loved ones because their existence is fundamental to our own. We do not do so, in the first instance, out of a sense of obligation, moral or otherwise, let alone as the result of deliberation; nor out of a will to repay kindnesses rendered; nor out of a virtuous character; nor, as Harry Frankfurt claims, out of "*disinterested* concern" for the loved one—a claim about the nature of love, about what "love is, most centrally,"[6] that, as the citation at the head of this chapter makes clear, even one of the greatest fathers of Christian love, Thomas Aquinas, would regard as incoherent.

Indeed, for Thomas genuine love for another is not only self-interested but, as we will see in Chapter 25, derived from *self-love*. And the highest love, which is for God, toward whom all genuine human love is oriented, is also the truest self-love. Similarly, for Augustine all love is motivated by the search for one's greatest flourishing or happiness, the perfection of which is the beatitude to be found in fellowship with God, or in our soul coming to rest in God, who is our ultimate good. For Augustine, to love oneself well *is* therefore to love God. And we love our neighbor, too, not in some formally disinterested way, unconnected to any desire, but for the sake of God. "Each man," he says, "insofar as he is a man should be loved for the sake of God, and God for his own sake."[7] Indeed, Augustine warns:

> First see whether you yet know how to love yourself [in loving God]; and then I will entrust your neighbor to you, whom you are to love as yourself. But if you don't yet know how to love yourself, I'm afraid you are only too likely to cheat your neighbor as yourself![8]

So, too, in repudiating the "quietist" insistence that pure love for God is without any self-interest, the Catholic Church under Pope Innocent XII claimed, on the contrary, that love for God is quite properly accompanied by hope of reward (and fear of punishment), such as getting to Heaven, avoiding Hell, and finding happiness. Thus the Church took the position that "even the highest form of altruistic love must have a motive of self-interest."[9] It is plainly an error to assume that Christian love necessarily seeks nothing for itself.

In short: love's self-giving, self-forgetfulness, and self-sacrifice are consequences of, and inescapably grounded in, self-interest. We surrender to our loved one only because we are motivated to love what we take to be truly good for us. The important distinction in love is not between whether love is self-interested or not, but between whether our self-interest is benighted or enlightened: whether we crave pleasures that sabotage our real flourishing, in the pursuit of which we love the wrong people and things, and close down our vision and attention to the right ones; or, by contrast, whether the object of our self-interest is our highest good: that which can be secured only by a wide-ranging, refined, and patient relationship to powerful sources of life that we experience as existing beyond us and in relation to which alone we can flourish. As Augustine warns: "Love, but be careful what you love."[10]

W. B. Yeats's poem "For Anne Gregory" magnificently mocks any expectation that we are loved for our own sake. A woman who wants to be loved "for herself alone," and not for her mesmerizing yellow hair, is told this:

> Never shall a young man,
> Thrown into despair
> By those great honey-coloured
> Ramparts at your ear,
> Love you for yourself alone
> And not your yellow hair.

The woman is then reminded that loving someone for their own sake is—as I argued in Chapters 1 and 2—the preserve of God; or, more precisely, of a God who is taken to be free of the neediness that propels human love:

I heard an old religious man
But yesternight declare
That he had found a text to prove
That only God, my dear,
Could love you for yourself alone
And not your yellow hair.[11]

Exile as Love's Inspiration

If love is joy aroused by the promise of home or rootedness in a world that we supremely value, then it follows that all love starts from the experience—of greater or lesser intensity—of homelessness or rootlessness. Indeed, insofar as we are all cast at birth into a world in which we are strangers and in which a genuine grounding for our life cannot be fully given but must be earned, often through prolonged trial and error, a primal experience of exile is the background to all love, even if we are dimly or seldom conscious of it.

And this in two ways: the pain of exile—to feel in exile, or to remember it—is the most powerful motivation to love (and be loved).

At the same time, to love is also to deepen our sensitivity to exile: for to glimpse a promise of home is to become more aware of our distance from it—and of the pain of that distance.

Exile is an extreme form of loss, and in particular of what since the eighteenth century has been called "alienation." It is intrinsic to exile, as it isn't to all loss, to feel debarred from the very source of our life, or of meaning in our life. Such a source isn't just an origin in time; it is a locus of belonging and purpose and vitality, to which we must experience an umbilical connection if those ends to which we are naturally disposed are to flourish.

And so we are cast into exile when what we lose—our country, our child, our system of belief, our whole culture, even (for a thinker such as Karl Marx) our very humanity—was the central source of meaning in our life. Such an obliterating loss means we are no longer able to have a place in a world that we supremely value. We can then only be spectators of our existence, going through the motions of an "as if" life, in which none of our thoughts or actions or projects, none of our ends and values, however admirable we (or others) find them, really engage us wholeheartedly, or are ultimately fulfilling, or make unquestionable sense to us. Any place of meaning and belonging that feels authentically ours will seem no more than a provisional possibility on the far side of the horizon—unless we encounter, as we do when we love, a fresh source and center of life that seems to offer us a genuinely new home.

Our lives begin, of course, in a primitive form of exile. We are born into a world not of our making at a time not of our choosing. It will gradually dawn on us that we are strangers in the land where we must eventually make our home—the land that will be the field of all our possibilities. This is a universal human experience: for such an early experience of exile inevitably pervades our lives, even if at most times we are unaware of it—one reason why I propose that the need for a promise of ontological rootedness is universal. And to the extent that love's hope cannot be finally and stably fulfilled—because no perfect anchorage in life is achievable or even identifiable—love repeatedly returns us to the experience of exile. Which, in turn, repeatedly renews our search for home and, perhaps, also clarifies our vision of what home is for us.

In the particular sensibility shaped by biblical monotheism, exile lies close to the beginning not just of any individual human life but of all human life. It is striking that in the Bible there is no mention of the word "love," in any of its Hebrew forms, until well *after* the banishment of Adam and Eve from the Garden of Eden[1]—in other words, until well after the moment when the drama of exile in the history of Western consciousness decisively begins. (We have to wait until God orders Abraham to sacrifice Isaac, later in the Book of Genesis, for love to make its explicit biblical debut: "Take your son, your only son, whom you love."[2])

In Eden—which in Hebrew means delight or bliss—there was harmony; but the text does *not* tell us that there was love. There was solitude for Adam before Eve appears, but not the drastically different condition of homelessness. God's reason for creating Eve is to provide a sustaining companion—a "helper as his partner"—for Adam: for "it is not good that . . . man should be alone."[3]

The Garden of Eden narrative is too abbreviated to be sure of the true nature of Adam and Eve's relationship before their expulsion. But, if I am right that love fundamentally involves a striving for ontological rootedness, and that this striving is what distinguishes instances of intimacy and attachment and sex and care that express love from those that express other bonds of devotion and need, then, contrary to almost all traditional interpretations of the Garden of Eden, I suggest that we cannot see the relationship of Adam and Eve before their expulsion as a model of love. God is therefore not yet speaking of the sort of intimacy that enacts love. Indeed, God's referring to Eve as merely a "helper" and his warning against the solitary life imply that, at this stage of Genesis, he is speaking only of the general human need for the intimacy and mutual care afforded by companionship and society. (Just as Aristotle remarks, in a similar vein, that we are by nature social creatures, disposed "to live with others." Indeed, Aristotle adds, even the most blessed person is not a solitary; for "no one would choose to possess all good things on condition of being alone."[4] The flourishing life, with all its virtues, is ineluctably social; it cannot be attained in isolation. But Aristotle, too, does not stipulate that living with others—community, intimacy, support, marriage—always and necessarily takes love's very specific form. As I argued in Chapter 1, there are many ways in which human beings can be bonded; and if we are too quick to call them all "love" on account of their intimacy or resilience or mutual devotion, we lose what is unique to each of them—as well as to love itself.)

In any event, within the Garden of Eden God is decidedly not creating romantic lovers who are searching, in and through each other, for a home— an existential grounding that they cannot secure in the world around them. Eve is no Isolde, and Adam no Tristan. Nor is God creating Aristotelian friends united by common virtues and dedicated to maximizing their human flourishing. Nor are Adam and Eve devoted to each other in self-sacrificing benevolence. Within the walls of the Garden of Eden neither ascending *erôs* nor perfect *philia* nor compassionate *agape/caritas* (as this expression of love comes to be understood after Augustine) has yet been born.

Moreover, though they might be husband and wife, we are hardly entitled to project onto them our modern, post-eighteenth-century, understanding of marriage as founded on love.[5] Indeed, in reply to God's question about eating the fruit, Adam speaks of "the woman whom you gave to be with me," words that hardly sing of a deep love.[6]

There is, in short, good reason why none of the Hebrew terms for love are used to describe their bond within Eden. In this world of primal bliss the motivation for love—the yearning for a promise of ontological rootedness—doesn't yet exist. By the same token, if indeed Adam and Eve do have sex within the Garden[7]—where a man and his wife are described as becoming "one flesh"[8]— rather than only after their expulsion when they come to "know" each other,[9] we should also not assume that any such sexual intimacy is a synonym for love, romantic or otherwise. Nor, clearly, do we have grounds to interpret their sexual relations as a stage on the ascent to a higher love.[10] In the first five books of the Bible, God is still far from becoming a Platonist.

But what does happen at this early stage in the Book of Genesis—and this is decisive—is that God's banishment of Adam and Eve creates the *possibility* for love to become a central virtue, even the central virtue, of the well-lived life. The catastrophe of banishment rings the starting bell for a historical drama of love in which men and women are forced to seek, each one for him- or herself, their own way of being at home on earth and, inseparably from this goal, a new relationship to their creative source (in God). The conditions for love to become one of the great goals of the flourishing life—the conditions for humans to search for a promise of ontological rootedness—appear only when Adam and Eve find themselves outside Eden, cast, like every newborn, into a world in which they are strangers and in which a genuine grounding for one's life is not given but must be progressively discovered or created, often repeatedly. In short, it is the exile of Adam and Eve from the Garden of Eden that creates the possibility for companionship to become love—for a bond of mutual support to become animated by love.

There is no way around it: exile from Eden—and from God—can be overcome and redeemed *only* through love. Love as return to a primal origin through a future-oriented attentiveness to the source of one's being. Love as recovery of an origin that never merely restores the *status quo ante* (as the myth of Aristophanes one-sidedly presents it as yearning to do), but is always a new relation to lineage and so to oneself.

Here again we see love's tremendous specificity; for of all the emotions—including emotions that are often conflated with love, as if they were just different words for it, such as benevolence and devotion and intimacy and sexual desire—love alone has the drive to respond to the pain of exile by rooting our lives in relation to a world that we supremely value; and love alone is dedicated to this goal as its intrinsic, defining purpose, its very raison d'être.

And so the search for love is especially urgent—and as a result often especially clumsy, even brutish—in those periods of our lives when we lose our own Edens: when the infant learns that its mother is not the infallibly available source of protection that it craves; when irreversible ruptures of consciousness occur as one stage of childhood or adolescence yields to the next; when we lose confidence in our vocation or way of life; when we discover that we are not wholeheartedly committed to those ends that we thought defined us; when our parents die; when our world, or culture, or religion, and its scaffolding of meanings collapse, or threaten to collapse.

These transitions might be culturally "constructed" in that the degree to which people speak of exile, the meanings they attach to it, and the extent to which they suffer from it will differ from one culture and time to another. But the point remains the same: the *experience* of exile—of its despair, and helplessness, and breakdown of meaning—is the most powerful (and, to the degree that it can never be stably overcome, enduring) motivation to love, however that experience comes about and however it is interpreted. For love's aim, uniquely, is to overcome isolation from any possibility of a meaningful home.

It is therefore surely significant that love becomes the supreme virtue in Hebrew scripture, with the commandment to love God with all one's heart and soul and might, later taken up by Jesus in the New Testament. For, as we will discuss in Chapter 26, in the Israelites we have a people whose very identity—uniquely—is structured by the absence of an indigenous home; whose Promised Land of Canaan belongs, quite explicitly, not to them but to God; and who have suffered long exile in Egypt and in Babylon. Indeed, their founding Patriarch, Abraham, is himself an exile from his ancestral home who, even after sixty-two years of living in the Promised Land, still calls himself "a stranger and an alien"[11] in this new home because, though God promised the land to his descendants, four hundred years of exile from Canaan will have to pass before they come to inhabit it.[12]

In short: Were not the Hebrews forced to recognize love as the supreme virtue precisely because they could never take a home in the world for granted, but had to earn it anew again and again? Was it not the depth of their experience of exile, and so the inextinguishable urgency of their search for a promise of ontological rootedness, that made it possible for them to hear the call for love to be not merely one virtue among others, but the highest virtue of all?

Why Some Epochs (and People) Value Love More Than Others

You could not be born at a better period than the present, when we have lost everything.

—SIMONE WEIL[1]

We are not really at home in our interpreted world.

—RAINER MARIA RILKE[2]

All human beings, I just suggested, have a disposition to love because all are thrust into a world not of their making or choosing, a world in which a secure sense of existence and home cannot be perfectly given and so must always be sought. As a result, some experience of exile or alienation from a world that affords a secure meaning and place is likely to be a universal—and by no means only a modern Western—phenomenon.

But the extent to which people think of themselves as alienated—and, crucially, to which they suffer from alienation—varies vastly from one individual, culture, and period to another. And it is this—the extent to which alienation is *experienced as a problem*, indeed as a problem that can undermine trust in life itself—that will determine the value of love at any particular time and place.

In other words, love's prestige will track the degree to which individuals, societies, or indeed whole epochs feel uprooted and provisional. (Like the meanings attached to love, or like the objects that are taken to be supremely worthy of love, its value will always be culturally created—will always be local to a particular time and place—however absolute it might feel.)

As we have seen, it can be no coincidence that the journey of love in the monotheistic tradition begins with the primal exile of humanity in Genesis—as expressed by the story of Adam and Eve's banishment from the Garden of Eden—an exile that can be overcome only through love for God and an acceptance of God's benevolence toward erring human beings.

Nor can it be a coincidence that love for God—and for "neighbor" for the sake of God—is so central to the New Testament, which vividly pictures this world as imperfect and not to be loved, and which therefore sees human life as intrinsically estranged from its only possible fulfillment: to be in the eternal presence of God. "Do not love the world or the things in the world. The love of the Father is not in those who love the world."[3] "Do not store up for yourselves treasures on earth, . . . but store up for yourselves treasures in heaven."[4]

Indeed, we are obliged by the narrative of alienation in Christian scripture to see ourselves as exiles—both *in* this world, which is not our real home, and *from* the next world, which we have yet to attain. (And we find Peter addressing the Christians he writes to in exactly these terms, as "aliens and exiles."[5]) Can it be any wonder that love—as the emotion whose very nature it is to search for, and respond to, a promise of home—will become the privileged emotion in this extraordinary eschatology?

Nor, perhaps, is it surprising that within Christian scripture love is most decisively exalted not by Jesus but rather in Paul's epistles, which invest death with unsurpassed immediacy and significance. Not just individual death, but the imminent demise of the world, which Paul, following Jesus, expects and which is the decisive horizon of all his thinking. This imminence of the end of the world dramatizes, to a degree that not even Jesus does, the picture of human life as fundamentally a condition of exile from the only true life: the heavenly life to come. Which Paul in fact portrays as a home:

> [W]e have a building from God, a house not made with hands, eternal in the heavens. For in this [earthly] tent we groan, longing to be clothed with our heavenly dwelling.[6]

So, too, it makes sense that for the greatest thinker of love in the Christian tradition, Augustine, the natural world is, by definition, a place of exile; and love is the passion to overcome this exile once and for all by seeking our genuine home, which is God. As he says in the famous opening of his *Confessions*: "You [God] have made us . . . for yourself, and our heart is unquiet until it rests in you."[7]

Finally, can it be a coincidence that the prestige of human love has risen ever higher in the West since the seventeenth and eighteenth centuries— in parallel with modernity's relentless litany of exhilarating but uprooting upheavals? Just four hundred years have bequeathed us the scientific revolution, which re-described the physical world through mathematically conceived laws, and progressively denuded it of divine or human qualities— indeed of any sense that the universe revolves around us or is oriented toward our good; the idea, most dramatically formulated by Rousseau, that each of us has an authentic self from which we have become alienated, so that, instead of being self-determining and self-affirming, we become enslaved to the will and recognition of others; the invention of "autonomy," given paradigmatic expression by Kant, in which the individual is self-consciously to legislate or endorse values for herself, regardless of what tradition or religion ordains, so tearing herself from their familiar moorings; the anxiety, articulated by

Marx and a succession of nineteenth- and twentieth-century thinkers, that men and women—and their relations to the world—have lost an essential humanity; the gradual (if far from complete) "death of God" and so of trust in salvation and redemption by divine love; the related collapse of divinely ordained values and conceptions of flourishing, along with their metaphysical groundings, none of which any longer seems authoritative or achievable, thus marooning, or repeatedly threatening to maroon, human beings in nihilistic despair and disorientation; the questioning of old unities as fundamental and hitherto as seemingly self-evident as "the self" and even the "I," increasingly regarded merely as useful fictions or logical presuppositions of experience, rather than as the real core of personhood; the concomitant struggle to discover one's own identity, and the immense onus on each of us sovereignly to create or choose our own way in life; the insistence on the fundamental equality and dignity of all human beings, and so the challenging of those hierarchies in which one's position was securely, if often humbly or humiliatingly, fixed; the relentless cult of the new, which implicitly or explicitly pronounces a death sentence on what already exists, merely because it already exists (and which is not identical with the cult of progress, for the new need not be conceived as a step toward a determined end, or even toward something better); a picture of life in which human beings are no more than a late product of evolution by natural selection, rather than made in the image of an omnipotent and omniscient God; and a view of the universe as utterly indifferent to human concerns and inhospitable to human meanings, rather than as a cosmic home, animated by intrinsic meaning and purpose, with humanity at its center and bonded to it in preexisting harmony.

Such breathtakingly vast and rapid transformations in how people think of human nature and its place in the cosmos have culminated in our modern preoccupation with alienation: alienation from world, from God, from community, from politics, from tradition, and from one's own self. Indeed, alienation—and its correlative: a sense of personal dispossession that impoverishes our human dignity—is arguably not just a contingent quality or founding cause of modern subjectivity, but is rather constitutive of it: in other words, the subject of modernity is constituted by the experience of loss and estrangement. Subjectivity as alienation; or even: subjectivity as exile.

And to these philosophical innovations must be added the closely related social, political, and economic revolutions that have also fostered a widespread sense of unending dislocation, loss, powerlessness, and loneliness: the upheavals of industrialization; the erosion of old gender, ethnic, and class roles; accelerating technological change; and, more recently, globalization, migration, international capital of vast mobility and power, the destruction of cultures and languages, and the rise of winner-takes-all markets, in which one country or even one company could win monopoly power—and then lose it again to another.

Despite the thrilling freedoms and the tremendous opportunities for personal, societal, and political renewal that such philosophical, social, economic, and scientific developments have made possible for so many; and the huge increases in knowledge, power, prosperity, mobility, equality, safety, and social security that they have fostered, few of us—even among those who have most benefited from this immense panorama of flux—can be deaf to the sounds of which Joyce's Stephen Dedalus speaks: "I hear the ruin of all space, shattered glass and toppling masonry, and time one livid final flame. What's left us then?"[8]

———

Love—and not any political ideology—has been the most resilient beneficiary of this gathering crisis of alienation, of which such figures as Rousseau, Feuerbach, and Marx already speak, and of the "disenchantment"—the *Entzauberung*, or voiding of magic, as Max Weber called it—that has accompanied it and that he called "the fate of our age."[9] It is a disenchantment often accompanied by the re-casting of all phenomena in terms of a naively reductive naturalism that mistakenly thinks there is no room in a scientific worldview for the sacred or for awe before a universe that seems to dwarf the possibilities of human understanding—a universe that as J. B. S. Haldane suggested is "not only queerer than we suppose, but queerer than we *can* suppose";[10] a universe that to this extent we experience as "sublime": as thrillingly presenting us with overpowering grandeur in the face of which we are nonetheless able to exist and flourish.

No other ideal has been as successful as love in enchanting this disenchanted world. Or at least in offering hope for its enchantment. Not by yet again seeing the world as ordered by a grand purpose or idea or meaning intrinsic to it, which can offer a redemptive finale to history—such as God, communism, freedom, nationalism, scientific progress, or the universal triumph of democratic liberalism. Nor by the always futile and usually destructive attempt by apostles of violent nostalgia to turn the clock back and regain the "wholesomeness" of a lost organic community, set in a natural world of forests and lakes with the spirit of which its members effortlessly commune. Rather, love enchants life by privatizing the sacred: by creating a shared space of supreme value and meaning, magical in its promise of hope and intimacy, which is constituted and controlled by the lovers themselves in accordance precisely with modernity's ethos of autonomy, though they are also permeable to each other—a sacred space, often conceived as fenced off from the enforced conformism of society; a sacred space so far sought principally in the romantic couple and more recently in the parent–child relation.[11]

Here the sense of the magical and the miraculous, which has been progressively (though never finally) evicted from the universe as a whole since the seventeenth and eighteenth centuries, may be rediscovered in the mingled inner worlds of the lovers, who take each other and their love to be charged not only with supreme value but also with the sort of power to bestow fortune (or, if love is betrayed, misfortune) on their lives that had once been attributed to spirits and potions and saints' relics and, above all, to the mysteries of divine grace. And this enchantment of the private can happen *without* the hubris of seeing human love as a bearer of those divine qualities that mark the sanitized conception of how God is said to love: without, that is, seeing genuine love as intrinsically unconditional, disinterested, enduring, and all-affirming of the loved one.

Indeed, far from seeking to overcome alienation by defying modernity, love seems uniquely able to work with the grain of two sides of modernity's divided soul: on the one hand, to achieve autonomy, in which we create, discover, or endorse demanding ends to which we as individuals are wholeheartedly committed, to the point where we can "do no other"; *and* on the other hand to attain a redemptive intimacy with other human beings in which the loneliness that can so easily befall the autonomous subject might be overcome, but which is nonetheless a project of self-determination, willed and secured by the individual through his or her own efforts.

On the one hand, therefore, love is well suited to the modern idiom of individual autonomy and self-creation. For though the meaning, value, and rituals that we ascribe to love are deeply conditioned by tradition and society, it is also notoriously subversive of all authority and custom and morality that get in its way. And so it readily sees itself as discovering, expressing, and cultivating the unique personal identity of the lovers in opposition to such authority—an identity organized around the fundamental values and ends to which they are committed and that shape the significance that events and things in the world have for them. In other words, love is naturally in tune with the drive to challenge the legitimacy of convention that is so central to modernity's sense of its own vitality.

On the other hand, love's urge to create "one soul of interwoven flame," to merge two lives, to discover a bond in which each party is a "second self" to the other, to submit to the law of the loved one in order to achieve true relationship—all this also enables the individual to find, through love, newly created or endorsed structures of belonging, which, like the promise that defines all love, are open-ended rather than finally achievable. And to do so in a modern idiom: that is, to create one's own private *Gemeinschaft*, one's own autonomously enchanted world, in a way that draws on, and in turn fosters, the identity, the self-conscious uniqueness, of the lovers. We think of ourselves, to this degree, as the sum of our own particular loves, of our own enchanted communities of two. Or of a few.

The conviction that we now live in a defiled era that has lost moral fiber and a strong, healthy community is hardly unique to our time. There have been many precursors to the modern fiction that human beings felt markedly less lonely and vulnerable in the pre-modern world, thanks to their robust social roles; strong extended families; the moral clarity given by religion and custom; an unchallenged metaphysical worldview that had not yet been shattered into specialized domains like knowledge, ethics, and aesthetics; and a well-ordered place in a universe imbued with an intrinsic purpose and ruled by a reliable demiurge, who also afforded people a meaningful death. Similar convictions are already expressed in the poetry of Hesiod, which, in eighth-century BCE Greece, looks back to a golden age, the earliest of the five ages of humanity (of which the latest is merely iron), when people lived "with a spirit free from care, entirely apart from toil and distress";[12] in Homeric epic, also from the eighth century BCE, where figures like Nestor lament that once there were heroes but today there are only lesser men; in the actions of those Athenians who condemned Socrates to death in 399 BCE for failing to honor their traditional gods and corrupting their young; as well as in the Roman poet Catullus in the first century BCE, who berates his age for incest, fratricide, impiety, and a host of other ills that have festered because people are no longer god-fearing.[13]

A kindred nostalgia extends all the way to Nietzsche's proclamation that the whole of Western civilization since Plato is decadent compared with the nobility and vigor of what came before; to Spengler's diagnosis of the decline and fall of the West; to Thomas Mann's *Zauberberg*—and beyond. We are not the first age to experience the world as disenchanted and corrupt, and our lives as alienated from stable and healthy sources of meaning.

Nonetheless, Western modernity is peculiarly prone to *suffer* from the consciousness of alienation and loss. In addition, its self-respect depends crucially on its self-contempt: its feeling of vitality is aroused to a considerable degree by its diagnosis of its own failings; and its belief in its own ethical integrity feeds on its self-criticism as ethically inadequate, or even as contaminated by unachievable, deluded, or empty values. In the West's self-understanding the present is always a time of alienation, and to that extent of corruption.

Here love steps smartly into the vacuum of belonging. For love, as I have characterized it, is *the* emotion that seeks, and responds with joy to, a promise of ontological rootedness in a world we supremely value. And so love, experienced in its modern form as an autonomously endorsed, sacred community of two (or a few), is the ideal response to the West's crisis of alienation: to its sense of homelessness in the world.

We may, therefore, predict that the more powerful is our sense of exile from compelling structures of belonging, and the more abandoned and disillusioned people feel—whether, most recently, by political and economic elites; or as a result of the vulnerability of intimate relationships to impatience, divorce, and sexual choice—so the more the prestige of love is likely to keep on rising: the more the atomized individual of contemporary modernity will look to love to discover his or her own manner of being at home in the world.

20 }

The Languages of Love

The word "love" is, and has historically been, used very widely to denote, variously, disinterested benevolence, selfless devotion, sexual intoxication, powerful attachment, a form of supreme valuing, desire for beauty, desire for the good, and so on. But, I am proposing, our experience of loving suggests that by no means every case of love is marked by these dispositions and desires, either singly or collectively. Indeed, if "love" were another name for any or all of them, we would have no need of the word. We could just as well call benevolence "benevolence" or sexual intimacy "sexual intimacy." Why call an instance of them "love"?

I suggest that we call an instance of these things "love" when the will to them is grounded in and inspired by a promise of ontological rootedness, rather than when they are, say, the manifestation of some other drive or need or of an excellence of character. In other words, we should consider reserving "love" to denote a very particular emotion: joy inspired by a promise of grounding for our life in a world that we supremely value. We should do so because, so I have argued, such a promise is the ground of all our great loves; it is what gets them going in the first place; it is what accounts for why we love one person and not another; it is what motivates the self-giving and search for relationship of a healthy love; and the need for it is, I claim, one of the greatest of human needs.

Such joy, inspired by a promise of ontological rootedness in a world that we supremely value, can, of course, be expressed in different forms: for example, romantic love, parental love, friendship love. It can take different objects: a person, a god, a work of art, a landscape, an ancestor. It can be rapturous or quiet; unqualified or admixed with pain, jealousy, and even disgust. And it can evoke different behaviors: self-giving or cruelty, devotion or rejection, care or destructiveness.

But though all love is grounded in this promise, and so has a common origin and aim, each of its major forms speaks its own dominant emotional language.

Thus the language of sexual desire, with its explicit physicality, possessiveness, desire to merge, and proneness to jealousy, dominates in romantic-erotic love; that of protection and nurturing in parental love; that of joint ideals and tastes and common ends and second selves and mutual well-wishing in friendship love; that of awe and reverence in love for nature or ancestors or the divine. Romantic love feels most vital when accompanied by the bittersweet triumph of surmounting obstacles to it; which is also true of love for God insofar as for some Christian, Islamic, and Jewish mystics its language is overtly romantic-erotic, speaking of longing and swooning, of embraces, and even of intercourse. (The twelfth-century abbot Rupert of Deutz dreams of kissing the crucified Christ "for a long time," and he goes on: "I felt how deeply he [Christ] appreciated this sign of love when in the midst of the kiss he opened his mouth so that I could kiss more deeply."[1]) Yet the sense that obstacles charge love with vitality and meaning is nothing like as prominent in love for art or landscape or even friends. And, as we saw in Chapter 12, all of these types of love, once they have been aroused by a promise of ontological rootedness, speak a common language of devotion to the law of the loved one, whom the lover necessarily sees as beautiful.

In other words, the dominant language spoken by each type of love will characterize both the way in which a promise of rootedness speaks to us *and* the kind of relationship that love, once aroused by that promise, then goes on to seek. In romantic-erotic love, for example, intoxication by physical beauty, by bodily vitality, by the tactile and the elusive, by the thrilling reality of flesh, and by the power and mystery of gender (including in homosexual loves) will govern how the loved one's promise of rootedness speaks to us. And it will also govern the language in which the dialogue of love evolves. For a dialogue between two people's lives can be conducted with remarkable complexity and finesse through the language of sex, which can afford not only unsurpassed intimacy with another person but also endless insight into their character, sensibility, taste, fears, imagination, strengths, and weaknesses.

To be clear: though these erotic languages are how the promise speaks or shows up, they do not *constitute* the promise. They do not point to the real ground of love, which always lies in the lineage, ethical home, existential power, and call to life that we see in the loved one. This is why the very same bodyliness can provoke disgust today, but erotic obsession tomorrow. Or the other way around, as on those occasions when Swann in Proust's *In Search of Lost Time* finds himself overcome by "the lack of enthusiasm, amounting almost to distaste, which, in the days before he was in love with Odette, he had felt for her expressive features, her faded complexion." "It's an odd thing," he says to himself of the previous night in bed with her, "but I actually thought her ugly."[2]

Though each form of love—erotic, friendship, parental—has a dominant language, it is not an exclusive language. One reason for our confusion about the nature of love is the insistence, for so much of the history of love, on hiving off ways of loving—such as self-giving love (*agape*); desiring, possessive love (*erôs*); and love as dedication to the flourishing of those experienced, in key respects, as equal and as second selves (*philia*)—into hermetically sealed types, which are even said, for example by theologians like Anders Nygren, referring to *erôs* and *agape*, to be mutually exclusive: "separate and mutually incompatible fundamental motifs."[3] But they aren't incompatible at all, either in principle or in practice. On the contrary, as I will suggest in Chapter 22, they are different modes of the same relation; different modes of attention to the loved one with the identical aim: to assimilate her presence.

The reality, therefore, is that most relationships of love speak several languages. For example, sexual desire, if of a sublimated form, might play a role, too, in the bantering playfulness that two friends can enjoy when they have attained an easygoing trust and pleasure in each other's company; or in relations between parents and their children, where, despite the immense power of taboo, it can express itself in a marked urge to touch, especially a parent or child of the opposite sex, which cannot be explained merely by the instinct to protect or be protected. There can be an erotic quality in love for landscape or art or food or wine, as in the desire to come close to them, to be taken over by them, to savor their colors and textures, to possess them, and even—especially in the case of music and landscape—to be one with them.

Conversely, the languages of parental nurturing, or of friendship's dialogue of joint ideals and second selves, are central to the richest erotic relationships. Mutual well-wishing, self-giving, and even self-sacrifice will be found in almost every type of love, as will the enjoyment of common ideals and tastes classically associated with friendship love. Awe or reverence might pervade friendships and, at times, parental love.

Or take jealousy. Though intense jealousy is often seen as the preserve of romantic love, indeed as evidence of its authenticity—for it would seem strange for romantic lovers to be relaxed about rivals—it pervades many other forms of love, such as friendship, filial love, parental love, and in particular, as I argued in Chapter 14, sibling love, a fact with which we moderns are oddly uncomfortable. Perhaps it is only because we have elevated romantic love to the supreme form of love since the late eighteenth century, seeing it as a litmus test of a life well lived, that jealousy, as proof positive of our romantic commitments, has come to seem as fitting to it as it seems inappropriate to most other relationships of love.

Yet the Bible is magnificent on divine jealousy: "you shall worship no other god, because the Lord, whose name is Jealous, is a jealous God."[4] *King Lear* is brutally eloquent on a father's jealousy of his beloved daughter's other affections. Parents' jealousy of their child's life—of his loyalties, erotic and non-erotic; of his talents, even when less marked than theirs; and above all of his youth—can be profound; and, to the extent that parenthood is held to be sacred, it is shrouded in denial and repression. (It is interesting to note that in the first edition of *Snow White* by the Brothers Grimm, the wicked stepmother who is jealous of Snow White's beauty and standing is actually written as her biological mother.[5]) Conversely, children's jealousy of their parents' bond can be overwhelming—and is closely related to the envy diagnosed by Melanie Klein as, along with gratitude, the most primitive emotion experienced in early infancy in relation to the mother.

Equally, friendships are potentially powerful arenas for jealousy, if seen as the mutually passionate devotion that they can be, rather than as the luke-warm or optional forms of love—the love for wimps—that, today, they are commonly regarded as being. One could, for example, imagine Jonathan and David, two of the soul friends mentioned in the Bible, being violently jealous of interlopers; or indeed Montaigne and Étienne de La Boétie, who from the moment of meeting discovered themselves to be "so taken with one another, so well acquainted, so bound together, that from that time on nothing was as close to us as each other."[6] Montaigne is clear that friendship of this order is necessarily exclusive:

> He who supposes that of two men I love one just as much as the other, and that they love each other and me just as much as I love them, multiplies into a fraternity the most singular and unified of all things, of which even a single one is the rarest thing in the world to find.[7]

Indeed, the intense friendships that were still common in the nineteenth century could and did nurse powerful jealousy of rivals; for they involved a passion that would today seem utterly out of place in a form of love—soul friendship—that is arguably the highest and yet has been relegated to the lowest. Respectable female friends would, for example, carve "their initials into trees, set flowers in front of one another's portraits," dance, kiss, hold hands, and send letters to each other saying that "the expectation once more to see your face again, makes me hot and feverish." And until late in the nineteenth century, friendships between heterosexual men might also involve remarkable physical intimacy and emotional intensity. In 1851, James Blake notes in his diary that he and a friend, while roommates, shared a bed "and in each other's arms did friendship sink peacefully to sleep."[8]

Above all—and here again the Bible, with its narratives of Cain and Abel, Isaac and Ishmael, Jacob and Esau, and Joseph and his brothers, is as eloquent as contemporary literature is reticent[9]—there is the jealousy of siblings, per-haps the most violent, insatiable, and unappeasable of any expression of this terrifyingly uncompromising emotion. And of course the most long-lived, for only the jealousy of siblings can last an entire lifetime: from the murderous resentment of some infants toward the very existence of the other; to their often-unceasing battles for parental attention, which can leave scars and vengefulness that fester far beyond their parents' deaths; to their bitterness at every new quality and success and recognition accrued by their brothers and

sisters, whether in childhood, in early academic, sexual, sporting, and professional achievements, or in the last exertions of old age. A defeated rival in
a romantic relation, who was once the object of furious jealousy, can give up
and disappear from view, but one can never disappear from view in the psyche
of a jealous sibling. Nor can the existential provocation that your life poses to
him, the disgust he feels at even your trivial successes, his fury at having had
to share the world with you at all, be assuaged by any kindness, by any ap-
peasement, or by any recognition that you might extend to him. Not even by
your death.

Love's polyglot nature, and the tendency of a powerful relationship of love to
express diverse modes of love—such as friend, erotic lover, and parent—that
have historically been segregated off from each other into distinct "types" of
love, is nowhere better seen than in that primordial love: for God. Though
love for God is often depicted in one-dimensional terms as that of a child to
an all-powerful father figure, in fact it is far richer than that. In the Bible and
other religious writings, God has been portrayed not only as father,[10] but also
as mother,[11] as spouse,[12] as lover,[13] as friend,[14] as nature,[15] as "neighbor,"[16] and of
course, in Christianity, as child.[17]

Nor is this many-sidedness of love for the divine confined to monotheism.
In Hinduism, for example, we see something similar: Krishna, Lord of the
Universe, is loved in five distinct ways. He appears, variously, as erotic lover,
as child, as friend, as elder or master, and as the one who is loved impartially
and dispassionately.[18]

And here too, each way of loving Krishna has its own preferred emotional
emphasis. As a lover he is, of course, the object of erotic passion (*priyata*).
As a child he is loved in a parentally affectionate way (*vatsalya*), marked by
protectiveness and nurturing. As a friend, he and his human lovers are in a
companionable relationship of equals (*sakhaya*), expressed in a confident and
easygoing familiarity. As a superior master or protective elder, love for him is
characterized by respect (*priti*). As the object of impartial love, a love of non-
distinction and purity (*shuddha*), the lover of Krishna feels peacefulness, because she is voided of her own self and its passions.

Love for God and love for Krishna: these primordial loves speak powerfully
of the polyglot nature of all love. They exemplify the reality that almost any
rich relationship of love—whether for the divine, for a parent, for a romantic
lover, for a sibling, for one's child, or for a friend—will encompass, with vastly
different degrees of emphasis, the possessive and jealous desire of *erôs*, the
self-giving of *agape*, the joint ideals of two individuals who are second selves
to each other typical of *philia*, and the awe and fear that mark love for God.

The Primacy of Loving over Being Loved

Love, we have claimed, is born at that moment when we glimpse in the other a promise, which they might be unaware of offering, of our own rootedness in the world—or, more precisely, in a world that we supremely value. This is the moment of wonder—even of revelation—when something, not yet nameable, about the other inspires in us an intensified faith in the vitality and reality, and therefore the validity, of our existence. Indeed, it is our joyful gratitude for such faith that unleashes love's tremendous will to idealize, and to give to, the loved one.

In the adult, this faith in the vitality and validity of our existence comes in the first place from *loving*, rather than from being loved. If there is a primary question of love, it is not, as the theologian-philosopher Jean-Luc Marion suggests, "Does anyone out there love me?" or "Do you love me?"[1] but on the contrary: "Is there anyone out there whom *I* can genuinely love?" So too Sartre is mistaken in thinking that "to love is to want to be loved";[2] as is Rosenzweig when he says that "the soul . . . attains being, a being visible to itself, only when it is loved";[3] as is my friend who, when his wife asks "Why do you love me?," answers: "Because *you* love me."

To be loved—to be a source of groundedness to another, through our mere presence to them, and as a result to be valued, celebrated, and embedded in their life as its indispensable center—fundamentally constitutes us as a self in infancy and childhood. It is of course crucial to our flourishing before we ourselves are old enough not merely to form attachments or to show altruism but to be able to love (an ability that is unlikely to be formed much before the age of eight[4]). And throughout our lives being loved—or even having the prospect of being loved by someone we value—confers on us the deepest serenity and well-being, turning paralyzing loneliness into the creative joys of intimacy.

But in the adult the most life-giving love, the love that really roots us in the world and gives our existence its sense of indestructible "there-ness"— the love that enables the soul, in the words of Rosenzweig that we just cited, to attain "being, a being visible to itself"—is always our own loving, even if unreciprocated, or even if we aren't sure whether we are loved back. Because love seeks ontological grounding in the world, and is inspired by a promise of such grounding, not to love at all is, in a crucial sense, not to exist. It is worse than to be unloved. "What is hell?" asks Dostoevsky's Father Zossima. And he answers: "The suffering of being no longer able *to love*."[5] And for this reason the courtesan Philine in Goethe's *Wilhelm Meister* is right to ask: "Wenn ich Dich liebe, was geht's Dich an?" "If I love you, what's that to you?"[6]

———

For the adult, therefore, loving is necessarily of greater value than being loved. Not just of greater moral value, as an unsurpassed source of generosity and sacrifice and attentiveness to others, or because it is noble to love without expecting reciprocity, but, in addition, of greater value to our own flourishing.

This is surely why the "gaze" or the "look" of love—that famous moment of meeting described in numerous poems and stories—is primarily about seeing and recognizing, rather than being seen and recognized. It is the look of lovers rather than of loved ones. The jolt that the look gives us comes more from realizing that we love than from feeling that we are loved.

This is true not just for romantic lovers but also for the encounter of soul friends, for a mother seeing her child—and for the believer face to face with God. Indeed, if loving is more fundamental to the adult's flourishing than being loved, then the strongest faith in God would be motivated more by the desire to love the divine than by the desire to be loved by it.

Belief in, say, the Christian God wouldn't be dependent, then, on merely infantile "longing for a father," as diagnosed by Freud; or on resentment by the weak toward the strong (and toward a world of loss and suffering), as Nietzsche claims; or on craving easy answers to questions such as "What values should I hold?," "Why is there something rather than nothing?," "Why are we here at all?," or "What is the meaning of life?," as "New Atheists" like Richard Dawkins insist. On the contrary, faith would arise out of a quintessentially *adult* desire—the desire to love another acknowledged as ineluctably other, as impossible to possess, as ultimately unknowable, and as calling us to the greatest responsibility.

And of course, in the case of the monotheistic God, this other is not just any worthy object of love, but rather the theoretically maximum possible object of love. For, by definition, the monotheistic God offers the maximum possible promise of ontological rootedness. As creator and sustainer of all that exists, God is conceived as the ultimate source of life and lineage; of ethical home; of power over our sense of existing; and of the call to our destiny—whether individually or as a community. And since God is also as other and as ungraspable as it is possible to be, the divine is the most demanding, rather than the easiest, of all objects of love. Far from being a necessarily infantile object of love, God is the adult object of love par excellence. (Moreover, even if God is nothing more than our wish fulfillment—a charge leveled by thinkers from Feuerbach to Freud to Dawkins but impossible to falsify or verify—the wishes from which the divine, as an object of love, is forged, the longings of which it is merely a projection, are those of the adult—the longing for grounding, for ethical home, for "the call"—rather than of the child.)

The capacity to love God—and so to experience the maximum possible promise of ontological rootedness in the world—is, as I argued in Chapter 16, not grounded in, or necessarily conditional on, divine benevolence or kindness. Indeed, God's greatest gift to those who believe in him is *not* his putative love but simply that he is there to be loved—that he makes himself available, through his command to love him with all our heart and soul and might, as our highest object of love.

22 }

Attentiveness: Love's Supreme Virtue

Conventionally, a sharp distinction is made between the moment that love is born—between falling in love, whether or not at first sight—and love's development—continuing or growing in love.

But such a distinction between falling and growing in love in no way entails that the *ground* of our love is different in both cases. In both it is the promise of ontological rootedness that inspires and sustains our love. In both the lover is transfixed by the promise of lineage, ethical home, power, and the call to being that she is certain she sees in the other. In both cases reflection, inference, and justification are covertly at work: for the mind can reflect and infer with lightning speed, especially when it thinks it has found what it most craves (or most fears). Which, I think, is why love at first sight is possible.

What *is* different between falling in love—in particular when we do so in an instant—and developing our love is that the latter is utterly dependent on what, in Chapter 12, I called love's supreme virtue: attentiveness.

What Is Attentiveness?

Attentiveness is an openness to the other marked by ardent patience, curiosity, and wholeheartedness. It is that courageous looking and discerning epitomized, at the limit, by Van Gogh's capacity to see nineteen distinct shades of white, according to Alasdair MacIntyre.[1] It enables us to see the promise of a loved one in an ever richer and more fine-grained way—and so to keep falling in love. It is the foundation of a relationship that enacts and refreshes our love.

In attending we wait intently, even without knowing what we are waiting for. We question minutely, often without knowing quite what we are asking about—indeed taking care not to ask questions that will conceal the loved one or cause her to conceal herself. Every small sign of her floods us with the force of revelation.

Yet the closer our attention takes us to her, the more we realize how un-bridgeable is the distance that separates us. How our knowledge of each other, like all real knowledge, enriches our ignorance—and by doing so provokes wonder. How much easier it is to become "one" in love than mutually to enjoy our insuperable two-ness. How each of us will never really understand why the other loves us: what they see in us; what they need from us; what they want to give us—for to have such understanding we would need to be the other, including all the history that has made her just the person she is with the needs and hopes she has (though to be her wouldn't of course guarantee self-knowledge). And to that extent even the most passionately reciprocated love always comprises two parallel relationships, in which, as Rilke puts it, there is no higher task than to be guardians of each other's solitude. For though we might experience ourselves as "one," this one is cemented, enticingly, by its mutual incomprehension. Two lovers are never in the same relationship. Their intimacy is richest from out of the depths of their lived solitude.

Attentiveness might sound simple: a passive capacity to receive, to obtain an image of the loved one's reality, as if the lover were like a camera or movie screen. But it is, in fact (like true obedience), intentional, willful, searching. Far from being "selfless," it demands the fully engaged presence of our self with all its affirmative and critical powers. For the more perspectives we have on the loved one, along with the drives and ends internal to those perspectives, the better we will grasp what she is calling on us to do. And, far from being dis-interested, attentiveness is structured by powerful, often overwhelming, per-sonal interest in discovering and affirming who she is.

Such attentiveness is the oxygen of love. Without it love becomes gruesomely anonymous: passion for another person whom it never takes the trouble to no-tice. Or rather *refuses* to notice. (Not noticing someone who impinges on us as powerfully as a loved one is necessarily a state of siege against them. Just as indifference to what comes close to us is often active resistance to it, rather than the lack of any interest.)

Without attentiveness the lover ignores, even resents, everything about the loved one beyond those of her qualities that give him immediate pleasure. For anything else—her vocation, her character, her friends, all the things she really cares about in her life and all the conditions for her flourishing, but also more trivial qualities, such as her eating and sleeping habits—all this is at best un-interesting and at worst a menace to such a lover, potentially threatening his hold over the loved one and taking her out of his line of sight, where he needs her to stay if her presence is to ground him. This is a relationship like that of Marcel, Proust's Narrator, to Albertine, or of Shakespeare's King Lear to his favorite daughter Cordelia: grasping, heedless, suspicious, monomaniacally focused on keeping her in his orbit and at his disposal.

But inattentive love is often less conspicuous than this. It is quite capable of being generous to the loved one, of willing and promoting her flourishing, and of assuming respectful responsibility for her life. In other words, love that lacks deep attentiveness doesn't necessarily lack a modicum of love's other virtues.

Two people can be bonded like this for years. To outsiders their love, especially if it is romantic, might look "perfect," "magical." To the lovers themselves something will seem namelessly wrong. Their intimacy will feel hollowed out by loneliness, famished in the midst of plenty. Everything that we think of as necessary to love will be there: devotion, generosity, responsibility, care. But without really looking at each other. They will be inseparable but they will never meet.

To What Is Attentiveness Attentive?

So what is love's attentiveness attentive to? The answer is: most fundamentally to the four conditions that arouse our love in the first place. It enjoys the loved one as a source of lineage; of an ethical home containing those ends that ground us, the lover, with stable purpose; of power over our sense of existing; and of a call to our destiny.

To be attentive to lineage is, as we said earlier, to be attuned to the loved one's taste, sensitivity, and emotional cleanliness—and so to the peculiar relationship and non-relationship to the world that it dictates.

To be attentive to the loved one's ultimate ends is to seek out those ideals and virtues and moral insights through which they attempt to find a reliable place in the world and through which the world comes alive to them.

To be attentive to their power over us—specifically, power to imbue us with those sources of security that we most crave and most painfully lack—is perhaps hardest of all, for we both bask in that power and fear, even loathe, it. It makes us feel especially vulnerable because only we, as lovers, are susceptible to it. For it speaks of our very particular conditions for rootedness. To everyone else—everyone who doesn't share those conditions—our loved one's power will be imperceptible. The way it thrills and terrifies us will be unknowable to them.

All these things—taste, sensitivity, emotional cleanliness, ultimate ends, ideals, virtues or dispositions of character, moral insights, and the sources of the other's existential power over us—together either constitute or speak of the law of their being: the unalterable law that, through love's attentiveness, becomes the law of our own being.

This is the law that must govern how we dedicate ourselves to the loved one. For to be devoted, even to sacrifice, to another in love is not to give whatever we feel like, or decide is good for them. Rather, loving devotion is to seek, honor, and give to them only what the law of their being legislates. This is what it is for love to be just. Whereas the greatest injustice we can do a loved one—the injustice that penetrates and wounds the depths of their soul—is not merely to refuse to see and honor who they are, but to see them as someone they are not. To praise, blame, and act toward them as the person they aren't. To align ourselves with an effigy.

Patient Waiting

In order for attentiveness to discover the law of the loved one and to make it our own, it must be as if purposeless: waiting indefinitely for the other, as Florentino Ariza waits fifty-one years, nine months, and four days for Fermina Daza in Gabriel García Márquez's *Love in the Time of Cholera*.[2] It should not jump in too quickly, like a eudaimonistic busybody, seeking to understand and promote her flourishing, as if a lover's devotion were identical to a protector's or a mentor's. Love's generosity is seen at least as much in open-ended patience, in delight that any truth at all is revealed to it, and in taking capacious joy in the loved one's existence, as in any practical steps to foster her well-being.

Even altruistic emotions, like compassion or pity, can be impatiently intrusive. As Nietzsche reminds us, compassion or pity is often a way of refusing to accept the person on whom we bestow it—of defending ourselves against her reality.[3] For if its concealed, perhaps unconscious, aim is to sweep out of sight her suffering, which we find unbearable, by in effect demanding that she cease to suffer in ways that burden us; if its real desire is to master the other person's distress, of whose true nature we can never be certain but that our compassion presumptuously assumes it has understood—then we aren't properly attending to who she most deeply and personally is, and so to her real needs. On the contrary, prompted by our aversion to any sign of distress, we turn away from who she is, without attempting to understand the real economy of her soul. We want to banish or re-mold those aspects of her that we find arduous, even offensive, to witness. We notice her sufferings and at once our compassion springs preemptively into action, seducing, maneuvering, cajoling them into our power. (Power that we might relish, not only for its own sake, but also because it distracts us from our own distress.)

In loving another, her good becomes our good. But it is not our business to turn our love into the command and control center of her flourishing. The magic of loving devotion lies in something less goal-driven and less interfering: in joyful recognition and affirmation of her existence; in offering oneself as a space for her being to take root in the world; in seeking, honoring, and so being just to, the law of her being insofar as it reveals itself to us. Attentiveness that conjures this magic is the greatest gift that lovers can bestow on each other. A gift that is, in turn, the ground of all love's other virtues and works, including all its particular acts of generosity and justice.

Erôs, Agape, and *Philia* as Modes of Attentiveness

As I suggest in *Love: A History*, attentiveness exists in at least three modes, which we can name *erôs, agape,* and *philia*.[4] Traditionally these words are used to designate three distinct types of love. *Erôs* is said to be desiring, self-interested, possessive, and conditional on the loved one's qualities. *Agape,* by contrast, is characterized as free of desire, disinterested, unpossessive, unconditional—indeed, it gratuitously confers value on the loved one—and, on some accounts, such as Anders Nygren's, as entirely spontaneous. Whereas *philia* is selective, grounded in similar qualities in the lover and beloved, and characterized by deep devotion to the flourishing of another who is experienced as a second self and whose life we crave to intertwine with our own, so striving to attain the "entireness," the "total magnanimity and trust" that Emerson sees as the essence of friendship.[5]

But *erôs, agape,* and *philia* are not best seen as distinct types of love, let alone as incompatible types.

All love has the quality of *erôs*: desiring, evaluating, possessive, self-interested, and conditional.

All love, like *philia*, is inspired and sustained by experiencing similar fundamental qualities in the loved one (from the most general, such as common humanity, or the possession of a "soul," to the most particular, such as those qualities of taste that are embodied in lineage and those values or goods that constitute ethical home; from a similarity that is roughly symmetrical to one that is grossly asymmetrical, where lover and loved one evince the relevant qualities to vastly different degrees). Yet, though inspired and sustained by what is similar, love *goes on* also to seek out and enjoy precisely what is different. To oversimplify: enjoyment of similarity is love's root; enjoyment of difference is its fruit.

Finally, as long as the single condition for love's existence—a promise of ontological rootedness—is fulfilled, it will, beyond that, be unconditional, though not disinterested: bestowing value on, and giving to, the loved one in the manner of *agape*.

As I pointed out in Chapter 17, to fulfill this single condition of love does not mean that we are dominated by *awareness* of our loved one's promise of ontological rootedness once love gets underway; and, still less, that we continually check that the promise is still active, or evaluate how well they live up to this condition.

Nor does our bestowal of value on our loved ones entail that we will love or affirm everything about them. We are always prisoners of our partial perspectives and values, and so cannot say Yes to everything we encounter in another. We cannot find everything good, as God does in Genesis. ("And . . . it was very good."[6]) In fact, to become unambivalently open to a loved one, to be attentive to the dark as well as the light, might foster ambivalence toward them—ambivalence that love should be strong enough to hold firmly in its sights without needing to deny.

If we, therefore, think of *erôs, agape,* and *philia* as naming compatible, indeed mutually reinforcing, modes of love's attentiveness, and consequently of devotion, all of which are present in the fullest love, then we can say that the attentiveness denoted by *erôs* is characterized by desiring, evaluating, searching, and possessiveness; that of *agape* by passionate, value-bestowing surrender to the loved one and in particular to the law of their being; and that of *philia* by an intimate identification with fundamental similarities that the lover sees in the loved one—notably in respect of taste, lineage, and the qualities that constitute ethical home—and to that extent by experiencing him or her as a second self.

Pride: Love's Enemy Number One

If attentiveness is love's principal virtue, then pride is the vice most inimical to love. Not good pride, in the sense of measured and realistic satisfaction with who we are—as expressed, in particular, in those ends, virtues, and achievements that we most care about and that define the self we have become; but rather pride that closes us to any realities that might challenge our self-regard—including the reality of loved ones.

Such bad pride will, without scruple, mangle those realities with falsehood and incapacitate our ability to heed them. Its unfailing valet is denial, and its most abundant creation is lies. Before such pride everything is forced to succumb—truthfulness, conscience, self-knowledge, vision, hearing—even, as Nietzsche pointed out, memory:

> "I have done that," says my memory. "I cannot have done that," says my pride, and remains inexorable. Eventually—memory yields.[7]

But pride also has subtler guises. Humility can be a form of pride. So can modesty. So can self-contempt. All of them can be ways of exalting our standards (which are so high that we cannot help failing in relation to them)—and so of exalting ourselves. As can any virtuous act that is done merely to secure our self-regard. Pride is the most liquid of the vices, able to insinuate itself into almost all our doings and valuings and feelings.

And so it will refuse to see everything that love's attentiveness craves to see: the loved one's taste, sensitivity, emotional cleanliness, ultimate ends, ideals, virtues, and all the sources of their existential power over us. It will deny them, down to their deepest reality.

At the limit, pride will reject precisely what attentiveness seeks and recognizes: the very existence of the other. It will ignore or disdain or falsify the law of her being, or otherwise refuse to hear and heed it. Under pride's deadening gaze the loved one will come to seem like a phantom—as if she

cannot exist. She will be reduced by pride to a collection of threatening qualities, emptied of being.[8]

Spirituality as Attentiveness

Taken to its extreme, attentiveness has another name: spirituality.

For spirituality—like love, one of the most elusive and abused words in
the lexicon (and for similar reasons)—is attentiveness of the highest intensity, clarity, and refinement. It can have as its inspiration God or a leaf or a
screaming child or a dying parent. It can be honed in the loneliness of the
desert; the peace of a pastoral setting; the chaos of the city; or the hubbub of a
hospital ward, surrounded by raving patients and harassed doctors.

What is essential to the spiritual, as to the sacred, is not that its object of devotion is taken to be supernatural rather than natural, or absolute rather than
contingent, or infinite rather than finite, or eternal rather than temporal—
though such transcendence might be the readiest way of picturing its radical
difference from our everyday distractedness. Instead, what defines spirituality is its depth and range of attentiveness, a maximal attentiveness in which
all three modes of attention—*erôs, agape,* and *philia*—are combined, each of
them at its purest, most powerful, most focused, and most patient. Spirituality
urgently desires the presence of the other, whose value is unquestionable, yet
waits for any sign of him indefinitely. It looks, touches, and listens posses-
sively, "drinking the loved one in," surrendering to her with every faculty. It
is seized by the iron conditionality of love—responding just to this one loved
one, whose place in our life cannot be substituted by anybody else (which
doesn't mean that we can't love other people just as intensely) and with whom
we share a unique and unrepeatable history. And yet, once this single condition of love—the promise of ontological rootedness—is satisfied, it repudiates
any further conditions.

Everything else that we associate with spirituality—its earthy contact with
"heavenly" things, its power of vision—is its *consequence*, not its inner nature,
which is nothing but pure attentiveness. Indeed, the seeming paradox of the
purest attentiveness is that the more precisely we attend to the loved one,
the more our gaze simultaneously overshoots her particularity—to alight on
a whole valued world that she brings into view. This is the valued world in
which love seeks to be grounded—and, at the limit, it might be identified with
whatever we take to be ultimately real: for example, God (Christianity), or
the eternal Forms (Plato), or nature (Spinoza), or fate (Nietzsche). Differently
put: the more personal love is the more impersonal it can also be in its ultimate
aim and motivation—a phenomenon to which we will turn in Chapter 24.

Love and Death

Because the spiritual is that extreme attentiveness where the being of the other floods us, and becomes foundational to our sense of existing, it can also be the point at which love becomes most closely connected to thoughts of death as the maximum loss of existing, of self, of the possibility to pursue any projects at all, and of the possibility of meaning. For the loved one's existence, by its sheer power, is able to evoke both their *and our* nonexistence—which, at the limit, is death: death as the penumbra of love.

The main reason why our loved one's presence can evoke nonexistence and therefore death isn't, as we might think, because the possibility of loss is intrinsic to all love—so that the greater our love, the more death, as the maximum loss, will cast a shadow over it. Nor does the loved one's evocation of death depend on seeing love as aiming at an eternal union—with, say, the romantic partner or with God—that, by definition, cannot be consummated in this life of space, time, and individuality; and so as attainable only by dying, only by *Liebestod*. Nor, too, need it rest on a conception of love as otherwise seeking its consummation in a realm that is no longer of this world, notably a conception structured by a Platonic "ladder of love" or *scala amoris*. Nor, finally, is love's relation to death, or to thoughts of death, necessarily motivated by its desire to "return" to an origin, and to that extent its urge to unravel the whole trajectory that the lover's life has taken since then.

Though these are all ways in which love can be associated with death—indeed in which love can be caused actively to seek death—there is a further, and I think deeper, relation between love and death: namely that in a very great love, when the loved one feels indispensable to the grounding of our life, we will tend to experience everything beyond their being as, at the limit, nonbeing, as collapse of our world, as emptied of the possibility of meaning, as the impossibility of our rootedness, as thrusting us into the absolute solitude that dying and death are (in that only we can die our death). Death—again, as the ultimate extinction of existing, of self, and of the possibility of action and meaning—potentially appears to us wherever our loved one cannot be;

wherever they are absent. It potentially appears to us, too, wherever we fail to respond to their promise of rootedness, and specifically to their call to our existence.[1]

Moreover, as I already suggested in Chapter 13, the loved one also confronts us, the lover, with our own nonexistence precisely by inspiring in us such a powerful sense of our existence. For the greater our sentiment of existing—the raw awareness that I am—the more clearly we experience the possibility of our not-existing.[2]

And not just the possibility but also the reality of our not-existing. To love is to be forced into awareness of those ways in which we contrive not to be alive and present in the world, in which we purge ourselves of vitality, in which the crushing power of what Freud called the "superego" holds us rigidly to standards against which it finds us hopelessly wanting. These standards—internalized from early figures of authority, above all our parents—don't necessarily have anything to do with our own flourishing. Rather they can constitute an airless habitat from which love, at its best, removes us, in order to transplant us to a home that is really ours and where we are called to our self-hood. Worse: this superego is in unholy tandem with a force for disintegration, along the lines of the "death instinct," also posited by Freud, which seeks to undo life not in the name of any ideals, however misconceived, nor even because it judges one's existence to be a crime, but simply to abolish the tension intrinsic to mental life—and so, at the limit, to abolish life itself.

Finally, death is love's hinterland in that the more we genuinely face the inevitability of our extinction—of our final banishment from life—the greater our impetus and power to search for grounding *in* life. The Greeks of the epic and classical ages understood this profoundly. They considered a *katabasis*—a descent by the living to the realm of the dead, to Hades—to prefigure a return to life with new and untold wisdom. Before we can grasp life, we must "go down": we must encounter the reality of death. As Homer's Odysseus is forced to do, before he can recover the home and the wife he loves.

If love is powerfully motivated by the experience of exile, as I argued in Chapter 18, then the prospect of this ultimate exile—from life itself—will be the ultimate motivation to achieve a love, or loves, that will anchor us in the world. Death must be faced not because it is either glorious or grimly inevitable, but because the eventuality of our own death is that horizon of certain finality that turns us back decisively toward life; because to look unflinchingly at death's certainty is to open up paths to our own most grounded and genuine relation to life. And if Heidegger is right that the authentic life is one that resolutely anticipates its death, then to the degree to which we achieve such anticipation we are strengthened in our capacity to love; and, to the degree to which love, in turn, compels such anticipation, love will enable us to live authentically.

Thus, to love is not only to become intoxicated with life but also, and insep-arably, to be pushed into painful awareness of death. Of course, we normally resist any such awareness with all our ingenuity of denial and distraction that, every day, enables us not to see abysses lying immediately before us; and our loved ones easily begin to repel us if they cannot maintain the unseeing coun-tenance, the reassuring narrowness, that obscures all such abysses.

Like the call to our destiny that we find too arduous to heed, or the transi-tion to a new home that we find too unsettling to make, so too the horizon of finitude with which our loved ones confront us can spur us to reject precisely them: precisely those we most love. For a very great love can thrive only if we can live out the tension, not to say contradiction, at its heart: the tension be-tween how love empowers us by intensifying our sense of existing and yet also humbles us by bringing to light our ontological fragility.

"Overshooting" the Loved One: Love's Impersonal Dimension

We rightly think of love as the most personal of emotions. Personal in its *origin*, in expressing who precisely we, as lovers, are: our taste, our character, our history, what we most deeply care about, what world we want to inhabit. And personal in its *object*: in its highly selective focus on our loved ones, and in craving as much of their particularity as we can possibly relate to, come close to, give to, and enjoy.

The four features that I have suggested ground and define love—identification with a lineage, the discovery of an ethical home, power over our sense of existing, and the call to our selfhood or destiny—speak of the deepest particularity both of the lover who responds to the promise and of the loved one in whom she glimpses it, whether we are talking about love for romantic partners, children, spouses, works of art, or God, to name just some of love's many possible objects. Indeed, since the eighteenth century, and in particular since Rousseau, we have thought of love as both reflecting and fostering the lover's individual "authenticity."

Yet because love craves rootedness in a *world* that the lover supremely values—because, at the limit, love strives to relate her to, or embed her in, an entire world to which she feels called or fated—there is also a sense in which the more personal love is, the more it also seems to transcend both lover and loved one. That is, it seems to have an origin beyond the particularity of the lover insofar as love involves experience of fatedness—as well as seeming to seek, or spill over toward, a reality beyond the loved one insofar as love seeks a whole valued world. And to that degree love can appear impersonal.[1] As if the direct relationship between lover and loved one is only part of what love is about—albeit its vital core, where the desires, intentions, hopes, and actions of the lover are most focused, most concentrated, most palpable.

What does this really mean? How can love be experienced as simultaneously personal and impersonal? How can the particularity of lover and beloved be love's inspiration and relentless focus *and yet* what love cannot help transcending?

It can be precisely because to feel grounded through love is to feel that, in and through our loved one, we belong, or are blessed with a promise of belonging, to a supremely valued world in which we yearn to make our home; a world that we see as the field of all possibilities for us; a world of which the beloved speaks or is the animating center, and to which they point or call us; a world that, as Rilke puts it, we see in the face of the beloved. Love gives us the strongest possible sentiment of our, and our loved one's, individual existence precisely by relating us to a whole—a whole that is necessarily elusive if only because of its scope, which is the horizon of this existence. (And so love for one individual in particular can transform our relationship to the world in general.)

Moreover, love's sense of being fated is why, in its origin, it is so often experienced as coming upon us like a bolt from the blue, as "larger than us." Love might make us feel magnificently free; yet we do not necessarily want to think of it as the product of a free will: of a will that is taken to be aware of alternatives, to choose between them, and to be capable of deciding otherwise. Rather we want love—and the loved one—to seize us with the force of destiny, a force magnificently indifferent to who we have been until now, indeed that will henceforth decide and define who we are. (In other words, I am not claiming that love is *in fact* not under our control; rather I am suggesting that even if, in some sense, it is a voluntary decision we experience it, to a great degree, as fated.)

Thus we feel exhilaratingly free in love not despite, but *because* of, our belief in its necessity. Our sense of freedom depends on our conviction that we have no choice in the matter. This is why the origin of love has, variously, been depicted as Cupid's arrow, divine grace, the machinations of gods, magic potions, and the gaze that seals destinies—all of them deliverances of powers beyond the lovers' control, powers that they can celebrate but not choose.

Here love is experienced no differently than many other moments in which the individual most intensely feels her power of existence and her freedom to be. The great statesman senses the hand of destiny that has chosen and guided him. The artist believes she is "in-spired" courtesy of an external power: the muse. The convert is struck down on the road to Damascus. The moral hero takes herself to be acting out of overwhelming compulsion.

It is not out of modesty, but out of immodesty, that we like to think of our small decisions as free and our largest ones as fated. And even the proudest will enjoy this sensation of humility: of surrender to an empowering force beyond their ken.

Unfreedom—in the form of necessity—dignifies everything that gives ultimate meaning to our lives: our most deeply held ends and values; our "choice" of vocation; our "choice" of spouse; our heroic acts. Great things feel destined.

Is this not true even of morality? Despite the insistence of Kant, and of much of Jewish and Christian tradition, that moral responsibility presupposes the idea of freedom of the will—a will sovereignly able to do otherwise—is it not rather the case, especially for our hardest moral decisions, that we take ourselves to have no choice? That responsibility is rather about wholeheartedly responding to the call that presents itself to us in the depths of our being? That when we hesitate before alternative paths the decision arrives, resolves itself, from within or from without? That deliberating and agonizing might clarify the options but they don't make the decisions? So that we say with Luther: "Here I stand. I can do no other."

—

If the first reason why love can seem impersonal precisely when it feels most personal is that we take it to originate from beyond rather than within us—to befall us as a destiny we cannot choose but by which we feel individually chosen—the second is this: the more arrested we are by the loved one's promise and thus by their particularity, the more our love can seem also to overshoot them. For in responding to a promise of rootedness in a world that we supremely value, our love for the other is, at the same time, a yearning for that particular world. And the loved one, by captivating our attention, sensitizes us to this world that they open to us and to which they, by their very existence, call or point us.

To be clear: this overshooting does not leave the loved one behind. The loved one is no ladder that the lover discards. On the contrary, it is her particularity, and it alone, that grounds the lover's love. His love must be grounded in her in order to see beyond her. In other words, to focus on her particularity and to see beyond her constitute the same movement: the more intense the one, the more intense the other.

Sometimes we express this by feeling that we love all creation when we love her. Sometimes we see her pointing beyond herself to a transcendent reality, not of this world—as in *La Vita Nuova* Dante sees Beatrice guiding him to the divine being; and as in *The Divine Comedy* he glimpses how, in opening the way to the heavenly realm, his very particular love for Beatrice, and for her alone, creates the possibility of participation in the universal "love that moves the sun and other stars," as the last line of the poem has it. Sometimes, in an utterly different idiom, which in no way posits a divine or final object of love beyond the lovers themselves, we express this double focus on the particular and the general as Tristan and Isolde do, by proclaiming that we—the combined "We" or the double "I" of love—*are* the world. ("Then I myself am the world," *selbst dann bin ich die Welt*,[2] they sing together at the summit of their passion—and it would be missing the point to see this as mere narcissism.)

Philosophers too—especially but not exclusively within secular and religious traditions influenced by Platonism's *scala amoris*—have given expression to this sense in which love, in focusing on the loved one, also aims for a reality beyond her, and we do not need to agree with their explanations of the ground of love to see that this is so.

It is there, paradigmatically, in Socrates's account of the ascent of love from desiring a beautiful individual to contemplating the absolute beauty that transcends all individuals.

It is there in Augustine's description of how genuine love (in the sense of *caritas*) for another person is ultimately for the sake of love for God.

It is there in Spinoza's idea that properly to love anything particular is to love it in relation to the whole—nature considered as a totality, or God—of which that thing is an inextricable part and from which it necessarily derives.

It is there in Schopenhauer's idea that genuine love—*Menschenliebe*, the selfless compassion that achieves a "wholly direct and even instinctive partic- ipation in another's sufferings"[3]—points us toward ultimate reality: the single, timeless, absolute, undifferentiated whole called "Will," from which each of us springs and that transcends all individuality or embodiment, including that of our loved ones.

It is suggested in Friedrich Schlegel's magnificent remark that it is only in a great love relationship "that a feeling for the world has really dawned on us."[4]

It is echoed in Kierkegaard's description of God as "the middle term" in all love between individuals—in other words, of God as the absolute source and standard of love, from which the love of two individuals derives its force and genuineness, and toward which it is ultimately oriented: "The God-relationship is the mark by which the love for people is recognized as genuine . . . God in this way not only becomes the third party in every relationship of [genuine] love but really becomes the *sole* object of love."[5]

It is there in Sartre's claim, cynically one-sided about love as he often is, that the loved one is "*only* a conducting body" that mediates between the lover and his world.[6]

It is there, explicitly, in Simone Weil's insistence that "what is sacred in a human being"—and the true focus of love for our neighbor—"is the imper- sonal in him."[7]

It is there in Levinas's notion of how our responsibility to one involves un- limited responsibility to everyone—including his ideal that in being respon- sible for others you are also responsible for their responsibility for you. For if you properly experience and respect the absolute otherness of a single indi- vidual, you will be led properly to experience and respect the absolute other- ness of all.

And because love proceeds in this way from an individual to a whole, we cannot love everyone in virtue of their being our "neighbor" unless we first love one or more people in virtue of their offering us a promise of ontological rootedness. Yet again we must be careful not to conflate love with benevolence, as if they were two words for the same thing. As a virtue of character benevo- lence can be extended equally to anybody, regardless of who they are. In this sense, we can be Good Samaritans to anyone. But as an expression of *love*, benevolence—and with it devotion and value—can be bestowed on people in general only as the result of being first bestowed on people in particular. Since love seeks and responds to a promise of ontological rootedness—grounded in recognition of a very specific lineage, ethical home, existential power, and "call," which cannot possibly be inspired by everyone, regardless of who they are—indiscriminate love, in the sense of devotion to, valuing of, and intimacy with anyone regardless of their qualities, presupposes discriminating love, which overshoots its chosen loved ones in its striving to embrace a whole valued world and all who are included within it. In other words, we can love humanity only if we first love human beings. Or if we first love God, conceived as the source of humanity and its ethical home. (It is not for nothing that Augustine, Thomas Aquinas, and numerous theologians have characterized love for neighbor as necessarily flowing from, and existing for the sake of, love for God.) Love for the particular is in every sense prior to love for the general.

In each one of these cases of "overshooting" a particular loved one, what is key about this larger world for which the lover yearns is not that it is conceived as located beyond this life of time, space, and individuation—in other words, as otherworldly in, for example, the manner of Plato's "ascent" story. The key is rather that the lover experiences this particular larger world that she values (whether conceived as transcendent or as immanent) as attainable only in and through her loved ones. In other words, she sees it as a sacred place that is both embodied by her loved ones and, at the same time, beyond them; a world to which they alone have the key and to which they alone can beckon.

This ambition to attain a whole world that is the field of all the lover's possibilities is, of course, so extravagant that it is no more likely to be achievable, or even to have a determinate aim, than it is feasible for the loved one to be securely "possessed." Here again we see how human love, as a trajectory toward a promised groundedness in a world that we supremely value, has no endpoint that can be finally and stably reached.

Can We Love Ourselves?

A man ought, in charity, to love himself *more* than his neighbor.

—THOMAS AQUINAS

Thou doest ill in loving thyself.

—MARTIN LUTHER

[Each of us] is his own best friend and therefore ought to love himself best.

—ARISTOTLE

Self-love, . . . as the principle of all our maxims, is precisely the source of all evil.

—IMMANUEL KANT[1]

In order to explore more deeply the nature of love as joy inspired by one who offers us a promise of rootedness, we must turn now to that notoriously problematic case over which philosophers and theologians have agonized for centuries: self-love, love's perplexing ugly sister.

In the first place, is self-love desirable? Isn't it at bottom a narcissistic self-concern in which your world shrinks to nothing more than your own perspectives, whims, and interests, and in which others exist only as impersonal sources of self-esteem and need satisfaction?

As the epigraphs at the head of this chapter suggest, even the Christian tradition, which is often assumed to condemn self-love outright, is divided on this question, and makes clear distinctions between good and bad instances of it, between loving yourself in the right way and in the wrong way. After all, the Bible already commands you to love your neighbor *as yourself*—suggesting that self-love is not only legitimate but is actually the measure and model of an impartial love for others.

And among Christianity's greatest theologians, we find many who regard good self-love as central to the well-lived life. Thomas Aquinas even claims that "a man ought, in charity, to love himself more than his neighbor."[2] By which he means that we are bound to love our spiritual nature, as distinct from our bodily nature, more than we love anyone else's; for it is closer to us than anyone else's can be.[3] Indeed, our love [*amicitia*] for ourselves is the model of our love for others. Love of neighbor, in other words, presupposes love of self.

Augustine too has a well-defined place for self-love, namely as whole-hearted commitment to one's own greatest good: love for God. "He who knows how to love himself loves God."[4] For only in loving God in the fullest degree do we achieve true happiness and self-fulfillment. "Man loves himself by relating to God as his maker" is how Hannah Arendt summarizes Augustine's position on good self-love.[5] By contrast, he excoriates any concern for oneself that disregards God and instead pursues merely worldly goods, which are perishable and therefore, he maintains, ultimately of no value. A human being, he says, "can relate only destructively to himself when he holds God's will in contempt" and so is "given over to himself" in a manner that ignores this supreme good.[6]

In other words, Augustine is saying that to love yourself well is to know what your greatest good is and to be completely devoted to it. To love your greatest good is not a *means* to true self-love, as if we are to focus first on loving God and then, armed with this relationship, we are in a stronger position to love ourselves. Rather it is the *same* as true self-love.

Whereas merely to do whatever gives you the most immediate satisfaction, or to protect your interests at the expense of others, will not enable you genuinely to flourish or be happy, and so cannot count as healthy self-love.

For Kierkegaard, echoing Augustine, "to love God is to love oneself truly."[7] And because to love God is—in imitation of God—to love your neighbor, he also identifies neighbor love with self-love: "to love yourself in the right way and to love the neighbor correspond perfectly to one another; fundamentally," he adds, "they are one and the same thing."[8] Or, more precisely (and convolutedly) put, good self-love is when you "love yourself in the same way as you love your neighbor when you love him as yourself."[9] By contrast, corrupt self-love is a turning away from God toward mere selfishness: "In the human psyche," Kierkegaard says, "there lies a selfishness that has to be broken if the God-relationship is truly to be won."[10]

———

Then there is the other, and perhaps better-known, side of the Christian tradition: the side that excoriates self-love, whatever its form. Luther is a perfect example of this. For him *any* interest in one's own flourishing or happiness is incompatible with genuine love, very much including love for God. Indeed he goes further: "To love," he proclaims, "is the same as to hate oneself"[11]— adding: "you will not be straightened out and made upright unless you cease entirely to love yourself, and, forgetting yourself, love only your neighbor."[12]

Although such exhortations to annihilate self-love already existed in the Middle Ages and earlier, it is in the particular Protestant tradition inaugurated by Luther—and *not* in the long Christian tradition preceding it—that we find the decisive origin of today's conviction that love for others must be free of all self-interest: the conviction, unwittingly taken over from that Protestant tradition by secular thinkers such as Frankfurt, who regard it as self-evident that love is intrinsically selfless or disinterested, that it "is not driven by any ulterior purpose"[13] or by the hope of "any benefit that [the lover] may derive either from the beloved or from loving it."[14]

Similar divisions between proponents and opponents of self-love exist in the wider philosophical tradition. For Aristotle, self-love, properly conceived, is central to being a virtuous person, and so is vital to our flourishing and a condition of love for others. Each of us, he says, "is his own best friend and ought to love himself best."[15] For Spinoza, self-love is not merely good but "the highest thing" for which we can search.[16] For Rousseau, in his concept of *amour de soi*, self-love is the healthy and innate drive of all living creatures to persist as the kind of creature they are—and it can be absolutely consistent with love for others. *Amour de soi*, which Rousseau holds to be "always good," "is a natural sentiment which inclines every animal to watch over its own preservation, and which, directed in man by reason and modified by pity, produces humanity and virtue."[17] For Nietzsche, "one thing is needful: that a human being should *attain* satisfaction with himself,"[18] else he will fall prey to the crippling emotion of resentment. For Simon Blackburn, good self-love includes "proper pride in our own achievements."[19] And this kind of life-enhancing self-respect or pride is indeed something that cannot be substituted (even if it can be encouraged) by the esteem of others, which might be what the great first-century BCE Jewish sage, Hillel the Elder, means when he says, "If I am not for myself, who will be for me?"[20]

By contrast, Aristotle condemns the common kind of self-love where people "assign to themselves the greater share of wealth, honors, and bodily pleasures; for these are what most people desire, and busy themselves about as though they were the best of all things."[21] According to Adam Smith, the eighteenth-century moralist Francis Hutcheson declares that self-love can "never be virtuous in any degree or in any direction." In fact, says Smith, "Dr. Hutcheson was so far from allowing self-love to be in any case a motive for virtuous action, that even a regard for the pleasure of self-approbation, to the comfortable applause of our own consciences, according to him, diminished the merit of a benevolent action."[22] Rousseau, for his part, excoriates that distortion of self-love which he calls *amour propre*, and which, he says, "inclines each individual to have a greater esteem for himself than for anyone else, inspires in men all the harm they do to one another, and is the true source of honor."[23] And Kant, that sternest advocate of the duties of the moral law, sees self-love, in the form of our natural desire for happiness, as "the source of all evil" when it becomes the principle of maxims that govern our will, and so impedes our obedience to morality. (Yet even Kant does have room for good self-love, both in the sense of a desire for happiness that does not impede our obedience to the moral law and also as respect for the dignity of our own humanity.[24])

———

Nonetheless, many of these traditional discussions of self-love, whether they are for it or against it, make the same error as discussions of love in general: they take "love" to be, variously, just another word for benevolence, or valuing, or esteem, or affirmation, or respect, or pride—directed in this case reflexively, toward oneself; and so they, too, lose sight of love's specificity.

As we have just seen, Kant does so in speaking of self-love in terms of self-respect or self-esteem. So does Rousseau when he characterizes good self-love, *amour de soi*, in terms of self-respect; and bad self-love, *amour propre*, in terms of bloated self-esteem or craving for self-esteem. And so, too, does Harry Frankfurt: "Loving ourselves," he says, "is the same thing, more or less, as being satisfied with ourselves."[25] Good self-love, he goes on, "is a condition in which we willingly accept and endorse our own volitional identity"[26]—in other words, those ends that we cannot help willing and that define who we are, whether they are good or "dreadfully and irredeemably wicked."[27] Such self-love is the "deepest and most essential . . . achievement of a serious and successful life."[28] Bad self-love, by contrast, is smug complacency or the conceit that we have successfully fulfilled our ambitions.[29]

But though pride, esteem, valuing, admiration, and affirmation can all be of the greatest value to our flourishing, they are *not* the same as love. And we will fail to understand either what they are or what love is if we conflate them. We know this from love for others, which is something more than—on occasion even distinct from—"being satisfied" with *them*, wholeheartedly endorsing their "volitional identity," taking "proper pride" in their achievements, or otherwise respecting and esteeming them. We can have such feelings for those we don't love. Conversely, we can genuinely love people without being satisfied with them, endorsing their core values, or taking proper pride in all their achievements—indeed, without even liking them.

Rather than being another word for self-love, pride in oneself is a virtue conducive to loving others; or, when it becomes hubris, a vice that obstructs love for others. Good pride is an empowering satisfaction in who one is—and, in particular, in those ends and achievements that one most cares about. It gives us confidence to open ourselves to the reality of others, including their perspectives and values and achievements, and so to notice a promise of ontological rootedness, if they are offering us one, and then to build a relationship of love with them.

By contrast, bad pride is a state of siege against any realities—of oneself and of others—that might question our self-regard; or that challenge the life we lead now. It is a state of siege employing denial, lying, pomposity, narcissism, and complacency, all of which close us to what we do not already see or embrace. Others then figure in our lives merely to endorse or echo who we are. Aside from that, their perspectives, values, and achievements mean nothing to us, even if we notice them. Bad pride is the enemy of love, for it prevents us from responding to the very promise of ontological rootedness in another for which we yearn.

Historically, therefore, much, perhaps most, discussion about good and bad self-love has actually been about good and bad pride, or about other emotions of self-esteem. It hasn't been about self-love at all.

———

But there is a prior question that is easily obscured by this long historical focus on distinguishing good self-love from bad: Is self-love even possible? Can we really be our own lover and beloved?

I think that we cannot. Not because we can't have powerful emotions toward ourselves. We clearly have many, such as esteem, respect, joy, contempt, pity, shame, guilt, concern, disgust, and, as we have just seen, good and bad pride. Indeed, in contrast to love, these feelings can be *more* powerful when directed inward, toward ourselves, than when directed outward at others. And in some cases, like guilt, they are necessarily reflexive.

Rather, self-love is impossible because it lacks love's intrinsic condition: the grounding presence of another whom we experience as radically distinct from us, and who remains so however much we also become a union, a "We." For love is a relation to such a grounding presence, which promises us a home—a horizon of possibilities; a source of life that is not already our own; a potentially benevolent existential power over us; an ethical home; a call to us—that is necessarily seen as a gift from without and so cannot be discovered within the compass of our own self, however multiple, sprawling, and fluid we take that self to be. Love, in its very structure, is directed at one who breaks into our life from outside and who is the origin of the promise that we cannot make to ourselves: one who embodies or points to that world, transcending the current borders that we take our life to have, to which we yearn to belong or to which we have been irresistibly called, and who elicits a devotion that casts us beyond ourselves. In and through the loved one, this promised world comes alive to us as a home—a home in which, at the same time, we can come to new life.

And so we will always experience the object of our love as larger than us, as transcending us, even if it is *not* a distinct being that we must think of as external to us—a person or god or landscape or work of art—but is rather, say, a vocation. If I feel that I am by nature a philosopher, or an artist, or a builder, or a mountain climber, what I experience as purely within the ambit of my being is my devotion to this vocation, my valuation of it, my capacity to pursue it— but *not* the object of my devotion, which, like every object of love, necessarily exceeds me, however much it also "is me."

Our love cannot therefore be elicited by ourselves: we cannot take ourselves as objects of our own love. At most we can feel toward ourselves a simulacrum of love, in the sense of joy at being someone who is able to be grounded in another and, through them, in a world that we supremely value. But this is, strictly speaking, self-esteem and not self-love. For love's rapture—a rapture that, it is worth noting, never has the same quality in what is called "self-love," or in any of the emotions of self-esteem, however strong they are—depends upon the lucky throw of encountering a source of being that we experience as standing beyond us and that calls or energizes us to new life.

No matter how deeply we come to share in the life of this loved one, and to regard his needs and ends and projects as our own, we will continue to refer them to a distinct self—a "second" self, or "another" self, to use Aristotle's word—with a history, a self-consciousness, and an embodiment that are, all three, different from ours. Or when lovers proclaim that they are merged into a union of interchangeable names—as Wagner's Tristan and Isolde do—there are always *two* who do so, each addressing the other as "you" (though they also think of each other as "me"), and each with his or her own embodied self-consciousness.

In the great friendships of history we see the same. However perfect the union, there are always two in it: "one soul in two bodies," as Augustine says of one of his youthful friendships,[30] a formula echoed by Montaigne eleven centuries later. "In the friendship I speak of," Montaigne says of his love for Étienne de La Boétie, "our souls mingle and blend with each other so completely that they efface the seam that joined them, and cannot find it again."[31] Through love, Augustine adds, speaking of *caritas*, lovers dwell inside *one another*.[32] So that, however we conceive of personal identity and its unique psychological unity or continuity, we will always see our loved one as originating from beyond its ambit.[33]

––––––––

There is, however, one scenario in which genuine self-love would become possible, though it is not one of which human beings, as we are normally constituted, are capable; and it is this:

If one could be a genuine union of lover and loved one—if, in an extreme psychological condition, one experienced oneself not merely as two souls cohabiting one breast, as Goethe's Faust famously describes his warring selves, but rather as *two distinguishable persons, each of whom also dwells in the other* (or as two souls inhabiting the breasts of two distinct selves, with separate lives and bodies and histories)—then, perhaps, one could love oneself with the same ardor and gratitude that fills one's love for others.

This, we might think, is akin to how Narcissus falls in love with himself when, as the Roman poet Ovid recounts it, he first sees his reflection in a still pool, where he is slaking his thirst after fleeing the desirous nymph Echo. But, of course, he doesn't really exemplify such an extreme psychological condition; for at that moment he takes himself to be seeing *another* person altogether. The beautiful youth looking back at him from the water, by whose lovely form he is smitten, is, he thinks, someone else:

Unwittingly he desires himself; he praises and is himself what he praises; and while he seeks, is sought; equally he kindles love and burns with love. How often did he offer vain kisses on the elusive pool? How often did he plunge his arms into the water seeking to clasp the neck he sees there, but did not clasp himself in them! What he sees he knows not; but that which he seeks he burns for, and the same delusion mocks and allures his eyes.[34]

Yet there is a far more powerful image of what I take to be genuine self-love than the myth of Narcissus, and this can be found in the Christian doctrine of the Trinity. Here, and particularly in interpretations of the Trinity as a "society," we find a model of precisely that extreme condition in which self-love becomes possible: that condition in which one person also experiences herself as two or more distinct people who are united in love. For the Trinity's "three persons," Father, Son, and Holy Spirit, can be said to love each other in just such an ultimate sense at the same time as being one. Their mutual love is also their self-love.

Indeed, according to this interpretation of the doctrine, the Trinity describes no less than the nature of God, whose three persons are distinct in that they dwell in each other and surrender to each other in love, and yet who are also one being in that this mutual indwelling and surrendering are total: three persons who are, in short, simultaneously different and identical. As the Council of Florence (1438–1445) declared:

> The Father is totally in the Son and totally in the Spirit. The Son is totally in the Father and totally in the Spirit. The Holy Spirit is totally in the Father, totally in the Son.[35]

Each person of the Trinity is therefore in the other and also distinguishable from the other in just the way that Jesus characterizes his relationship with the Father: "I am in the Father, and the Father is in me." And he goes on: "The words that I say to you I do not speak on my own; but the Father who dwells in me does his works."[36]

Since two or more human persons cannot be, at the same time, totally in each other, irreducibly distinct, and also one being, they cannot fulfill the conditions for self-love in the way that the persons of the Trinity do.

And so what is normally called "self-love" is, I have suggested, really good or bad pride, or other emotions of self-esteem, involving delight in our powers, joy in our existence, confidence in our ultimate ends, wholehearted pursuit of our desires and values.

Nonetheless, to love another does foster a very particular sort of self-esteem or self-relatedness—especially though not exclusively when our love is reciprocated: namely as one who can rescue herself from the dullness and terror of solipsism by responding with joy to a promise of groundedness in a world that she supremely values; as one, that is, who can find in that world a home, a field of possibilities, and a call to her being; and who can therefore give her life a new trajectory of meaning. Another's recognition or affirmation of her will *not* suffice to bring about this self-esteem if she herself does not love.

The self-esteem made possible by our love for another is, in other words, quite specific. We don't come, through loving, to a deeper affirmation even of everything that we deem good or praiseworthy about ourselves. To love doesn't necessarily make it easier to value our bodies or our minds or our virtues or our ends or our achievements; and we abuse love if we demand that it be a source of such far-reaching affirmation.

To love another does, however, allow us to become as open as we can be to *their* esteem for us—and by the same token to their love for us. Only when we love another can their esteem for us enduringly inspire our esteem for ourselves: only then can it be truly effective. To the point where we can be sure whom we love by the degree to which even their subtlest recognition of us inspires joyful self-affirmation and becomes a deeper confirmation of our existence. Whereas all praise by those we don't love is a short-lived thrill, a recognitional endorphin shot, which will eventually wear off, leaving our self-esteem as dependent as it ever was on honors, status, and applause.

Taken together, these two paths to self-esteem that love opens up for us—valuing ourselves as one who can be grounded in the world through love, and enabling the esteem of loved ones to be truly effective—afford us a sense of peace and of belonging that is among the deepest to be found.

But since these paths to self-esteem are opened up by love, they are at least as rare as love itself is. Indeed, any genuine self-esteem or good pride, as distinct from self-centeredness or bad pride, is difficult; and even the brashest confidence is possible only by rigorously concealing or ignoring self-doubt. For self-esteem is far from identical with self-centeredness: with putting ourselves first, seeking to maximize our pleasure regardless of the cost to others, or protecting our interests at their expense. Rather, self-esteem—as a deeply felt critical relation to one's virtues and vices, ends and lack of ends, achievements and failures—is secured through the trial and error of successfully negotiating one's way through an intractable world into which one has been cast and in which one's groundedness will always remain fragile and provisional, however much recognition and prestige and power one manages to win. Far from being natural or easy, therefore, such self-esteem—and in particular the kind that is fostered by love of another—belongs to the most hard-won achievements of a well-lived life.[37]

PART III

Narratives of Love
as Rootedness

Introduction

I argued in Part I that something is missing in the six major conceptions of love that have emerged in the Western world—or, more precisely, in all those parts of the world that are heir to the confluence of biblical and Greek thought—since ancient times. What is missing is an answer to the question "what is the ground of love?" that can explain love's brute particularity: why, for example, of all those we find beautiful or good or virtuous or sexually attractive or kind or altruistic, we love only a very few; or why this person and not that one feels like our "other half" or our "second self." Without addressing this question head-on, there can be no satisfactory understanding of the nature of love.

Nor do we answer our question by shifting the focus from the qualities of the loved one to the qualities of the lover. It doesn't suffice, for example, to characterize love in terms of devotion, generosity, attachment, possessiveness, intimacy, respect, or kindness. For to do so is always to beg the question: When are these motivated by love and when, by contrast, do they reflect, say, dispositions of character or other forms of attachment? And how does devotion or generosity or jealousy or attachment differ when it is found in a relationship of love—structured and colored as it then is by love's ontological yearnings along with the peculiar joy and awe that accompany those yearnings when faced with a promise of satisfaction—as distinct from a relationship motivated by, say, altruism or duty or social solidarity? And why does a particular relationship of love, marked by self-giving, devotion, and intimacy, get going in the first place?

I then proposed in Part II that an answer to the question "what is love?" that better identifies love's very specific ground and aim can be given in terms of our universal human need to experience an inviolable grounding for our life in a world that we supremely value. Love, I suggested, is joy inspired by those in whom we see a promise of "ontological rootedness," joy that motivates the possibly lifelong search for a relationship with them.

I now want to show that we find key elements of such an answer to the question of the ground of love in those two great sources of the Western spirit: Athens and Jerusalem; and in particular in Greek epic poetry and Hebrew scripture. In each of them, we find myths that connect love to the search for, and the promise of, home in a world we supremely value—"myths," in this sense, being not falsehoods but structures of revelation: narratives through which fundamental realities of the human condition, and of the ethical, symbolic, and motivational order that governs it at any given place and time, are spoken and made comprehensible, whether or not the events they recount actually happened.

In Greek epic we find it in Homer's *Odyssey*: in Odysseus's journey back from the Trojan war to his homeland, Ithaca—a journey motivated by longing to return to his wife, his land, his son, his kingship, and his parents, all of them, I will suggest, facets of one love, of one promise of home.

In the Bible we find a paradigmatic expression of love inspired by a promise of ontological rootedness in the response of Abraham to God's call to travel to an unknown land, far from his ancestral home: the land of Canaan, where his true home is to be discovered and where his destiny is to unfold.

My purpose in this part of the book is not to put forward or claim an original interpretation of these famous narratives, but only to show how they explicitly or implicitly articulate the idea that love, in its very structure, is a response to a promise of ontological rootedness, which in turn involves identification with a lineage, discovery of an ethical home, the loved one's power over our sense of existing, and the call to our selfhood or destiny. In the one case, this response is a journey to a new territory, radically removed, perhaps inconceivably distant, from our actual origin and so at the outset uncharted; whereas in the other, it leads to renewed relationship with the place where we started: a return to the loved one that, through a fresh encounter with them and the arduous journey needed to achieve it, is a way of going forward with our love and as a result with our life.

And so it is to God's call, embodied in his covenant with Abraham, the Patriarch from whom all three monotheisms descend, that we first turn.

The Bible: Love as a Discovery of Home

Covenant is central to the Bible. In covenant, God promises himself to human beings as the highest possible object of love: as the ultimate grounding of the lives of all those who receive this promise; a grounding that is also the foundation for a community of love among them—and that deeply recognizes human dignity, integrity, and responsibility. Human beings, for their part, are to be obedient to the law that structures this promise—obedience that demands ceaseless attentiveness to God and to what he calls on them to do; obedience without which they could not attain the promise of groundedness.

Two key covenants of Hebrew scripture—of the Old Testament—are those made by God with Abraham and with Moses. Here we find articulated precisely the promise of ontological rootedness that I have sketched: the promise of home in a world that the lover supremely values, in this case through the establishment of a land and a lineage ordained by God himself; the discovery of an ethical home in the form of divinely revealed law, which, far from being constructed merely out of a set of commands to be slavishly followed, speaks of the fundamental existence, the innermost spirit, of the loved one, in which the lover may anchor himself and be called to himself; the forward-looking structure of love in the form of promise and hope; the idea that love is inspired by the loved one's power to make and rescind the promise of belonging on which the lover's sense of existing depends and without which he would, at the limit, be nobody; the terror that is constitutive of love—and is evoked more consistently by the loved one's presence than by his absence; the potential jealousy and violence and inconstancy with which all love has to reckon; the experience of exile in motivating the search for groundedness in the world; and, behind all this, the lover's sense of being called to his destiny by the loved one. In exemplifying all these elements of what I take to be the fundamental structure of love, the covenants with Abraham and Moses that we find in Hebrew scripture are, I suggest, truly the *Urtext* of love.

Let us look, then, in more detail at how the narrative of covenant illustrates four of these key elements of ontological rootedness: home in a world that we supremely value; promise as the structure of love; the experience of exile as motivating the search for groundedness in the world, and so as sustaining and enriching our openness to love—and in particular, to the promise that grounds it; and love's consummation—its success in attaining a relationship with the loved one—as conditional on the self-mastery to make their law our own.

Home

What do the covenants with Abraham and Moses fundamentally offer? They offer a home in this world containing within it vast new possibilities, not least of which is a world-creating system of ethics, an entirely new lineage—the people of Israel—whose historic calling it is to live and exemplify this system of ethics, and a profound spiritualization of human nature.

It is an extraordinary home in that it is constituted not by whatever land and lineage and morality one happens to have been born into and raised in, which is the norm for human beings, but, on the contrary, by a new land, a new lineage, and a new morality, all of which are divinely ordained out of the mysterious working of God's will. Home is ultimately a relation to the great anchoring and originating power that is God, whose law must be heeded if the promise of rootedness—the promise of love—is to be fulfilled.

This is deeply odd, perhaps unparalleled in history: a home in the world that is divinely given by means of covenants that are gratuitous in the sense that no right to them can be assumed. Indeed, those covenants and the home they promise must be deserved afresh by each generation, not because won by force of arms or superior cunning, but rather by dint of moral scrupulousness.

On the one hand, therefore, the Hebrews are denied the rootedness taken for granted by most human beings—the rootedness afforded by being born into a particular place, lineage, and morality. On the other hand, they are promised the maximum rootedness conceivable: in a land, a lineage, and a moral order vouchsafed by the source of all life, of all land, and of all possible home. By God.

God's promise of home—this combination of place, kin, and law—is to structure human beings' love for God. The aim of the covenants with Abraham and Moses isn't, of course, to inspire God to love—or to teach God the nature of love, or the responsibility and selfhood that are prerequisites for it—but rather to inspire and teach humans to love. Beginning with love for God: the primordial love; for, as I argued in Chapter 7, every other expression of love—for our romantic partner, for our parents, for our children, for our country, for nature, for art—is, in its motivation, aim, and form, a special and partial case of love for God.

Promise as the Structure of Love

The Bible reminds us again and again how promise—the future-oriented structure of love—is fundamental to covenant.

First, and most obviously, none of the founding Patriarchs sets up a permanent home in the Land: it remains promised; not yet inherited. Abraham, Isaac, and Jacob are merely sojourners or strangers in Canaan; while Moses never sets foot there. They are all on their way to the fulfillment of the promise, as love is always a movement on its way to rootedness.

Second, when the Land is reached it doesn't become the finally achieved possession of the Israelites. As in all love, there is no endpoint at which home is secured once and for all, and so at which love's orientation to the future ceases. The covenants are not about holding God to his gifts: the Israelites, like any lovers, are not freeholders with owners' rights over their loved one and his gifts. Indeed, the Land is quite explicitly *not* Israel's.[1] Canaan is, as it were, merely leased, subject to contract. It returns to God in the Sabbatical and Jubilee years. It belongs to the loved one—to God—and cannot be lived in without his continued blessing.

Third, the way of love is strewn with difficulties, some of them self-inflicted. Abraham's progeny will take four generations—four hundred years—to reach Canaan. There will be captivity in Egypt before the Israelites can begin the journey to Canaan. There will be forty years of wandering in the desert. Even after settling the Land, there will be the exile of further captivity in Babylon, following the destruction of the First Temple in Jerusalem in 586 BCE, and so the need to reach the Land once again. Then there will be nearly two millennia of expulsions and dispersions after the destruction of the Second Temple in 70 CE. It is perhaps no surprise that the word "Hebrew," *ivri*, means literally "one who crossed over," who has come from there to here.[2]

Love as Motivated and Sustained by Exile

Rootedness is promised; it isn't guaranteed. Because, as covenant shows us, whether we, as lovers, attain the rootedness promised by the loved one is dependent on our preparedness to be displaced—even to be in exile—and is conditional on aligning ourselves with the law of the loved one.

We have already seen how, early in Genesis, the loss of the original home—Eden—motivates the long search for a homeland, which actually begins twenty generations later with God's covenant with Abraham.

So, too, when Abraham receives the covenant he must leave his ancestral home in ancient Mesopotamia. For the most fruitful home, the home in which he and his offspring may blossom with vast new possibilities and energies—in which they will live out the call to their destiny, to their "I will be"—is not to be found there. And so God says to Abraham: "Go from your country and your kindred and your father's house to the land that I will show you."[3]

To find our new home, structured by the law of the loved one, we have to leave our old life and its no longer vital customs and laws. Indeed, Abraham must, in addition, abandon his inherited lineage and found a new one: a lineage in which those who receive the promise can ground their lives and also find a trajectory into the future. His displacement or exile must be not only outer but, in a certain sense, inner as well. And to mark this seminal crossover, from the old home of habit to the new home of destiny, God renames him: Abram becomes Abraham.[4]

Even after sixty-two years living in the Promised Land, Abraham, we should recall, still calls himself "a stranger and an alien"[5]—an alien who resides in the Land but does not have ownership over it, and so lacks any irrevocable guarantee of home.

Abraham's offspring, in their turn, will discover that exile is a precondition for attaining God's promise of progeny and land: "Know this for certain," God says to Abraham, "that your offspring shall be strangers in a land that is not theirs, and shall be slaves there, and they shall be oppressed for four hundred years."[6]

Moses, too, receives the covenant while still at Sinai—in other words, not in the Land.

In short: we cannot find the most fertile rootedness-in-the-world unless we have first had the experience of being uprooted from an original, habitual habitat. The most authentic groundedness presupposes experience of radical displacement—a displacement that, at the extreme, is experienced as exile: exile both from the original habitat we had to leave and from the new home that we have tasted as sojourners but not stably attained.

At the same time, as I suggested in Chapters 5 and 18, to love is also to continually refresh our sense of displacement or exile: for to glimpse a promise of home is to become more sensitive to our distance from it. Because love's hope cannot be finally and stably fulfilled—because no perfect anchorage in life is possible or even identifiable—love repeatedly returns us to the experience of displacement. And so there is no consummation of love in which displacement is finally overcome, once and for all; no consummation in which we can be certain never again to be "a stranger and an alien" in the home that is most authentically ours.

Love's Consummation as Conditional on Heeding the Law of the Loved One

If the first condition for love's consummation—for maximally attaining the loved one's promise of groundedness—is the experience of displacement or exile, the second is to hear and heed the law of his being and precisely what it calls on us to do. This is only partly to do with the explicitly conditional element of divine love: "If you heed these ordinances, by diligently observing them, the Lord your God will maintain with you the covenant loyalty that he swore to your ancestors; *he* will love you."[7] It is, more fundamentally, as I argued in Chapters 12 and 22, because *we* cannot love—we cannot be in a relationship of love—unless we hear the law of the loved one and strive to make it our own; unless we attune ourselves to this law that speaks of his being, the being in relation to which we root our lives in the world. Indeed, love is not only compatible with law; it is centrally a *search* for law.

The point of obeying the law of God's being is, in other words, *not*, in the first place, to evoke his favor or secure his blessings. (For beyond all conditionality attached to divine favor, such favor cannot be taken for granted even if we obey every law he issues: ultimately, he will favor us if he favors us.[8]) It isn't even just to cleave to a supreme morality, or authority for a morality: human beings can find—and, in numerous societies from Homeric Greece to Heian Japan, and through many philosophers from Aristotle to Hume, from Spinoza to Kant and beyond, have found—their own binding moralities, their own tables of virtues and vices, without any ultimate reliance on divine command. They have grounded such moralities in tradition, in the cult of ancestors, in conceptions of human nature, in reason, and in happiness—none of which need appeal to divine authority.

Rather, the overriding purpose of obedience to God's law is *to enable us to love him*. Once we love him—once we detect the promise of rootedness in and through him—we will inevitably wish ever better to hear, to discover, and to align ourselves with, the inner law of his being—to "keep his statutes and his commandments."[9] For only thus can the promise of ontological rootedness that he holds out be seized.

This is not the obedience of a zombie. For such a creature does not do things with all its heart and all its soul;[10] it does not take the law of the loved one "to heart" or invest itself in its deeds as a self-conscious and self-responsible agent. The point of obedience is not to bribe the loved one with rote following of laws to whose particular inner nature we are indifferent; for, as every unrequited lover knows, the other's love cannot be bought. The point is that the obedience of an autonomous person, who has made the loved one's law his own, is the only obedience that can root the lover in the being of the loved one, so enabling lover and loved one to be bound in a relationship of dialogue and practice. It is a rootedness and a relationship that can be sustained even when the loved one occasionally disappears, as of course the Hebrew and Christian God does. For though he might disappear ontologically, he never disappears ethically: his law, as sign of his being, always remains present.

Such obedience to the law of the loved one is, in a deep sense, for the lover's "own well-being."[11] As I have argued elsewhere, submission to law and possession of law in the sense of self-legislation—obedience to law and whole-hearted assent to it—can be two sides of the same coin. An absolute dichotomy between obedience and autonomy in morality is, to that extent, a false one. On the contrary: obedience is fundamental to autonomy.[12]

(As an aside, we should point out that Jesus does *not* alter this primal significance of the law, spoken of in Deuteronomy and elsewhere in the Hebrew Bible, as the necessary and irreplaceable condition for reaching, hearing, and understanding the ways of God—and so for loving God. What he does is to offer himself as the radically new path to achieving just this condition. So that divine law becomes what it was always intended to be: not an alien rulebook, but a bond with God endorsed by each individual as her own autonomous law. And in thus becoming autonomously endorsed by the individual, rather than standing over against her as merely imposed, the law becomes a source of freedom. Not freedom from the law, but freedom through the law.

In other words, contrary to one traditional way of framing the distinction between the Christian and the Hebrew scriptures—the "New" Testament and the "Old"—Jesus does not turn the law into an outdated, no longer necessary, route to God, but on the contrary he guides human beings in the incomparably difficult task of grasping, living by, and in a sense becoming the law. "Do not think that I have come to abolish the law," he warns those who think they are being offered relief from the rigors of Hebrew scripture: "I have come not to abolish but to fulfill. For truly I tell you, until heaven and earth pass away, not one letter, not one stroke of a letter, will pass from the law until all is accomplished."[13] In the Gospel of Luke, Jesus echoes these sentiments: "everything written about me in the Law of Moses and the Prophets and the Psalms must be fulfilled."[14] The rather later Gospel of John repeats this same point in the specific context of love: "this is his [God's] commandment, that we should believe in the name of his Son Jesus Christ and love one another, just as he has commanded us."[15] And when the rich young man in Matthew's Gospel asks Jesus what he needs to do to have eternal life, Jesus tells him to "keep the commandments."[16] It is therefore deeply mistaken to claim that Jesus inaugurates a Christian tradition that breaks entirely free of the law in opposition to a Jewish tradition that is dogmatically bound by the law.)

Finally, the unfolding of love's promise is contingent on circumstances utterly beyond our control—the reasons for which we might not immediately or ever understand. Thus Abraham's descendants cannot settle in the Promised Land "until the fourth generation" because "the iniquity of the Amorites is not yet complete"[17]—in other words, because the Amorites, who live in Canaan when it is promised to Abraham, have not yet been pernicious enough to forfeit their right to the land.

Nor does Abraham initially understand the reason for this four-hundred-year delay in the gift of the land[18]—and this incomprehension of the ways of

God, as generally of the ways of a loved one, is symbolized by the fact that the promise is given to Abraham while he is in a deep sleep (*tardemah*).[19]

In addition, attaining the promise of the loved one can be inescapably contingent on what our forefathers have done. This might seem perverse to an age that imagines, in the fashion of Jean-Paul Sartre's existentialism, that "to be is to *choose oneself*"; that "nothing comes to [human reality] either from the outside or from within which it can *receive or accept*."[20] But, as the Bible recognizes, the foolish ways of ancestors can indeed imperil the lives of their successors, whose goals and values and actions and destinies cannot be entirely self-chosen. God himself says, in giving the Ten Commandments, that children will be punished "for the iniquity of parents, to the third and the fourth generation of those who reject me"; just as he will bestow "steadfast love to the thousandth generation of those who love [him] and keep [his] commandments."[21]

God's words here remind us that the lives of our parents, their parents, and their parents' parents are written into our souls, and *will* have consequences, for good or ill, in our own lives—consequences that might, indeed, emerge for the first time only with us; that their deeds, their values, their experiences, their ways of flourishing, and their ways of coming to grief are the raw materials out of which we must create ourselves. Freedom is to be found in deeply assimilating an inheritance out of which we can forge something radically new only to the extent that we have first struggled to make it our own. And to make it our own, we need to make its resources and its strengths relevant to the challenges of the contemporary world in which we are set. Perhaps this is what Goethe means when he writes:

> What you have inherited from your forefathers,
> Earn it, in order to possess it.[22]

Our individual responsibility extends therefore not just to what we take ourselves to have autonomously chosen and to be directly accountable for, but also to that far larger reality that is given to us and with which we cannot help reckoning if we are to become authors of our lives: a personal heritage, a surrounding world into which we are thrown by birth and by the circumstances of life, and an inner world—our individual selfhood—many or most of whose defining virtues, vices, questions, answers, drives, tastes, and reverences are not at all of our own making or choosing—but for which we nonetheless have to take responsibility. Radical freedom is possible only if, in our own interests, we struggle to be responsible for—to take "active ownership" of; to be agents capable of exercising control over—this given totality by which life confronts us.

Such radical freedom—the privilege of such far-reaching responsibility— might not be possible in each generation. For to absorb the past to the point where it is so deeply understood by our whole being that it can genuinely animate and structure our ultimate ends and values and actions can take work, patience, and education too prolonged for even the longest life span.

In particular, genuine love and the concentrated devotion it involves—"*all* your heart, and *all* your soul, and *all* your might"—is so hard and demands such accumulated wisdom and experience that it might be the fruit only of many generations. Not every generation in a family will necessarily be capable of love. And even when one generation is capable of it, the effort of responsibility for a long moral inheritance—and so for a whole history of fateful choices, deeds, and experiences—might cause its members to slip back into carelessness and forgetfulness. As Nietzsche clearly recognized, the temptation, for generations as well as for individuals, to return to passivity and slavery of spirit is ever present. For, as the endless journeying of the Patriarchs and the Israelites underlines, to love well is not a matter of merely celebrating a promise offered by the loved one, or seeking a relationship with him or her of comforting stability, but involves tremendous effort and risk, patience and responsibility. Throughout the exodus from Egypt, the Israelites yearn, again and again, to return to the pharaoh, and so to slavery. When, after many generations have failed to live up to his covenants, God asks his people pleadingly, "What wrong did your ancestors find in me that they went far from me, and went after worthless things, and became worthless themselves?,"[23] the answer is surely that they found the effort, the risk, the patience, and the responsibility too arduous. Laziness and harlotry of spirit—the delicious temptations of fresh satisfactions and easy rewards—readily seduce us from the promise. Even when an overwhelming promise of love is staring us in the face, golden calves beckon everywhere.

Most accounts of human love in Hebrew scripture focus on the two great love commands—the commands to "love God with all your heart and soul and might" and to "love your neighbor as yourself"—as well as the erotic love of the Song of Songs, the friendship love of Jonathan and David or Ruth and Naomi, the paternal love of Abraham for Isaac of which God speaks ("your only son whom you love"), and other explicit biblical invocations of love, whether descriptive or normative. I have suggested that, in addition to these well-known and direct invocations of love, Hebrew scripture's overarching narratives of covenant articulate a truer model of the nature of love—and in particular of what grounds it; of *why* we love—than any of the other dominant models in the Western tradition that I outlined in Chapter 3: those that we find in Plato, in Aristotle, in the "sanitized" version of Christian *agape*, in contemporary ethics—especially where love is conceived as disinterested concern for the welfare of another for their own sake or as wholehearted commitment to one's highest ends—or in naturalism from Lucretius to Freud to evolutionary psychology.

For once we think of love as responding to a promise of ontological rooted-ness, as potentially involving radical displacement to a far horizon of unfore-seen possibilities, as vastly intensified by exile in both its motivation and the clarity of its vision, as identifying with a lineage, as consummated only through obedience to the law of the loved one, as discovering an ethical home, as a call to the responsibility of a new personal destiny, as a relation to a great source of existential power, and as pervaded by terror of the loved one's presence even more than of their absence, we can see that in the covenants with Abraham and Moses we arguably find the paradigm of all love. It is, indeed, ironical that the structure of covenant in Hebrew scripture—which is so unique to one specific people, involves such an exclusive historical consciousness, and is the very basis of election—should be a model that best answers the question of why human beings, at any place and time, should love, but this is precisely what I propose it is.

The *Odyssey*: Love as a Recovery of Home

When we turn from the Bible to another great founding text of Western cultures—Homer's *Odyssey*, thought to have been composed in the eighth century BCE—we again find a remarkable narrative of love as the search for home.[1] Except that, in this case, the journey of love takes the lover back to a fresh encounter with his original home, rather than forward toward an entirely new territory.

At the outset of the epic, Odysseus, king of Ithaca, a hero of rich character—wise and reckless, compassionate and cruel, patient and intemperate, a master of masks who will lie about almost anything, especially his identity—has already been away from his land, his throne, his wife Penelope, his son Telemachus, and his mother and father for seventeen years, prosecuting the Trojan War for ten and subsequently marooned on the goddess Calypso's island for a further seven. And he yearns to return to all of these: to land, to kingship, to spouse, to heir, and to parents.

These are not separable loves. Rather they are facets of one love: facets of the yearning for home that sustains Odysseus's perilous journey.

In kingship we find the lineage that inspires Odysseus's love. In Penelope's richly complex nature—she is far more than the merely dutiful wife of so many accounts of the *Odyssey*—we find a wily, tenacious, and tough-minded operator, as capable as her husband of charm and manipulation; and, in particular, we find the moral heroine who raises loyalty to the status of a heroic virtue, and who, together with the goddess Athena, is the lodestar of Odysseus's entire journey in search of home. In Ithaca we find the power that gives existential weight to Odysseus's life: for the land of Ithaca signifies the hoped-for recovery of his family, his people, his *oikos* (that evocative Greek word for home, which can denote not just where I dwell, or what belongs to me—*oikeios*—but what is at home with me, what is part of me, what is proper to me or truly particular to me, even what my lineage is).[2]

All of these—Penelope, kingship, the land of his family and people—experienced by Odysseus from his position of long exile, constitute a call to a new relation to his homeland—and to that degree, I will suggest, to a new inner way of being beyond that of warrior and voyager: a new way of being forged by his overwhelming experience of the loyalty of his *oikos* and his people—and, above all, of his wife.

And all of them are brought together in the person of Telemachus, Odysseus's young son and heir, the figure who embodies their future: the future of the royal line, of the land, and of its people. Indeed poignantly so: for the epic tradition tells us that Odysseus has known him only as a baby, before departing for the Trojan War; and so Telemachus is all future to Odysseus (and, perhaps, the other way around: Odysseus is all future to Telemachus, the father whom he has never consciously encountered). And just as the future trajectory of any relationship of love is utterly opaque—despite our frequent conviction that, precisely in love, we can see the "ever after"—so, significantly, Telemachus's personality is less clearly drawn than that of either of his parents. Yet he is at the center of no less than four of the *Odyssey*'s books and speaks more than any of its other characters except Odysseus himself.[3]

The way home is, of course, no simple matter for Odysseus, no straight line. It takes him ten years: as long as the Trojan War from which he is returning. Indeed, when the poem begins, he despairs of ever reaching Ithaca:

> [S]training for no more than a glimpse
> of hearth-smoke drifting up from his own land,
> Odysseus longs to die.[4]

And the voyage is riddled with obstacles, the overcoming of which by the wily hero contributes to the transformative power of his return: the return that is the purpose of his journey of love.

In other words, overcoming these obstacles isn't just proof of his love; it doesn't merely stress-test a love that was already fully formed. Rather it gives new form and life to Odysseus's love for Penelope and Telemachus and the other key figures of his *oikos*, above all by captivating him with the rooting power of loyalty: their loyalty to him, and his own loyalty to them, which these obstacles deepen and draw out of him.

In the course of his journey and arrival home, Odysseus is transformed from what the classicist Bernard Knox calls, disingenuously, an "illiterate pirate," whose virtues are predominantly those of the heroic ideal—the pursuit of honor and glory through war—to a man whose already many-sided character is now complicated and enriched by the very different heroism of loyalty to intimates who constitute a foundation of his world, a foundation from which all larger heroic pursuits might in turn draw strength. By the end of the *Odyssey* kin and *oikos* in general, and Penelope in particular, cease to be merely Odysseus's household or hinterland, dependent on the hero and in many ways indistinguishable from him,[5] and become, in a much more conscious way, his ethical home, a home on which, as we will see, he discovers his own profound dependence. And this discovery reanimates his love for wife, land, kingship, and, one might conjecture, that embodiment of them all: Telemachus, his son.

———

What, then, are the obstacles that mark the hero's journey and transform his love for home?

Most conspicuously they are the encounters that threaten death and destruction: menacing monsters like the one-eyed Cyclops, or like Scylla and Charybdis; sea storms and giants that pulverize the hardiest vessels; cruel and all but invincible immortals like the goddess Circe; the Sirens who lure passersby to death with their knowing words and the sweetness of their songs; the vengeful sea god Poseidon. Any one of these might destroy the lover and terminate his journey of love.

Yet the heart of the drama doesn't lie with such deadly dangers. We sense that Odysseus's dare-devilish courage, his craftiness, his adroit spirit,[6] and the timely intervention of gods, especially his patron goddess Athena, will ward them off.

Perhaps this reflects the reality that destructiveness isn't always the greatest threat to love—even if it is the most obvious threat.

Instead, love often finds itself in gravest danger from its counterfeits—where the lover is confused, disoriented, and weakened by the temptations of false coinage. Of these counterfeits the most perilous are those where the lover deceives himself that he loves, rather than where he is deceived that he is loved.

And it is precisely here that we see Odysseus's clarity of purpose: his immunity to all such counterfeits; his determination not to be seduced into tarrying with those he doesn't love, notably Calypso, Circe, and Nausicaa, though they might amuse and delight and flatter and give; his wholehearted dedication to returning to where his love really lies. For his journey of love—his return home—seems most at risk when he stumbles on exquisite offers of sex, of kingship, of power, of property, of prestige, and even of that prize not normally bestowed on Homeric warriors: immortality. Offers, we should note, that far from necessarily bearing malign intent are often extended out of love for him, or if not of love then of desire and respect for a man of such godlike character.

But, for all their potential joys, these offers never arouse Odysseus to genuine love: he can find in them no promise of ontological rootedness, though, like the promise of immortality, they might come from a nymph-goddess such as Calypso. And so the feeling they inspire in him might be gratitude, or sexual pleasure, or comfort and ease—but it isn't love.

Yet the power of his love for Penelope and for Ithaca shows itself precisely here. For though he cannot always be as unflinching in resisting temptation as he is in cheating destruction—proposals of sex from goddesses cannot easily be turned down—in the end his love for home prevails (if sometimes with a little nudging from a god or from his comrades) over the distraction and for-getfulness that would obscure it. Indeed Odysseus exemplifies how love can be the most clear-sighted of all emotions, the least deluded.

Entertained for one year by the lovely witch-goddess Circe—deceitful, se-ductive, and able to transform men into animals at whim: she tries to turn Odysseus into a pig in an attempt to capture him for herself[7]—he is finally reminded by his crew that he must leave. Home calls:

> [M]y loyal comrades took me aside and prodded,
> "Captain, this is madness!
> High time you thought of your own home at last,
> if it really is your fate to make it back alive
> and reach your well-built house and native land."[8]

Though Circe has plied him not just with her sexual favors but also with "sides of meat and heady wine,"[9] his men bring his thoughts back to home, and he begs Circe to let him go:

> My heart longs to be home,
> my comrades' hearts as well. They wear me down,
> pleading with me whenever you're away.[10]

To which Circe answers:

> Royal son of Laertes, Odysseus, old campaigner,
> stay on no more in my house against your will.[11]

Even when we see him, after yet another shipwreck, rescued by the beau-tiful princess Nausicaa, whose father, King Alcinous, has offered him her hand, along with kingship, robes, territory, and jewels, he remembers his true goal: Ithaca—which encompasses Penelope, father, throne, people, son. Though Nausicaa has saved his life, he spurns her, along with all the riches and status that are her dowry. Magnanimously, she accepts that he will leave:

> Farewell, my friend! And when you are at home,
> home in your land, remember me at times.
> Mainly to me you owe the gift of life.[12]

And the hero replies:

> Nausicaa, daughter of generous King Alcinous,
> may Zeus the Thunderer, Hera's husband, grant it so—
> that I travel home and see the dawn of my return.
> Even at home I'll pray for you as a deathless goddess
> all my days to come. You saved my life, dear girl.[13]

We don't know how Nausicaa really feels about Odysseus's departure. We know only that this girl would like someone like him to be her husband; and we may suppose that Odysseus feels lastingly grateful to her for saving his life when she found him stranded, starving, and exhausted on her island.

But for those who are spurned, gratitude offered in lieu of love is likely to be experienced not as courtesy but as mockery. Gratitude only rubs salt in the wounds of rejection.

———

So, too, when the sea-nymph and goddess Calypso embroils Odysseus for seven years in her erotic magic, closing in on him like an oyster around a pearl and concealing him from the world to which he yearns to return—"*calyptō*" (καλύπτω) means "to cover" or "to hide"[14]—we sense his gathering despair at being marooned on this island of sensuality, though she loves him and has restored him to health. And so instead of relishing his long sexual intimacy with her, he increasingly participates in it out of necessity and against his will: "he'd sleep with her in the arching cave—he had no choice— / unwilling lover alongside lover all too willing."[15] Day after lonely day he pines for his homeland, sitting on the shore, "wrenching his heart with sobs and groans and anguish, [and] gazing out over the barren sea through blinding tears."[16]

Calypso's promise isn't to be refused lightly. She offers not just sexual joy, not just her beauty, not just her love and care, but also immortality without aging: among the rarest prizes that a Homeric hero could attain. For even the hero whose deeds have won him the ultimate prize of eternal glory, which turns him into a subject for the tales of the singers, will, in almost every case, eventually die—and this mortality distinguishes him absolutely from the deathless gods.[17]

Indeed, nothing shows Odysseus's overriding yearning for Penelope, and for the home that she represents, as clearly as his rejection of the prize of immortality for the sake of a wife who he cannot be sure has remained loyal to him, indeed who might have remarried in his long absence, as she was fully entitled to do.

Odysseus tells Calypso that he is well aware of what she is proffering—and of Penelope's inability to match it. He acknowledges that he is rejecting divine beauty for the sake of an aging matron; an immortal goddess for the sake of a mortal human. Nonetheless, he wants only to return home:

> "Ah great goddess,"
> worldly Odysseus answered, "don't be angry with me,
> please. All that you say is true, how well I know.
> Look at my wise Penelope. She falls far short of you,
> your beauty, stature. She is mortal after all
> and you, you never age or die . . .
> Nevertheless I long—I pine, all my days—
> to travel home and see the dawn of my return."[18]

Calypso might nonetheless have been inclined to detain Odysseus at her pleasure, so consigning him to a kind of oblivion; but Hermes, messenger of the gods, has already conveyed to her Zeus's order to release him at once:

> Now Zeus commands you to send him off with all good speed:
> it is not his fate to die here, far from his own people.
> Destiny still ordains that he shall see his loved ones,
> reach his high-roofed house, his native land at last.[19]

And so the nymph-goddess sends Odysseus on his way, even helping him construct a seaworthy raft—but not before they have once again made love:

> [T]he sun set and the darkness swept the earth.
> And now, withdrawing into the cavern's deep recesses,
> long in each other's arms they lost themselves in love.[20]

———

Even more obviously than Abraham's journey to the Promised Land, Odysseus's voyage begins far from his true home.

When Abraham sets out for Canaan his journey begins at his habitual home, which he must leave in order to reach his new home, the place where his destiny will be enacted, as will the destiny of the Israelite lineage that he is called upon to found.

By contrast, the epic of return recounted in the *Odyssey* begins on Calypso's island, a place far from any sense of home, and one that Odysseus cannot come to see as home. Moreover, the path to Ithaca will pass through that realm of ultimate exile: from life itself. For on the way Odysseus is told to go to Hades, the Underworld, in order to be guided to Ithaca by the blind seer Tiresias, who also prophesies what will await him at home. Here he is compelled to wrestle with the horror of death, learning from slain heroes like Achilles that there is no joy in this realm[21] and chancing upon the heart-rending shade of his mother, who has died in his absence out of longing for her son. The merest form of life, as the slave of a pauper, Achilles tells Odysseus, is preferable to being king of all the dead.[22] For the Homeric hero there is glory in dying but no joy in death.[23] Even the gods, who will never have to suffer this disintegration, abhor it.

And so the divine will, which supervises so much of the action in the *Odyssey*, has decreed that he cannot return home except by tarrying in the place furthest from it, the inhabitants of which never return, the place that the Greeks locate literally at the edge of the world. Before he can head for Ithaca, Circe tells him,

> [A]nother journey calls. You must travel down
> to the House of Death and the awesome one, Persephone,
> there to consult the ghost of Tiresias, seer of Thebes,
> the great blind prophet whose mind remains unshaken.

> Even in death—Persephone has given him wisdom,
> everlasting vision to him and him alone . . .
> the rest of the dead are empty, flitting shades.[24]

Grief-stricken by this news, Odysseus relays Circe's order to his men:

> You think we are headed home, our own dear land?
> Well, Circe sets us a rather different course . . .
> down to the House of Death and the awesome one, Persephone,
> there to consult the ghost of Tiresias, seer of Thebes.[25]

And he continues:

> Back to the swift ship at the water's edge we went,
> our spirits deep in anguish, faces wet with tears.[26]

In his encounter with the Underworld, with its "endless, deadly night,"[27] the hero is overcome by the emotion least familiar to him: fear. When he comes to depart from Hades, it is not with smug satisfaction at returning to life but rather in terror at what he has seen. "The dead," he says, "came surging round me, hordes of them, thousands raising unearthly cries, and blanching terror gripped me—panicked now that Queen Persephone might send up from Death some monstrous head, some Gorgon's staring face!"[28]

Odysseus's fear speaks not of cowardice, but on the contrary of his courage to confront the reality of death. For to look directly at death, to glimpse the other side of life without turning away, is, for Greeks of the epic and classical ages, a path to blessedness, prefiguring a return to life with new wisdom that cannot be gained in any other way. As I argued in Chapter 23, this place of the most extreme exile—its darkness, its helplessness, its hopelessness, its destruction of the body—must be faced as fully as a human being can in order for him or her to attain the promise of home: in order for love to be maximally fulfilled. Death must be faced not because death is glorious, but because death and the eventuality of our own death is that horizon of certain finality that turns us back decisively toward life; because to look unflinchingly at the inevitability of death is to open up paths to our own most grounded and genuine relation to life.

And Odysseus's journey home must pass, too, through that other intense experience of isolation and loss: nakedness. When Nausicaa and her gaggle of friends find him washed up on her island, shipwrecked, starving, and reduced to a beggar, he is at his most vulnerable. Dazed on the beach, a middle-aged, exhausted wreck of a man, he has been stripped of life's most basic protections: food, clothing, shelter, dignity, and companionship of the soul. He has become Nobody.[29]

Odysseus's total loss of his world—of a place, a role, and what today we call an "identity"—is a turning point for him. Like his sojourn in Hades, it reignites his will to return home: a will of which this time he doesn't need to be reminded, as he did when stranded with the seductive Circe. In his moment of greatest vulnerability he cannot be tempted by gifts of status, youth, and wealth. Offered all three by the great-hearted King Alcinous, he wants none. Instead he begs Alcinous to set him on his way home:

> [A]t the first light of day, hurry, please,
> to set your unlucky guest on his own home soil.
> How much I have suffered . . . Oh just let me see
> my lands, my serving-men and the grand high-roofed house—
> then I can die in peace.[30]

The magnanimous Alcinous—whose name can be read to mean "the strong minded"—accepts his entreaty:

> Odysseus,
> now that you have come to my bronze-floored house,
> my vaulted roofs, I know you won't be driven
> off your course, nothing can hold you back—
> however much you've suffered, you'll sail home.[31]

And so here in the *Odyssey*, as in Genesis, we see that the agony of displacement or exile is central to the journey of love: that it not only lies at the beginning of love, motivating the search for ontological rootedness in a world that we supremely value, but that it also besets the lover throughout the journey, steeling him or her to overcome the inevitable obstacles to fulfilling a promise of home.

———

What of reaching home? Isn't this a moment of cathartic joy? Isn't attaining the shores of one's true home the end of the drama of homecoming? Again, as with Abraham and Isaac and Jacob, the answer is No. For the Hebrews there is to be exile again and again: establishing the home to which they have been called is a never-ending task—a task that is, in every sense of the word, *unsettling*. For Odysseus, there is also to be further loss of his homeland; for Teiresias has prophesied that he will have to leave Ithaca yet again.

Indeed, reaching home after the Trojan War is only the beginning of the end of that particular journey, and brings with it a cascade of fresh burdens and tears. The *Odyssey* belongs to those poems that speak of *nostos* (νόστος): poems about the homecoming of Homeric heroes.[32] Far from being an unalloyed delight, homecoming is often pervaded by *algos*: pain of body or mind. It is as if "nost-algia" denotes not just the pain of separation from home but also the pain of recovering home: the pain of discovering potentially insuperable obstacles both to reaching it *and* then to inhabiting it afresh.

For Odysseus the burden of return comes, above all, in the form of his outrage at the unscrupulous suitors who are wooing Penelope and who have settled uninvited into his palace, where they are living at his expense. These ultimate spongers, brutal and brazen, and happily humiliating the ruling family, are the elite of Ithaca, whose ambition is to persuade Penelope that her husband is dead; to murder his son and heir Telemachus; and to ensure that one of their number seizes the throne. Disguised by the goddess Athena as a beggar in order not to be recognized by them, Odysseus will set about killing all one hundred and eight.

And, even before he is confronted by the suitors, there are the tests of recognition—and of loyalty—of those closest to him: his servant, the swine-herd Eumaeus; his son Telemachus, whom he already encounters outside Ithaca in Eumaeus's hut; his dog; his old nurse Eurycleia; his wife; and his father. We sense that, through each of these figures, he must reestablish a relation to his homeland in which he trusts. In almost every case he disguises himself, or lies about his identity, in order to ensure that these anchors of his old life have remained true. In almost every case their recognition of Odysseus triggers a breakdown: his father Laertes faints; so too does Penelope; his hunting dog Argos dies; his son sobs. And Odysseus himself sheds many tears: when he encounters his father (an occasion on which, for once, he is unable to lie, though he tries to at first); when he sees his faithful dog lying moribund on a heap of dung; and, not least, when he meets and recognizes his son Telemachus. At that moment, Odysseus and Telemachus:

> cried out, shrilling cries, pulsing sharper
> than birds of prey—eagles, vultures with hooked claws—
> when farmers plunder their nest of young too young to fly.
> Both men so filled with compassion, eyes streaming tears.[33]

These are moments of existential power. In recognizing and in being recognized again, Odysseus's very existence seems to be given new depth—a development heralded, perhaps, by those images of rebirth, such as dawn, that greet his landfall at Ithaca. In particular, in being recognized by Penelope he has arrived back in a home that, in his experience of it, is radically different to the one he left: a home at the center of which is a "noble wife," as Athena refers to her,[34] who he now knows will never cease to wait for him, despite every reasonable expectation that he is dead and her waiting futile. This is waiting not in the sense of docile fidelity, but rather in the sense of the single-minded attentiveness—as heroic in its endurance as any heroism of men in battle—that, we have seen, is love's supreme virtue.

———

The *Odyssey* is a work profoundly concerned with ethics, at one pole of which is the noble and wise Penelope and at the other the wicked and disloyal suitors. Virtue is rewarded—Penelope gets her husband back; while vice is punished—the suitors are killed. And beyond this concern with justice the *Odyssey* raises loyalty to the status of a heroic virtue—every bit as heroic as a warrior ethic—and in particular shows us how this virtue is tested and exalted in Odysseus's homecoming, making his return not merely a recovery of his family and native land but also a deeper encounter with them and, to that extent, with the ground of his being.

Nonetheless, the *Odyssey* should not be interpreted as a journey of redemption from darkness to light, from ethical imperfection to ethical perfection, from matter to spirit; nor one where suffering is given meaning and value by issuing in a higher good. To see it this way would be to impose onto a world of Homeric heroes a Platonic ladder of love, or still less appropriately a Judeo-Christian eschatology, that is utterly alien to them. Odysseus is no Augustine, eschewing the false religion for the true.

Rather, loyalty—his own for wife, father, son, and people; and, even more so, theirs for him—is central to the ethical home that he discovers as a result of his journey and return to Ithaca. It is a virtue embodied, above all, in the person of Penelope;[35] indeed it is she, we may surmise, who really opens Odysseus's eyes to the idea of loyalty as a *heroic* virtue, rather than merely as a taken-for-granted fidelity between him and his *oikos*. And to that extent she, so to speak, confronts him with a rival ethical world—an ethical world that he is compelled, by the power of loyalty in driving his journey and shaping his homecoming, to make his own. In this way Penelope might be seen as the joint hero of the story, and ethically its real hero: as enriching Odysseus's warlike, honor-driven genius (though he remains no less scheming, deceiving, and disguising); and so as enlarging him ethically, giving him a new sense of place in his old world, and, though we know from Teiresias's prophecy that Odysseus will have to leave Ithaca again, bestowing on him a vision of life beyond war and wandering—beyond all his feats of endurance, self-control, and tactical ingenuity. Like the ethical home sought by all love, this is one that the lover already values but can secure for him- or herself in a full way only in and through the loved one.

Odysseus's recovery of Ithaca and of his kin is therefore a discovery of precisely this: the heroism of loyalty; the blessings of an ethical home linked to lineage; and the way in which love yearns for those very blessings. In this sense he has returned to the same country but, inwardly, to a new world. For even when love involves a trajectory of return, rather than of going forward to a new home, the *status quo ante* cannot be recaptured: the lover and their relationship to the loved one have, in returning, become irreversibly transformed.

PART IV

How Is Love Related to Beauty, Sex, and Goodness?

Why Beauty Is Not the Ground of Love

What of the beauty that, in so much of the Western tradition, from Plato to Edmund Burke and beyond, has been seen as the central inspiration and ground of love? Not just of erotic or romantic love but also of love of landscape or art or morals or science—or anything. What is going on when we encounter someone of tremendous beauty, whether of body, or character, or wisdom, or "soul," and at once fall in love with him or her?

No experience has been more consistently recorded. In countless poems and stories, men and women declare themselves to be in love precisely with another's beauty. The joy and awe that beauty evokes in us are so powerful, and the vitality of love seems to flow so directly from it, that, surely, as Plato's Diotima says, beauty must be love's true ground? For isn't love's ultimate object to be in constant union with absolute beauty—to contemplate it, to possess it, and so give birth to beauty in beauty?[1]

As in Dante's vision of Beatrice, or Odysseus's sighting of the young Nausicaa on the island of the Phaeacians, beauty stuns and besieges us with new life. And it does so in seemingly contradictory ways: it shines a merciless light on reality—*and*, as Nietzsche insisted, it conjures illusions that protect us from realities that might otherwise destroy us. It liberates and it imprisons, consoles and unsettles, empowers and overwhelms. It can inspire the clearest sight and the wildest falsehood. It can guide us to truth and goodness—and it can delude and corrupt. Or it can do all of these things. Beauty is by no means "*only* the promise of happiness"[2] as Stendhal famously claims ("La beauté n'est que la promesse du bonheur"), though the awareness of beauty and the feeling of happiness are surely closely connected.

———

And yet we must ask: Is beauty the real *ground* of love? Is it what ultimately inspires and sustains love? If it were, we would love everyone and everything we find beautiful—which we do not. We would love people and things in proportion to their beauty—which we do not. We would love our neighbor as ourselves because we find him or her beautiful—which seems implausible. We would love our children strictly according to their beauty, which isn't what happens. We would love God principally because we find God beautiful, which isn't necessarily the case, *pace* Augustine. (Indeed, in neither the Old nor the New Testament is beauty claimed as a fundamental feature of God, let alone as a ground for loving God.) And we would never love what we find coarse or ugly. Which, I will argue in Chapter 31, isn't true either.

What, then, is going on when we believe we are falling in love with someone because of their beauty?

What is going on, I suggest, is this: their beauty rivets us to them; it disarms our usual state of inattentiveness to people and things; it is the siren call that opens our eyes and ears to another. So that *if* they offer us a promise of rootedness—the true inspiration for love—we are now far more likely to notice it and surrender to it.

In other words, beauty (or creation in beauty) isn't the actual ground of our love—contrary to the vastly influential tradition stemming from Plato's *Symposium*, if not earlier, that insists it is. Instead, beauty lures us into the other person—in whom we then either glimpse the four conditions of genuine love, or we don't.

Proust magnificently evokes this luring into the other person, this hijacking of our attentiveness, when Marcel catches sight of the girl serving milk at a train stop:

> I could not take my eyes from her face which grew larger as she approached, like a sun which it was somehow possible to stare at and which was coming nearer and nearer, letting itself be seen at close quarters, dazzling you with its blaze of red and gold.[3]

When we do then glimpse, or believe we glimpse, the four conditions of genuine love, we might imagine we are falling in love with the other person's beauty because this is what first stuns us into really seeing them—because falling in love so often seems to be triggered by beauty. But this is to make the error of assuming that just because one experience regularly precedes another, the first must be the real ground of the second.

Or we might imagine that beauty is the ground of love because, like love, it occasions such intense pleasure; and because, like love, beauty seems to offer us a *promise* (here Stendhal is right): a promise of happiness in the person of the loved one; and a promise of fecundity, inspiring the creation of children, art, laws, and thought, or the discovery of fresh ways of being. Like love, beauty draws us into the future.

But the real relation between beauty and love is just the opposite of the view that Plato articulates. Rather than being the necessary ground of love, beauty is the necessary *consequence* of love.[4] It is, in a special sense to which I alluded in Chapter 20, one of two universal languages of love, the other being devotion to the law of the loved one: languages that love speaks—or, if it is to develop beyond a mere stance, must learn to speak—once it has been aroused by a promise of home or ontological rootedness. We will always see a loved one as beautiful—even if, before we loved them, we found them ugly; indeed, even if we love them *for* their ugliness. (And so, as I will suggest in Chapter 31, we can find beautiful what we also experience as ugly.)

In short: we will necessarily find beautiful those we love, but we will not necessarily love those we find beautiful.

We know how perilous beauty is as a guide to love—and how love and the desire for beauty can seek quite distinct things—from that all-too-familiar situation when, drunk on someone's beauty, we rush into the closest intimacy with them, but find ourselves unable to love them. When the thrill of their beauty leads us to discover their fascinating, seductive, delicious inner world, which we long to linger in and explore; and yet this same world—infuriatingly, appallingly—does not arouse our love. When it dawns on us that beauty's promise of happiness and love's promise of rootedness can point in very different directions. When it becomes obvious that the poets who lament the fickle relations between love and beauty are right.

What happens then to us, children of Plato?

On the one hand, our will to love, press-ganged by an ancient tradition into seeing beauty as love's true ground, and in particular into seeing erotic beauty as the ground of a deeper love, feels marooned. We might even—perversely—resent the other's beauty, which has drawn us into a loveless land in which we see no future.

Or else we feel humiliated by, and perhaps guilty about, our failure to love. We blame ourselves for being unable to love that person. They as loved one and we as lover have both failed, it seems to us, to make good on the Platonic promise that to possess beauty—to be inspired to create or give birth in beauty—*is* to love.

Or we take a very different trajectory. As Diotima's marionettes, we decide that, after all, we do—we *must*—love them. If we don't fully experience this love, this can only be because we fear it, or resist it, or haven't tried hard enough to love, or are captive to unhealthy templates of relating that bar us from genuine love. And so we begin the great game of pretense in which we will ourselves to discover a love for the other commensurate with our delight in their beauty, and hope that with sufficient patience and effort we will develop an attachment strong enough to call love. In thus striving to love, but being unable to, we fixate on their beauty as the pole star that should guide us to the promised land of love. Which it stubbornly fails to do.

This might be why Stendhal says that "Men who cannot love passionately are, perhaps, those who feel the effect of beauty most keenly."[5] Believing with Plato that beauty is the real ground of love, the less such people can love the more they cling to beauty as a promise of love (and the more, perhaps, they persuade themselves that their enjoyment of beauty is proof that they *do* love). Beauty with its big bold brushstrokes is all that they are capable of noticing in another. They do not and cannot, Stendhal implies, look beyond the door that it opens.

For that is the role of beauty in love: it opens a door to the other, so that *if* they are offering us a promise of home or ontological rootedness, we are able to see it.

29 }

How Important Is Sex to Love?

If love is neither grounded in beauty nor motivated by desire for beauty, or to possess the beautiful, or to create in beauty, then still less can love, even in its romantic-erotic form, be identical with sexual desire: that craving to touch, behold, evoke, explore, enjoy, possess, and be possessed by, another's bodyliness and the whole person of which it speaks.

For the qualities that inspire sexual desire are by no means the same as the qualities that inspire love. We find many more people sexually desirable than we love. And we can passionately love people without finding them sexually desirable—as is surely the case (*pace* the early Freud) for, say, filial, parental, and friendship love.

So what is the relation of sex to love?

Sex or sexual desire has, I suggest, two quite distinct roles in the drama of romantic-erotic love.

First, like beauty, sex (or sexual desire) rivets us so intensely to another person that we are able to see their promise of ontological rootedness, and so to fall genuinely in love with them. In our everyday twilight of attentiveness we don't notice who they really are. We see little more than their erotic penumbra. Sex, however, coaxes us into such intimacy with them and arouses such desire for their presence that if they are offering us a promise of ontological root-edness we will now be more likely to notice it—especially after orgasm, in those intervals between sexual satisfaction and new desire that are marked by heightened, often painfully refined, sensitivity to the other's reality. Though sex and sexual attractiveness are neither the ground nor the ultimate inspira-tion of love, they awaken and train the gaze that is then able to see the promise.

In other words: it is the promise of rootedness, not the intoxication of sex or sexual desire, that awakens love—and that marks the transition from erotic delight to erotic love. (This transition is, if we attend to it, palpable. It is the moment when we notice something else about the other that arouses the de-sire for a more far-reaching union than sex alone can achieve. This "something else" is a source of life with which we deeply identify; ethical home; the power to deepen our sense of existing: power to intensify the reality and vitality, and therefore the validity, of our existence, as we experience it, including the power to give us the security that we lack and most crave; and the charisma of their presence that calls us to ourselves and evokes our passion to nurture their life.)

Second, sex is a supreme expression of love—once love has been aroused. It is at the heart of the dialogue of two lives that unfolds in erotic love; a privileged way—on occasion *the* privileged way—of enacting their intimacy and their need for one another; and a profound exploration of and delight in the other person, very much including what is ungraspable in them. For sex does not just express and intensify an intimacy that is already there, but relishes and brings to awareness precisely what is alien in the other—teasing and testing and striving to overcome it. As Ibn Hazm (994–1064), a medieval Islamic scholar, puts it in his treatise on love *The Ring of the Dove*, once love is established between two people physical intimacy "completes the circuit" between them, allowing "the current of love to flow freely into the soul" of each.[1]

And when a sexual dialogue of intimate pleasures morphs into a language of love it becomes, like all love's dialogues, at its heart existential. What is then at stake for both lovers is their pathos of existing, each for himself or herself, each for the other, and each as a "We." All their sexual communication, all their sexual exploration of each other's being, now has raw existence as its major theme—the joy and power of existence, but also the fear, the dread, and the fragility—a theme that the pleasures of lovemaking express and reinforce.

So that when sex expresses love it arouses in the lovers not only erotic intoxication but also, beyond that, a deeper sense of existing: of the power and vitality of their being in the world. Just as when love is expressed in acts of generosity or devotion or mutual support—recognizing each other's achievements, consoling each other's sadnesses, nurturing each other's ends—the lovers experience these acts not only as "kindnesses" that strengthen their bond of trust, but, over and above that, as bearing existential import: as giving their beings, as individuals and as a union, a new force, density, groundedness.

Within erotic love, therefore, sex is the channel through which each lover is filled with the reality of the other—the reality, known and unknown, familiar and alien, that he or she must deeply feel if the other's promise of rootedness is to be realized. Through sex lovers feel they are physically grasping—becoming bodily attuned to—the lineage, ethical home, existential power, and call to being of the other. And thus also grasping how they are returning to themselves.

Sex, in other words, can open a path to love; it is a central language of love; but it is never the actual ground of love.

The whole relation of sex to love is a minefield because sex plays so many other roles—which can abut love or cohabit the same relationship as love—that we easily confuse one with the other. The reproductive instinct; the drive for pleasure; the craving for intimacy; the attraction to power and vitality and confidence; the elation of another's succumbing to one's own power; the thrill of creating a cocoon of oneness that can shut out society and complexity; the joy of feeling one's bodily reality and vigor; the fantasy of flirting with and then cheating death; the delight in another's smell, taste, and texture; the urge to possess someone on whom we are vulnerably dependent; the euphoria of being desired in return (especially in a society in which self-esteem is so dependent on being sexually attractive): these are just some of the origins or catalysts or roles of sexual desire that need have *nothing* to do with love. And in all of them our imagination, and its capacity to bestow erotic charisma on our lover, is key to arousing—or dampening—desire.

Since sex can play any and all of these roles in a single relationship, erotic love is almost always a composite of thoroughly different emotions: in particular *love*, inspired by a promise of ontological rootedness; *physical pleasure* and its anticipation, inspired in particular by a beautiful body and by various types and degrees of power; and the *reproductive urge*, responsive to indicators of biological or social fitness, some but not all of which will coincide with those characteristics that we find erotically alluring. In other words, a rich erotic relationship is usually several relationships proceeding in parallel—sometimes conversing, sometimes competing, sometimes ignoring each other—each of them bringing different desires, different needs, different expectations, and different tastes to bear on a single bond.

Yet love and sex have become hopelessly entangled in our minds, to the tremendous detriment of love in particular, because an ancient tradition—articulated above all by Plato and the Christianization of Plato, and taken to its extreme in nineteenth-century Romanticism—has given love the job of expressing, dignifying, and controlling sexual desire by being its supreme fulfillment. For that same tradition, from Plato to Proust and beyond, has told us that the unruly urge sexually to possess another, which can be the cause of so much frustration, anger, and misunderstanding, is, or should be, only the starting point of a journey of love, which will culminate in a state of grace, transcending sexuality as bodily desire yet thoroughly dependent on its driving energy, such as a vision of absolute good (Plato); the creation of beautiful children or of fine moral, intellectual, or artistic achievements (Plato again); the integration of the psyche (Freud); or a narrative of our life that can redeem its pain and suffering (Proust).

If, however, sexual desire or fulfillment should fail to lead to love, if we should have the famous feeling of emptiness precisely where we hoped, or felt a duty, to find love, then we must tell ourselves that this is emotionally impoverished sexual desire—mere lust rather than love, to use the hackneyed distinction.

Or else we must *pretend* that we are in love. A pretense that is, at first, not hard. For the aliveness, the intoxication, the happiness, the intimacy, the thrilling mutual recognition afforded by purely sexual delight do indeed mimic those afforded by love, though they have an utterly different source.

And out of gratitude for such delights, and hope that they will continue, as well as out of determination to love—determination forged partly by a craving for love and partly by immense cultural pressure to turn sex into love—we might embark on a relationship marked by virtues and activities—devotion, giving, intimacy, the sharing of everyday life—that bear many of the hallmarks of love without actually being grounded in love. After all, such virtues and activities are, as I have already suggested, not monopolized by love, and can appear in many other forms of relating.

But a bond that is predominantly forged by sexual desire can be interpreted and lived as if it were a relationship of love only for as long as such desire— along with the joys and intertwining of lives that it makes possible—endures. As soon as desire cools or is experienced by one or both lovers as too narrow a foundation for intimacy, the reality that they are not in a relationship of mutual love will inevitably assert itself and they will realize, even if just silently, each for him- or herself, that they are professing one sort of bond while actually being in another. For if two people do not offer each other a promise of ontological rootedness, sex will never bring them to mutual love, no matter how magical it is.

———

Conversely, and at the same time, romantic love has become tyrannized by the expectation that it be relentlessly expressed and endorsed by sex. Romance, whether hetero- or homosexual, is compelled to prove itself by its sexual vitality—and becomes demoralized, even delegitimized, when it fails to do so. Sexual satisfaction is therefore press-ganged into being a litmus test of romantic love's success—again with an inevitable cost in the form of damaging pretense and relationships of genuine love unnecessarily discarded.

Of course, pretense is far more difficult when we love without feeling sexual desire than when we feel sexual desire without loving. Unlike love, sexual passion can't be faked for long. And, also unlike love, the giving, devotion, and intimacy peculiar to sex cannot credibly be expressed in any other sort of relationship. We can't imagine that our bond is essentially sexual if it isn't. In this respect there is something strikingly honest about sex.

It is therefore time for a much more far-reaching divorce between romantic-erotic love and sex than even the sexual revolutions of the twentieth and twenty-first centuries have afforded, so that they may each be allowed to live and develop without being forced to march in lock step, or to serve as litmus tests for each other. So that, as was the case in medieval courtly love, it is in no way mandatory for passionate romantic-erotic love to express and prove itself through sex, let alone to do so invariably. So that we can recognize that love can be deeply erotic without necessarily being sexual.

The greatest beneficiary of this further liberation will *not* be sex—which has been vastly, if incompletely, liberated in the past one hundred years—but love itself, still trapped, as I argued in Chapter 1, in a conceptual time warp dating from the nineteenth century. For though sex has, to a great extent, been unshackled from constricting servitude to love, love has not been released from unhealthy servitude to sex. Most of the great revolutions in "free love" in the Western world have freed how we think of sex far more successfully than they have liberated how we think of love. For all the structures of power, prejudice, inclusion, and marginalization that still pervade and control it, sex is far less dominated by marriage, by heterosexuality, by moralities of stigma and shame, by parental control, by fear of disease, and even by inequalities in power between the genders than it was a half century, let alone a century, ago; while contraception and fertility technologies are increasingly breaking its link to reproduction. Sexual morality has obviously been transformed out of all recognition from times as recent as the late nineteenth and early twentieth centuries, when the clitoris and ovaries of healthy women might be excised as a cure to the "insanity" supposedly induced by masturbation, which, it was feared, would lead to neurasthenia, epilepsy, convulsions, melancholia, blindness, paralysis, and eventual death;[2] or when unmarried pregnant girls would be deemed mentally subnormal and incarcerated in psychiatric asylums.[3]

By contrast, love today—especially on the dominant view that I critique (the view of love as secularized *agape*)—is recognizably similar to love a century and more ago. Paradoxically, by vastly expanding the field of possible partners, itself the result of love's accelerating independence of social, religious, familial, and other external authorities, each successive revolution in love since the nineteenth century, from divorce to contraception, from gay love to feminism, has become a fresh opportunity to pursue and so to entrench that modern ideal of human love as unconditional, spontaneous, disinterested, and all-affirming of the loved one. In other words, the liberation of our *practice* of love—its ever-greater freedom to establish relationships of choice that seek mutual autonomy and self-creation—has facilitated the ossification of our prevailing *conception* of love, which has become increasingly yoked to a hubristic and unworkable ideal of secularized *agape*.

30 }

The Real Relation between Love and Beauty

Beauty, I argued in Chapter 28, is not in itself the ground of love: it is not what ultimately inspires and sustains love. Indeed we find many more people and things beautiful than we love. Rather its role in inspiring and sustaining love is to hijack our attention so that we are then receptive to love's actual ground: the promise of ontological rootedness.

Yet once love has got going, another and deeper relation of beauty to love opens up. In the very special light of the promise we see in them, we will necessarily find beautiful those we love. Indeed we will be prone to idealizing their beauty (and goodness) in a way that easily becomes delusional and obsessive. For we cannot love someone and then find no beauty in them—whether in their body, their virtues, their taste, their strengths, their vulnerabilities, or their gestures and mannerisms. To see beauty in them is of a piece with the intense gratitude we feel for their existence. Each of these judgments—of gratitude and of beauty—confirms the other.

Why do we necessarily see beauty of some kind in those we love? When we glimpse in the loved one a promise of rootedness—a lineage with which we deeply identify, an ethical home, existential power over us, and the call to being—why do we, on this account, find them luminously beautiful?

The answer, I suggest, is that, taken together, these four conditions of love point to the central feature of anyone and anything we call "beautiful" (as distinct from merely attractive or delightful): their spellbinding power to speak of, to witness, to disclose, to gesture toward, what most fundamentally concerns us—whether we celebrate or abhor it; whether we feel empowered by it or mortally threatened by it; whether we find it significant or trite—because our life can flourish, we believe, only if we become intimately attuned to it, keep it vividly in view, find a living bond to it.

What most fundamentally concerns us—as individuals, as an age, and as a culture—is, therefore, by no means only what we most desire or value or idealize or honor. It is also what we find most problematical, fearful, alienating, trivializing, empty, and *ugly*, in our own life or society, in the spirit of our

174

times, or, more generally, in life and existence; and yet what we feel compelled to face, understand, reckon with, and even affirm if we are to be vitally and creatively engaged in the world in which we find ourselves.

Beauty is, therefore, the power to speak of—to coax to vivid presence; to inhabit and reveal—those realities of our life, our age, our existence, that we, as individuals, take to be most central to it: realities to which we crave, or feel called, to find a living, nourishing, affirming, masterful, immersive relation—whether we desire or dread them (or both), whether we find them attractive or repellent, good or evil, profound or superficial. Thus, we might experience those realities as deeply harmonious or—like Dmitri Karamazov's profession of the beauty of Sodom and the Madonna—as warring opposites: conflicting but equally vital axes of existence, for both of which the "heart burns."[1] We might see them as unique to our age, or as "timeless." But in all of these cases beauty is centrally about the charisma of spokesmanship—a spokesmanship that can take innumerable forms, only one of which is direct mimetic representation. (It can take time to come to see that a person, a work of art, a landscape, even a god, thus speaks to us, which is why we are often not seized by their beauty at first; but when we do see it we can change, in a moment, from seeing no beauty in them to being overwhelmed by their beauty—and so to craving constant communion with them.)

And so we will call "beautiful" whoever and whatever has this power to speak of or disclose what is most central to the world as we experience it and to which we crave this living relation. Indeed, to be offered access, if only imaginatively, to such people or things—to "possess," or imagine oneself possessing, them and their power in any way—is the source of that intense pleasure occasioned by all beauty, a pleasure to which thinkers such as Stendhal and Nietzsche have drawn attention but the precise origins or grounding of which they have not identified. It is a power that bestows life—and calls us to life. And it is a power that, in contrast to many traditional ways of thinking about beauty, does not necessarily see it as, in any way, a symbol of morality, or as equivalent to the good.

Moreover, if beauty is the power to speak not only of what is, for us, of the greatest significance and consequence (whether we value or abhor it), but also of what we find trite and trivial, yet so fundamental to the world into which we are cast and in which alone we can flourish that we cannot help seeking a living relation to it, then we can see why though beauty always occasions pleasure— the pleasure of achieving, through beauty's powers of presentation and revelation, vital engagement with such realities—beauty does not always move us. We are moved only by the beauty that speaks of what we personally most care about: what is most deeply in accord with our own taste and concerns and ends and hopes. For there is much that we find beautiful but that leaves us cold: the beauty, for example, of what we see as pointless perfection—the perfection of things that fail to engage us; or beauty that speaks ingeniously, intensely, rivetingly, of what we find frivolous.

Indeed, if beauty is this power of spokesmanship, then we are not wholly free, as individuals or as a class or age or culture, to decide what we find beautiful and what we don't. The world that is given to us in the time and place in which we live—the world into which we happen to be cast—will to a great degree determine and constrain the range of what we can find beautiful. By the same token, it is not possible for us to experience as beautiful just *anything* that people living in other times and places have called beautiful, no matter how "open" we are to it, or how flexible are our individual standards of beauty.

———

We can now see why what we find beautiful will be far more extensive than what we love. For love is inspired only by worlds that we supremely value and that we experience as promising a genuine home: worlds that when disclosed or revealed or promised by loved ones will cause us to find them beautiful. Whereas we can find beautiful not only these worlds captured or pointed to by love but also whatever speaks charismatically of those other worlds, or inheritances, or idioms, or features of life and existence, to which we believe we must become deeply attuned if we are wholeheartedly to live and flourish in the times into which we have been born.

To the extent that we see those other worlds as beautiful, they come to be imbued for us with an overwhelming sense of necessity, as Kant says (though for different reasons). Not purposiveness—which Kant also ascribes to a judgment of beauty—but necessity. Just as the beauty of a sandstorm in a desert evinces not purposiveness but necessity. Indeed, if we experience the necessity of such worlds intensely enough they will become sacred to us.

And whatever speaks forcefully, intoxicatingly, insistently, of those worlds can be terrifying—whether they are worlds that we wish to make our home (the worlds sought by love); or whether they are worlds of horror, or perhaps of banality, that appall us but that we feel compelled to come to terms with, and even to affirm, if we are to live fully and well (those other worlds that, when powerfully spoken of or disclosed, we find beautiful but cannot love).

This is why we so often find power beautiful, especially when it is overwhelming and yet does not harm us. The mighty event, once underway, has an aura of sublime necessity that defies all human willpower to the contrary. It is unstoppable. (The reason, perhaps, why the composer Stockhausen could, shockingly, find in the destruction of the World Trade Center on September 11, 2001, "the greatest work of art that is possible"[2] from the hands of Lucifer.)

In other words, beauty, like love, can inspire not only joy but also fear—and, again like love, less by the threat of losing its object than precisely by its presence. Far from being a condition of painless calm, in which all willing has ceased and "happiness and unhappiness have vanished,"[3] as Schopenhauer holds, contemplating the beautiful person or thing can overwhelm the senses, driving emotions to confusing extremes and causing dizzying anxiety.

Stendhal, who speaks of beauty as the promise of happiness, also gives voice to just this fear and turbulence that beauty can arouse, in this case after encountering the frescoes of Volterrano in the Basilica di Santa Croce in Florence. "As I emerged from the porch of *Santa Croce*, I was seized with a fierce palpitation of the heart (that same symptom which, in Berlin, is referred to as an *attack of nerves*); the well-spring of life was dried up within me, and I walked in constant fear of falling to the ground."[4] And Rilke writes of beauty:

> Beauty is nothing
> but the beginning of terror, which we still are just able to endure,
> and we are so awed because it serenely disdains to annihilate us.
> Every angel is terrifying.[5]

Beauty is, of course, more than *nothing but* the beginning of terror, just as it is more than *nothing but* the promise of happiness. Indeed, the terror and the happiness that beauty arouses in us are two sides of the same coin: for beauty's power to symbolize, to signify, to point to, to disclose, to render intelligible or experienceable—"graspable"—those worlds, whether we find them good or bad, in relation to which we crave a living bond is itself both terrifying and exhilarating, a source of awe as well as of joy.

———

Clearly, much of what most deeply matters to human beings—what realities they feel they must reckon with, come close to, and make their own—and so what they will find beautiful, will vary from one epoch and one culture and one person (and even one stage in that person's life) to the next. There can be no eternal standards of beauty or universally agreed judgments of beauty.

For one epoch or type of sensibility, beauty might be said to lie predominantly in harmony and symmetry, as Aristotle holds,[6] for another in dissonance and asymmetry; for one in eternity and permanence, as in Diotima's vision of absolute beauty, for the other in transience and becoming; for one in order and for the other in chaos; for one in wholeness or perfection, as in Aristophanes's account, and for the other in the unfinished or the imperfect, as in the Japanese aesthetic of *wabi-sabi*; for one in the elegant and the ornamental, as Mannerism conceived the beautiful,[7] and for the other in the jarring and the spare; for one in clarity and light, for the other in the obscure and the dark; for one in perfection, for the other precisely in the dignity of the imperfect and the imperfectable; for one in tradition, for the other in the destruction of tradition. (Or, since many, perhaps most, epochs are transitions, or mosaics, of sensibility, beauty might, at any given time, be identified with combinations of these standards.)

And so we can find beautiful what we also see as ugly. We can even find profound (Duchamp's urinal) what, under another aspect, we find trivial (any ordinary urinal). A person or a work of art or a cityscape that, looked at in one way, we find ugly can, looked at in another way—as symbolically presenting a reality in which we are, or yearn to be, at home—be experienced as beautiful.

In sum, beauty is the power to disclose or display those realities and sensibilities, whether they are seen as timeless or time-bound, as universal or local, as good or bad, as reassuring or frightening, as significant or trivial, to which we are driven, consciously or not, to find a living relation if we are to be anchored, and so to flourish, *in the time and place we inhabit*. Of all that we find beautiful—of all such disclosed realities and sensibilities—we are, as I suggested earlier, moved only by the beauty that speaks of what we personally most care about: what is most deeply in accord with our own taste and concerns and ends and hopes.

Beauty isn't, therefore, an essence. Nor can it be encapsulated in Keats's elegant symmetry: "Beauty is truth, truth beauty—that is all / Ye know on earth, and all ye need to know." Nor is it related, as Kant says it is, to the formal "purposiveness" that the free play of the imagination and understanding sees in an object—*as if* the object were expressly arranged for our appreciation[8] (but only "as if," for Kant insists that our pleasure in the beautiful is experienced as entirely disinterested, in other words as free from any desire for the beautiful object's existence). And still less is beauty nothing but "pleasure regarded as the quality of a thing," or "pleasure objectified," in Santayana's question-begging definition;[9] or "that quality or those qualities in bodies by which they cause love, or some passion similar to it," in Burke's equally question-begging, Platonic definition.[10] Nor is it adequately characterized as "simply and solely that which is an end in itself," or "that of which the admiring contemplation is good in itself," as G. E. Moore says of the beautiful.[11]

We do not choose the circumstances—the era, the society, the parental heritage, the life events, the hopes and disappointments, the sensibility, the style, the prevailing ethic—into which we have been born or that most powerfully impinge on us; and to that extent we have no control over what we find beautiful. In an age (or period in our life) of violent alienation, of *Zerrissenheit*, of dissonance, we might find beauty in anyone or anything that presents this reality in such a way that we are able to find a life-giving relation to it. Or that, at least, articulates it such that we feel we can begin to grasp it. And, by contrast, at such a time, any contemporary presentation of the world as threaded by calm, proportion, harmony, elegance, innate purposiveness, and perfection will seem insipid, pointless, uncourageous, pretentious, inauthentic, even mocking. A stale idiom. Like *kitsch*.

That what we find beautiful speaks of, and to, what most concerns us is why beauty can, though it need not, symbolize our morality—in a way very different, of course, to Kant's concept of beauty as a symbol of the morally good (both aesthetic judgment and morality, for Kant, being marked by the nobility of disinterestedness as well as by a claim to universality). For to the extent that those ends and norms that, taken together, we call "morality" express what most deeply matters to us as well as what we feel we must reckon with if we are to have confidence in life—very much including those aspects of life that we find terrible, meaningless, and yet intrinsic to it—we will find morality beautiful.

A person whom we deeply love is the paradigm of beauty thus conceived. For love is grounded in a very particular promise of confidence in and mastery over life: the promise of rootedness in the world.

Perhaps Sappho, the bisexual love poetess, agrees that beauty is inspired by love—and not the other way around—when she says:

> Some say thronging cavalry, some say foot soldiers, others call a fleet the most beautiful sights the dark world offers, but I say it's whatever you love best.[12]

31 }

Can We Love the Ugly?

We cannot be done with our opposition to the long tradition that deems beauty to be the real ground and inspiration of love until we have gone one step further and asked this next question: Can we love people—or things: for example, works of art—*because* they are ugly?

The question here is obviously not the one that has amused or alarmed generations of poets, such as Lucretius. It has nothing to do with delusion: with seeing as beautiful what, were we not in love, we would find hideous:

> We often see mis-shapen, disgusting women
> Regarded as charming, indeed, you might say worshipped . . .
> A dark girl looks like honey; an unwashed one is natural;
> The cat-eyed bitch is a goddess; the stringy one is a sylph;
> The undersized, undergrown one a minute gem;
> The overgrown monster has an extraordinary dignity.[1]

Of course, many of the passions—not just love—can idealize. All powerful desire, whether it is needy or generous, creative or destructive, taking or giving, can turn its object into a paragon of good or bad. All love can gild the loved one with so many perfections that the lover either ends up "blind" to their imperfections, or has transformed their ugliness into beauty, and now deems nothing more beautiful than their pockmarked face.

The question we want to ask is rather this: Can we love someone *despite* continuing, in love, to find them ugly (as well as beautiful)? Quite clearsightedly. In other words, without imagining away their ugliness.

And more radically still: Can ugliness itself be an inspiration and object of love?

The conventional answer to both questions is No.

Again, Plato lays the groundwork for this answer with the greatest precision. If, as he writes in the *Symposium*, the object of love "is to procreate and bring forth in beauty," and if one can bring forth or give birth "only in beauty and never in ugliness," it follows that there cannot be love of ugliness.[2] Whether of

180

body or soul or anything else. In Plato's wake, Augustine asks: "What is it that entices and attracts us in the things we love?" And he answers: "Surely if beauty and loveliness of form were not present in them, they could not possibly appeal to us."[3] These views are echoed today, even more explicitly, by Alexander Nehamas, who insists that it is "impossible to be a friend of someone you actually find physically repulsive, even ugly."[4]

But is this right?

We surely can love people despite and, I will argue in a moment, even *for* their ugliness. And without deluding ourselves about it. Again: this is surprising only if we assume that beauty, or creation in beauty, is necessarily the ground of love. If, on the other hand, beauty—and in particular physical beauty—isn't at all love's real ground, and if love is in fact concerned with something very different—ontological rootedness—then it ceases to be absurd to love others whom we find ugly, whether physically, morally, or otherwise.

To understand this, there is no need to invoke, as much of the tradition does, some mysterious capacity of love gratuitously or spontaneously to bestow value on the loved one, without any grounds or conditions, in the way that God is said to love. If beauty isn't a necessary condition of love in the first place, then why shouldn't we love someone whom we find physically ugly? Or even, in some respects, ugly in soul?

We spot in them a lineage with which we powerfully identify. We see an ethical world that echoes our own and in which our ultimate ends find a home. We feel grounded by their existential power, in the way I discussed in Chapters 6 and 10. We feel that their whole being embodies the maxim attributed to Augustine: *Amo, Volo ut sis*—"I love you; I want you to be." We feel called to our genuine selfhood. Why would we not love them merely because they are ugly? Their ugliness is as nothing compared with these great gifts.

Such love of another, despite finding them ugly, is neither absurd nor deluded.

And we can go further: if their ugliness in some way expresses, as human "deformities" so nobly can, the true structure of the world as it confronts us—if it expresses what is ineluctably jagged, misshapen, impaired about the world, *including ourselves*, but in such a tenderly uncompromising way that it draws us close to what we normally ignore or flee—then we can love them precisely for embodying, straightforwardly and courageously, a fuller, richer reality than that which we normally choose to inhabit. Strange though it sounds, their ugliness offers us the thrilling privilege to come to terms with, even to celebrate, those troubling "imperfections" that are constitutive of any world that is open to us fully to live in. They are our guides to so much of the world—and of ourselves—from which we have turned away in fear. And so we love them *for* their ugliness.

Similarly, we are not being sentimental when we love, say, the very severely handicapped child with whom we can barely communicate and in whose presence we are unrelievedly distressed. We love him—and on that account find him beautiful—not just because his incapacity has wrought a searingly gentle innocence that is barely available to those engaged in normal commerce with the world; not just because we are moved by the unknowing dignity with which his life perseveres; but precisely for his extreme disability, which speaks openly, even brazenly, of a world that is also disabled, a disabled world that we must affirm if it is to be our home, a disabled world that is the only world we have.

Thus, contrary to the condescending view—though it thinks of itself as charitable—that love for such a handicapped child is a compassionate response to the horror of his condition, which confers dignity on it (and fortifies us against the pain and fear that it arouses in us), in fact we love him for his power to disclose and affirm those infirmities of the world from which we take flight at the price of not fully living in it.

Love is not the same as compassion, as Arthur Schopenhauer, one of the early secularizers of Christian *agape*, claims it is; and our love for the severely incapacitated is not, most fundamentally, an act of generosity or compassionate insight. Rather it is grounded in their power to bring into view—usually with utmost gentleness and necessarily free of all vanity and of all desire to be recognized or pitied—incapacities with which we must discover a tranquil and affirming intimacy if we are to be richly at home in the world.

In short, thanks to love's clearsightedness—genuine love is, at root, never "blind"—we love the handicapped for the majesty of their endurance, for revealing so powerfully a human world that is itself handicapped, for compelling us (without the use of any force, but merely through their presence to us) to attend to it, and so for teaching us how to be at home in it.

———

Such power of spokesmanship belongs, we saw in the previous chapter, to the nature of beauty. This is why we can find beautiful—and love—what, at the same time, we see as ugly or troubling. His handicap can appear to us in double aspect: we find its extreme misshapenness unsettling—and yet, in its power to speak of a whole world that we yearn to affirm, overridingly beautiful.

Similarly, we can love a work of art for its ugliness; in other words, not only one that depicts something ugly but, more controversially, one that we find ugly in its language and composition and manner of disclosure. If we love (rather than merely find technically dazzling) one of Picasso's horribly distorted paintings of Jacqueline at the same time as it repels and disturbs us, isn't the reason, at least in part, that it relates us to our dissonant, destructive era in such a way that, rather than overwhelming us with terror or disgust, we feel a heightened ability to grasp it and be intimate with it? Such disclosure of what repels or terrifies us cannot be achieved just by an act of will on our part; it can be vouchsafed only by works of art or people or aspects of nature that present these troubling realities to us with irresistible power, and so afford us a firmer orientation with respect to the very problematical world to which they belong.

Our capacity to love what is ugly—even for its ugliness—might be just what Shakespeare gives voice to in his "Dark Lady" sonnets. Whether or not we take him to be mocking conventional love poems with their perfected loved ones, this speaker seems wholly capable of loving a woman without any idealizing or "crystallizing"—without first needing imaginatively to transform the ugly into the beautiful:

> My mistress' eyes are nothing like the sun;
> Coral is far more red than her lips' red;
> If snow be white, why then her breasts are dun;
> If hairs be wires, black wires grow on her head.
> I have seen roses damask'd, red and white,
> But no such roses see I in her cheeks;
> And in some perfumes is there more delight
> Than in the breath that from my mistress reeks.
> I love to hear her speak, yet well I know
> That music hath a far more pleasing sound;
> I grant I never saw a goddess go;
> My mistress, when she walks, treads on the ground:
>   And yet, by heaven, I think my love as rare
>   As any she belied with false compare. (Sonnet 130)

32 }

Can We Love Evil?

The malice was loathsome, and I loved it. I was in love with my own ruin, in love with decay: not for the thing for which I was falling into decay but with *decay itself.*

—AUGUSTINE, *THE CONFESSIONS*[1]

It is rare to love what we take to be ugly, but far more common to love what we see as evil.

Augustine recalls that he had enjoyed committing theft in his youth, not because it had served some pleasurable end, such as living more comfortably, possessing a trophy that his friends lacked, or showing generosity to someone from whom he wanted something, but rather for the sake of doing evil for no purpose. ("There was no motive for my malice except malice."[2])

Why is this so? Why are human beings able to love evil as an end rather than just as a means?

Not, in the first place, because of the pleasures of transgression: cheating the constraints that bind everyone else; outwitting the power of society and other authorities; enjoying a shot of freedom, or respite from boredom and conformity, anonymity and impotence, alienation and banality.

Nor, even, because of lust for cruelty, revenge, and bloodletting. Or relief in discharging aggressive drives. Or delight in power over someone weaker who knows he's at your mercy—powerful though all these impulses can be. For what we are talking about here is *love*: love of what you yourself take to be evil.

Rather we will love evil as an end in itself to the extent that the evil act or the evil person speaks seductively of those fundamental realities of life—be they destructive or banal, heroic or tedious—that are off limits to the morality we ourselves endorse, or that oppress us with their stubborn persistence, but that, *at the same time*, we see as intrinsic to our humanity, or to the society in which we are compelled to live, and so to any world in which we can be capaciously and wholeheartedly at home.

We will then be tempted to embrace these realities even at the cost of sacrificing whatever else we value most highly.

This is the essence of attraction to the perverse, which, as Edgar Allan Poe puts it in his short story "The Imp of the Perverse," is a "primitive impulse" of the human heart. Echoing Augustine, he says:

> I am not more certain that I breathe, than that the assurance of the wrong or error of any action is often the one unconquerable *force* which impels us, and alone impels us to its prosecution. . . . [T]his overwhelming tendency to do wrong for the wrong's sake . . . is a radical, a primitive impulse—elementary.[3]

To love evil as an end is not, in other words, the same as being attracted to it because it offers a role in life to those who feel "lost" or angry, alienated from their societies, and lacking in meaning; and, still less, because its partisans see it not as evil but rather as their version of the good (all of which are possible relations to evil and all of which are familiar explanations for why people turn to crime and terrorism).

For what is explicitly sought here is not a role in life, or an identity for its own sake, or a higher good for the sake of which crimes may be committed, but evil itself, as a sovereign driving force constitutive of the world—a force that has been recognized from the ancient Zoroastrians to the Manicheans; from the Gospel of John, which speaks of people loving "darkness" and of evildoers hating "the light,"[4] through Christian heresies such as the Cathar movement of the thirteenth century, to Freud's concept of the "death instinct" as the impulse to destroy life and return to an inorganic state.

This motive for love—to find grounding in destructiveness as a fundamental and purposeless reality of life—is perhaps the deepest wellspring of the criminal mind; and, if we are to understand the horrors of which the most genuine love is capable, we cannot conceal it from ourselves.

But such concealment is just what a long tradition, perhaps the most influential form of which is that stemming from Plato and Aristotle, insists on. "The *only* object of men's love is what is good," writes Plato; and we would cut off our own arms and legs if we found them to be diseased. For to possess beauty is to possess the good—and love's desire is for nothing other than "the perpetual possession of the good."[5]

Aristotle agrees: we do not genuinely love what is evil, he insists. "What is evil neither can nor should be loved."[6] So too Augustine. We can, he says, love only what God has created in human beings (including their potential for redemption), which is by definition good; but we cannot love what they freely choose to do that is bad: "We love what God created, the man and not the error," as he pithily puts it.[7] We love him "as man," not "as sinner."[8]

In other words, for this tradition we can love evil only if we do not recognize it as evil, only if we mistakenly think it good or pleasurable or freedom-giving for us. Or we can love evil people for the specks of good that we find in them. But we cannot love what *we take* to be evil.

How, though, could we possibly experience evil as offering us a home in the world?

The answer, again, is: to the extent that we crave to affirm life as a whole, and not just that slice of it endorsed by our own morality. To the extent that we see the evil person as possessing the vitality, power, freedom, and courage to embody life in this broad sense and to impose their will on it. To the extent that we perceive their power and courage as available to protect *us* (even if for now, until we have persuaded them that we love them, it is directed against us). To the extent that the criminal or terrorist has genuine existential power over us (the hostage-taker again)—and so forces upon us the conviction that we must find a way of affirming them, if only to master our fear of them. To the extent that we take joy in destruction and even see the evil loved one as venting our destructiveness on the world by proxy. In all these ways we can find in evil, or the doer of evil, a path to home in the world.

And so this terrible love recognizes evil as evil, and is inspired and vitalized by it. Such love does not merely mistake evil for good, or vice for virtue. It says with Satan in Milton's *Paradise Lost*: "Evil, be thou my good."

Nor does it need to see evil as a necessary step on the way to what is good: to virtue, redemption, creativity, truth, insight. As when, for example, the artist feels justified in abandoning his family to poverty and loneliness so that he can develop as an artist wherever he finds his best inspiration: the case of Gauguin. Or when, in the "just war," killing is necessary to achieving a more humane order. Or when destruction of a corrupt social order is held to clear the way for one of integrity. Or when terrorists or dictators claim that murder is a necessary means to a morally great end. Ultimately, loving evil is not about needing to break eggs in order to make omelets.

Nor, too, do evil acts necessarily arise, as Freud ingeniously claims they can, out of guilt. Freud's paradoxical idea is that guilt *precedes* the crime: the adult commits a criminal act in order to rationalize—and so to relieve—an oppressive sense of guilt left over from the infant's Oedipal urge to kill his father and have sex with his mother.[9] Since this urge has been repressed and thus "forgotten," the adult commits a conscious crime in order to provide an object—an explanation—for his primal guilt, which is unbearable as long as it lacks a crime to justify it. But this theory, too, ignores the direct, unmediated attraction to evil in the adult: the way in which evil can actually ground a human being in the world.

Such unmediated attraction to evil finds in what it recognizes as evil— murder; the death of others; apocalyptic destruction; violent power for its own sake—an essence of life and world no less fundamental than, say, the fact of finitude, to which Augustine traces the very possibility of evil, an essence of life expressed by gloating Dionysus in Euripides's *The Bacchae*, whose only drive is to foment destruction, madness, and death.[10] Expressed, too, by Joseph Conrad's Professor in *The Secret Agent*, who, driven by thoughts that "caressed the images of ruin and destruction," always carried on him an explosive device, strapped to his chest, that could be detonated at whim.[11] Expressed, possibly, by Iago's will to destroy Othello. And expressed, perhaps most powerfully of all, in the Bible, when God says of himself: "I form the light, *and* create darkness: I make peace, *and* create evil [ra]: I the LORD do all these things."[12] One of the great moments of divine self-revelation in scripture—and, because it jars with modernity's sanitized view of God as a source only of compassion and loving-kindness, one of the most resolutely ignored.

The last passage, from the Book of Isaiah, is so potent because it speaks of the world in its totality: its darkness as well as its light, its evil as well as its good. And it does so, of course, from the point of view of its creator—the God who, in Genesis, had deemed it all "very good."

There are those who, in order to feel vibrantly at home in a world filled with evil, seek to celebrate it and align themselves with it. Not as voyeurs, by describing or depicting it, let alone by grudgingly "facing imperfect reality," but rather by themselves enacting it: by becoming one, as master or slave, with the stubborn horrors of banality, emptiness, destruction, nonbeing, and, since the "death of God," the absence of any intrinsic meaning or purpose. They are intoxicated by what they see as the charismatic independence of spirit needed to give voice to such horrors through action, in the face not just of opposed social norms but—more alluringly still—in the face of *their own* opposition to those very horrors. And so for them enactment of evil, and of its inevitability, is indispensable to being genuinely at home in the world as it is, rather than as the morality that they might also espouse, even passionately espouse, prescribes how the world should be.

This, indeed, is the deepest yearning of the criminal mind: to be at home in a world of ineliminable evil. It is not to transgress for its own sake; or to create a new society; or to show contempt for life-denying morality; or to rebel against order and meaning. For the true criminal evil is never embraced merely, or even primarily, as a means to a better world; and certainly never merely as a means of protest. The will to evil, as theologians like Augustine and Thomas Aquinas so clearly saw, and that the atheist Freud echoes with his idea of the "death instinct" (which he introduces in order to explain the immensity of human destructiveness), is above all a will to the absence of structure and being—a will to nothingness. And a will to recognize and affirm nothingness as a central reality of the given.

Thus, the death camp commandant might see mass murder as evil and, at the same time, enthusiastically endorse it. To him, his victims are merely an occasion, and their alleged mendacity merely a plausible justification, for his actions; but they are not the ultimate cause or aim of those actions, nor therefore the real focus of his interest. Indeed, there are times when he must be puzzled why it is *them* he is destroying. For this ultimate criminal is deeply bound up with a larger purpose than his victims. He thinks he loves the world—he thinks of himself as a natural lover—by showing that he, just one ordinary or not so ordinary man, can affirm and be the equal of the horrors intrinsic to it: injustice, indifference, destruction, cruelty, resentment, envy, and the ruthless desire for power. More: he prides himself on his courage—and his vision—to affirm the necessity of what he also dreads, and finds in this affirmation a source of vitality, of joy, of meaning, of peace—and, crucially, of his own laudable integrity. And so, we may conjecture, he discovers in evil a way of being at home in the world.

Such is Peter Verkhovensky in Dostoevsky's *Devils*. Though Verkhovensky poses as a revolutionary, though he might appear to claim, in his bouts of bragging, that total destruction is a *means* to purging Russia of what he takes to be its stultifying ills so that a new, purified community may be born, his actions suggest otherwise. Namely that for him violence itself is salvific, even beautiful, because it expresses, affirms, brings him close to, dimensions of life outlawed by morality. Thus he tells his hero Stavrogin: "We'll proclaim *destruction* . . . why, why again is this little idea so fascinating?"[13]

This "little idea" is so fascinating to him, we may conjecture, precisely because it is extraordinary that any activity as potentially simple and quick as destruction can also, to its perpetrators, promise a path to oneness with ultimate metaphysical realities. (And destroying is indeed the simplest path to metaphysical consolation available to human beings.) Unlike a revolutionary, Verkhovensky does not seriously try to justify the ruin he brings to others by some higher social or redemptive purpose to which it is supposedly necessary.[14] He loves destroying because to unravel existence, to produce nothingness, is to be threatened by nothing; because, through it, he feels the power to be aligned with, to be the equal of, to face down—whether in anger or delight, resentment or celebration—what he takes to be the ultimately purposeless, meaningless, formless nature of ultimate reality: something like Schopenhauer's impersonal Will. A mind like his is ecstatic that one puny individual's destructiveness can afford him such intimacy, such oneness, with a world that is itself entirely indifferent to the decay and disintegration to which everything living within it finally succumbs. And so the destroyer can feel comfort, safety, even joy in the face of what the rest of humanity—the humanity of morals; the humanity that craves to purify the world of this whole dimension of indifference, decomposition, and evil—finds nauseating and terrifying. As a result, in Verkhovensky there is no flicker of hope that either his own destructiveness *or* the world's might somehow be redeemed. To redeem reality would be to escape it. Such redemption is for cowards.

And yet, as I have suggested, there is also the type of criminal who, at the same time as reveling in these consolations of evil, is loyal, often passionately so, to the morality against which they are rebelling; and for them destructiveness alone is hard to endure. This is the case with Stavrogin, that beast of prey with claws, who does have an obstinate sense of morality for all his flouting of it; who is somehow in search of redemption from evil and from his "ungovernable wildness"; and who, unlike Verkhovensky, is finally destroyed by his crimes and his conscience.

We don't know whether Stavrogin ever ceases to love evil. But we do know that he sees evil as evil, and that in the end his commitment to morality, the violation of which so intoxicates him, cannot endure it. Recalling in despair his rape of a twelve-year-old girl and his indifference to her subsequent suicide, he hangs himself in his own loft.

Stavrogin, with what Dostoevsky calls his "superhuman strength," affirms evil in the spirit of Nietzsche's ambition to achieve *amor fati*—love of fate. This is the spirit that can see, or wishes to see, everything in life as such and in our own life in particular, including every impulse to good and bad, as beautiful and as lovable, not because it might turn out to foster a noble end, such as artistic creativity, but simply on account of its brute *necessity*.[15] This, too, is the spirit in which another great Dostoevskian character, Dmitri Karamazov, professes equal love for the beauty of the Madonna and the beauty of Sodom.[16] So that if we are to say what Nietzsche calls the "most wantonly extravagant Yes to life," which he claims is "not only the highest insight but also the *deepest*,"[17] we must love it all: the necessity that spawns everything that exists, the evil as well as the good, the will to nonbeing as well as the will to being, the dark as well as the light.

PART V

The Child as the New Supreme Object of Love

Of all that I've done in my life, I'm most proud to be your dad.
—BARACK OBAMA *to his daughters in his farewell speech to the nation as president of the United States*

Out of everything I've accomplished, my proudest moment, hands down, was when I gave birth to my daughter Blue.
—BEYONCÉ

Introduction

The starting point of this book is to ask: "What is love?" In particular: "What is love's purpose and motivation?"; and "What is the good that love, uniquely, realizes or constitutes?" These, I suggested, belong to the most common of all questions—and, at the same time, to the most unanswered or dogmatically answered. (And to that degree they are questions about which we have ceased to think.)

For a dominant answer is one or another variant of "secularized *agape*," which, to the extent that love is seen as unconditional or spontaneous in its origin, sidesteps all questions about its ground— its ultimate purpose and motivation—or deems such questions to be otiose.

Indeed, we saw that instead of investigating what the unique ground of love is—and so how this emotion, which, out of the same passion, can be simultaneously the most clearsighted and the most deluded, differs from, say, *any* intense form of altruism or sexual desire or attachment or intimacy or devotion or compassion (to one or more of which it is so often equated), or from our life's ultimate ends and core values; why we love just one or a few people, and not necessarily those who are kind or loving to us; and, moreover, why we love at all—instead of asking these fundamental questions, reflection on love today is overwhelmingly concerned with characterizing genuine or successful relationships, and the virtues and practices internal to them, *once* love has got going. But this is to put the cart before the horse: for, at the level of its fine-grained experience, we can't characterize what is *specific* to a relationship of love, or to a wholehearted commitment to an object of love, or to the virtues and practices that mark such a relationship or commitment, or to the nature of the "We-ness"—the "common venture"—that marks the intertwining of two lives, and we can't therefore determine what it takes to succeed (or why we fail) in love, unless our understanding is guided by a conception of what the particular ground of love is—and so of what is peculiar to its goal, inspiration, and intentions, as distinct from those that characterize other types of attachment or desire.

What Sorts of Answers Have Been Given So Far to the Question "What Is Love?"

I then identified six basic types of answer to the question "What is love?" that have been given so far in the West since ancient times: since biblical and Greek thought, the major origins of Western love. These are:

1. Love as responsibility for our "neighbor," rooted in and for the sake of love for God.
2. Love as desire for supreme beauty or goodness.
3. Love as yearning for wholeness—for our (unique?) other half.
4. Love as friendship: as dedication to the well-being of another person, experienced as a second self, who is alike in virtue or otherwise similar in key respects to the lover.
5. Love as idealizing those we sexually desire or regard as reproductively suitable.
6. Love as divine: as belonging to the nature of God; and, during the nineteenth century, as "sanitized" of all destructive or vengeful qualities, so that divine love comes to be seen as purely unconditional, disinterested, enduring, and all-affirming of the loved one. This picture of how God is said to love is then secularized, so that these four qualities are deemed to be sovereign human powers rather than attainable only by the gift of divine grace.

This sixth and last conception of love prevails today, in its secularized form. In other words, human love has been ascribed all those sovereign powers, such as unconditionality, disinterestedness, and the capacity to affirm everything about the loved one, that were once reserved for God. The concept of "*agape*" has been torn from the theological foundation that alone gives it sense, and in particular from the idea that human love can exhibit such divine qualities only if enabled to do so by the unknowable workings of God's grace. And so a way of loving that was once seen as dependent, in whole or in part, on a divine gift is now taken as our natural birthright; and powers to love that, by definition, transcended human nature are now seen as *defining* human love at its most genuine.

Though none of the other traditional conceptions of the nature of love has been—or could be—press-ganged into mimicking the divine to this extent, they too, I suggested, cannot fully account for the tremendous selectivity of love, whether for friends, children, spouses, works of art, landscapes, God, or any of its other many possible objects and expressions. For we love far fewer people than we find beautiful or good or sexually attractive, or to whom we are benevolent or powerfully attached. Love's specificity is precisely what has been lost in the history of Western love, and to understand it we need to dig down to love's ultimate ground, to its fundamental motivation and aim.

Love: Toward a New Understanding

So how might we think of love in a way that does justice to its powerful specificity: to what really motivates it; to what it seeks; to the sorts of relationships it nurtures; to the reality that, of all those we value, we love very few? Put another way: What evokes the famous "look" of the lover? What does his or her "gaze" *recognize* in the loved one (for love always involves the amazement of recognition)?

In Part II of this book, I sketched a conception of love as the joy inspired by whomever or whatever we experience as rooting our life, and attempted to explain what such rooting amounts to. Love, on this picture, is grounded in the promise of "ontological rootedness," rather than in sexual or reproductive arousal, along with its triggers such as smell or physique or tactile stimulation, as promulgated by naturalistic traditions from Lucretius's characterizations of erotic desire, through Schopenhauer's sexual love, to the libido described by the early Freud, to evolutionary psychology; or in beauty, or goodness, or virtue, as the great traditions descending from Plato and Aristotle hold—though we will see beauty or goodness in an object that holds out such a promise.

What, then, is it to experience another as offering us a promise of ontological rootedness?

It is, I proposed, to experience them in four ways:

> First, we glimpse in them a source of life, a lineage or heritage, with whose sensibility we deeply identify.

Second, we have the sense that the loved one offers us an ethical home: that they embody those ultimate values and virtues that are most crucial to our sense of being stably at home in the world *and* that, of all our ethical commitments, we feel least able to live out on our own.

Third, we feel that they possess decisive power to deepen our sense of existing—power to intensify the reality and vitality, and therefore the validity, of our existence, as we experience it. This is the power—a power that at the limit feels like one of life or death—by which love is always inspired and to which it is unfailingly attracted—one of the reasons why hostages can fall in love with their captors.

And fourth, we experience the presence of the loved one as calling us to life, to our destiny, to our individual "I am" or "I will be." This fourth experience presupposes the first three; for if we can sustain them—our powerful identification with the loved one's lineage, with the ethical home they offer us, and with their power over our sense of existing— then we are prepared to feel called into an authentic relationship with both them and ourselves. And so to feel commanded to become not only who we are but also who *they are.*

This very particular ground of love—this very particular structure of experience and intentionality—can be found in the widest variety of bonds, from friendship to romance, from parental love to filial love, from kindness to a stranger to other relationships of altruism, from unrequited love to unrequitable love such as for art or nature or a vocation or country. Yet all of these relationships can also have nothing to do with love: a colleague might be a model of altruism and yet not love us; a parent (or child) might be cruel and deeply love us; a romance might be energized by the life-giving joys of sex, but be empty of love; or it might be empty of sex and yet express the love of both partners' lives.

Narratives of Love as a Promise of Home or Rootedness

I then suggested, in Part III, that my conception of love as a joyful response to a promise of ontological rootedness is powerfully articulated in two of the West's founding texts, both of them archetypal narratives of love—primordial "myths," or structures of explanation, that allow a phenomenon like love to become intelligible—which may be interpreted precisely as connecting love with the search for, and the promise of, home in a world that we supremely value: first the covenant between God and Abraham in the Bible, in which Abraham learns that his true home and destiny are not where he was born or now lives, nor where his kin and father's house are, but rather far away in Canaan; and, second, Odysseus's journey home from Troy to Ithaca, recounted in Homer's *Odyssey.*

In the first type of case, home is an entirely new territory, inconceivably removed from one's actual origin and so at the outset completely uncharted; in the second, the journey takes us back to a fresh encounter with the place where we started—and that, perhaps, we never genuinely made our own, or the possibilities of which we never fully lived. In both cases, love involves a displacement—and in the case of an Abraham a radical displacement—from the *status quo ante*.

What Is the Relation between Love and Sex, and Love and Beauty?

In Part IV, I used my proposal that love is grounded in a promise of ontological rootedness to try to take a fresh look at the relation of love to beauty and sex. I argued that sex is never the ultimate ground of love, and that, *contra* Plato's Diotima, nor is beauty (or creation in beauty). Instead beauty and sex rivet our attention to another so powerfully that we are better able to see in them a promise of ontological rootedness, if it exists.

In addition, sexual joy and ascriptions of beauty are expressions of love, for we inevitably see beauty in one we love and sex itself is one of the main languages of love, or at least of romantic-erotic love. Thus, in coming to see what roots us as beautiful, love is able to see beauty in people or things that we also find ugly. Moreover, I suggested, ugliness—like evil—can be loved, without in any way being imaginatively transformed into beauty, if it speaks of a world in which we seek to be at home.

In concluding, we must turn from our guiding question "What is love?" (and, in particular, "What is the ground of love?") to the further question: "What is the supreme object of love?" In other words, what sort of object of love, what kind of loved one, is taken to be most worthy of love, or to offer the purest possibilities for loving?

Like the *value* of love, which, I argued in Chapter 19, is not fixed, but varies between epochs or cultures, depending on the degree to which they suffer from exile and alienation, so too the archetypal *object* of love is not fixed but changes from one historical time and place to another.

For Plato's Diotima it was absolute beauty; for Aristotle it was the perfect friend; for Plotinus it was the "One," the source of everything else: its ultimate efficient and also final cause; for Augustine, and of course during many centuries of Christian dominance, it was God; for the troubadours of medieval Europe it was the (usually unattainable) Lady, repository of virtue; for Spinoza it was nature considered as a whole; from the late eighteenth century it became the romantic-erotic partner—or, more rarely, nature or art; for psychoanalytic thinking (in all its diversity) it is the parent, or rather an internal representation of the parent: some internalized primal figure who comes to stand for the parent; but now, in a historic change, it is, I suggest, coming to be the child.

Though we are not yet anywhere near its downfall, modern romantic-erotic love, which reached its apogee around the middle of the nineteenth century with works such as *Tristan und Isolde*, and, in its ideals and ways of feeling, pushed "the long nineteenth century" right through the twentieth and then on into the twenty-first, is inexorably drawing to a close as our archetypal love. Instead, the must-have form of love, the one without which a life is deemed to be ultimately impoverished whatever its other achievements—or its other loves—and the one by which people's capacity for genuine love is most critically assessed by their peers (and so by themselves) is gradually changing from romance to parenthood. By the same token, the child is displacing the romantic lover as our most sacred object; and the parent–child bond is taking over from the romantic couple as the most sacred relationship. And so to violate the child—or the parent–child bond—is now the ultimate sacrilege, today's equivalent of desecrating the divine. (Indeed, such violation is one taboo that few artists and writers, seeking to question entrenched norms or to shock their publics into such questioning, will dare to challenge.)

To be clear: it isn't that the value we attach to love has declined. On the contrary, the prestige of love is still increasing—and will continue to increase—because human beings are ever more conscious of their alienation from enduring sources of meaning and belonging: alienation that love, with its capacity to deeply ground individuals in their own chosen and self-determining communities of two or a few, is perhaps uniquely able to overcome and redeem. It is just that, as we will see, the idiom of romantic love is becoming ever less suited to the temper of our times, while the idiom of parental love is becoming ever more finely attuned to it.

In short: at life's gravitational center we find love; and at love's gravitational center we find—increasingly—the child.

Why Parental Love Is Coming to Trump Romantic Love

If this is true, we are witnessing a revolution without precedent: for, in all of Western history, the child has never been the archetypal object of love.

Children have, of course, been loved, often deeply. In the Bible, Abraham loves his son Isaac; and Jacob loves Joseph—above all his other children. The Prodigal Son is evidently doted on by his forgiving father. The images of Mary holding the infant Jesus, which we find in so much European painting and sculpture, often depict her loving intimacy (rather than only her pious care). A mother's love for her child, Aristotle says, epitomizes the virtue of doing and wishing what is good for a loved one for his own sake, and of grieving and rejoicing with him.[1]

Moreover, the prestige of children—and stigmas against childlessness—have been reflected in the fertility cults of many societies, as well as in prayers to overcome barrenness, such as Hannah's appeal to God for a child in the Old Testament,[2] or Elizabeth and Zacharias's in the New.[3] In Genesis, God orders Adam and Eve, and later Noah and his sons, to "be fruitful and multiply."[4] And parents have, at most times, taken joy in producing heirs as well as pride in preserving their family, clan, or community.

Yet until well after the rise, in the mid- to late eighteenth century, of what is often (if terminally vaguely) called "modernity"—the sensibility that sets up as supreme values individual autonomy, self-reflective authenticity, personal identity as a never-ending construction site, equality and emancipation, rational planning, and perpetual novelty along with its associated destructiveness of what has been hitherto; and that is marked at every turn by the overthrow of traditional social hierarchies and, in much of the Western world, by the slow "death of God"—until well after the rise of this modern period, the child is not commonly a *special* object of love in the West, and certainly not its highest object. And nor, until well after then, was childhood seen as the primary locus of the sacred, and so as incompatible with valuing children as economic assets.

On the contrary, for much of the nineteenth century children continued to be widely regarded as economic assets, and had few rights in law. Incredible though it might now seem, child labor was abolished in the United States only in the early twentieth century, until when "ten year old boys were commonly found in the blinding dust of coal breakers, picking slate with torn and bleeding fingers," while "thousands of children sweltered all night for a pittance in the glare of the white-hot furnaces of the glasshouses."[5] In the nineteenth century, orphanages in the United States routinely supplied child laborers by way of so-called orphan trains.

At the same time in London, dead infants "littered parks and roadsides."[6] Newspapers and individual witnesses reported, often in sensationalist terms, that the city was "clogged with the corpses of innocents and stained by their blood, inhabited by a swelling population of murdering mothers,"[7] and replete with "thoroughfares obstructed by the detritus of unwanted babies."[8] Again, incredibly to our contemporary ears, in England, "of the 5,314 cases of homicide recorded by the Registrar General between 1863 and 1887, 3,355"—a full sixty-three percent—"concerned a child under 1 year of age."[9] In other words, according to such statistics, children were more likely to be murdered than any other age group. And in the late eighteenth and early nineteenth centuries, they were given to foundling homes on a massive scale, especially in southern Europe.[10]

Moreover, only decades before that, a Venetian infant who was thought to be illegitimate might be abandoned or killed.[11] This was also a time when the sale of children as slaves was still prevalent in western Europe, as it had been for two thousand years and as it remains today in some other parts of the world.[12]

In all these periods offspring were, of course, often desired, anticipated, welcomed, protected, boasted of, and indeed loved. Already in the nineteenth century there was a strong cult of motherhood in the middle classes in, for example, England, with mothers prepared to devote everything to their children. By the 1860s, child murder was coming to be regarded as signifying a deep national disorder, which threatened the communications networks, hygiene, and moral stature of Britain.[13] Yet such valuing, care, and love of children was consistent with, and perhaps in part even motivated by, their role as healthy specimens able to contribute to the family's economy, to its social prestige, to looking after parents in their old age, and, at least in the case of the nobility, to the continuation of lineage. To love children and to value them for their economic or social utility were not, for the great part of Western history, regarded as incompatible, as they clearly are today. In short, we don't need to go back as far as Socrates, for whom it was a mark of the *inferior* soul that he or she "surrenders to pleasure and sets out in the manner of a four-footed beast, eager to make babies,"[14] to see that a conception of the child as the supreme repository of the sacred, and of love for the child as the supreme expression of love, is the radical exception in Western history and possibly in world history.

———

So what might account for this epochal change, which dawns, with remarkable suddenness, between the mid- to late nineteenth and the early twentieth centuries, when, as the sociologist Viviana Zelizer has shown, children under fourteen went from being objects of "utility" to objects of "sentiment," from being valued for their economic contributions to the family to being "economically 'worthless' but emotionally 'priceless' "?[15] What happened between the time when the newborn was "welcomed as the arrival of a future laborer" and the beginning of an era when, as Felix Adler, first chairman of the US National Child Labor Committee, declared in 1905, to profit from children is to "touch profanely a sacred thing"?[16] And why has this transformation gathered such momentum since then that today the child is becoming the archetypal object of love?

In terms of love as a joyful response to a promise of ontological rootedness, the question is this: Why does the child—rather than God, or the romantic lover, or the spouse, or nature, or art—now offer the most potent promise of finding a home in the world?

We should eliminate from the start four tempting, because obvious-seeming, explanations: that in celebrating childhood we are seeking a sanctuary of innocence from a venal world; that the near elimination of child mortality in much of the West has made it "safe" to risk profound attachments of love to one's children; that we are in the grip of a new fertility cult; and that, with the "death of God," we now hope for immortality in our offspring rather than in a life to come.

A Search for Innocence?

Our age is unlikely to be capable any more of seeing childhood as a realm of pure innocence—unlikely, in part, because the unparalleled violence of the twentieth century made it hard to regard human nature, at any stage of its development, as intrinsically and incorruptibly good; and in part because the tremendous influence of Freud and his successors (whether for good or ill) has not exempted childhood from a view of the psyche as pervaded by destructive and brutally self-centered impulses.

Freud's account of the jealous, manipulative, erotically driven, possessive infant, hate-filled toward its parents on account of their inevitable absences, destructive of rivals for their attention, and residually narcissistic even as it becomes an adult, is too ingrained in our contemporary consciousness for us to cleave to any straightforward view of children as intrinsically innocent in the sense of either goodness, or naivety, or lack of cynicism, or freedom from sexual desire, greed, cruelty, hatred, violent intent, and all those anxieties, cravings, corruptions, and sufferings that we would like to confine to the adult world.

In addition, if the child internalizes the values and ideals and experiences of its parents, and later of society more broadly—if mother and father plant their ego and superego in it, as much of the psychoanalytic tradition suggests—then it is already infiltrated by an adult world that cannot be seen as innocent in any of these senses. So that whatever innocence children are taken to have is necessarily challenged by their absorption of the larger world into which they have been cast—a world from which no amount of "protected space" can shield them.

It has therefore become ever harder to see children as filled only with un-corrupted naturalness and open-hearted humility—in other words, to see them in terms of an ideal of childhood that, in its modern version, dates from the eighteenth century and finds its greatest spokesmen in Romantics such as Jean-Jacques Rousseau, William Blake, and William Wordsworth. Much though we might wish to insist on their intrinsic innocence, after Freud an image of children such as Wordsworth's can feel one-sided at the least, if not outright deluded:

> [T]railing clouds of glory do we come
> From God, who is our home:
> Heaven lies about us in our infancy![17]

So, too, does a distant predecessor of this view of childhood as close to the divine, articulated by Jesus himself:

> Unless you change and become like children, you will never enter the kingdom of heaven.[18]

The Decline in Child Mortality?

Nor is the increasing sacredness of the child the result of a decline in child mortality, which now allows parents to risk an intensity of loving attachment to their children that they avoided when many or most infants didn't survive. For it wouldn't be true to claim that parents were not attached to their children in previous times: their grief at the death of a child is well documented, even in periods of very high infant mortality.[19]

If the child became the supreme object of love merely because declining in-fant mortality rates made loving attachments less risky for parents, we should expect to have seen a leveling off of this historic trend ever since survival could be more or less assured. But this doesn't appear to have happened. On the contrary, the sacralization of the child, and of love for the child, has continued apace, and arguably with greater vigor than ever.

A New Fertility Cult?

Moreover, the sacred status of the child is also not the consequence of a modern fertility cult.

If a fertility cult were at work parents would strive to have the maximum number of children—or at least of healthy children. More prestige would attach to having five than to producing just one. Whereas in much of the Western world exactly the opposite is happening: the ever-greater moral significance of parental love is coinciding with a demographic crisis. People are refusing to have large families at the same time as they are turning the child into the repository of the sacred.

In fact, the gathering moral weight of parenthood might be contributing to declining birthrates in some countries and social groups, if only by compelling parents to "get it right" with each child. Which means that their devotion, time, and money are better concentrated on few children than spread thinly between many. It might even be inhibiting people from having children at all, or at least causing them to wait until they are certain of doing so for the "right" reasons, or until age forces their hand. And this is particularly so for women, still very much regarded as emotionally the more crucial parent, and therefore more subject to society's unforgiving strictures should they be deemed to fail, despite the fact that men are increasingly participating in childrearing.

Indeed, women today are under a massive double pressure: the sacred status of the child is raising the stakes of motherhood ever higher; and, at the same time, the pressure—and the opportunity—to play a full part in the world of career and work are also ever greater. To have a child whom she loves in the correct way *and* to pursue a successful career are both seen, to an unprecedented degree, as central to a woman's personal fulfillment—to her leading a genuinely flourishing life. We are not just speaking, therefore, of the practical challenges of managing a family and a career, formidable though they can be; for this double pressure is, above all, moral.

In addition, if a fertility cult were the reason for the child becoming the supreme object of love, this would almost certainly undermine the attractiveness of adoption or stepchildren—and even associate them with shame. Yet this, too, does not seem to be happening. There is no clear sense that children must be one's biological offspring in order for them to be regarded as sacred or supremely lovable. Indeed, all the reasons that I will propose for this ever-growing phenomenon apply just as well to the stepchild or the adopted child as to the biological child.

Seeking Immortality through Our Children?

Finally, the cult of the child as the archetypal object of love is not fundamentally about seeking immortality through one's children in an age when traditional promises of immortality—in an afterlife guaranteed by a loving God, or through heroic deeds that will survive the hero's death, or in a romantic union that can be perfected only beyond this world—are no longer widely believed; or if they are believed fail to give our lives the intense meaning and moral significance that they once did.

For if today's cult of the child were centrally about a desire for immortality, one might expect this, too, to be reflected in an urge to have more children, while stigmatizing adoption, stepchildren, and infertility, which do nothing for a parent's immortality, at least in a biological sense. But that is not the case either.

Instead, in today's secular times we seek immortality in our reputation, and especially in the memory of others who are likely to survive us—including but not limited to our children. To paraphrase W. H. Auden's elegy to Yeats,[20] we become—or hope to become—our admirers. Our postmortem existence is to be a memory trace in those who outlive us. And the trace we want to leave is not so much one of courage, as in archaic societies such as those of pre-Christian Greece and Rome, as one of love. Our indestructible legacy is to be our loving and our being loved—a reality to which many a funeral oration attests.

For all except the most famous, any such immortality will, of course, be brief; for those who remember us will themselves soon be dead.

———

Far from being aimed at immortality, love of the child in the contemporary West is fundamentally about locating the sacred in *the finite life of the individual*, instead of in its transcendence. It is about finding the purest love in an exclusively worldly setting that contains none of those otherworldly overtones, none of those strivings for transcendence—such as the desire of lovers to "merge" and so to be rid of their individuality along with the banality of everyday life—with which romantic love is inextricably associated.

Indeed, unlike romantic love in its heyday, parental love is to be as down to earth as it is possible for love to be, entirely unconcerned with dualisms such as body/soul, sexual/spiritual, earthly/heavenly, and temporal/eternal, or with ambitions to transfigure the first of each of these pairs into the second, or the second into the first: dualisms that so energize romantic love from Dante to Wagner and beyond, but that no longer speak as urgently to our world. Specifically, parental love pursues, for the sake of both child *and* parent, today's thoroughly secular way of conceiving the ideal of an autonomous, egalitarian individual—an ideal, originating in the eighteenth century, to which the idiom of romantic love has become, as we will see, far less well suited.

Who is this ideal individual?

She chooses, or at least willingly endorses, her ends, values, and the actions conducive to them. And, in doing so, she identifies and cultivates her particular tastes and needs. Together with such sovereignty goes the modern ethos of equality, very much including equality between the genders, respect for people as ends in themselves (and so for their feelings and perspectives), compassionate empathy, and mastery of life's risks and dangers. Parental love is to foster each of these goals, on the part of parents as well as of their children.

For a long time romantic love was the perfect vehicle for the first two of these ambitions: sovereignty and equality.

Well into the twentieth century, romantic love was *the* realm in which the individual could define herself and defy convention. A realm in which she could be ethically autonomous, authentic, and cocooned from society with its entrenched values and ambitions and structures of power. A realm in which the lover could cultivate her own self in the act of total devotion to her loved one.

Romantic love crashed through barriers between classes: only here was it legitimate for the royal to worship the commoner, or the wealthy the pauper, or the bourgeois the manual laborer.

It set itself against all authority that obstructed it—from Church, to ethnic clan, to parents on whose social and economic ambitions for their children's marriages it could bring ruin.

It subverted inequalities between women and men: for in romantic love women too could choose and reject and, to that extent at least, be free. They might even be seen as the superior party: erotically the more charismatic, ethically on a pedestal, more knowledgeable about the ways of love, guardians of its flame, mistresses of its realm.

And yet, even if we see romantic love as having gone some way toward eroding gender inequalities, it went—and could go—only so far. For love to go further in fostering equality between men and women, it increasingly turned to the child as the center of its attentions. One might think that it could have turned to passionate friendship; but, for good reasons, to which we will come, it didn't.

Parental Love and the Ideal of Autonomy

We "fall" into a romantic commitment, whereas we decide to have—or not to have—a child.

Parental love is autonomous to a degree that romantic love never can be—even when we've methodically set about finding the "right" partner. And though this autonomy of parental love is especially marked in an era of reliable contraception, it was always, in a much lesser way, true before that.

Thus, to fall romantically in love with someone whom we once hated, or otherwise against our will, is no slur on our love, and might even be regarded as a mark of its authenticity (Benedick to Beatrice in Shakespeare's *Much Ado about Nothing*: "I do suffer love indeed, for I love thee against my will"). By contrast, love for our children feels compromised if it flourishes against our will, or if we initially loathed them, as Tristan and Isolde initially loathed each other.

Moreover, the inequality of power between parents and their children and the intense dependence of children upon their parents' care conspire to make parental love the epitome of personal responsibility. Whereas high romantic love, throwing caution to the winds in pursuit of its passion, can be—and can revel in being—the epitome of irresponsibility.

In addition, parental love cultivates the loved one's—the child's—sovereign individuality; while romantic love, when its lovers seek to merge, threatens or even dissolves it.

Such contrasts reflect the very different ways in which we think of parental and romantic commitments. Parental commitments are dignified by being autonomous, consciously chosen, and responsible; romantic commitments are dignified by being fated, not consciously chosen, and—often—irresponsible. (No matter how calculatingly we might search for our ideal romantic partner, no matter how many criteria we might expect them to meet, we nonetheless expect the love itself—the *experience of loving*—to bear these features of falling, of inevitability, of incaution, of spontaneity, of being swept away. The whole point of all that meticulous calculation, the whole point of all that targeted searching for the "right person," is to set us up for the ideal experience of spontaneous love; and—as far as possible—not to leave fate to chance.)

Indeed, the more moral meaning that we ascribe to childhood, the more we are expected to choose parenthood rather than to fall into it. The child's sacred status; the unlimited liability for children's emotional needs that parents are taken to have; the way we now see a whole human life as fundamentally shaped by its early experiences; the tremendous power to facilitate or engineer a child's future happiness, success, and competitive prowess that is widely (and perhaps exaggeratedly) attributed to good "parenting"—all this means that having a child has become a moral decision of a typically modern kind: one that is genuine only if reflectively endorsed as the product of an autonomous will.

And today's intense moralization of childhood has practical consequences too. Parents are keenly aware of how much of their own lives they must devote to each child if their responsibilities are to be upheld—and recognized by society as upheld. They are not just to meet their children's emotional needs and to cultivate their authentic selves; not just to foster their ethical autonomy, including as responsible citizens and consumers; not just to be a role model with exemplary values or to ensure that they are always there for them—always caring, listening, and loving. In addition, they are to mold their children into (middle-class?) success stories—into their society's future "human capital"—investing in education, hobbies, housing, and health, as well as in what are taken to be legitimate material entitlements, for as long as it takes, which can mean well into their children's early twenties if not beyond. Whether so much parental supervision and availability is, in fact, an inspired way to raise flourishing human beings—and one must severely doubt that it is—the manic managerialism of contemporary parenting does, in turn, make it all the more proper that parenthood be experienced as the product of choice rather than of chance.

We are, of course, in a stronger position than ever to exercise such choice. Contraception, fertility aids, *in vitro* fertilization, sperm donation, the vanishing of social norms that tied sex to reproduction and marriage, the possibility for many LGBTQ couples to adopt or give birth—all these moral and technical developments, still in their infancy, have given us unprecedented control over whether and when to have children.

The upshot is clear: if having children is increasingly a decision that we reflectively endorse, then loving them is increasingly the consequence of such a sovereign decision. It is to love in a manner consistent with the modern idiom of autonomy that goes back to Kant.

Neither of the two previous types of supreme love in the Western world can be experienced as so autonomous in origin: certainly not romantic love, as we have seen, which is dignified by, to a great degree, *not* being chosen; but not love for God either. For, as in romantic love, we might fall in love with the divine against our will, and even after bitter opposition, as St. Paul's conversion on the road to Damascus shows—driven not by a conscious decision but by what we take to be external forces that overwhelm us.

And the upshot for romantic love is equally clear: if, in keeping with the idiom of autonomy as it is expressed today, we try to turn romance into a decision that is to be reflectively endorsed; if we "seal the deal" by visiting our lawyer rather than by being carried away into the sunset; if we see romantic love in the way we have come to see parental love, as micromanaging the happiness and success of our loved ones, complete with goals, road maps, and benchmarks—then it will feel inauthentic, and so will lose its hold over us. Which is just what we are experiencing in the Western world as the traditional conception of the "fatedness" of romance is forced—impossibly—to serve our contemporary ideal of autonomous choice.

Childhood and the War on Risk

To this ideal of autonomy must be added a closely related reason for the suitability of the child as today's supreme object of love: the determination of our age to eliminate risk; to make the whole of life a safe space. Comfort and safety, we should note, are no longer merely practical goals driven by the human instinct to maximize pleasure and minimize pain; they have become moral imperatives of the first order.

This is not a recent phenomenon—one born, say, in the 1950s with the emergence of mass consumerism, or in the 1990s with "zero tolerance" toward crime. Like the ethos of autonomy, it becomes a central theme of the Western mind in the eighteenth and nineteenth centuries. As Nietzsche presciently observed in 1882, the modern Western world—those peoples whose heritage is, centrally if by no means exclusively, the history of Christianity and of its various secularized forms—is pervaded by a "*religion of comfortableness*"[21] that is single-mindedly devoted to conquering suffering and the causes of suffering. Not in some distant utopia or in another world altogether, such as Heaven, but right here and now, in a life of "happiness" achieved through the security of family, career, health, equality, and practical convenience.

Such happiness isn't to be achieved by *redeeming* our sufferings—through seeing them as essential to some great good that they, and perhaps only they, can bring about: a good such as artistic creativity or moral virtue or enlarged consciousness or indeed romantic love. Though lip service might be paid to the power of suffering to foster such greater goods, to the slogan "no gain without pain," another, stronger ideal rules: happiness is to be achieved by *vanquishing* suffering. By striving for zero tolerance toward pain, especially lasting pain, whether physical or psychological.

As a supreme value, love has, not surprisingly, become pressed into active service in this war on risk. Love must not merely be pursued in as risk-free a way as possible; it must itself be our ultimate refuge from risk. So that love, which so easily becomes the most perilous emotion, is expected, on the contrary, to be the safest.

———

Here, too, parental love comes into its own. And here, too, it trumps romantic love. It wins on *moral* grounds.

Whereas romantic love must be prepared for risk—whereas it knows that it must constantly confront the possibility of loss, betrayal, rejection, and other obstacles to its consummation; indeed that such obstacles feed its energy and its sense of its own validity—parental love is duty bound to strive for safety. Despite the tremendous differences in their conceptions of love, for couples such as Paris and Helen of Troy, the medieval troubadour and his Lady, Lancelot and Guinevere, Shakespeare's Romeo and Juliet, and Tolstoy's Anna Karenina and Count Vronsky, it is axiomatic that love, precisely at its most genuine, is unconcerned with danger—and even seeks dangers to overcome in order to prove its *bona fides*. In contrast, it is axiomatic that parental love is centrally devoted to the control of danger—for both lover and, in particular, loved one. The proverb "all is fair in love and war" is as unsuited to parental love as it is a staple of romantic-erotic desire—even if, nonetheless, many parents end up disappointed in their children or children estranged from their parents.

And so the child—as the paragon of human vulnerability, for whom any suffering is undeserved—increasingly demarcates the battlefield on which the West's war on risk is being fought. The most morally urgent love is therefore necessarily directed at the child. As the totemic object of our new religion of safety, it must at all costs be protected from risk, suffering, trauma. Society can be judged safe only to the degree that the child is safe (so that the democratic State, which follows like a sniffer dog wherever the values of the age lead, now makes the safety of the child one of its paramount concerns). And parental love is deemed to be successful, even genuine, only to the degree that it strives—and manages—to make the child invulnerable. No effort can be spared, no vigilance can be too great, when it comes to the security of a child—though it might end up shielding him from opportunity and learning and discovery as well as from danger.

This much is perhaps obvious to a contemporary reader. Less obvious is that love of the child serves the safety of the parent too. For in no other type of love is the lover's devotion extended from such an overwhelming position of superiority—at least until the child reaches the threshold of adulthood.

So, for example, in love for God, we are the absolutely inferior party, at the mercy of an all-powerful, all-knowing power, who might, moreover, disappear in our hour of need.

In romantic-erotic love, the lover is vulnerable to rejection, indifference, betrayal, rivals, and a panoply of destructive possibilities at the hands of the loved one.

In love for nature, whether she is seen as Mother Earth, or as the sublimely terrifying force, indifferent to human concerns, depicted by Kant and Burke and many eighteenth- and nineteenth-century poets and painters, the lover is, again, the fundamentally weaker party. (Indeed, human puniness—the finite in the face of the infinite—is integral to the "romance" of mighty nature, as in the paintings of Caspar David Friedrich.)

In ideal friendship, as paradigmatically depicted by Aristotle in his conception of "perfect" *philia*, there is, by definition, parity between the two parties in terms of those qualities that ground their love for one another, and so (as Aristotle himself notes) this kind of reciprocal love is out of the question if one party is significantly inferior to the other and, moreover, is to a degree a part of the other, as, Aristotle says, a child is to its parent. Which means, he says quite explicitly, that "it would be absurd for a man to be the friend [*philos*] of a child."[22] In other words, what Aristotle takes to be the highest form of love—reciprocated, perfect friendship, grounded in the ethical equality and independence of the two parties—cannot, he thinks, exist between parents and their children.

Moreover, parental love, as it is conceived today, is manifestly devoted to maintaining "borders" between lover and loved one. And so it avoids the thrilling if often dangerous erosion of individuality, the porous selfhood, that is the signature and even the goal of the other great forms of love. No matter how intense its devotion, it eschews any yearning to "merge" with the loved one, as we find in romantic love. Nor does it see the loved one as a "second," possibly indistinguishable, self in the manner of friendship love, as described by such writers as Aristotle and Montaigne. Nor does it involve the kind of passionate, awe-filled submission that we find in love for God—not to mention the craving to fuse with God expressed by so many mystics: to be absorbed into God "with greater violence and efficacy than a torrent of fire [absorbs] a single drop of the morning dew," as St. John of the Cross writes, or to become one and the same liquid, "like rain falling from heaven into a river," as St. Teresa of Avila puts it.[23] On the contrary, such impulses would be repudiated as perversions or betrayals of love for one's children. Respectful distance and clear boundaries are to be maintained. Indeed, such respect is seen not as a restriction on love but as a sign of love.

Finally, in parental love the risk of being repudiated or betrayed by the loved one is less than in any other form of love. Until the child has reached early adulthood its need for mother and father is so great that it cannot emotionally abandon them—even if its love, let alone gratitude, cannot be counted on after that; and arguably the parent is the only lover who can never be truly abandoned. For in one internalized form or another, a child remains loyal to its parents for its whole life, even when it thinks it is rejecting them, often speaking and dreaming of them on the day of its own death.

For all these reasons, parental love today is talismanic of the war on risk. Such love is focused on the safety of the loved one to a degree unrivaled by any other expression of love. And however much parents, for their part, claim to be, and are, slaves of their children, and terrible though rejection by them is—"How sharper than a serpent's tooth it is / To have a thankless child," rages King Lear—the reality is that their love is very much less vulnerable to destructiveness, wrath, or betrayal than is any other form of love. Today's safety-obsessed, hypervigilant "helicopter parents" are as far from the death-devoted hearts of Tristan and Isolde as it is possible to get.

The Child as Parent of the Adult

The primacy of childhood in our contemporary consciousness, and so in love, is still further enhanced by the conviction, taken to an unprecedented extreme in our time, but again deeply rooted in eighteenth- and nineteenth-century thought, that an emotionally healthy childhood is the key to a flourishing life and love the key to a flourishing childhood; that the child's psychological well-being or misery is the overwhelming determinant of the adult's; that from its experiences, and in particular from the quality of its early attachments, emerge the templates for how, as adults, we will live and love and value and relate to others, as well as our possibilities of becoming authentic, self-creating, self-respecting, autonomous individuals—in other words, of achieving the dominant modern conception of what it is to flourish.

On this view, therefore, the adult is constituted by the history of her childhood, which is in turn central to any narrative that can structure her life and explain or redeem its difficulties. To that extent the child is parent to the adult; and like every parent remains over in the life to which it gives rise.

In its bare elements, this view goes back to Aristotle, who conceives of childhood as the potential to give rise to an adult manifesting, in their mature forms, traits and functions that characterize flourishing human nature. It is a potential that must be cultivated, in particular, by rigorous education in the virtues, such as courage—and not least by fostering motives for virtuous activity, such as pleasure in noble and just behavior.

By contrast, our modern emphasis on fostering the individual autonomy of the child, on the development and health of its inner emotional life, and on its need for the right sort of loving intimacy is first gestured at by Rousseau in his 1762 pedagogical treatise *Emile*, with its insistence that only through meticulously mentored self-discovery will the child give rise to an authentic adult: a human being who, with single-minded integrity, is sovereign in his or her values and tastes, rather than one who, as he puts it in the *Second Discourse*, lives in and through the opinion of others, and whose sense of existing is nourished exclusively by their judgments. It is expressed by Wordsworth's famous line "The Child is Father of the Man"; reflected in Alyosha Karamazov's rapturous injunction to the group of boys at the end of Dostoevsky's *The Brothers Karamazov*: "You must know that there is nothing higher, or stronger, or sounder, or more useful afterwards in life, than some . . . beautiful, sacred memory, preserved from childhood. . . . If a man stores up many such memories to take into life, then he is saved for his whole life";[24] turned into an engineering manual of baby and child care by Dr. Spock; and richly developed (though without Wordsworth's or Dostoevsky's sense for the joys of childhood) by Sigmund Freud, Melanie Klein, John Bowlby, and other psychoanalysts, as well as by the hugely influential ideas of Piaget and his followers, which see human development as marked by clear stages, each of which takes place between certain ages and each of which is as vital to the formation of an adult as it is irreversible.

It would surely be mistaken to see childhood merely as a series of experiences in which the foundations of adulthood are laid, if only because children have powers, such as the ability to acquire languages, to train memory, and to master complex physical and mental challenges like learning to play a musical instrument, that adults usually cannot match to anything like the same degree. Nonetheless, in thinkers such as these we find the seeds of today's conviction that the experiences of childhood determine, in great degree, the ends and powers and contentments of a human life, that parental love is vital to discovering and fulfilling the individuality of each child, and that the quality of its early attachments forges a model of relating that will govern all its adult interactions. For if childhood is the crucible of the individual's flourishing then, to the extent that love is a moral emotion and central to the well-lived life, love's natural focus must be the child.

The onus thus placed on parental love is obvious, but also hard to overstate. From birth—and perhaps even in the womb—the infant, and thus the whole life to which it will give rise, is deemed to be minutely dependent on its parents' and, above all, its mother's unblemished devotion. Psychological health, physical health, the capacity to become a self-respecting, autonomous individual—all these and more can be sabotaged without the right attentiveness and attachment. In this feverish environment and under the tremendous pressure it places on mothers in particular, any woman who fails to experience a rush of protective love on holding her newborn, or who doesn't feel complete only when she is with her baby, might well judge that she has already betrayed her child's life as well as her own, biologically determined, instinct to care for and to become viscerally attached to her young.

Indeed, according to the attachment theorist John Bowlby, an infant isn't just critically *dependent* on his mother for nurturing love; he is so helpless that, in crucial ways, he *is* his mother:

> It is not surprising that during infancy and early childhood these functions [the capacities for self-regulation] are either not operating at all or are doing so most imperfectly. During this phase of life, the child is therefore dependent on his mother performing them for him. She orients him in space and time, provides his environment, permits the satisfaction of some impulses, restricts others. *She is his ego and his super-ego.* Gradually he learns these arts himself, and as he does, the skilled parent transfers the roles to him. This is a slow, subtle and continuous process, beginning when he first learns to walk and feed himself, and not ending completely until maturity is reached. . . . Ego and super-ego development are thus inextricably bound up with the child's primary human relationships.[25]

This immense power that our age rightly or wrongly, for good or ill, ascribes to the parent—and specifically to good (enough) parental love—and the corresponding malleability and vulnerability that it sees in the child do not, however, entail that the child is regarded as a paragon of goodness or psychic health that can be ruined only by inadequate parenting. On the contrary, as we saw earlier in this chapter, the psychoanalytic tradition, in particular, has taught our age, with astounding success, to see childhood as anything but innocent, whether in the sense of good, or naive, or free from violent and narcissistic drives.

Even the capacity to love, Freud suggests, is not innocent in its origins. For it is dependent on the infant's primal trauma, and the anger it unleashes, of learning that his caregivers aren't always available when he wants them—a trauma that forces upon him awareness of the independent selves of others, which is, in turn, a precondition of love. Since love's possessive ambitions cannot be perfectly or finally fulfilled, Freud tells us, anger and destruction are always latent in its desiring.

Freud here, as so often, echoes that other "master of suspicion," the philosopher Friedrich Nietzsche, who had already claimed, though for different reasons, that hatred is the womb of love, indeed that Christianity's entire "religion of love" is motivated by aversion to nature, to strength, to life itself. So that:

> [From] the profoundest and sublimest kind of hatred, capable of creating ideals and reversing values, the like of which has never existed on earth before—there grew something equally incomparable, a *new love*, the profoundest and sublimest kind of love.[26]

So much of what we value, Nietzsche suggests, originates in its opposite—or, rather, in what we take to be its opposite: truth in falsehood, selflessness in selfishness, purity in lust.[27] Also good in evil and forgiveness in resentment. As exhibit 1 of this thesis, he cites St. Paul, the great apostle of love—and arguably the inventor of universal "Christian love"—who, as Nietzsche portrays him, is also the high priest of hatred, a man consumed by resentment and an "extravagant lust for power," who despised the Jewish law that he also felt compelled to fulfill—a cruel man who had been complicit in the stoning of St. Stephen, the first Christian martyr.[28]

———

To such philosophical and psychoanalytic doubts about the very possibility of pure innocence, or of intrinsic human benevolence, must be added our era's experience of genocide, totalitarianism, and world war, disseminated by a mass media with global reach, which has left us in no doubt about the evil of which the most ordinary human beings are capable—human beings who might at the same time be loving parents, loyal spouses, sensitive aesthetes, and kindhearted members of their own communities. Mistrust of human motives—right back to the infant's intrinsic potential for anger and violence, and to the colonization of its psyche by an indelible parental heritage—has become the contemporary equivalent of Augustine's doctrine of "original sin." And to face this putative reality—that there is no stage of development before which the human soul is certain to be innocent—is a matter not of regrettable cynicism but of laudable integrity.

It is, therefore, not only unlikely that the child has become our supreme object of love in the expectation of reconnecting to a condition of pure innocence but possible that the very opposite is the case: namely that the child has become love's most urgent focus precisely out of the conviction, whether well founded or not, that childhood can be the crucible of human horror, the hotbed of life-long resentments and hatreds, the determinant of war and peace in the adult psyche. If so, it is here, in cultivating the "Father of the Man," or the parent of the adult, that love as a moral emotion will have its greatest work to do.

The Woman as Lead Lover?

Does the cult of parental love mark a radically new phase in the history of love, where, for the first time, the woman—to the extent that she takes herself to be and is taken to be the primary parent—is decisively in charge as lover, rather than as beloved?

Or, by contrast, is the new archetype of parental love the latest manifestation of the old order, imprisoning women more securely than ever in a traditional identity of mother and principal caregiver?

On the face of it, the elevation of the child to the highest object of love promises to catapult the woman into supremacy in love. Not the compromised supremacy of, say, medieval courtly love—the love of the troubadour for his Lady—or indeed of much of the romantic tradition to which it gave rise, where her power derives from the position of *loved one*, able only to test, accept, or reject the devotion of a lover, who is always conceived as male, who always takes the initiative in love, and who has made all the decisions about what is to count as "woman," as feminine. (A male who, moreover, in the tradition of courtly love arguably reduces the woman to a formal ideal, over the construction of which she has no say.) Rather the woman's new supremacy would lie in being the principal *lover* in what has become the most valued relationship of love; in being the one who legislates what success and failure in love consist in, who determines the style of loving from out of her own nature, and who is, to that extent, a genuinely autonomous subject in the field of love. Motherhood would no longer be merely the living of a role ordained by patriarchy; instead its quality of devotion would be defined, discovered, and directed by the woman, who is in effect the high priestess of the new sacred—namely, the child.

Yet the extraordinary moral and sacramental significance of the child today, together with the demand that it inhabits as safe a space as it is possible to create, might cut both ways. It might also exert immense pressure on the mother, because of her position as childbearer—and also as the parent conventionally deemed to be psychically, biologically, and symbolically the primary figure for at least the early infant—to fulfill precisely the ideal ascribed to women by a male-dominated history: to be perfectly self-giving, self-sacrificing, and self-effacing—a servile support structure for the propagation of the species; to be the raw matter of a culture and an ethic to which men have given the form. ("Matter" shares the same Latin root—*mater*—as "mother.") And so rather than liberate her from a traditional identity as dutifully servicing a culture defined, created, and so far operated largely by men, the sacramentalization of the child might entrench, oppressively so, that very identity.

For the cult of parental love does continue, to a great degree, to hold the mother responsible as the main guarantor of her children's lives: to defend them from risk and danger; to ensure that their experiences prepare them to be parent of the adult; to be engineer-in-chief of a new and successful human life; to maintain the fiction that they are loved unconditionally and equally; to raise them as paragons of the modern ideals of autonomy and authenticity.

Fathers might be playing an ever more important role in all these tasks, as well as in the day-to-day practicalities of childrearing. The father might, in some cases, also abandon his career for homemaking, leaving the mother freer to pursue hers. Nonetheless, if parents are judged by a watchful society, or later by their adult children, to have failed in their duties, then the mother, to the extent that she is still seen as primary and unsubstitutable in the physical-emotional relationship to the child, is likely to be first in the moral firing line. Today's idea of a "loose woman" is one whose devotion to her children society deems insufficiently rigorous.

Can she, under such intense pressure to perform, ever discover a manner of loving that is genuinely her own? And would it be any wonder if the extraordinary moralization of parenthood drives increasing numbers of women to decide not to have children at all, even if as a result they feel a terrible sense of loss? Though, on the one hand, the sacred status of the child and the supreme value attached to parental love compound the pressure on women to bear or adopt children, should we be surprised if, on the other hand, the stakes of motherhood are now so high that they are becoming a serious deterrent to embarking on it? If, therefore, turning the child into the highest object of love ends up in a demographic crisis?

———

At the same time, another, quite distinct, development is, I suggest, afoot. Parental love—the form of love in which disparities of power between the parties are most marked, or at least most obvious—is also emerging as the laboratory of a revolutionary and perhaps impossible experiment underway in the contemporary West, though it is so far largely implicit and unacknowledged: to see if love can be purified of *all* power.

The aim of this experiment goes far beyond that long-standing attack, in the West, on traditional hierarchies and their entrenched inequalities of power, which, though with many reversals, has spawned repeated crises of political legitimacy, flatter and more transparent hierarchies, and a growing refusal to tolerate sexual exploitation—among numerous other consequences. For this embryonic experiment is not just about seeking equality of power in love relationships; not just about freeing them from their concealed as well as overt disparities and impositions of power. In addition, its goal is to achieve forms of intimacy that are *in no way* structured by relations of power; and are, instead, animated by the ideal of respect for the ungraspable Otherness of the loved one. This is an Otherness that love is to affirm precisely by not expecting in any way to grasp it, in the sense of either possessing or understanding it—an Otherness that is taken to be traduced by all exercise of power.

Any such goal, however elusive, of liberating relationships of love from the brutal struggles for recognition and control that so easily colonize and corrupt them must go together with—indeed, presupposes—the forging of a greatly intensified sensitivity to the workings of power in *all* human relations.

There is nothing fanciful about positing such a new sensitivity to the workings of power: for it has been in the making ever since the seventeenth century, pioneered by such thinkers as Spinoza and Hobbes—the first of whom holds that love, as passion, is aroused by those we experience as empowering; while the latter sees "a perpetual and restless desire" for power as "a general inclination of all mankind."[29] In particular, it was deepened in the nineteenth and twentieth centuries by the very figures who most radically developed the hypothesis, now widely taken to be incontrovertible, that power is the key to understanding human relations and who would have ridiculed any attempt to rid love of its fundamental determination by power: figures such as Nietzsche, who diagnoses and celebrates "will to power," or the drive to increase one's power, as motivating all human relationships and as *the* prism through which they are to be understood and evaluated—very much including those based on altruism, humility, pity, self-denial, and charity;[30] Leopold von Sacher-Masoch, after whom "masochism" is named and whose novels—and actual life—groundbreakingly explore a victim's lust to be humiliated on terms defined by him, not by his tormentor; Marcel Proust, with his incomparable depictions of the dynamics and horrors of erotic possessiveness as it seeks to dominate not merely another body but, more hopelessly still, another consciousness that it experiences as terminally elusive and deceptive;[31] Sigmund Freud, for whom love always involves a battle to control those crucial individuals whose loss we relentlessly fear, beginning in the "oral" stage of infancy when we attempt cannibalistically to incorporate the loved one into our own psyche;[32] Jean-Paul Sartre, who insists that love is necessarily a conflict between sadism and masochism as each lover attempts to steal the freedom of the other; and on to Michel Foucault, who depicts love in general and sexuality in particular as a paradigm expression of social power—as "an especially dense transfer point for relations of power"—to the extent that sexual permissiveness is, for him, no liberation but rather a fresh expression of society's surveillance and control of the body and of "the life of the species."[33] Indeed Foucault—for whom, in one of his voices, even peace is a form of war: one way in which a generalized war can manifest itself—is arguably the culmination of this modern disposition to see every aspect of life—from the construction of our notions of selfhood, illness, knowledge, and health, to the ways in which we experience intimacy, self-giving, and self-surrendering, to our values and aesthetic preferences—as structured and established by power relations or by the striving for power.

Yet even if it is impossible to purify love of power relations—even if every attempt to repudiate power merely gives way to, or manifests, new forms of power; even if every relationship of love, including parenting, inevitably remains full of power struggles—nonetheless the pursuit of the *ideal* is of momentous significance in developing further this consciousness of the workings of power in human relations. And it can be no coincidence that the paradigm for a new type of relationship, cleansed of power, is parental love. Here, precisely where the natural inequality of power is at its greatest, or at least at its most unmasked, we have the test case for eviscerating love of its will to power and filling it instead with a will to the sovereign Other, marked by responsibility and respect. Here we are not merely to seek the minimum possible inequality where for centuries there was institutionalized superiority of one party—the male parent over the female, and both parents (or the extended family) over the child; not merely to substitute "negotiation" for command and persuasion for force when there are the inevitable conflicts to resolve; but, far more ambitiously, to try to find a way of loving that is not structured by power at all, that somehow sidesteps altogether the exercise of power, and that is no longer to be understood in terms of an ontology of power. (Which is a far cry, indeed, from those eighteenth- and nineteenth-century hierarchical families of which the husband was absolute ruler, let alone from pre-revolutionary France, where fathers had the right to imprison children to compel obedience.[34] Not to mention the license given to parents in the Bible to kill a "stubborn and rebellious son who will not obey his father and mother," even after they discipline him.[35])

The upshot of this will to eviscerate love of the will to power is that even, perhaps precisely, those elements of a love relationship that most obviously invite the consciousness of power—protectiveness, possessiveness, setting standards of right and wrong and taste—are now to become a way for the parent to cultivate the singularity of his or her children and to call them to their own sovereign individuality, a way that is as free as possible of power and of the feeling of power.

In this spirit, the parent is to teach her children but also to learn from them, to instill her interests but also to acquire theirs, to develop them but also to develop through them, to induct them into her heritage but in doing so to induct herself into it afresh; and, of course, ever more perfectly to identify with their successes and failures. To instill an ethic in one's children is therefore not only to enable them to realize their own unique way of being, but also to see them as a mirror and so, potentially, as a corrective to one's values as a parent, or to one's ability to live out those values. And to this extent to raise one's children is also, quite deliberately, to be raised by them.

———

And there is a second reason why it might be no coincidence that parental love is the laboratory for this historic experiment. Precisely because the traditional identity allotted to women was that of mother and primary caregiver—whether or not they were actual mothers—it is here, in the role of mother, that women have a so far uncontested position from which to drive a revolution in power. Precisely because parental love is the one expression of love in which the woman—insofar as she takes herself to be, and is taken to be, primary caregiver and lover—is deemed first among equals, if not supreme (whether that supremacy is seen as biologically or as culturally determined), she is strongly placed here to further that revolution.

But such a revolution will not only take the form of seeking a reversal of power relations in love, or more broadly in society, so that now the woman is the more powerful. For a reversal readily flatters, imitates, and to that extent entrenches the order that it overturns. The profounder revolution is to go on to create new ways of living that step outside the terms of the old order. Which here means to turn a relationship of love defined by power, and understood in terms of power, to one defined by its striving to be free from power. This would extend beyond redressing traditional inequalities to create a genuinely new value in the realm of love.

If—and it is obviously a big if—parental love succeeds in being the testing ground of an attempt, however ultimately futile, to cleanse love of power, and if the woman is seen as the lead lover in this relationship and as the one who defines its goals and terms, then it is possible that the cult of the child as the new archetypal object of love will go together with a radical redefinition of the role of the feminine within love as a whole—and so, perhaps, within society more widely.

Since this cult is still in its early stages, it is far too soon to say to what extent elevating the child to our supreme object of love will enable the woman, for the first time in Western history, to define the love relation—indeed not just any love relation but the now-archetypal love relation; to what extent, by contrast, it will turn her into merely a puppet leader whose very self-conception and self-evaluation as mother is a male creation; and to what extent love can be freed from traditional power relations, and perhaps from all power relations. In the inescapably ambiguous way of most revolutions, it will probably afford both a genuine liberation and also a new guise for traditional roles and values.

Becoming Rather Than Being (or Why Love for the Child Is Never Consummated)

For previous supreme objects of love—God; the romantic couple; the Lady of courtly love; or the absolute beauty or goodness of which Plato speaks—it made sense (or seemed to make sense) to envision a moment when love was "consummated" or an endpoint where it was "completed." A destination at which love could aim, even if it could never be reached or indeed clearly conceived; a finality that would give meaning and urgency to all of love's strivings: such as to rest in God, or to achieve union with the erotic lover, or to behold the pure, eternal essence of beauty.

Love for the child does not, however, admit of such consummation or completion. It posits no endpoint that is its perfect—even if unattainable—fulfillment and that animates all its strivings. It does not even have sacramental moments equivalent to marriage or death or Damascene conversion: moments that thrust into view a terminus for love to aim at and that mark the journey toward love's completion, as marriage can do in romantic love or death can do in love for God.

Instead it is intrinsically open-ended; it is always "becoming," incomplete, ongoing. (To speak in a certain philosophical, but not very illuminating, jargon: its being is its becoming.) Its time, unlike the way we experience climactic moments in romantic love, doesn't "stand still" but is in perpetual motion. It chimes with modernity's veneration of the new: our reverence for the instant when a life, an act, a thought that has never existed before comes into being; our reverence for possibility, for the radical event, for the open horizon, for the contemporary and even more for what is not yet. After all, every child is a fresh life; an embodiment of indeterminacy: of something that has not been before. (Here our modern sensibility is almost exactly the opposite of the archaic, where only what has already existed commands prestige and awe.[36])

This turn away from the conviction that love can have an identifiable consummation or completion chimes, too, with a key feature of recent modernity: its dwindling belief in progress—in other words, its calling into question the credibility of final ends, such as the perfectly just society or the victory of liberal democracy or the triumph of communism, toward which history is supposedly a linear path and in the light of which every event might be grasped as a step forward or as a step back. Indeed, we see here how the cult of the new is not the same as the cult of progress; how the two can come radically apart. For when the cult of the new becomes a celebration of endless and unpredictable becoming, which cannot, even in principle (let alone in imperfect practice), have a predetermined end—moreover, which refuses any such end and sees itself as defiled by the search for one—it turns into the enemy of the idea of progress, whether that idea takes modern secular form or traditional religious form.

And we see just this coming apart in the case of love for the child, which is perfectly attuned to the cult of the new yet at the same time is defiantly not a love that is expected to progress toward a final end at which it is deemed complete. As a result, no "ladder of love"—as Plato and his legions of successors, from Augustine to Proust, present it—in which desire is progressively purified, can conceivably describe the history of love between a parent and their children, or imbue that love with normative direction, or give meaning and value to every stage on the way—as it can for traditional conceptions of romantic love or of love for God.

In short, love of the child is the first archetypal love in two millennia of Western thought to move decisively beyond Plato: no longer to partake at all in ambitions to overcome becoming for the sake of being (in the sense of the perfect, ultimate, unchanging essence of the good), time for the sake of eternity, the particular for the sake of the whole, the individual for the sake of the absolute. And it is, in that sense, the first to be resolutely anti-metaphysical.

Childhood and the Affirmation of Ordinary Life

Just as parental love is in tune with an era that affirms becoming over being, so too it chimes with our contemporary affirmation of the everyday, which we also see in art (Hannah Arendt speaks of the "modern enchantment with 'small things'" preached, for example, by "early twentieth-century poetry in almost all European tongues"[37]); with letting the here and now, precisely in its "ordinariness," come to power and presence; with the striving to celebrate rather than to transcend the mundane; with enjoying what is regular and near rather than reaching for the grandiose and the distant. So that if our culture still has any patience or desire for the notion of "transcendence," it is as the immanent intensely experienced, or as our capacity to rise above narrow self-interest to focus on large, generous ends.

As every exhausted parent knows, love for your child, unlike romantic love, is not manifested or proved by exiting daily life—let alone by yearning to transcend the limits of space, time, and individuality. Nor would it make any sense to say that parental love's fundamental aim is to attain the *quies*, or perfect peace, that Augustine sees as the goal of the highest love. The opposite is the case: *quies* is out of the question!

And so with the child the sacred has withdrawn from the absolute or the cosmic—God, Nature as a whole, History, Freedom—where it once resided, or to which it unfailingly pointed. Nor is any larger love, such as for God, generally taken to animate love for your child: to be the love for the sake of which you love your child.

On the contrary, parental love is resolutely down to earth. Its arena is this everyday world and no other. And whereas the dominant sense of previous archetypal loves—notably, love for God and romantic love—was hearing or sight, which can be imagined to reach beyond the worldly, for parental love hearing and sight are co-dominant with touch, which cannot. From the lover's vision of absolute beauty described by Socrates in Plato's *Symposium*, to the famous "gaze" or "look" of love (the only way, according to Victor Hugo, in which one falls in love[38]), to the troubadours' paeans to their Ladies, to the mystics' images of God, vision is how love, for much of its history, has imagined its relation to the loved one—though we all too easily forget the importance of hearing, which is arguably the supreme sense in the Bible, especially in the Old Testament, and is also central to romantic love, which trains its ears on the beloved, listening out for anything she wants to say to us, including with her look.

Sight and hearing have been accorded this status in the history of love—stretching back both to its Greek sources in Plato and Aristotle and to its biblical sources in Hebrew and Christian scripture—not because those two senses have somehow been privileged in themselves, but rather because the greatest things have been held to be the most remote and elusive. Of all the senses, only they are taken to have access to those distant, unworldly, unquotidian, and sometimes transcendent perfections typically sought by romantic love or by love for the divine. By contrast, touch is confined to what is earthbound and indeed nearby: it is, with taste and smell, a "this-worldly" sense par excellence, unable to reach beyond the immediate (and scorned by Aristotle, in both his treatise on the soul and his *Nicomachean Ethics*, as the lowest of all the senses, with sight as the highest).[39]

If it sounds strange to say that touch does not belong to the dominant senses of romantic-erotic love, we should recall that some of the supreme narratives of such love unfold without any sex, and sometimes without any touching at all. A medieval troubadour might not even hold the hand of his Lady, let alone have sexual intercourse with her; for though he might crave such consummation his higher goal is to perfect his devotion and desire. Dante's love for Beatrice in *La Vita Nuova* is powerfully erotic, yet he barely touches her; in fact, for most of the time she is beyond his reach, in Heaven, "a vision of a soul in glory."[40] Jake and Brett in Ernest Hemingway's *The Sun Also Rises* draw ever closer to one another without consummating their love. So too Lily Bart and Lawrence Selden in Edith Wharton's *The House of Mirth*.

But it is impossible to imagine a passionate parental love that *never* holds the newborn baby, the infant, the child, the adolescent . . . ; that loves entirely through sight and hearing. Indeed, can there be any form of love to which touch is more essential? Touch is surely the sense best suited to a world in which great things, very much including our ultimate objects of love, are no longer taken to be inaccessible or ineffable. And in which our relation to such things is no longer governed by what Nietzsche called a "pathos of distance."

And so for the kinds of reasons that I have sketched in this chapter—among them the role of parental love in relocating the sacred to this finite, everyday life; in fulfilling our contemporary ideals of autonomy and equality; in waging war on suffering and risk; in shaping those early stages of life that have come to be seen as the key to human flourishing; in favoring an idiom of "becoming" over "being"—for such reasons the child is, I suggest, the quintessentially modern object of love. Love for the child, in its contemporary form, is the first archetypal love not dependent on traditional religious or otherwise dualistic categories; the first genuinely to reflect the death of God; the first not to be marked even by shadows of the divine.

The Conservatism of Romantic Love

If romantic love is beginning to lose its place as our archetypal love, this isn't because we fail at it too often. It isn't because romantic relationships so often end in disappointment, anguish, and frustration.

Great ideals seldom lose their spell merely by failing to fulfill their promises. Or by demanding too much of their votaries. Only a change of *taste* can be certain to dethrone an ideal.

And this, as we have just seen, is precisely what is happening: the idiom of romantic love—as it has been conceived for two centuries or more, including its yearnings to transcend the everyday and the temporal; its sense of itself as a plaything of fate; its intrinsic danger—is becoming ever less suited to the taste and temper of the times.

Unlike parental love, romantic love isn't taken to be the product of decisions that we reflectively endorse; and there is a limit to the degree to which it—the choice of partner, the course of relationship, the distribution of power—can be planned and managed and negotiated before it loses its romantic character altogether. It is too stormy, impulsive, and vulnerable to loss and rejection to succeed in minimizing suffering; or to be in the vanguard of an all-consuming war on risk; or to maximize control over our lives; or to foster the emotional continence that we so prize in practice (for all our celebration of self-expression, for all our affirmation of contingency, and for all our talk of taking risks for love). Its identification of love with radical freedom, and so with danger, is out of place at a time of increasing emphasis on safety—and thus on love as a search for safety. Its craving for union is at odds with our ethos of the inviolability of the individual and his or her sacrosanct "borders." Its erotic energies hardly make it a laboratory for stripping love of power and possessiveness, or for nurturing a will to the sovereign Other. Its striving for transcendence of the ordinary does not sit easily with our reification of the everyday. Its sense of timelessness is out of kilter with an age in which time is life's crucial axis (an age in which, to many, it is unacceptable, even meaningless, to think of actions, events, and values *sub specie aeternitatis*). Its search for completion clashes with a modern idiom of endless "becoming," powerfully expressed by such thinkers as Herder in the eighteenth century, Nietzsche in the nineteenth, and Derrida, among many postmodernists, in the twentieth. Its ambition to create a cocoon of oneness that shuts out the world is not in tune with the defiant worldliness of our era.

By contrast to parental love, romantic love speaks to the preoccupations of another age that is now passing. This was an age that began, explicitly, with Spinoza in the seventeenth century but, in reality, much earlier, with the Neoplatonism of the Italian Renaissance: an age that strove to bring into a more harmonious and less hostile relation than so much Christian theology had permitted such hallowed oppositions of a God-centered worldview as body/soul, nature/divine, sensual/spiritual, particular/universal, temporal/ eternal, and becoming/being. It sought to overcome the hostility, even incompatibility, between these opposites that theologians like Augustine had insisted on because, right into the high Romanticism of the nineteenth century, men and women were still *troubled and inspired* enough by them to crave ways of resolving, without dissolving, the dichotomies animating them.

Today, however, such opposites no longer inspire or trouble us as deeply and as widely as they once did. Perhaps they no longer genuinely speak to us—including to many religious believers. Nor do they seem fundamental to conservative vocabularies and worldviews. And so the passion to reconcile them—to see them as essential to each other, rather than as radically discontinuous realms; to find ways of bringing them into intimate relation, rather than merely to overcome the first in each pair for the sake of the second—has ceased to be urgent, or even relevant.

This has been a body blow to romantic love; for it derived much of its tremendous energy from precisely those dichotomies. Indeed, the revolutionary power of romantic love did not lie only, or even primarily, in its ability to subvert conventional morals, including conventional conceptions of marriage, along with the duties and social barriers imposed by class, clan, family, ethnicity, religion, wealth, and power. In addition, it lay in its extraordinary, perhaps unique, capacity to revitalize in secular form—or at least in a form that did not need to refer to a deity or to obligations to a deity—a traditionally religious order, structured by just such dichotomies as body/soul, carnal/spiritual, and earthly/heavenly. It did this by making each element in these pairs the key to the true fulfillment of the other: the body the key to the soul, the soul to the body, the sensual to the spiritual, and the spiritual to the sensual.

———

Thus, the amazing innovation of romantic love since its flowering in the late eighteenth century (an innovation with roots in the heyday of courtly romance in the thirteenth century) was to turn two realms that had once been seen as incompatible enemies into compatible friends, while preserving the traditional distinction between them, indeed using precisely that distinction to energize each of them. Thanks to romantic love, therefore, sex could be not just an inferior stage on the way to the spiritual, as of course it could already be in Plato's ladder of love, but could become the *privileged path* to the spiritual. And conversely, and even more strikingly, the spiritual could become embodied in the sexual, turning sex from an abomination, as it is for Augustine and his enormously influential legacy, into something sacred, and making possible the full flowering and meaning of the erotic. So that by the turn of the nineteenth century, a Romantic like Friedrich Schlegel could write, in his novel *Lucinde*, that "In the solitary embrace of lovers sensual pleasure becomes once more what it basically is—the holiest miracle of nature." And could go on to proclaim:

> This moment, the kiss of Cupid and Psyche, is the rose of life. Inspired Diotima revealed to Socrates only the moiety of love. Love is not merely the quiet longing for eternity: it is also the holy enjoyment of a lovely presence. It is not merely a mixture, a transition from mortal to immortal: rather it is the total union of both.[1]

Though romantic love is intrinsically progressive in its subversion of conventional morality and society—its crashing through prohibitions imposed by class and clan and Church and convention, including, most recently, obstacles to same-sex, transgender, and inter-ethnic love and marriage—such language confirms that at another level, at a metaphysical level, it is intrinsically conservative.

This conservatism has been part of its attraction since the late eighteenth century. For as well as being very modern in some of its aims—such as the self-conscious way it takes itself to cultivate the lovers' identity, authenticity, freedom, and equality; and so to disdain ingrained social roles and rules—romantic love *also* attempts to preserve the traditional oppositions of a religious world order that modernity has otherwise deemed moribund. Indeed, the remarkable paradox of romantic love is that its power to undermine convention has depended, in part, on precisely its intense conservatism: its genius at breathing new life into the metaphysical "opposites" that have structured the Western spirit since Plato and the Platonization of the great monotheisms.

By contrast to this metaphysical conservatism, romantic love's privileging of traditional heterosexual structures of loving along with oppressive or unequal gender relations and interpretations of marriage, which have marked so much of its history, is not *intrinsic* to it; and so is not where it can most enduringly uphold tradition. As the supreme form of love since the late eighteenth century, romantic love has certainly been co-opted for these conservative purposes and saturated with their norms, entrenching, for example, male power at the expense of female autonomy, as thinkers such as Simone de Beauvoir and Shulamith Firestone have powerfully argued. But rather than being constitutive of it, these conventional purposes and norms are contingent features of romantic love, which, on account of its huge prestige, has been an ideal vehicle for preserving precisely such traditional gender identities and inequalities.

Indeed, romantic love could be—and to a formidable degree is being—recast to foster equality of both gender and sexual identities, if not yet to the extent of the "confluent love" proposed by Anthony Giddens;[2] and it doesn't seem unreasonable to expect that its powerful elective affinities and will to freedom will radically subvert traditional gender identities and inequalities, just as, in the past, they have so often ended up subverting conventional social barriers.

___

Yet it would be a mistake to think that only romantic love can disrupt moral and social conventions. For doesn't all love strive to select its loved ones wherever the qualities that are taken to ground it are to be found? Even if those qualities are located beyond the social or normative world from which each lover hails. In that sense, isn't all love potentially in tension with prevailing culturally constituted categories?

Imagine, for example, that in the nineteenth century passionate friendship love had acquired the prestige of romantic love. Imagine that it had become the norm for two friends to pine for each other in just the way that romantic lovers, such as Tristan and Isolde or Lancelot and Guinevere or Vronsky and Anna Karenina, did, or for them to be prepared to die for each other, as, according to Plato's *Symposium*, Achilles died to avenge the honor of his friend Patroclus in the Trojan War. Imagine that such friendships had been celebrated in numerous poems and stories. And that they had been held up as one of the noblest goals of a human life, as of course Aristotle did. Then friendship might have come to seem subversive and innovative in just the manner of romantic love. For friendship love grounded principally in the characters of the friends could, if allowed to, have ignored entrenched distinctions of class and clan and power and wealth and ethnicity and indeed of gender as surely as romantic love has ever done. Friends, too, can create a little community of two, or of more than two, based purely on the ethical world they share, which can shun, challenge, and transgress the norms of the society beyond them as well as can any romantic couple. Friendship love could have democratized the private sphere in the way that, as Anthony Giddens notes, romantic love has done.[3] Nothing about a person's intrinsic character, or about the attraction of similar types of character to each other, respects class and convention any more than sexual attraction respects them. The prince and the pauper could be "perfect" Aristotelian friends no less than they could be romantic lovers.

This is no idle speculation because, of course, exactly such friendships have been celebrated. Some of the passionate friendships that are recounted in the Bible, like Ruth and Naomi,[4] or Judah and Hirah,[5] *do* cross deep boundaries of ethnicity or clan. Ethnic divisions are breached by Ruth and Naomi, the one a Moabite and the other an Israelite. As they are by Judah, an Israelite, and Hirah, an Adullamite. Or, even more radically than such human bonds, friendship has been thought capable of reaching across a gulf as vast as that between the human and the divine, as in Thomas Aquinas's conception of friendship with God.

Indeed, that great skeptic of the priority of friendship in the pantheon of love, C. S. Lewis, has stated its subversive potential very clearly. "Authority frowns on friendship," says Lewis. "Every real friendship is a sort of secession, even a rebellion."[6]

Aside from friendship, other forms of love can also be deeply subversive, and, in their cumulative effect, arguably more so than romantic love has been. Love for God has possibly undermined ancient social norms and political hierarchies more than any other expression of love. And for good reason. After all, love for God, especially "with all your heart and soul and might," as commanded in the Bible, involves the idea that human beings crave, and owe overriding loyalty to, a being superior to *any* earthly political or social order— human beings who are also seen as essentially equal in their possession of a God-given soul or reason or createdness. In his letter to the Galatians, Paul is categorical about this: there is, he famously declares, no distinction between Jew and Greek, slave and free, and, indeed, male and female: for "all of you are one in Jesus Christ."[7] Jesus Christ, he continues elsewhere, "has broken down the dividing wall, that is, the hostility between [formerly divergent groups]," who are henceforth "members of the household of God . . . with Jesus Christ himself as the cornerstone."[8]

So, too, love for neighbor, as commanded in the Bible—and as implicitly universalized by Paul, and explicitly by Augustine—can be interpreted as ascribing an equality to individuals that is potentially threatening to social and class barriers. As is the compassionate love, or *Menschenliebe*, articulated by Schopenhauer, which, in seeing beyond the delusions of individuality to the suffering common to all individuals—in experiencing others as an "I once more"[9]—regards all human beings as equally deserving of our love. Indeed, such compassionate love has clear ethical priority over, and so intrinsically challenges, our participation in worldly life and our conventional obligations to society.

———

Romantic love has *appeared* to have a monopoly on the subversion of moral and social convention—a monopoly that other forms of love allegedly cannot challenge—only because the prestige it has been accorded gave it the necessary freedom to occupy this position. And it has had this prestige—it has been the paradigm of love since around 1800—not because no other forms of love could have been subversive in these ways, but because of its unique power to meet a need of its time—a need no longer as urgent, or even urgent at all: namely, as I just proposed, to enable the familiar dichotomies of religious tradition to be preserved in a manner that appealed to a new, secular age; in other words, to enable such dichotomies as body and soul, nature and divine, particular and universal, to be reconciled by making each member of these pairs the key to the fulfillment of the other. Thus, those dichotomies could be preserved without any longer making reference to God or demanding that the first member of a pair—the "earthly" one—be repudiated for the sake of the second—the "heavenly" one.

In this way, for example, sexual desire could be seen not as chaining lovers to the carnal or the earthly, but rather as transporting them into a transcendent domain beyond the purely carnal and earthly. And, in doing so, sexuality itself is not devalued as mere *cupiditas*, but, on the contrary, is made sacred. Far from being a path to damnation, sexual desire is a path to salvation. Richard Wagner expresses this vividly in a letter to Mathilde Wesendonck, a married woman with whom he was certainly in love, in December 1858:

> [T]he path of salvation that leads to the total quietening of the will [pro-ceeds] through love, and moreover not through an abstract *Menschenliebe* [in other words the traditional *caritas* of Christian thinking, or the com-passionate lovingkindness of Schopenhauer] but through a love that re-ally germinates out of the ground of *Geschlechtsliebe* [sexual love], i.e. the attraction between man and woman.[10]

In the same month Wagner even drafted a letter to Schopenhauer in which he insisted that "the natural tendency to sexual love represents a way to salvation, to self-knowledge, and to self-negation of the will."[11]

We must repeat how remarkable this thought is: sexual love leads to self-negation of the will; the most extreme desire leads to the most extreme release from desire. In other words, not only are the two domains of desire and denial of desire no longer discontinuous, but the former is dignified by being the royal route to the latter.

As I suggested, this kind of reconciliation of formerly warring opposites is where romantic love is most innovative. And yet, we have seen, it trades on an ancient idiom: those religious dichotomies that it conserved in the process of challenging them. Though today some of us can still see the point of, in-deed the need for, contrasts between body and soul, material and spiritual, earthly and transcendent (even if we don't conceive such contrasts in terms of discontinuous realms), few any longer agonize about them, or crave ways of reanimating or reconciling them, with anything like the fervor of a nineteenth-century Romantic like Wagner. In other words, Romanticism's radicalism has become, in great part, irrelevant.

In our time, romantic love is, to some degree, being recast as bespoke erotic intimacy—which is now largely purged of such traditional dichotomies as body/soul or earthly/transcendent, and is expected to flower into well-managed and respectfully "negotiated" relationships of mutual devotion that succeed in reconciling spontaneity with predictability. But to the extent that an idiom changes, attempts to repeat in updated form the old, established one—in this case high romance, with its ideal of union, its rejection of the quotidian, its redemptive promise, its radical freedom, its intoxicating riskiness—can begin to feel formulaic, sentimental, effete, banal. So that, at the same time as romantic love remains intensely compelling, speaking as it does of a heritage so recent and potent, it can also seem artificial—as if, somehow, we are merely going through the motions—because it is no longer in tune with the deepest needs and sensibility of the age.

Why Isn't Friendship the New Archetypal Love?

Surely, we might ask, friendship love is just as attuned as parental love to the taste of our times, and so has a worthy claim to succeed romantic love as our archetypal love? Surely this most ancient of loves—which in Homer's portrayal of Achilles and Patroclus, Aristotle's description of perfect *philia*, and Montaigne's paeans to his friend Étienne de La Boétie, is the unsurpassed love—succeeds in avoiding the transcendental temptations of romantic love or of love for God every bit as well as does parental love? Surely, friendship too can cultivate individual autonomy; very much affirms everyday life; doesn't envisage an endpoint at which its aims would be fully attained; and, to that degree, accords with an ethos of open-ended "becoming"? And insofar as ideal friendship has been regarded, since Aristotle, as dependent on the mutually recognized equality—especially ethical equality—of its participants, could it not contribute (contrary to Aristotle's convictions) to founding a more equal love between the genders?

Friendship love is, indeed, all these things. As Aristotle already depicts it, it is explicitly a relationship of equals; it is located and achievable only in everyday life; it is based on mutual well-wishing, respect, intimacy, trust, disclosure, dialogue, and therefore the maximum possible sharing of the interests and ends of both parties. And, more recently, that great thinker of the German Enlightenment, Gotthold Ephraim Lessing, praises friendship, Hannah Arendt tells us, as "the central phenomenon in which alone true humanity can prove itself."[1] Friendship love is, on the face of it, superbly attuned to the spirit of our age and overdue for a great revival.

But the reason friendship is not about to become our supreme form of love is that it cannot rival love for the child, as this is conceived today, in at least three key respects: in its suitability to wage war on risk; in its perceived power to foster human flourishing; and in its devotion to maintaining "borders" between lover and loved one.

Unlike love for the child, love for a friend would be seen as insipid rather than strong if devotion to our friend's welfare were centrally concerned with his or her safety—or if we experienced our day-to-day relationship as totemic in the fight against risk and vulnerability.

Unlike love for the child, friendship cannot be deemed to be the type of love that is most critical to the flourishing of the adult—given that, in our age, the conditions for such flourishing are held to lie so decisively in the early stages of life.

And unlike love for the child, friendship is not committed, as one of its sacred principles, to maintaining the distinctness between lover and loved one. Indeed, for Aristotle, in the most perfect friendship each of the friends sees the other as a "second self"—so forming that union or "entireness," that "semblance of my being, in all its height, variety, and curiosity, reiterated in a foreign form," of which Emerson speaks. And to that extent an erosion of borders between them is not just permissible but a sign of the genuineness of their bond. To the point where, as Montaigne puts it, if my friend demands that I reveal to him secrets that I have sworn to tell no one, I can do so with impunity because, as my second self, he is, in effect, me. Everything that is mine is therefore his: my soul, my secrets, my thoughts, my possessions. Each of our wills, says Montaigne, speaking of his friendship with Étienne de La Boétie, plunges into the other friend and loses itself there:

> I say lose, in truth, for neither of us reserved anything for himself, nor was anything either his or mine.[2]

In this exalted conception of friendship love, such dissolution of borders is central to the ethical value of the relationship, a mark of its success. The precise opposite can be said of the parent–child relationship, as we think of it today: nothing could be worse than to regard the other as me. Here too, in the controlled, even negotiated, manner in which we conceive today of respect and intimacy and equality in relationships, the child decisively trumps the friend as a candidate for our archetypal object of love.

Conclusion: The Child as the First Truly Modern Archetypal Object of Love

The new supremacy of love for the child, I have argued, can be understood only in relation to the deepest ideals of modernity, all of them with roots going back at least to the late eighteenth century.

Philosophically, love of the child dovetails with the ideal of autonomy—the autonomy of the parent, we should note, as well as of the child itself; with the striving for equality, based on the maxim of respect for everyone as an end in him- or herself; with the ambition to achieve ever-greater safety and security; with our reification of the immanent and the everyday; with a growing urge to prioritize touch over sight, love's traditionally privileged sense; and with a marked reverence for time and transience and, by the same token, with an attack on the ancient veneration of the permanent and the absolute: in short, with the favoring of an idiom of endless "becoming" over eternal "being."

Psychologically, the priority of parental love is fostered by the tremendous emphasis on childhood as the key to a flourishing life: as incubating not only the ends and values we will espouse as adults but also our capacity to pursue them. At the same time, our belief in the immense vulnerability and plasticity of the infantile psyche makes it *the* crucial battleground in the war on risk, and so *the* necessary focus of love as a moral emotion.

Sociologically, the priority of the child is arguably a natural correlate of the feminist revolution, very much including the demand for an end to women's emotional subservience in matters of love (though, as I suggested earlier, it can at the same time entrench that subservience). It is also a natural correlate of the increasingly provisional nature of the couple, whether married or not, which shrinks the nuclear family down to its irreducible core of each parent's relationship to his or her children. And it reflects and enhances the intense sensitivity of our age to the workings of power in all human relationships—including those based on compassion and altruism—and a corresponding will to find a way of relating that is, impossibly perhaps, free of power.

These are just some of the ideals and realities of the contemporary world to which, taken together, the priority of the child as an object of love is uniquely attuned—and that make the child the first truly modern object of love. To have children and to love them in accord with these ideals and realities has come to be regarded as an achievement of individual self-realization, much as romantic love used to be so regarded. The childless are criticized not so much, and certainly not only, for failing, selfishly, to contribute to their society's future or to devote themselves to the welfare of others, as for failing to live *their own* lives fully: for missing out on a dimension of the flourishing life, indeed on a secular sacrament, that cannot be made up by any other achievement, including by any other love.

———

Through all this, however, our guiding conception of the *nature* of love—of what love seeks, what grounds it, and what we are to expect from it—remains stuck in precisely the nineteenth century time warp that I discussed in Part I. Genuine love is still, on the dominant view I have been contesting, seen as unconditional, disinterested, enduring, and affirming of the loved one in all their particularity. All that has changed is that the paradigm instance of such love is now taken to be parental, rather than romantic. So that if any love can—and must—bear these qualities, and to the highest degree, then it is love for one's children.

Harry Frankfurt is an eloquent spokesman for this new received wisdom, concisely expressing not only today's prevailing conception of love but also its application to the child as our new archetypal object of love. "[T]he love of parents for their infants or small children is the species of caring that comes closest to offering recognizably pure instances of love," he proclaims.[1] By "pure" he means disinterested and not conditional on who they are: "the particular value that I attribute to my children," he says, "is not inherent in them but depends upon my love for them."[2] Indeed, he adds, "I can declare with *unequivocal confidence* that I do not love my children because I am aware of some value that inheres in them independent of my love for them."[3] Moreover, he began loving them even before they were born, which he takes as confirmation that his love for them cannot be a response to any value he recognizes in them.

Yet Frankfurt doesn't ask whether his children do, in fact, embody value that might arouse his most intense love. For children fulfill one of the great ends of the flourishing human life, especially as it is conceived in our times, namely to become a parent—indeed, to excel as a parent. Moreover, parents can be deeply ontologically rooted in the world through their child, who develops a lineage that is not only biological and social but also ethical and aesthetic—embodying qualities and values and, in the broadest sense, tastes that orient their (the parents') lives and yet that they might feel they themselves have barely realized; and who also has existential power over its parents of the kind that arouses and sustains love, for its mere presence bestows numinous depth on their existence and anchorage for their life, without which they can feel adrift no matter what their other sources of grounding.

In addition, for those who hold, with Plato's Diotima, that love centrally seeks immortality,[4] children can be conceived as offering a parent a way of being immortal (though, as I have said, I neither think that love's fundamental aim is immortality nor see this as a reason for our contemporary cult of the child). Furthermore, if one agrees with Aristotle that children constitute "other selves" whom parents naturally love as they love themselves,[5] then a child could be, almost precisely, what Proust's Narrator calls "that prolongation, that possible multiplication of oneself [which I would gloss as the very fact of one's existence], which is happiness"[6]—and beyond this, of course, the opportunity for a fresh start: for a life that is endowed and nourished by one's own life as a parent, yet is a new beginning.

None of these perceptions of value need be narcissistic in that it prevents a parent from seeing her children as independent beings, with a life and reality, interests and needs, loves and fears, fundamentally distinct from her own. Nor, of course, does it entail that her love for them cannot elicit the most powerful devotion to their well-being. On the contrary, we would expect such "other selves" or "second selves," in Aristotle's terms, to elicit exactly this devotion.

In addition, children embody many potent sources of value that contemporary Western society, independently of any particular parent, imputes to them. As we have just seen, these include the child's role in relocating the sacred to this finite, everyday life; in fulfilling our contemporary ideals of autonomy and equality; in waging war on suffering and risk; in favoring an idiom of "becoming" and transience over "being" and permanence; and in being the key to a flourishing adult life. To see childhood as instantiating such defining values and idioms of our age is already to assign it prodigious power in grounding us as parents in the world, and so in evoking our love, even before we have begun to relate to the individuality of our own, actual children.

By the same token we can indeed find ourselves loving our unborn children when they are still in the womb, or even before they are conceived, and so while they remain figments of our imaginative longing. We can feel love for an unconceived child merely by imagining its conception. But again this doesn't confirm that parental love is unconditional, disinterested, and never dependent on the value it recognizes in the loved one, as Frankfurt, in line with a dominant view of love today, thinks it does; rather it is the result precisely of the overwhelming value that each of us, including this author, as a creature of our times, already recognizes as inhering in *any* child of our own, even if it is yet to be born.

Instead of seeing how parental love, like all human valuing and feeling, expresses the particular historical period and culture in which it is located, Frankfurt, in keeping with the prevailing spirit of our age, writes as if the priority and purity of parental love were a timeless given. But this cannot be the case, for if parental love were in no way a response to the culturally determined value that parents recognize as inhering in their children, then why is it so weakly thematized before the nineteenth century? Why does no great thinker in all the centuries before then share Frankfurt's "unequivocal confidence" that love for our children is unmotivated by any inherent value that we recognize in them? Why do great masters of love from Plato to Kierkegaard, from Aristotle to Thomas Aquinas, not also take it as self-evident that parental love is the purest of all human love?

It isn't necessary to go as far back as those ancient Greeks and Romans who "exposed" unwanted, unhealthy, or unattractive infants—that is, abandoned them to their deaths—to know that childhood has not always been treated as sacred, nor parental devotion to children's welfare as a supreme ethical obligation. Nor do we need to look beyond the West to, say, those Hindus of India who killed infant daughters at birth in the hope of trying again for male offspring, or to the days when "the Japanese likened infanticide to thinning the rice plants in their paddies," or to foraging societies in Latin America like the Ache of Paraguay who might bury alive a baby merely because it was born with little hair, in order to find confirmation of this historical reality.[7] As we have already seen, in nineteenth-century England and America child labor was rife, infants might be left out to perish, and children had few rights in law.

Thus, as an extreme exception to the historical norm, parental love in the West has today not only become the archetypal love, but has also been pressed into the service of a modern ideal of love modeled on a "sanitized" conception of divine love—modeled, in other words, on a recent picture of divine love as a purely spontaneous outpouring and giving and affirmation and benevolence that is unconditionally and unalteringly available to the loved one—with perhaps more moral force than even romantic or marital love had to bear at the height of its prestige.

When a romantic lover deviated from the ideal, such as through infidelity, falling out of love, or a self-seeking neediness that made the life of his loved one a misery, social tolerance was often at hand. Violent jealousy of rivals might even be excused, and sometimes admired, as a "crime of passion." Brutal possessiveness might be taken as a sign, albeit pathological, of love's authenticity. By contrast, for a parent to violate the ideal of unconditional and disinterested love, or to inflict such jealousy or possessiveness on his children, is a moral failing for which there is no mitigation, save perhaps the imperfect love that he received in his *own* childhood.

The upshot is clear: we are applying ever more zealously a conception of love that is in its essence religious—because directly modeled on how God is said to love—to a supreme object of love that has never been seen in more avowedly secular terms. Modernity's desire to abandon the religious collides here with its desperation to retain it. And so the great innovation in love of our time—the emerging supremacy of parental love—has become the latest way of pursuing and entrenching precisely this traditional, late-Christian ideal.

Indeed, it is especially tempting to apply this template of divine love to our conception of parental love because the disparity of power between parent and child really is God-like in a way that has no parallel in romantic love, or in any other form of love.

The problem, of course, is that if only the love that God is said to bestow can coherently be understood as intrinsically unconditional, unchanging, disinterested, and capable of affirming everything about the loved one, then to claim that we can love our children in any such way is not merely hubristic. Worse, it is to deceive them about love right from that primitive phase of infancy when they first become capable of experiencing the world (including others, both care-givers and care-destroyers) as recalcitrantly distinct from them and as demanding from them the search for relationship. It is to offer children promises of how they are loved, and of what love can be, that will necessarily be betrayed.

And when it touches on matters of trust in their caregivers, or in other crucial anchors of their lives, children are damaged by nothing more than by deception, even if unintended. If they need to, they can virtuosically go with its flow, leading double lives in which they both believe and mistrust, both enact and resist, the lies by which they are given to understand they must live. Yet they are too finely and subtly sensitive to truth and falsity, in particular in matters of love and loyalty, to remain oblivious to, and so untarnished by, expectations that cannot be fulfilled and that they are not yet in a position to interrogate or repudiate. Though they must be protected from encountering the many horrors of the outside world, with all its cruelty and violence and abuse, such protection is neither the same as nor entails deception.

To mislead children in matters of love is especially serious because love is not a specialized emotional need, which can be split off from the rest of life, but rather structures one's entire sense of existing and one's whole horizon of felt possibilities. If love is the emotion that seeks and responds to a promise of ontological rootedness, and if what is at stake in love is the depth, intensity, and vitality with which one experiences one's existence—and inseparably from that, any possibility of meaningful relatedness to the world and others—then to offer children a false prospectus of the nature of love is to sabotage their lives in a most fundamental way, leading to deep confusion, detachment, mistrust, and anger, directed at themselves, at their primary caregivers, and eventually at the world more widely. Given children's inherent sense for untruth in matters of love, such falsehood cannot count as a "protective illusion" that provides a sense of safety, but will, on the contrary, end up undermining their confidence in a reliable world.

In reality, love for children is, like all human love, conditional, partial, inconstant, often unequal, with one child loved over the other, and far from all-affirming of each child in his or her full particularity. In all these respects it can feel frighteningly inscrutable and unpredictable to children—despite protestations by their parents that they love them "equally but differently," as the cliché has it.

Good parents will certainly protect, respect, and nurture the lives of all their children equally. Excellence at parenting is to do just that: maximally to promote the flourishing of all your children in the way that is best for each. But, if they are honest with themselves—and this will be tremendously hard in an age when we have internalized the maxim that we must love our children equally, indeed that "nature" has somehow instilled such an equal love in parents, any doubting of which can occasion extreme guilt—they will notice that they do not and cannot love all of them as equally as they can protect and defend and respect each of them.

As we have insisted from the outset, love is not identical to protection and nurturing and respecting, just as it is not synonymous with benevolence, or devotion, or generosity. To be on the receiving end of benevolence extended out of a virtuous character is, as an experience, utterly different to being on the receiving end of benevolence extended out of love.

Parental love's terrifying potential for selectivity stems, as all selectivity in love does, from the degree to which the loved one, in this case the child, embodies a promise of ontological rootedness: for example, the degree to which, as I suggested earlier, the child is seen, or imagined, by its parents to develop a lineage that is not only biological and social but also defined by an ethical and aesthetic taste that orients their lives and yet, for them, remains poignantly un-realized. As I just noted, a good parent will foster the flourishing and protect the lives of all her children equally; but she will most love those who inspire in her the deepest sense of groundedness: of at-homeness in her hoped-for world. By contrast, her love will not be enhanced by their other virtues, talents, successes, kindnesses, and sundry attractive qualities—nor, conversely, will it necessarily be diminished if, like the Prodigal Son, they are feckless and faithless; or, like Charlie Roberts and Dylan Klebold, they are mass murderers.

It is therefore cruelly ironical that love for children, which supposedly embraces the moral presupposition that the adult will never deceive the child with false promises, is now the flag carrier for the lie of unconditional, disin-terested, impartial, and all-affirming love.

Children obviously cannot escape the reach of such lies—except, at great danger to their own development, by a deep withdrawal into themselves, an urgent splitting of their psyche, and a radical dissociation from their parents as well as from a whole mistrusted world. But in doing so, in seeking such invulnerability, they cast themselves into an oblivion of loneliness where the possibility of embracing stable meaning and joy and hope cannot exist—or can exist only through revenging themselves on the world by ever more subtly and decisively turning their back on it, perhaps by engaging with it in a coldly detached, "as if" way, which risks no wholehearted devotion; perhaps to the point of refusing to recognize the world as an arena for any sort of committed future.

In romantic love, as in friendship love, there is the possibility of escape: you can end relationships or flee into new ones. In marriage, you can take refuge in impassive companionship, separate living, a myriad of practicalities, and, in our times, divorce. In love for art and nature and ancestors, and in other unrequitable loves, no one else can be hurt by a bond permeated by false promises and expectations.

Children, by contrast, have no such means of escape. Their love for their parents, biological or foster, cannot be redirected, without loss, to anyone else. Nor can their parents' love for them be substituted, without loss, by any other love. There is, in other words, no relationship in which the dangers of conceiving love as secularized *agape* are more real than in that of parents and their children. And yet there is no relationship in which there is greater social pressure to profess and believe precisely this conception. In this respect it is, today, almost impossible for us not to be parrots of the *Zeitgeist*.

Which is the latest and most compelling reason why we need to cease modeling human love on a sanitized picture of divine love as unconditional, disinterested, unchanging, and capable of affirming everything about the loved one—and, instead, to discover a way of conceiving it that does justice to the specificity of its all-too-human aims and to the kinds of relationships and lifelong trajectories that they structure. This is a specificity to which, I argued in Part I, none of the six principal conceptions of love that have emerged in the Western world since ancient times is fully true.

Others might not agree that love is centrally about the search for a promise of ontological rootedness; and that such a promise offers a lineage or source of life with which we powerfully identify, an ethical home that we crave to make our own, power to deepen our sense of existing, and a call to selfhood. They might not agree that to discover a promise of ontological rootedness is to create a space of supreme value and meaning where, in and through a relationship with another, the world, as a horizon of unfolding possibilities for our life, opens to us—a sacred, "enchanted" space, which today is experienced as constituted by the lovers themselves in accordance with modernity's ethos of autonomy.

But whether or not they do agree that an understanding of love—of the structure of experience common to its many expressions—lies in this direction, it is vital, precisely because love belongs to the supreme ends of a well-lived life, that we return with fresh eyes and ears to the long-neglected question that

Plato imagined the Greek god of fire, Hephaestus, husband of the goddess of love, Aphrodite, asking star-struck lovers who thought they knew exactly what love seeks: "What is it, mortals, that you hope to gain from one another?"[8]

In short: What is the good that love, uniquely, realizes or constitutes? What is love's ultimate purpose and motivation? What do we hope to find in the other and to give to them? Why therefore do we love those we do? Indeed, why do we love at all?

Questions, not answers, are sovereign. Any answers offered in this book are as nothing compared with the importance of living with these guiding questions—making them one's constant companions. Only by approaching such questioning afresh might love, honored for its specifically human qualities, rather than for divine powers that we hubristically arrogate to it, enchant—in new, privately constituted ways—our now long-disenchanted world.

NOTES

Prelims

1. Stendhal, *The Private Diaries of Stendhal*, ed. and trans. Robert Sage (London: Victor Gollancz, 1955); diary entry: December 10, 1801, p. 17.

2. Paul Tillich, *Dynamics of Faith* (London: Allen & Unwin, 1957), p. 1.

3. Simon May, *Love: A History* (New Haven, CT: Yale University Press, 2011), pp. 6–10.

4. I variously use he/him/his, she/her, or they/them/their as a pronoun for the lover and the loved one. For God, I use gender-neutral pronouns wherever possible, except where referring to texts, such as the Bible or the writings of canonical theologians, that employ the male pronoun in the original.

Chapter 1

1. Robert Solomon, *About Love: Reinventing Romance for Our Times* (Lanham, MD: Rowman & Littlefield, 1994), p. 197.

2. Robert Nozick, "Love's Bond," in *The Philosophy of (Erotic) Love*, eds. Robert C. Solomon and Kathleen M. Higgins (Lawrence: University Press of Kansas, 1991), p. 417.

3. Eva Illouz, *Why Love Hurts: A Sociological Explanation* (Cambridge: Polity Press, 2012), p. 18.

4. Erich Fromm, *The Art of Loving* (London: HarperCollins, 1995), p. 26.

5. Arthur Schopenhauer, *The World as Will and Representation*, vol. I, §66, trans. E. F. J. Payne (New York: Dover Publications, 1966), p. 374. Schopenhauer calls such compassionate love *"Menschenliebe."*

6. David Hume, *A Treatise of Human Nature*, ed. L. A. Selby-Bigge (New York: Oxford University Press, 1978), vol. 2, 3.3.4, pp. 607–608, n. 2. Hume also remarks that love and esteem "arise from like causes," but goes on to qualify this claim: "The qualities, that produce both [esteem and love], are agreeable, and give pleasure. But where this pleasure is severe and serious; or where its object is great, and makes a strong impression; or where it produces any degree of humility and awe: In all these cases, the passion, which arises from the pleasure, is more properly denominated esteem than love." We might, however, doubt whether this is the right distinction to draw between the causes of love and esteem. After all, love for God seems to be aroused by precisely the qualities that, Hume says, excite esteem as distinct from love. In the passage to which this is a footnote, he writes that "Good sense and genius beget esteem: Wit and humor excite love"—which is surely wholly inadequate as an understanding of what grounds love (p. 608).

7. See John Gottman, *The Science of Trust* (New York: Norton, 2011); and John Gottman and Nan Silver, *What Makes Love Last?* (New York: Simon and Schuster, 2012). John Gottman and colleagues have developed the "Specific Affect Coding System" and the "Turning System," which measure the relational dynamic between couples and reference

"Turning towards" and "Turning away" from the other as indicators of whether a marriage is likely to last, or not. See, for example: J. M. Gottman and J. L. Driver, "Dysfunctional Marital Conflict and Everyday Marital Interaction," *Journal of Divorce and Remarriage*, Vol. 43, No. 3–4 (2005), pp. 63–78; J. M. Gottman and J. L. Driver, "Turning Toward versus Turning Away: A Coding System of Daily Interactions," in *Couple Observational Coding Systems*, eds. P. K. Kerig and D. H. Baucom (Mahwah, NJ: Lawrence Erlbaum Associates, 2004), Chapter 13; and J. Coan and J. Gottman, "The Specific Affect Coding System," in *The Handbook of Emotion Elicitation and Assessment*, eds. James A. Coan and John B. Allen (New York: Oxford University Press, 2007), Chapter 16.

8. Baruch Spinoza, *Ethics*, trans. and ed. G. H. R. Parkinson (London: Everyman, 1992), III, proposition 59s, p. 126.

9. Felix Warneken and Michael Tomasello, "The Roots of Human Altruism," *British Journal of Psychology*, Vol. 100, No. 3 (August 2009), pp. 455–471.

10. Charles Darwin, *The Descent of Man and Selection in Relation to Sex* (London: John Murray, 1901), p. 203.

11. Arthur C. Danto, *The Abuse of Beauty: Aesthetics and the Concept of Art* (Chicago: Open Court, 2003), pp. 22–23.

12. Fernando Pessoa, *A Centenary Pessoa*, eds. Eugénio Lisboa and L. C. Taylor (Manchester: Carcanet Press, 1995), p. 74.

13. Simon May, *Love: A History*, pp. 1–5 and 11.

14. Franz Rosenzweig, *The Star of Redemption*, trans. William W. Hallo (Notre Dame, IN: University of Notre Dame Press, 1985), p. 306.

15. Friedrich Nietzsche, *The Antichrist*, §19, in *The Portable Nietzsche*, ed. and trans. Walter Kaufmann (New York: Viking, 1976), p. 586.

16. Friedrich Schlegel, *Lucinde*, in *Friedrich Schlegel's* Lucinde *and the Fragments*, trans. Peter Firchow (Minneapolis: University of Minnesota Press, 1971), p. 113.

17. Matthew 25:31–46; cf. 13:41–42.

18. Ephesians 1:3–6.

19. Romans 9:22.

20. Anders Nygren, *Agape and Eros*, trans. Philip S. Watson (Philadelphia: The Westminster Press, 1953), pp. 726 (my italics), 75, and 78.

21. M. Jamie Ferreira, *Love's Grateful Striving: A Commentary on Kierkegaard's* Works of Love (New York: Oxford University Press, 2001), p. 78.

22. Søren Kierkegaard, *Works of Love: Some Christian Deliberations in the Form of Discourses,* ed. and trans. Howard V. Hong and Edna H. Hong (Princeton, NJ: Princeton University Press, 1995), p. 3.

23. Søren Kierkegaard, *Works of Love*, pp. 9–10.

24. Søren Kierkegaard, *Works of Love*, p. 159.

Chapter 2

1. Irving Singer, *The Nature of Love*, Vol. I: *Plato to Luther* (Chicago: University of Chicago Press, 1984), pp. 3–5.

2. Harry Frankfurt, *The Reasons of Love* (Princeton, NJ: Princeton University Press, 2004), pp. 38–39.

3. Harry Frankfurt, *The Reasons of Love*, p. 38.

4. Harry Frankfurt, *The Reasons of Love*, pp. 39–40 *passim*.

5. André Comte-Sponville, *The Book of Atheist Spirituality*, trans. Nancy Huston (London: Bantam, 2009), p. 204.

6. C. S. Lewis, *The Four Loves* (London: Collins, 2012), p. 1.

7. Max Scheler, *The Nature of Sympathy*, trans. Peter Heath (London: Routledge & Kegan Paul, 1954), p. 148. Thus, Scheler says: "preference and rejection belong to the sphere of 'value-apprehension' (and indeed to the apprehension of grades of value) whereas love . . . cannot be reckoned as [an act] of apprehension at all."

8. Jean-Luc Marion, *The Erotic Phenomenon* (Chicago: University of Chicago Press, 2007), p. 81.

9. For example, Troy Jollimore, in a very interesting study that does ask about the ground of love, specifies the "properties in virtue of which the beloved is loved" as being "in large part attractive qualities such as charm, intelligence, humor, physical beauty, moral virtue, and so forth—the sort of universalizable qualities in terms of which a person's attractiveness or desirability is typically assessed." But such qualities do not, at least in the general way in which Jollimore evokes them, possess the specificity required to account for why we fall in love with, or otherwise begin to love, one person rather than another; or why, as he puts it, we come to "appreciate" any given set of qualities in one person and not another, when they both possess qualities of these kinds. And though he adds that "love is also a response to a nonuniversalizable, nonassessable property, [namely] that of *being a subject in the world*," this property, too, is cast too generally to explain love's tremendous selectivity. After all, we can see many people as being a "subject in the world," in Jollimore's sense, without loving every one of them. See Troy Jollimore, *Love's Vision* (Princeton, NJ: Princeton University Press, 2011), pp. 25–26; cf. 75, 123, 124, 125, 130–131.

10. Harry Frankfurt, *The Reasons of Love*, p. 79.

11. Harry Frankfurt, *The Reasons of Love*, p. 61; cf. p. 42.

12. Harry Frankfurt, "Autonomy, Necessity, and Love," in *Necessity, Volition, and Love* (Cambridge: Cambridge University Press, 1999), pp. 133–134, my italics.

13. Harry Frankfurt, "On Caring," in *Necessity, Volition, and Love*, p. 170.

14. Harry Frankfurt, *The Reasons of Love*, p. 40.

15. Indeed, the confusion is compounded when it comes to self-love, which Frankfurt insists is also disinterested "in the clear and literal sense of being motivated by no interests other than those of the beloved" (*The Reasons of Love*, p. 82). Since in self-love we are both lover and beloved, this means, for Frankfurt, that it is motivated by no interests other than our own and yet is in no way "for the sake of any benefit that [the lover] may derive either from the beloved or from loving it" (p. 61). It is hard to understand what such self-love really involves.

16. J. David Velleman, "Love as a Moral Emotion," *Ethics*, Vol. 109, No. 2 (January 1999), pp. 338–374, p. 366, my italics.

17. J. David Velleman, "Love as a Moral Emotion," pp. 365–366.

18. J. David Velleman, "Love as a Moral Emotion," p. 355.

19. J. David Velleman, "Love as a Moral Emotion," p. 360.

20. J. David Velleman, "Love as a Moral Emotion," p. 372.

21. J. David Velleman, "Love as a Moral Emotion," p. 371.

22. J. David Velleman, "Love as a Moral Emotion," p. 372.

23. J. David Velleman, "Love as a Moral Emotion," p. 372.

24. Martha C. Nussbaum, *Upheavals of Thought: The Intelligence of Emotions* (Cambridge: Cambridge University Press, 2001), p. 527. See also pp. 161–165, 494–499, 523–524, 548–549, and 559–560.

25. See, for example, Martha C. Nussbaum, "Transcending Humanity," in *Love's Knowledge: Essays on Philosophy and Literature* (New York: Oxford University Press, 1990), pp. 365–391, especially pp. 386–389.

26. Quoted by Hannah Arendt in *The Origins of Totalitarianism* (New York: Harcourt Brace Jovanovich, 1973), p. 301.

27. This, too, is of a piece with the idea that love is unconditional (though, of course, you can also believe that genuine love endures even if you don't think it is unconditional). For if love isn't grounded in any qualities of the loved one, then no change in our loved one and no sudden belief that we as lovers had been deluded about him could in any way affect our love.

28. Aristotle, *Nicomachean Ethics*, 1165b15, in *The Complete Works of Aristotle*, vol. 2, p. 1842.

29. Nozick thinks, however, that love is eventually "no longer dependent upon the particular characteristics that set it off," which, I will suggest in Chapter 17, is not the case: the conditions of love that inspire it in the first place never stop grounding it, whether or not they remain in the forefront of one's consciousness. Robert Nozick, *The Examined Life* (New York: Simon & Schuster, 1990), p. 76.

30. Troy Jollimore, *Love's Vision*, pp. 140–142.

31. Franz Rosenzweig, *The Star of Redemption*, p. 304.

32. "The work of love in recollecting one who is dead is a work of the freest love." Søren Kierkegaard, *Works of Love*, p. 351.

33. Friedrich Nietzsche, *The Gay Science*, §347, trans. Walter Kaufmann (New York: Random House, 1974), p. 287.

34. And also less a result of the commoditization of love than I once thought it was, as when I wrote in *Love: A History* that moving on is "fuelled by the spread of consumerism to love" (p. xii).

35. By "object" I am, of course, referring not to the loved one as "objectified," but rather to (the field of possibilities of) who the other is and what they do, the "who" and "what" with which love seeks to be in living relation.

36. Harry Frankfurt, *The Reasons of Love*, p. 43.

37. *Psychologies Magazine*, UK edition, November 2014. Pitt adds, "I care about them [his children] more than I care about myself, which I think is the real definition of love."

38. Isaiah Berlin, *The Roots of Romanticism*, ed. Henry Hardy (Princeton, NJ: Princeton University Press, 1999), p. 1.

Chapter 3

1. Michel de Montaigne, "Of Friendship," in *The Complete Works: Essays, Travel Journal, Letters*, trans. Donald M. Frame (London: Everyman's Library, 2003), p. 169.

2. Alexander Nehamas, "The Good of Friendship," *Proceedings of the Aristotelian Society*, Vol. 110, No. 3, Part 3 (October 2010), pp. 267–294, p. 292.

3. Harry Frankfurt, *The Reasons of Love*, p. 39.

4. Leviticus 19:18.

5. Leviticus 19:34.

6. Rabbi Hillel in *Babylonian Talmud*, ed. and trans. I. Epstein (London: Soncino Press, 1935–1948), Shabbath 31a.

7. Luke 6:27–28.

8. Cited in Oliver O'Donovan, *The Problem of Self-Love in St. Augustine* (Eugene, OR: Wipf and Stock, 2006), pp. 121–122.

9. See my *Love: A History*, pp. 111–114.

10. Søren Kierkegaard, *Works of Love*, p. 49.

11. Deuteronomy 6:5.

12. Luke 10:27. Jesus says, "You shall love the Lord your God with all your heart, and with all your soul, and with all your strength, and with all your mind; and your neighbor as yourself."

13. Matthew 5:48.

14. Plato, *The Symposium*, trans. Walter Hamilton (Harmondsworth: Penguin, 1951), 206b7–206b8, 206e, p. 86.

15. Plato, *Symposium*, 206a11–206a12, 210e–211e, 212a; p. 86, pp. 93–95.

16. G. W. F. Hegel, "A Fragment on Love," in *The Philosophy of (Erotic) Love*, eds. Robert C. Solomon and Kathleen M. Higgins (Lawrence: University Press of Kansas, 1991), p. 120.

17. Marcel Proust, *In Search of Lost Time*, Vol. 5: *The Captive and The Fugitive*, trans. C. K. Scott Moncrieff and Terence Kilmartin (London: Chatto & Windus, 1992), p. 113.

18. Baudelaire, *Journaux intimes* (I, 700), cited in Joanna Richardson, *Baudelaire* (London: John Murray, 1994), p. 50.

19. Plato, *Symposium*, 189a–193d, pp. 58–65.

20. Sigmund Freud, *Standard Edition of the Complete Psychological Works of Sigmund Freud*, Vol. XX: *Inhibitions, Symptoms, and Anxiety*, trans. and ed. James Strachey (London: The Hogarth Press, 1959), p. 122.

21. See, for example, Aristotle, *Nicomachean Ethics*, in *The Complete Works of Aristotle*, vol. 2, 1166a31–1166a33, p. 1843; 1168b7, p. 1847; 1170b6, p. 1850; and 1245a34–1245a36, p. 1974. See my *Love: A History*, Chapter 4, for a more extensive discussion of Aristotle's conception of friendship love.

22. Aristotle, *Nicomachean Ethics*, 1170b11–1170b12, in *The Complete Works of Aristotle*, vol. 2, p. 1850.

23. Lucretius, *De Rerum Natura*, trans. C. H. Sisson (Manchester: Carcanet, 1976), Book IV, lines 1079–1083, p. 132.

24. Arthur Schopenhauer, *The World as Will and Representation*, vol. II, p. 554.

25. Beckett, in fact, misquotes Augustine in an interview with Harold Hobson. See Harold Hobson, "Samuel Beckett: Dramatist of the Year," in *International Theatre Annual*, Vol. I, ed. Harold Hobson (London: John Calder, 1956), p. 153.

26. Benedict XVI, *Deus Caritas Est*, encyclical letter (Vatican: Libreria Editrice, 2005), Part I, sect. 11.

27. Romans 5:5.

28. Augustine, *De spiritu et littera*, 32:56, cited in Oliver O'Donovan, *The Problem of Self-Love in St. Augustine*, p. 130, my italics.

29. Thomas Aquinas, *Summa Theologiae*, Vol. 23: *Virtue*, trans. W. D. Hughes (London: Eyre & Spottiswoode, 1969), 1a2ae, question 62, art. 1, pp. 137–139.

30. Baruch Spinoza, *Ethics*, V, proposition 36, p. 218.

31. Søren Kierkegaard, *Works of Love*, p. 10.

32. Søren Kierkegaard, *Works of Love*, p. 126, my italics.

33. Søren Kierkegaard, *Works of Love*, p. 63.

34. For a discussion of Luther's conception of love through divine grace and for references to these citations from Luther, see my *Love: A History*, pp. 87–88 and 90–91.

Chapter 4

1. Harry Frankfurt, "On Caring," in *Necessity, Volition, and Love*, p. 170.

2. Deuteronomy 10:12.

3. This kind of criticism of Plato's ascent story of love is famously made by Gregory Vlastos in "The Individual as Object of Love in Plato," in *Platonic Studies* (Princeton, NJ: Princeton University Press, 1981), pp. 3–42.

4. Plato, *Symposium*, 189a–193d, pp. 58–65.

5. Michel de Montaigne, "Of Friendship," in *The Complete Works*, 1.28, p. 169.

6. 1 Samuel 18:1.

7. Jasper Griffin, *Homer on Life and Death* (Oxford: Oxford University Press, 1980), p. 168.

8. Quoted in Griffin, *Homer on Life and Death*, p. 200.

Chapter 5

1. "[C]lad in sweet humility she goes. / A thing from heaven sent, to all she shows / A miracle in which the world can share." Dante Alighieri, *La Vita Nuova*, Chapter XXVI, trans. Barbara Reynolds (Harmondsworth: Penguin, 1969), p. 76. In *The Divine Comedy: Paradiso*, Canto I, we hear Beatrice explain to Dante the form or structure of the whole created order, and its resemblance to God.

2. "Welt war in dem Antlitz der Geliebten—, / aber plötzlich ist sie ausgegossen: / Welt ist draußen, Welt ist nicht zu fassen." Rainer Maria Rilke, *Selected Poems*, trans. Susan Ranson and Marielle Sutherland, ed. Robert Vilain (New York: Oxford University Press, 2011), pp. 252–253.

3. "Ein höchst verworrenes Quartier, ein Straßennetz, das jahrelang von mir gemieden wurde, ward mir mit einem Schlage übersichtlich, als eines Tages ein geliebter Mensch dort einzog. Es war, als sei in seinem Fenster ein Scheinwerfer aufgestellt und zerlege die Gegend mit Lichtbüscheln." (My translation.) Another translation of this aphorism can be found in "One-Way Street," in Walter Benjamin, *Reflections: Essays, Aphorisms, Autobiographical Writings*, trans. Edmund Jephcott (New York: Schocken Books, 1978), p. 82: "A highly embroiled quarter, a network of streets that I had avoided for years, was disentangled at a single stroke when one day a person dear to me moved there. It was as if a searchlight set up at this person's window dissected the area with pencils of light."

4. Walter Benjamin, "A Berlin Chronicle," in *Reflections*, p. 5.

5. I owe this formulation to Peter Demetz, in "Introduction" to Walter Benjamin, *Reflections*, p. xvii.

6. Simone Weil, *The Need for Roots*, trans. A. F. Wills (London: Routledge, 1997), p. 41, my italics.

7. Friedrich Nietzsche, *Twilight of the Idols*, "Skirmishes of an Untimely Man," §8, in *The Portable Nietzsche*, p. 518. ("Das Wesentliche am Rausch ist das Gefühl der Kraftsteigerung und Fülle." Nietzsche, *Götzendämmerung* [Stuttgart: Alfred Kröner Verlag, 1954], p. 135.)

8. I explore this point in Chapter 18.

9. Genesis 12:1–3.

10. Virgil, *The Aeneid*, trans. David West (London: Penguin Books, 1990), Book 4:347, p. 91. I owe this reference to William Fitzgerald.

11. John of the Cross, "Ascent of Mount Carmel," Prologue, in *The Collected Works of St. John of the Cross*, trans. Kieran Kavanagh and Otilio Rodriguez (Washington, DC: ICS Publications, 1991), p. 114, my italics. I am grateful to Edward Howells for this reference.

12. Thus, in Plato's *Symposium* we read both of the drive to claim or reclaim an original union, expressed in Aristophanes's myth, and also of a future-oriented impulse, described in Diotima's account of the ascent of love to contemplating absolute beauty. See my *Love: A History*, Chapter 3, for an account of this double movement articulated in the *Symposium*. Far from being incompatible, the conceptions of love attributed by Plato to Aristophanes and Diotima are, therefore, in key respects complementary, though with the crucial qualification that, as Socrates himself says, love will desire only another half or a whole that is *good* (*Symposium*, 205d–205e, p. 85).

Chapter 6

1. Virgil, *The Aeneid*, 4:347, p. 91.

2. Plotinus, *Enneads*, trans. Stephen MacKenna (London: Penguin, 1991), I.6.8, pp. 53–54; cf. *Enneads*, V.9.1, pp. 425–426. In *Enneads*, VI.9.9, pp. 545–547, Plotinus also speaks of the soul's love for the One. The "possibility" of all other things means the power of generation and translates "δύναμις πάντων," which we find in various Enneads, for example V.1.7, pp. 355–356; V.3.15, pp. 381–383; V.4.2, pp. 388–340.

3. Cited in Oliver O'Donovan, *The Problem of Self-Love in St. Augustine*, p. 131.

4. Thomas Aquinas, *Summa Theologiae*, Vol. 16: *Purpose and Happiness*, trans. Thomas Gilby (London: Eyre & Spottiswoode, 1969), 1a2ae, question 4, art. 8, pp. 114–115.

5. Thomas Aquinas, *Summa Theologiae*, Vol. 19: *The Emotions*, trans. Eric D'Arcy (London: Eyre & Spottiswoode, 1967), 1a2ae, question 28, art. 2, and for fuller discussion, 1a2ae, questions 26–28, pp. 63–107.

6. Thomas Aquinas, *Summa Theologiae*, Vol. 19: *The Emotions*, p. 93.

7. *Sophist*, 263e3–263e5, where Plato speaks of reasoning being the silent dialogue of the soul with itself; cf. Plato, *Theaetetus*, 189e4–190a7.

8. Christine M. Korsgaard, *The Sources of Normativity* (Cambridge: Cambridge University Press, 1996), pp. 100–102.

9. I thank Daniel Rynhold for encouraging me to think about this limit case of the loved one as captor and its relation to ethical home, as well as for very valuable comments on this book more widely.

Chapter 7

1. Genesis 1:26–27.

2. Genesis 12:1–2, my italics.

3. Genesis 11:30 and 21:1–2.

4. Augustine, *City of God*, trans. William Babcock (New York: New City Press, 2013), Book XIII, Chapter 2, p. 69.

5. Genesis 12:1; cf. Isaiah 51:1–2.

6. Exodus 19:3.

7. Exodus 19:6; Leviticus 19:1–2.

8. Acts 9:1–19; cf. Acts 22:6–21.

9. Romans 8:28; cf. 11:29. The call from God is also a trope in many other religious settings—for example: in Augustine's conversion, reported in his *Confessions*, Book VIII, pp. 184–208; in Teresa of Avila's call to a "second conversion," described in her *Life*, Chapter 9 (Teresa of Avila, *The Life of Saint Teresa of Avila by Herself*, trans. J. M. Cohen [London: Penguin, 1957], pp. 67–70); and Ignatius of Loyola's call, on his sick bed after being wounded as a young soldier, recounted in his *Reminiscences*. See Ignatius, "Reminiscences," in *Saint Ignatius of Loyola: Personal Writings*, trans. Joseph. A. Munitiz (London: Penguin, 1996), pp. 13–17. I owe these references to Edward Howells.

10. Deuteronomy 6:5.

11. See especially pp. 8, 9, and 11–22.

12. For example, Paul Fiddes argues that "a God who creates 'out of love' has needs to be satisfied," needs that include being loved by human beings. Paul S. Fiddes, "Creation Out of Love," in *The Work of Love: Creation as Kenosis*, ed. John Polkinghorne (Grand Rapids, MI: Wm. B. Eerdmans Publishing Co., 2001), pp. 167–191, see p. 169. Vincent Brümmer also proposes that God desires and needs our love. Cited by Paul Fiddes, p. 170.

13. *Babylonian Talmud*, Shabbat 133b. See my discussion of this and related questions in Simon May, *Love: A History*, p. 18.

Chapter 8

1. I owe the Rilke and Plato citations to Hannah Arendt, "Martin Heidegger at Eighty," trans. Albert Hofstadter, *The New York Review of Books*, Vol. XVII, No. 6 (October 21, 1971), pp. 50–54. The citation from Dante is from *The Divine Comedy: Paradiso*, ed. and trans. Robin Kirkpatrick (London: Penguin, 2012), Canto 1, lines 110–111.

2. Thomas Mann, "Reflections of a Non-political Man," in *Pro and contra Wagner*, trans. Allan Blunden (London: Faber & Faber, 1985), p. 56.

3. Friedrich Nietzsche, *Beyond Good and Evil*, §231, in *Basic Writings of Nietzsche*, ed. and trans. Walter Kaufmann (New York: Modern Library, 1968), p. 352.

4. Plato, *Phaedrus*, 249d, in *Euthyphro, Apology, Crito, Phaedo, Phaedrus*, trans. Harold North Fowler (Cambridge, MA: Harvard University Press, 2005), p. 483, my italics.

5. Cited in Hannah Arendt, *Love and Saint Augustine*, eds. Joanna Vecchiarelli Scott and Judith Chelius Stark (Chicago: University of Chicago Press, 1996), p. 51.

6. Friedrich Schlegel, *Lucinde*, in *Friedrich Schlegel's* Lucinde *and the Fragments*, p. 113.

7. Søren Kierkegaard, *Works of Love*, p. 107: "love is a relation between: a person—God—a person; . . . God is the middle term." And: "The God-relationship is the mark by which

the love for people is recognized as genuine . . . God in this way not only becomes the third party in every relationship of [genuine] love but really becomes the sole object of love" (pp. 120–121).

8. See my *Love: A History*, p. 208.

9. Simone Weil, *Gravity and Grace*, trans. Emma Crawford and Mario von der Ruhr (London: Routledge, 2002), p. 40, my italics.

10. Song of Songs 3:4; cf. 8:2 and 8:5.

11. Confucius, *Analects* 1:2.

12. Mencius, *Mencius*, trans. D. C. Lau (London: Penguin, 2004), Book VII, Part A, 15, p. 148. The references to Chinese words and their elaborations within square brackets are added by me. This comment on Mencius is deeply indebted to Christopher Ryan.

13. Ruth 1:16–17.

14. Marcel Proust, *In Search of Lost Time*, Vol. 2: *Within a Budding Grove*, p. 433, my italics.

15. Isaiah 51:1–2.

16. I owe this reference to Isaiah and Maimonides's comment on this passage, which is to be found in *Guide to the Perplexed*, I, 16, to Lenn E. Goodman, *Judaism: A Contemporary Philosophical Investigation* (New York: Routledge, 2017), p. 117.

17. Plato, *Symposium*, 192d–192e, pp. 63–64.

18. "wiedererholtes Herz ist das bewohnteste: / freier durch Widerruf freut sich die Fähigkeit . . . / . . . Ach der geworfene, ach der gewagte Ball, / Füllt er die Hände nicht anders mit Wiederkehr: / rein um sein Heimgewicht ist er mehr." The English translation is mine. Two alternative translations of this all but untranslatable verse are given in Rainer Maria Rilke, *The Selected Poetry of Rainer Maria Rilke*, ed. and trans. Stephen Mitchell (London: Picador, 1987), p. 293: "only the won-back heart can ever be satisfied: free, / through all it has given up, to rejoice in mastery . . . / . . . Ah the ball that we dared, that we hurled into infinite space, / doesn't it fill our hands differently with its return: / heavier by the weight of where it has been"; and in Rainer Maria Rilke, *Selected Poems*, ed. Robert Vilain, pp. 268–271: "heart that has convalesced makes the most lived-in home; / strength returned knows delight all the more boundless . . . / . . . Ah, the thrown-ball that is risked in the upward soar, / does it not fill the hands differently on return: / pure, round its native weight, it has more."

19. T. S. Eliot, "Little Gidding," lines 237–241, from *Four Quartets* (London: Faber & Faber, 1959).

Chapter 9

1. If I may quote one of my aphorisms, in Simon May, *Thinking Aloud: A Collection of Aphorisms* (London: Alma Books, 2009), p. 144.

Chapter 10

1. Walt Whitman, *Democratic Vistas*, in *Leaves of Grass (I) and Democratic Vistas* (London: J. M. Dent & Sons, 1912), p. 329. I owe this parallel with Rousseau, Wordsworth, and Whitman to Lionel Trilling, *Sincerity and Authenticity* (Cambridge, MA: Harvard University Press, 1971), p. 92, italics mine.

2. Simon May, *Love: A History*, p. 252.

Chapter 11

1. Martin Heidegger, *Being and Time*, trans. John Macquarrie and Edward Robinson (Oxford: Blackwell, 1962), 275, p. 320.

2. "Tristan und Isot, ir und ich . . . niwan ein Tristan und ein Isot," in Gottfried von Strassburg, *Tristan und Isot*, lines 18352 to 18357, quoted in Denis de Rougemont, *Love in the Western World*, trans. Montgomery Belgion (Princeton, NJ: Princeton University Press, 1983), p. 135, n. 2.

3. Jean-Jacques Rousseau, *Julie, or The New Heloise*, trans. Philip Stewart and Jean Vaché (Hanover, NH: University Press of New England, 1997), Part Six, Letter VII, p. 555.

4. Gottfried von Strassburg, *Tristan*, trans. A. T. Hatto (London: Penguin, 1967), p. 264.

5. To the extent that the "maternal" may be identified with home, which is of course a controversial question, my conception of home might open a path toward meeting a major demand of some contemporary feminists, notably Luce Irigaray: namely, to restore, and no longer to repress, the maternal (the repression of which, according to Irigaray, is fundamental to the operation of a patriarchal order and marks the entire history of a Western tradition founded on "an original [symbolic?] matricide"). For, as I argue in the text, this conception of home is incompatible with the idea of a domestic cocoon that shuts out the world and in particular the public sphere—and so it would reject any conception of the maternal as a self-renouncing guarantor of such a cocoon of stability, standing stolidly in the background. Instead it would see the maternal as (creating) a potentially unsettling realm where the lover is called to their destiny; a "mother-land" to be progressively discovered, over which there is no question of sovereignty, and within which the lover would come to see any possible life-trajectory of theirs as necessarily unfolding. (For Irigaray's conception of the "original matricide," see Luce Irigaray, *Sexes and Genealogies*, trans. Gillian C. Gill [New York: Columbia University Press, 1993], p. 11; cf. *Je, Tu, Nous: Towards a Culture of Difference*, trans. A. Martin [London: Routledge, 1993]. I am interested here in Irigaray's diagnosis of this original matricide, but, in my own conception of love, I do not follow her response to this problem, nor her own approach to thinking about the nature of love in, for example, *The Way of Love*, trans. Heidi Bostic and Stephen Pluhacek [London: Continuum, 2002].)

Chapter 12

1. As Liddell and Scott's *Greek-English Lexicon* (abridged version, 1966) translates it.

2. In *Love: A History* I attempt to show what Hebrew scripture teaches us about how "loving demands unreserved submission to the laws of the ultimately inscrutable loved one," thus making the law of their being one's own. See p. 31; cf. pp. 29–37. I also argue that, for Jesus, love and law are inseparable, and that the widespread conviction that the New Testament sees love only as a spontaneous gift entirely free of law is untrue: p. 84.

3. Jeremy Waldron, "When Justice Replaces Affection: The Need for Rights," *Harvard Journal of Law and Public Policy*, Vol. 11 (1988), pp. 625–647, see p. 644.

4. Jeremy Waldron, "When Justice Replaces Affection," p. 647.

5. Robert Burton, *The Anatomy of Melancholy* (London: Chatto & Windus, 1891), Third Partition, Section II, Subsection V, p. 609.

6. Denis de Rougemont, *Love in the Western World*, pp. 42 and 46, latter italics mine.

7. Fernando Pessoa, "Salutation to Walt Whitman," cited in Harold Bloom, *The Western Canon* (New York: Harcourt Brace, 1994), p. 489.

8. Job 8:8–10, my italics.

9. Martin Buber, *I and Thou*, trans. Walter Kaufmann (Edinburgh: T&T Clark, 1970), p. 66. Kaufmann prefers "You" to "Thou" as a translation of the German "Du," given how easily "Thou" collapses, he thinks, into affectation and jargon.

10. Angelika Krebs, "Between I and Thou—On the Dialogical Nature of Love," in *Love and Its Objects: What Can We Care For?*, eds. Christian Maurer, Tony Milligan, and Kamila Pacovská (Basingstoke: Palgrave Macmillan, 2014), pp. 7–24, see p. 12.

11. Niko Kolodny, "Love as Valuing a Relationship," *Philosophical Review*, Vol. 112, No. 2 (April 2003), pp. 135–189, see p. 136.

12. Martin Buber, *I and Thou*, p. 66.

Chapter 13

1. Søren Kierkegaard, *Works of Love*, p. 154.

2. Simon May, *Love: A History*, pp. 249–250.

3. "Du im Voraus / verlorne Geliebte, Nimmergekommene," "You, beloved / lost in advance, the never-arrived," from "Uncollected Poems, 1912–1922," in Rainer Maria Rilke, *Selected Poems*, pp. 110–111.

4. As Kant puts it: "the sublime is that, the mere capacity of thinking which evidences a faculty of mind transcending every standard of the senses." Immanuel Kant, *Critique of Judgement*, trans. J. C. Meredith (Oxford: Oxford University Press, 2007), Book II, section 25, 250, p. 81.

5. Immanuel Kant, *Critique of Judgement*, Book II, section 28, 261, p. 91.

6. Edmund Burke, *A Philosophical Enquiry into the Origin of Our Ideas of the Sublime and Beautiful* (London: Routledge & Kegan Paul, 1958), Part I, Section VII, p. 39.

Chapter 14

1. Plato, *Symposium*, 212a5–212a6, p. 94.

2. Marcel Proust, *In Search of Lost Time*, Vol. 5: *The Captive and the Fugitive*, p. 111.

3. Proverbs 27:4.

4. Samuel Beckett, *Proust* (1931), in *The Selected Works of Samuel Beckett*, Vol. IV: *Poems, Short Fiction, Criticism*, ed. Paul Auster (New York: Grove Press, 2010), p. 534.

5. To use Tamra Wright's vivid term. See Tamra Wright, "Self, Other, God: 20th Century Jewish Philosophy," *Royal Institute of Philosophy Supplement*, Vol. 74 (July 2014), pp. 149–169, see p. 150.

Chapter 15

1. Terri Roberts, *Forgiven: The Amish School Shooting, a Mother's Love, and a Story of Remarkable Grace* (Bloomington, IN: Baker Publishing, 2015), p. 130; and Andrew Solomon, *Far from the Tree* (London: Chatto & Windus, 2013), p. 595.

2. W. H. Auden, "Canzone," in *Collected Poems*, ed. Edward Mendelson (London: Faber & Faber, 1976), p. 256.

3. Søren Kierkegaard, *Works of Love*, p. 107.

4. Søren Kierkegaard, *Works of Love*, p. 120.

5. Harry Frankfurt, *The Reasons of Love*, p. 79.

6. As the Bible makes clear, this does not stop people, including prophets, from lamenting, pleading against, and even indicting God's indifference and injustice in the face of suffering. In Jeremiah 12:1, the prophet complains: "You will be in the right, O LORD, when I lay charges against you; but let me put my case to you. Why does the way of the guilty prosper? Why do all who are treacherous thrive?" In Psalms 10:1–2 and 13, we read: "Why, O LORD, do you stand far off? Why do you hide yourself in times of trouble? In arrogance the wicked persecute the poor—let them be caught in the schemes they have devised . . . . Why do the wicked renounce God and say in their hearts, 'You will not call us to account?'" And Job cries: "I loathe my life; I will give free utterance to my complaint; I will speak in the bitterness of my soul. I will say to God, Do not condemn me; let me know why you contend against me. Does it seem good to you to oppress, to despise the work of your hands and favor the schemes of the wicked?" (Job 10:1–3). I owe these citations to Jeremiah Unterman, *Justice for All: How the Jewish Bible Revolutionized Ethics* (Lincoln: University of Nebraska Press, 2017), p. 134.

7. I owe this point to M. I. Finley, *The World of Odysseus* (New York: NYRB Classics, 2002), p. 143.

8. It is interesting to note that in Judaism love of God and fear (awe) of God are separate commandments even though they are often spoken of together and sometimes used as synonyms. Maimonides regards them as separate. I owe this point to Kenneth Seeskin (private correspondence).

9. M. I. Finley, *The World of Odysseus*, p. 143.

10. E. R. Dodds, *The Greeks and the Irrational* (Berkeley: University of California Press, 1992), p. 18.

11. M. I. Finley, *The World of Odysseus*, p. 143; cf. E. R. Dodds, *The Ancient Concept of Progress and Other Essays on Greek Literature and Belief* (Oxford: Oxford University Press, 1973), p. 140. The remark about it being incongruous (literally "out of place") to love Zeus comes in Aristotle's *Magna Moralia*, II, 1208b30–1208b31 (in *The Complete Works of Aristotle*, vol. 2, p. 1913).

Chapter 16

1. Numbers 25:1–9.

2. Numbers 12:1–10. I owe these last two examples to Louise Anthony, "Does God Love Us?," in *Divine Evil? The Moral Character of the God of Abraham*, eds. Michael Bergmann, Michael J. Murray, and Michael C. Rea (Oxford: Oxford University Press, 2011), pp. 38–39.

3. Joshua 6:16–17, 20–21.

4. Exodus 17:14–16; cf. Deuteronomy 25:17–19, and 1 Samuel 15:1–23.

5. 1 Samuel 15:3–4.

6. Matthew 25:41.

7. The nearest the Old Testament comes to an explicit concept of Hell is *Sheol*, the underworld where the dead exist in a form of sleep, "the land of gloom and deep darkness, the land of gloom and chaos, where light is like darkness" (Job 10:21–22). Death, as the

"land of no return," is not a site for reward or punishment, for the most part, in the Hebrew Bible. In the later Jewish apocalyptic tradition, however, eternal damnation is posed as a threat, though rarely. At the end of the Book of Daniel (12:1–2) we read: "But at that time your people shall be delivered, everyone who is found written in the book. Many of those who sleep in the dust of the earth shall awake, some to everlasting life, and some to shame and everlasting contempt." And, in the Rabbinic tradition, the Babylonian Talmud "contains graphic descriptions of afterlife states, particularly of Hell (*gehinnom*), where the wicked will be tortured in many horrifying ways." Keith Ward, *Religion and Human Nature* (Oxford: Oxford University Press, 1998), pp. 240 and 244. See also Dan Cohn-Sherbok, "The Jewish Doctrine of Hell," in *Beyond Death*, eds. D. Cohn-Sherbok and C. Lewis (London: Macmillan, 1995), pp. 56–62.

8. Matthew 13:41–42.

9. Matthew 5:21–22.

10. Jesus also speaks of vengeance in this world. In the "Parable of the Ten Minas," he decrees that those who reject his rule are not merely to be punished but to be killed: "as for these enemies of mine who did not want me to be king over them—bring them here and slaughter them in my presence" (Luke: 19:27).

11. Augustine, "The Predestination of the Saints," in *Answer to the Pelagians IV, The Works of St. Augustine, Vol. I/26*, trans. Roland J. Teske (New York: New City Press, 1999), Section 21, p. 202; cf. Section 24, p. 169: "And when infants die, with that [original] sin either removed by the grace of God or not removed by the judgment of God, they either pass by the merit of rebirth from evil to good or pass by the merit of their origin from evil to evil." I owe these references to Edward Howells.

12. Augustine, "The Gift of Perseverance," in *Answer to the Pelagians IV, The Works of St. Augustine, Vol. I/26*, Section 25, p. 206.

13. Thomas Aquinas, "Predestination," in *Summa Theologiae, Vol. 5: God's Will and Providence*, trans. Thomas Gilby (London: Eyre & Spottiswoode, 1967), 1a, question 23, art. 3, p. 117.

14. Thomas Aquinas, *Summa Theologiae, Vol. 5: God's Will and Providence*, p. 117.

15. Romans 9:22, my italics.

16. Romans 9:13.

17. Matthew 22:14.

18. John 21:20.

19. I develop the argument that God's love is not necessarily unconditional at greater length in *Love: A History*, Chapter 7.

20. This is how, for example, Eleonore Stump justifies God's order to kill the entire Amalekite people, including all their children. This order, Stump claims, employing a thought experiment, could have been necessary to forming the Israelite people as a people possessing moral agency, and so able to be united with God. It achieved this aim by teaching the Israelites "what will not work to enable a people to become just, good, and loving" (p. 197). In other words, to ward off or cure a severe spiritual sickness, God might be willing "to endure even the infliction of great suffering on a person, or on a people." And this, Stump says, makes God not a purveyor of genocide but "loving" (p. 207). See Eleonore Stump, "The Problem of Evil and the History of Peoples: Think Amalek," in *Divine Evil?*, pp. 179–197, and her response to Paul Draper: pp. 204–207.

21. 1 Corinthians 15:22.

22. Job 2:10.

23. "And in fact there is a continuity between our elementary likings for things and our loves for people. Since 'the highest does not stand without the lowest' we had better begin at the bottom, with mere likings; and since to 'like' anything means to take some sort of pleasure from it, we must begin with pleasure." C. S. Lewis, *The Four Loves*, p. 13.

24. From *Nationalökonomie und Philosophie* (1844). Published in Karl Marx, *Die Frühscriften* (Stuttgart: Alfred Kröner Verlag, 1953), pp. 300–301, quoted in Erich Fromm, *The Art of Loving*, p. 20.

25. Niko Kolodny, "Love as Valuing a Relationship," pp. 135–136, my italics.

26. Niko Kolodny, "Love as Valuing a Relationship," p. 154.

27. Niko Kolodny, "Love as Valuing a Relationship," p. 171, my italics.

28. Luke 6:32.

Chapter 17

1. Thomas Aquinas, "Angelic Love," in *Summa Theologiae*, Vol. 9: *Angels*, trans. Kenelm Foster (London: Eyre & Spottiswoode, 1968), 1a, question 60, art. 5, p. 197.

2. Genesis 22:1. Cf. Hilary Putnam, *Jewish Philosophy as a Guide to Life* (Bloomington: Indiana University Press, 2008), pp. 73–76.

3. God's calls to Moses and Jacob are cited in, respectively, Exodus 3:4 and Genesis 46:2.

4. Quoted by Hannah Arendt, *The Origins of Totalitarianism*, p. 301.

5. Simone Weil, *Gravity and Grace*, pp. 64 and 65.

6. Harry Frankfurt, *The Reasons of Love*, p. 42.

7. Augustine, *Christian Doctrine*, I, 27, 28, quoted in Hannah Arendt, *Love and Saint Augustine*, p. 36.

8. Augustine, "Sermon 128," in *Sermons 94A–150, The Works of St. Augustine, Vol. III/4*, trans. Edmund Hill (New York: New City Press, 1992), 128:5, p. 295; cf. "Sermon 90A" (Mainz 40), in *Sermons, The Works of St. Augustine, Vol. III/11*, trans. Edmund Hill (New York: New City Press, 1997), pp. 77–86. I owe this reference to Oliver O'Donovan, *Finding and Seeking: Ethics as Theology*, vol. 2 (Grand Rapids, MI: Wm. B. Eerdmans, 2014), p. 50.

9. Anthony Kenny, *Aristotle on the Perfect Life* (Oxford: Oxford University Press), p. 54, n. 15.

10. *Commentaries on the Psalms* 90, 31, 5. Cited in Hannah Arendt, *Love and Saint Augustine*, p. 17.

11. W. B. Yeats, "For Anne Gregory," in *The Oxford Anthology of English Poetry*, Vol. 2: *Blake to Heaney*, ed. John Wain (New York: Oxford University Press, 2002), pp. 582–583.

Chapter 18

1. Genesis 3:23.

2. Genesis 22:2.

3. Genesis 2:18.

4. Aristotle, *Nicomachean Ethics*, 1169b16–1169b19, in *The Complete Works of Aristotle*, vol. 2, p. 1848; cf. 1097b11, p. 1734.

5. As Stephanie Coontz says in her magisterial study of the history of marriage, "not until the late eighteenth century, and then only in Western Europe and North America, did the notion of free choice and marriage for love triumph as a cultural ideal." Stephanie Coontz, *Marriage, A History: How Love Conquered Marriage* (New York: Penguin Books, 2006), p. 7.

6. See Genesis 3:12. I am grateful to Daniel Rynhold for this point.

7. There is a long-standing, indeed fierce, debate about whether Adam and Eve had sex in the Garden of Eden. See, for example, Gary Anderson, "Celibacy or Consummation in the Garden? Reflections on Early Jewish and Christian Interpretations of the Garden of Eden," *The Harvard Theological Review*, Vol. 82, No. 2 (April 1989), pp. 121–148. I am grateful to Rachel Adelman for this reference.

8. Genesis 2:24.

9. Genesis 4:1.

10. The first case of romantic love in the Bible is probably when Isaac loves Rebecca, near the end of Genesis (24:67).

11. Genesis 23:4.

12. Genesis 15:13.

Chapter 19

1. Simone Weil, *Gravity and Grace*, p. 177.

2. From the first "Duino Elegy," in Rainer Maria Rilke, *Duino Elegies and The Sonnets to Orpheus*, ed. and trans. Stephen Mitchell (New York: Vintage, 2009), p. 3.

3. 1 John 2:15.

4. Matthew 6:19–20.

5. 1 Peter 2:11.

6. 2 Corinthians 5:1–4.

7. Augustine, *The Confessions*, trans. Maria Boulding (New York: New City Press, 1997), Book I, 1, p. 39.

8. James Joyce, *Ulysses* (London: The Bodley Head, 1993), p. 20.

9. Max Weber, "Science as a Vocation," in *Max Weber's "Science as a Vocation,"* eds. Peter Lassman and Irving Velody (London: Unwin Hyman, 1989), p. 30.

10. J. B. S. Haldane, "Possible Worlds," in *Possible Worlds and Other Essays* (London: Chatto & Windus, 1927), p. 286. I owe this reference to Robert Jackson.

11. As the anthropologist Clifford Geertz remarks in a very different context, "the shattering of larger coherences . . . has made relating local realities with overarching ones . . . extremely difficult." "If the general is to be grasped at all," Geertz writes, "and new unities uncovered, it must, it seems, be grasped not directly, all at once, but via instances, differences, variations, particulars—piecemeal, case by case. In a splintered world, we must address the splinters." Clifford Geertz, "The World in Pieces: Culture and Politics at the End of the Century," in *Available Light: Anthropological Reflections on Philosophical Topics* (Princeton, NJ: Princeton University Press, 2000), p. 221.

12. Hesiod, *Works and Days*, Loeb Classical Library, 57, ed. and trans. Glenn W. Most (Cambridge, MA: Harvard University Press, 2006), lines 109–120, p. 97.

13. "[A]fter Earth was stained with crime unspeakable / And all evicted Justice from their greedy thoughts, / Brothers poured the blood of brothers on their hands, / Sons no longer grieved when parents passed away, / Father prayed for death of son in his first youth / So as

freely to possess the bloom of a new bride, / Mother, lying impiously with ignorant son, / Dared impiously to sin against divine Penates. / Our civil madness by confounding fair with foul / Has turned away from us the Gods' forgiving thoughts." Catullus, 64th poem, in *The Poems of Catullus,* ed. and trans. Guy Lee (Oxford: Oxford University Press, 2008), lines 397–406, p. 103.

Chapter 20

1. Quoted in Bernard McGinn, "The Language of Love in Christian and Jewish Mysticism," in *Mysticism and Language,* ed. Steven T. Katz (New York: Oxford University Press, 1992), pp. 202–235, see p. 203.

2. Marcel Proust, *In Search of Lost Time,* Vol. 1: *Swann's Way,* p. 371.

3. Anders Nygren, *Agape and Eros,* p. 722.

4. "Take care not to make a covenant with the inhabitants of the land to which you are going, or it will become a snare among you. You shall tear down their altars, break their pillars, and cut down their sacred poles (for you shall worship no other god, because the Lord, whose name is Jealous, is a jealous God)" (Exodus 34:12–14).

5. In the introduction to a republication of the first editions of the fairy tales, Jack Zipes suggests that the character was changed from a mother to a stepmother in 1819 "because the Grimms held motherhood sacred." *The Original Folk and Fairy Tales of the Brothers Grimm: The Complete First Edition,* trans. and ed. Jack Zipes (Princeton, NJ: Princeton University Press, 2014), p. xxxvvi.

6. Michel de Montaigne, "Of Friendship," in *The Complete Works,* p. 169.

7. Michel de Montaigne, "Of Friendship," in *The Complete Works,* p. 172.

8. Stephanie Coontz, *Marriage, A History: How Love Conquered Marriage,* pp. 184–185.

9. The jealousy of Cain and Abel, Isaac and Ishmael, Jacob and Esau, Joseph and his brothers, and Leah and Rachel (in the Old Testament) and of the Prodigal Son's brother (in the New Testament) are just some of the prominent examples of sibling rivalry and hatred in the Bible. Envy and jealousy are on Paul's list of "the works of the flesh" (Galatians 5:19–21). And many other passages warn against hatred of one's sibling, regardless of its source; for example: "All who hate a brother or sister are murderers, and you know that murderers do not have eternal life abiding in them" (1 John 3:15).

10. "Look at the birds of the air; they neither sow nor reap nor gather into barns, and yet your heavenly Father feeds them" (Matthew 6:26). "For us there is one God, the Father, from whom are all things and for whom we exist" (1 Corinthians 8:6).

11. "As a mother comforts her child, so I will comfort you" (Isaiah 66:13), in the Old Testament. And in the New Testament Jesus laments maternally over Jerusalem: "Jerusalem, Jerusalem . . . How often have I desired to gather your children together as a hen gathers her brood under her wings" (Matthew 23:37).

12. "For your Maker is your husband, the LORD of hosts is his name" (Isaiah 54:5); and "As the bridegroom rejoices over the bride, so shall your God rejoice over you" (Isaiah 62:5). The culmination of the New Testament is the "marriage feast of the Lamb," in which the people of God are "prepared as a bride adorned for her husband" (Revelation 21:2).

13. For example, there is a long history of allegorical interpretation of the Old Testament book Song of Songs, an erotic love story between a young couple, as a metaphor for the love of God. This is true of the Jewish interpretative tradition, from the Aramaic Targum through

to Rashi. In the Christian tradition, John of the Cross, in *The Dark Night of the Soul*, says, "I abandoned and forgot myself, laying my face on my Beloved." John of the Cross, "The Dark Night," Prologue, "Stanzas of the Soul," in *The Collected Works of St. John of the Cross*, p. 359.

14. God speaks to Moses "as one speaks to a friend" (Exodus 33:11); and the New Testament reminds us that "Abraham . . . was called the friend of God" (James 2:23). Thomas Aquinas speaks of friendship with God: "it is clear that charity is a friendship of man and God." Thomas Aquinas, *Summa Theologiae*, Vol. 34: *Charity*, trans. R. J. Batten (London: Eyre & Spottiswoode, 1975), 2a2ae, question 22, art. 1, pp. 6–7.

15. Spinoza and St. Francis of Assisi are two good examples.

16. Jesus's parable of the sheep and the goats expresses the idea that we can love God in loving the stranger: "Truly I tell you, just as you did it to one of the least of these who are members of my family, you did it to me" (Matthew 25:37–40).

17. Luke 1:1–21, 1:26–38; and Philippians 2:5–8.

18. I am indebted to Edwin Francis Bryant, *Krishna: A Sourcebook* (New York: Oxford University Press, 2007), pp. 414–418, for these distinctions in love for Krishna, as well as to communications with Jessica Frazier.

Chapter 21

1. Jean-Luc Marion, *The Erotic Phenomenon*, p. 40; cf. pp. 20, 38–39. Indeed, Marion insists on the priority of this question to the point of claiming that "[t]o give up on asking (oneself) the question 'Does anybody love me' or above all to give up on the possibility of a positive response implies nothing less than giving up on the human itself" (p. 21).

2. Jean-Paul Sartre, *Being and Nothingness*, trans. Hazel Barnes (London: Routledge, 2007), p. 398.

3. Franz Rosenzweig, *The Star of Redemption*, p. 182.

4. Erich Fromm, for example, claims that we cannot genuinely love before eight and a half to ten years old (Erich Fromm, *The Art of Loving*, p. 31): "For most children before the age from eight and a half to ten, the problem is almost exclusively that of *being loved*—of being loved for what one is. The child up to this age does not yet love; he responds gratefully, joyfully, to being loved." This is also about the age when Martin Hoffman suggests we are first capable of genuine reciprocity in care for another. Martin L. Hoffman, *Empathy and Moral Development* (Cambridge: Cambridge University Press, 2000), p. 242.

5. Fyodor Dostoevsky, *The Brothers Karamazov*, trans. Richard Pevear and Larissa Volokhonsky (London: Vintage, 1992), Book VI, Chapter 3(i), p. 322, my italics.

6. Johann Wolfgang von Goethe, *Wilhelm Meister's Apprenticeship*, ed. and trans. Eric A. Blackall (Princeton, NJ: Princeton University Press, 1995), Book IV, Chapter 9, p. 139.

Chapter 22

1. Cited in Alasdair MacIntyre, *Edith Stein: A Philosophical Prologue, 1913–1922* (Lanham, MD: Rowman & Littlefield, 2005), p. 20.

2. Gabriel García Márquez, *Love in the Time of Cholera*, trans. Edith Grossman (New York: Penguin Books, 2007), p. 61.

3. For a discussion of Nietzsche's nuanced views on the types and functions of pity, some of which he praises, see my *Nietzsche's Ethics and His War on "Morality"* (Oxford: Oxford University Press, 1999), pp. 37 and 53.

4. Simon May, *Love: A History*, p. 248.

5. Ralph Waldo Emerson, "Friendship," in *Essays: First Series* (London: Routledge, 1883), p. 206.

6. Genesis 1:31.

7. Friedrich Nietzsche, *Beyond Good and Evil*, §68, p. 270.

8. It is surely significant that Greeks from Homer to Plato condemned overweening pride—"*hubris*"—as a catastrophic vice, which destroyed the "virtues of courage, temperance, justice, and wisdom that buttressed the political order and made the good life possible" (Michael Eric Dyson, *Pride* [New York: Oxford University Press, 2006], pp. 13–14). And significant, too, that Christian tradition is also filled with so many dire warnings against this vice. For Augustine, pride is the beginning of all sin, obstructing what he takes to be human life's supreme goal and good: the soul's return to God. ("It was pride, then, that hindered the soul's return": Augustine, "Sermon 142," 3, cited in Hannah Arendt, *Love and Saint Augustine*, p. 90). Pride is the root of Adam's sin in eating the forbidden fruit: "pride it was that turned him from wisdom," the wisdom of understanding his stupidity and Eve's "to love their own power to excess and to desire equality with God." A soul is diminished, says Augustine, "proportionally to its desire for self-aggrandizement." (Cited in Oliver O'Donovan, *The Problem of Self-Love in St. Augustine*, p. 96.) And in the sixth century CE Pope Gregory I decreed that pride is the root of all evil, which, once it captures a human heart, surrenders it to be laid waste by the other great sins (Michael Eric Dyson, *Pride*, p. 10).

Yet we cannot get rid of bad pride entirely. Some of the truths that such pride conceals would, if one held them constantly in view, sap one's vitality, one's capacity to flourish, and one's will to flourish. These could be truths about the horrors of human nature, including one's own; truths about one's own lack of real talent; truths about the love and loyalty of those close to us, or about our love for them; truths about our real motives for entering or leaving relationships—motives that we might wish to see as purer and more principled than they actually are; indeed truths about pride itself—and its innumerable pretenses, including pretenses to modesty. Thanks to pride we can survive realities that might otherwise destroy us.

Chapter 23

1. I am influenced here by Heidegger's concept of *Sein zum Tode*, "being-towards-death," in which he conceives death as "the possibility of the impossibility of any existence at all . . . the possibility of the impossibility . . . of every way of existing"—though I take him to mean something very different to what I intend here. Martin Heidegger, *Being and Time*, p. 307.

2. And conversely: the duller our sense of existing the duller our sense of not-existing.

Chapter 24

1. I briefly introduced this thought of the "impersonal" in love and the related idea of "overshooting" in the concluding chapter of *Love: A History*, p. 246, and will develop it now in some detail.

2. Richard Wagner, *Tristan und Isolde*, Act 2, scene 2.

3. Arthur Schopenhauer, *On the Basis of Morality*, §18, trans. E. F. J. Payne (Indianapolis, IN: Bobbs-Merrill, 1965), p. 163.

4. Friedrich Schlegel, *Lucinde*, in *Friedrich Schlegel's Lucinde and the Fragments*, p. 113.

5. Søren Kierkegaard, *Works of Love*, pp. 120–121, my italics.

6. Jean-Paul Sartre, *Being and Nothingness*, p. 584, my italics.

7. Simone Weil, "Human Personality," trans. Richard Rees, in *The Simone Weil Reader*, ed. George A. Panichas (New York: McKay, 1977), p. 317.

Chapter 25

1. The references to these citations are: (1) Thomas Aquinas, *Summa Theologiae*, Vol. 34: *Charity*, 2a2ae, question 26, art. 4, pp. 128–129, my italics; (2) Martin Luther, *Lectures on Romans*, cited in Anders Nygren, *Agape and Eros*, p. 712; (3) Aristotle, *Nicomachean Ethics*, 1168b9–1168b10, in *The Complete Works of Aristotle*, vol. 2, p. 1847; (4) Immanuel Kant, "Religion within the Boundaries of Mere Reason," in *Religion and Rational Theology*, ed. and trans. Alan W. Wood and George di Giovanni (Cambridge: Cambridge University Press, 1996), 6:45, pp. 90–91.

2. Thomas Aquinas, *Summa Theologiae*, Vol. 34: *Charity*, 2a2ae, question 26, art. 4, pp. 128–129.

3. Thomas's argument here proceeds via two distinct propositions: first, good self-love is love of our own spiritual nature; and, second, we are closer to ourselves (by "unity") than anyone else is to us (by "union"). Since, he claims, "union" presupposes "unity," it follows that love of neighbor presupposes love of self. I am grateful to Oliver O'Donovan for pointing this out to me.

4. Augustine, *The Trinity*, trans. Edmund Hill (New York: New City Press, 1991), Book XIV, 4, 17, p. 384.

5. Hannah Arendt, *Love and Saint Augustine*, p. 50.

6. Cited in Oliver O'Donovan, *The Problem of Self-Love in St. Augustine*, p. 95. O'Donovan is quoting from *The City of God*, Book XIII, 21.

7. Søren Kierkegaard, *Works of Love*, p. 107.

8. Søren Kierkegaard, *Works of Love*, p. 22; cf. pp. 52–53.

9. Søren Kierkegaard, *Works of Love*, p. 23.

10. Søren Kierkegaard, *Works of Love*, p. 361.

11. Quoted in Anders Nygren, *Agape and Eros*, p. 711. Nygren claims that for Luther love of one's neighbor "has the task of completely dispossessing and annihilating self-love" (p. 713).

12. See Martin Luther, *Lectures on Romans*, trans. and ed. Wilhelm Pauck (London: SCM Press, 1961), p. 408.

13. Harry Frankfurt, *The Reasons of Love*, p. 79.

14. Harry Frankfurt, *The Reasons of Love*, p. 61; cf. 42.

15. Aristotle, *Nicomachean Ethics*, 1168b9–1168b10, in *The Complete Works of Aristotle*, vol. 2, p. 1847.

16. Baruch Spinoza, *Ethics*, IV, proposition 52s, p. 176.

17. Jean-Jacques Rousseau, "Discourse on the Origins of Inequality," in *Discourse on the Origins of Inequality (Second Discourse), Polemics, and Political Economy*, trans. Judith Bush, Roger D. Masters, Christopher Kelly, and Terence Marshall (Hanover, NH: University Press of New England, 1992), pp. 1–95, p. 91. See also n. 12, p. 36.

18. Friedrich Nietzsche, *The Gay Science*, §290, p. 233.

19. Simon Blackburn, *Mirror, Mirror: The Uses and Abuses of Self-Love* (Princeton, NJ: Princeton University Press, 2014), p. 187.

20. *The Sayings of the Jewish Fathers*, ed. and trans. Joseph I. Gorfinkle (New York: Block Publishing, 1923), 1:14, p. 36.

21. Aristotle, *Nicomachean Ethics*, 1168b15–1168b17, in *The Complete Works of Aristotle*, vol. 2, p. 1847.

22. Adam Smith, *The Theory of Moral Sentiments*, ed. Knud Haakonssen (Cambridge: Cambridge University Press, 2002), Part VIII, Section II, Chapter III, §§12–13, p. 358.

23. Jean-Jacques Rousseau, "Discourse on the Origins of Inequality," p. 91.

24. Immanuel Kant, *Religion and Rational Theology*, 6:45–46, p. 90, long footnote. I am also indebted to Henry E. Allison, *Kant's Theory of Freedom* (Cambridge: Cambridge University Press, 1990), p. 124.

25. Harry Frankfurt, *The Reasons of Love*, p. 97.

26. Harry Frankfurt, *The Reasons of Love*, p. 97.

27. Harry Frankfurt, *The Reasons of Love*, p. 98.

28. Harry Frankfurt, *The Reasons of Love*, p. 68.

29. Harry Frankfurt, *The Reasons of Love*, p. 97.

30. Augustine, *The Confessions*, Book IV, 11, p. 99.

31. Michel de Montaigne, "Of Friendship," in *The Complete Works*, p. 169.

32. Cited in Oliver O'Donovan, *The Problem of Self-Love in St. Augustine*, p. 131.

33. In *Love: A History*, I suggested that self-love could be "the joy of feeling oneself to be a rooted being—and of being *able* to be a rooted being" (p. 10). But I now think this is wrong; indeed, in confusing self-love with self-esteem it makes the same mistake as much of the tradition does. Since, on my theory at least, love is necessarily a relation to a ground beyond oneself, what I called "self-love" in that work is really joy that one is and can be rooted in a world that one supremely values. In other words, it is joy in possessing a capacity to be rooted—and so is a form of self-esteem. But this is by no means the same as the emotion we feel toward the *source* of such a promise of rootedness.

34. Ovid, *Metamorphoses*, Book III, trans. F. J. Miller (Cambridge, MA: Harvard University Press, 1977), lines 424–432, p. 155.

35. Quoted in Jürgen Moltmann, "God's Kenosis in the Creation and Consummation of the World," in *The Work of Love: Creation as Kenosis*, ed. John Polkinghorne, pp. 137-151, p. 141. My discussion of the Trinity is indebted to Moltmann. As he puts it elsewhere: "The Son is other than the Father, but not other in essence. . . . [God] communicates himself to his like *and* his Other." Jürgen Moltmann, *The Trinity and the Kingdom of God*, trans. Margaret Kohl (London: SCM Press, 1981), pp. 58–59.

36. John 14:10; cf. John 10:38.

37. Another error of many traditional accounts of what has been called "self-love," whether they are religious or secular, is their assumption that we cannot help loving ourselves. As the theologian Karl Barth quips, "God will never think of blowing on this fire [of self-love], which is bright enough already" (Karl Barth, *Church Dogmatics: The Doctrine of the Word of God*, vol. 1, part 2, eds. G. W. Bromiley and T. F. Torrance [Edinburgh: T&T Clark, 1956], 3.2, §18, p. 388). Or, as Harry Frankfurt puts it in his secular terms: "We are moved more *naturally* to love ourselves, and more *heedlessly*, than we are moved to love other things"; indeed, he adds, "our inclination towards self-love . . . is exceptionally difficult

to overcome or to elude." (Frankfurt, *The Reasons of Love*, p. 81, my italics). In reality, the opposite is the case: assuming that what these accounts call self-love is actually self-esteem or self-affirmation, we are, I think, moved more naturally and heedlessly to esteem or affirm others than to esteem or affirm ourselves.

Chapter 26

1. Leviticus 25:23.

2. And it presumes crossing the Euphrates from "beyond the river" (*be'ever ha-nahar*): see Joshua 24:2. I owe this point about the meaning of "Hebrew" (*ivri*) to Rachel Adelman.

3. Genesis 12:1.

4. Genesis 17:5.

5. Genesis 23:4.

6. Genesis 15:13.

7. Deuteronomy 7:12–13, my italics. Cf. "Now, therefore, if you obey my voice and keep my covenant, you shall be my treasured possession out of all peoples" (Exodus 19:5).

8. In the sense, perhaps, that God says, "I will be gracious to whom I will be gracious, and will show mercy on whom I will show mercy" (Exodus 33:19). All divine favor or grace has this intrinsically inscrutable structure.

9. Deuteronomy 4:40.

10. Deuteronomy 6:5.

11. Deuteronomy 4:40.

12. Simon May, *Love: A History*, pp. 8, 26–31 *passim*, 247, 255.

13. Matthew 5:17–18.

14. Luke 24:44.

15. 1 John 3:23.

16. Matthew 19:17.

17. Genesis 15:16.

18. Genesis 15:13.

19. Genesis 15:12–14. I owe this point to Rachel Adelman, who offers a detailed explication of the significance of Abraham being in a deep sleep in her paper "On the Nexus between Homeland and Exile" (unpublished work).

20. Jean-Paul Sartre, *Being and Nothingness*, p. 463.

21. Exodus 20:5–6.

22. "Was du ererbt von deinen Vätern hast, / Erwirb es, um es zu besitzen." Johann Wolfgang von Goethe, *Faust: Der Tragödie erster Teil*, "Nacht." (My translation.) Alternatively translated: "The things that men inherit come alone / To true possession by the spirit's toil," Goethe, *Faust: Part One*, trans. Philip Wayne (Harmondsworth: Penguin, 1981), lines 682–683, p. 53.

23. Jeremiah 2:5.

Chapter 27

1. All citations from the *Odyssey* are from the English translation by Robert Fagles (New York: Viking Penguin, 2006), and given as the Book number followed by line number to be found in this translation.

2. Agamemnon's *oikos* denotes his bloodline—not just his extended household, along with its territory and possessions. I owe these points about the connotations of *oikos* to Antony Makrinos.

3. I owe this point about Telemachus being at the center of four books of the *Odyssey* to Stephanie West in *A Commentary on Homer's* Odyssey, Vol. 1: *Introduction and Books I-VIII*, eds. Alfred Heubeck, Stephanie West, and John B. Hainsworth (New York: Oxford University Press, 1998), p. 51.

4. *Odyssey* 1.69–71.

5. M. I. Finley remarks that for the Homeric hero, one's kin or family were normally "indistinguishable from oneself." M. I. Finley, *The World of Odysseus*, p. 119.

6. "Adroit" translates *polymētis* (πολύμητις—also translated as "of many counsels"). This disposition is related in spirit to others that are prominent in the *Odyssey*, such as *polytropos* (πολύτροπος—versatile, of many ways) and *polymēchanos* (πολυμήχανος—cunning, resourceful, inventive, rich in devices).

7. *Odyssey* 10.351–356.

8. *Odyssey* 10.519–523.

9. *Odyssey* 10.526.

10. *Odyssey* 10.533–535.

11. *Odyssey* 10.537–538.

12. *Odyssey* 8.518–520.

13. *Odyssey* 8.522–526.

14. This comment on the etymological allegorization of "Calypso" is highlighted by Eustathius. See Antony Makrinos, *Eustathius' Commentary on Homer's* Odyssey, PhD thesis (London: University College London, 2004), p. lxxxv.

15. *Odyssey* 5.171–172.

16. *Odyssey* 5.174–175.

17. M. I. Finley, *The World of Odysseus*, pp. 139–140.

18. *Odyssey* 5.236–243.

19. *Odyssey* 5.125–128.

20. *Odyssey* 5.249–251.

21. *Odyssey* 11.466–540.

22. *Odyssey* 11.554–573.

23. Jasper Griffin, *Homer on Life and Death*, pp. 100–101.

24. *Odyssey* 10.539–545.

25. *Odyssey* 10.619–622.

26. *Odyssey* 10.626–627.

27. *Odyssey* 11.21.

28. *Odyssey* 11.723–727.

29. *Odyssey* 6.139–152, 7.250–256.

30. *Odyssey* 7.257–261.

31. *Odyssey* 13.3–7.

32. Indeed, the *Odyssey* itself also refers to the stories of the returns of Agamemnon, Nestor, Aias (Ajax), and Menelaus. In addition, an epic poem about the returns of the Greek heroes of the Trojan War has been lost and is known to us mainly from a summary by Proclus, the Neoplatonist philosopher of the fifth century CE. I owe this point to Stephanie

West in *A Commentary on Homer's* Odyssey, Vol. 1: *Introduction and Books I–VIII*, eds. Alfred Heubeck, Stephanie West, and John B. Hainsworth, p. 53, n. 10.

33. *Odyssey* 16.246–249.

34. *Odyssey* 13.432.

35. The twelfth-century Byzantine scholar Archbishop Eustathius, writing in a Neoplatonist vein, goes as far as to allegorize Penelope as "moral philosophy," avidly sought by the "philosopher" Odysseus, who is tormented by his separation from her. Eustathius, *Commentary on the Odyssey*, I.17.7ff. See *Eustathii Archiepiscopi Thessalonicensis Commentarii ad Homeri Odysseam*, vol. 1, ed. J. G. Stallbaum (Cambridge, first published 1825, digitally printed version 2010). I owe this point to Antony Makrinos, *Eustathius' Commentary on Homer's* Odyssey, pp. lxxxv–lxxxvi.

Chapter 28

1. Plato, *Symposium*, 211d–211e and 212a, pp. 94–95.

2. Stendhal, *Love*, trans. Gilbert and Suzanne Sale (Harmondsworth: Penguin, 1975), p. 66n, my italics.

3. Marcel Proust, *In Search of Lost Time*, Vol. 2: *Within a Budding Grove*, pp. 270–271, cited by Elaine Scarry, *On Beauty and Being Just* (Princeton, NJ: Princeton University Press, 1999), p. 7.

4. I briefly introduce this thought in my chapter on Plato, "From Physical Desire to Paradise," in *Love: A History*, pp. 52; cf. p. 242, and will develop it and some of its implications in the current chapter and in the following three.

5. Stendhal, *Love*, p. 70.

Chapter 29

1. Ibn Hazm, *The Ring of the Dove*, trans. A. J. Arberry (London: Luzac, 1953), p. 59.

2. John Studd, "A Comparison of 19th Century and Current Attitudes to Female Sexuality," *Gynecological Endocrinology*, Vol. 23, No. 12 (December 2007), pp. 673–681, see p. 674.

3. Anthony Giddens, *The Transformation of Intimacy: Sexuality, Love and Eroticism in Modern Societies* (Cambridge: Polity Press, 1992), p. 77.

Chapter 30

1. Fyodor Dostoevsky, *The Brothers Karamazov*, Book 3, Chapter 3, p. 108.

2. Anthony Tommasini, "Music: The Devil Made Him Do It," *The New York Times*, September 30, 2001.

3. Arthur Schopenhauer, *The World as Will and Representation*, vol. I, §38, p. 197; cf. pp. 198–199.

4. Stendhal, *Rome, Naples and Florence*, trans. Richard N. Coe (Richmond: Calder Publications, 2010), p. 302.

5. "Denn das Schöne ist nichts / als des Schrecklichen Anfang, den wir noch grade ertragen, / und wir bewundern es so, weil es gelassen verschmäht, / uns zu zerstören. / Ein jeder Engel ist schrecklich." Rainer Maria Rilke, *Duino Elegies*, 1, ed. and trans. Stephen Mitchell (New York: Vintage, 2009), pp. 2–3.

6. Aristotle, *Metaphysics*, XIII, 1078a36–1078b1, in *The Complete Works of Aristotle*, vol. 2, p. 1705.

7. According to Arthur Danto, *The Abuse of Beauty*, p. 142.

8. Immanuel Kant, *Critique of Judgement*, Book I, §5, 218, p. 49.

9. George Santayana, *The Sense of Beauty* (New York: Dover Publications, 1955), §11, pp. 31 and 33.

10. Edmund Burke, *A Philosophical Enquiry into the Origin of Our Ideas of the Sublime and Beautiful*, Part II, section I, p. 57.

11. The two quotations from Moore are cited in Arthur Danto, *The Abuse of Beauty*, pp. 28 and 46.

12. Sappho, 6—in *The Poetry of Sappho*, trans. Jim Powell (Oxford: Oxford University Press, 2007), p. 6.

Chapter 31

1. Lucretius, *De Rerum Natura*, IV: 1155–1165, p. 134.

2. Plato, *Symposium*, 206c–206e, pp. 86–87; cf. 201a, p. 78.

3. Augustine, *The Confessions*, Book IV, 13, 20, p. 105.

4. Alexander Nehamas, *A Promise of Happiness: The Place of Beauty in a World of Art*, The Tanner Lectures on Human Values, delivered at Yale University, April 2001, p. 203; cf. p. 205.

Chapter 32

1. Augustine, *The Confessions*, Book II, 4, 9, p. 68, my italics.

2. Augustine, *The Confessions*, Book II, 4, 9, p. 68.

3. Edgar Allen Poe, "The Imp of the Perverse," in *The Complete Illustrated Stories and Poems of Edgar Allen Poe* (London: Chancellor Press, 1988), p. 440.

4. John 3:19–20.

5. Plato, *Symposium*, 205e–206a, p. 86, my italics. Plato's statement about beauty and good being interchangeable ("let us change our terms and substitute good for beautiful") comes at 204d13–204e2, p. 84.

6. Aristotle, *Nicomachean Ethics*, 1165b15, in *The Complete Works of Aristotle*, vol. 2, p. 1842.

7. Quoted in Oliver O'Donovan, *The Problem of Self-Love in St. Augustine*, p. 30.

8. Quoted in Oliver O'Donovan, *The Problem of Self-Love in St. Augustine*, p. 32.

9. Sigmund Freud, "Criminals from a Sense of Guilt" (1916), in *Standard Edition of the Complete Psychological Works of Sigmund Freud*, Vol. XIV: *Some Character-Types Met with in Psycho-Analytic Work* (London: The Hogarth Press, 1957), pp. 332–333.

10. I owe this parallel with Dionysus to Joyce Carol Oates. See Joyce Carol Oates, "Tragic Rites in Dostoyevsky's *The Possessed*," in *Contraries* (New York: Oxford University Press, 1981), pp. 17–50, see p. 18.

11. Joseph Conrad, *The Secret Agent* (London: Penguin Classics, 2007) p. 246.

12. Isaiah 45:7 (King James version), my italics. *Ra* (or *r'*) can also be translated as woe or disaster.

13. Fyodor Dostoevsky, *Devils*, trans. Michael R. Katz (Oxford: Oxford University Press, 2008), p. 446, my italics.

14. I owe this point about Peter Verkhovensky to Sarah Young, and thank her for very valuable comments on my references to Dostoevsky.

15. Nietzsche stresses that to love fate—*amor fati*—is to love "necessity" (*Ecce Homo*, "Why I Am So Clever," §10, in *On the Genealogy of Morals and Ecce Homo*, ed. and trans. Walter Kaufmann [New York: Random House, 1969], p. 258); indeed, it is to see beauty in necessity (*The Gay Science*, §276, p. 223). As I argue in "Why Nietzsche Is Still in the Morality Game," he does not say that *amor fati* involves loving every single event that necessity determines. In this Nietzschean vein, I propose in that article that "to affirm life is to look with joy upon one's life as a whole, conceived as necessary (or fated) in all its elements, without justifying it or desiring an alternative to it." In other words, "the primary object of affirmation is our individual lived life as a whole," and affirming this whole is "consistent with loathing, or 'saying No' to, particular experiences or events in it." In my "Why Nietzsche Is Still in the Morality Game," in *Nietzsche's* On the Genealogy of Morality: *A Critical Guide*, ed. Simon May (Cambridge: Cambridge University Press, 2011), pp. 81 and 100; cf. 81–82, 95–98.

16. Fyodor Dostoevsky, *The Brothers Karamazov*, p. 108.

17. Friedrich Nietzsche, *Ecce Homo*, "The Birth of Tragedy," §2, p. 272.

Chapter 33

1. Aristotle, *Nicomachean Ethics*, 1166a4–1166a9, in *The Complete Works of Aristotle*, vol. 2, p. 1843.

2. 1 Samuel 1:11.

3. Luke 1:13–14.

4. Genesis 1:28 and 9:7.

5. Walter I. Trattner, *Crusade for the Children: A History of the National Child Labor Committee and Child Labor Reform in America* (Chicago: Quadrangle, 1970), pp. 11–12, quoted in Hugh D. Hindman, *Child Labor: An American History* (New York: M. E. Sharpe, 2002), p. 51.

6. David F. Lancy, *The Anthropology of Childhood*, 2nd ed. (Cambridge: Cambridge University Press, 2015), p. 56, n. 21, and p. 29.

7. Josephine McDonagh, *Child Murder and British Culture, 1720–1900* (Cambridge: Cambridge University Press, 2003), p. 123.

8. Josephine McDonagh, *Child Murder and British Culture, 1720–1900*, p. 124.

9. Colin Heywood, *A History of Childhood* (Cambridge: Polity Press, 2001), p. 74.

10. Colin Heywood, *A History of Childhood*, pp. 77–82 *passim*.

11. David F. Lancy, *The Anthropology of Childhood*, p. 34.

12. David F. Lancy, *The Anthropology of Childhood*, p. 54.

13. Josephine McDonagh, *Child Murder and British Culture, 1720–1900*, p. 124.

14. Plato, *Phaedrus*, 250e.

15. Viviana A. Zelizer, *Pricing the Priceless Child: The Changing Social Value of Children* (Princeton, NJ: Princeton University Press, 1994), pp. 3 and 7. Zelizer's focus is US society between 1870 and 1930.

16. Viviana A. Zelizer, *Pricing the Priceless Child*, pp. 5–6.

17. William Wordsworth, "Ode: Intimations of Immortality from Recollections of Early Childhood."

18. Matthew 18:3.

19. See, for example, Linda Pollock, *A Lasting Relationship: Parents and Children over Three Centuries* (London: Fourth Estate, 1987), pp. 123–132, and Robert Woods, *Children Remembered: Responses to Untimely Death in the Past* (Liverpool: Liverpool University Press, 2006). I am grateful to Colin Heywood for these references.

20. In his poem "In Memory of W. B. Yeats," W. H. Auden writes of his fellow poet's demise: "The current of his feeling failed; he became his admirers." See W. H. Auden, *Selected Poems*, ed. Edward Mendelson (London: Faber & Faber, 1979), pp. 80–83.

21. Friedrich Nietzsche, *The Gay Science*, §338, p. 270.

22. Aristotle, *Eudemian Ethics*, VII, 1239a5–1239a6, in *The Complete Works of Aristotle*, vol. 2, p. 1963.

23. John of the Cross, *A Spiritual Canticle of the Soul and the Bridegroom Christ*, trans. David Lewis (London: T. Baker, 1919), p. 239. Teresa of Avila, *The Interior Castle, or The Mansions* (London: T. Baker, 1921), p. 272. I owe these references to Irving Singer, *The Nature of Love*, vol. I, p. 222.

24. Fyodor Dostoevsky, *The Brothers Karamazov*, p. 774.

25. John Bowlby, *Maternal Care and Mental Health*, World Health Organization Monograph Series, No. 2 (Geneva: World Health Organization, 1951), p. 53, my italics. Quoted in Inge Bretherton, "The Origins of Attachment Theory: John Bowlby and Mary Ainsworth," *Developmental Psychology*, Vol. 28, No. 5 (September 1992), pp. 759–775.

26. Friedrich Nietzsche, *On the Genealogy of Morals*, Essay I, §8, p. 470.

27. Friedrich Nietzsche, *Beyond Good and Evil*, §2, pp. 199–201. See my discussion of how, for example, the will to truth might arise out of the will to deception, in *Nietzsche's Ethics and His War on "Morality,"* pp. 161–163.

28. I owe this point about Paul and Stephen to G. W. Bowersock, "Who Was Saint Paul?," *The New York Review of Books*, Vol. LXII, No. 17 (November 5, 2015), pp. 21–23.

29. Thomas Hobbes, *Leviathan*, ed. J. C. A. Gaskin (Oxford: Oxford University Press, 1996), Book XI, p. 66.

30. Indeed, Nietzsche says, "life itself is *will to power*"—and all psychology is to be understood in terms of the "*development of the will to power.*" Friedrich Nietzsche, *Beyond Good and Evil*, §§13 and 23, pp. 211 and 221.

31. For a consideration of Proust's depiction of the impulse to possess, its futility, and its relationship to jealousy, see my *Love: A History*, pp. 215–234, especially pp. 216–218, 222–224, and 227–228.

32. Sigmund Freud, "Lecture 31," in *Standard Edition of the Complete Psychological Works of Sigmund Freud*, Vol. XXII: *New Introductory Lectures on Psycho-Analysis*, trans. and ed. James Strachey (London: Hogarth Press, 1964), p. 63.

33. I owe these references to Michel Foucault to Anthony Giddens, *The Transformation of Intimacy*, pp. 18–19 and 169–171.

34. Stephanie Coontz, *Marriage, A History: How Love Conquered Marriage*, p. 152.

35. Deuteronomy 21:18–21. This license to have one's errant child stoned to death was never put into practice as far as we know. I owe this point to Kenneth Seeskin.

36. This archaic sensibility is beautifully described by Mircea Eliade: "In the particulars of his conscious behavior, the 'primitive,' the archaic man, acknowledges no act which has not been previously posited and lived by someone else, some other being who was not a man. What he does has been done before. His life is the ceaseless repetition of gestures

initiated by others." Mircea Eliade, *The Myth of the Eternal Return*, trans. Willard R. Trask (Princeton, NJ: Princeton University Press, 1974), p. 5.

37. Hannah Arendt, *The Human Condition* (Chicago: University of Chicago Press, 1958), p. 52.

38. "We scarcely dare say these days that two persons fell in love because their eyes met. Yet this is how one falls in love and in no other way." Victor Hugo, cited in Stephen Kern, *The Culture of Love: Victorians to Moderns* (Cambridge, MA: Harvard University Press, 1992), pp. 19–20.

39. For example: "Now sight is superior to touch in purity." *Nicomachean Ethics*, 1176a1–1176a3, in *The Complete Works of Aristotle*, vol. 2, p. 1858.

40. Dante Alighieri, *La Vita Nuova*, Chapter XLI.

Chapter 34

1. Friedrich Schlegel, *Lucinde*, in *Friedrich Schlegel's* Lucinde *and the Fragments*, pp. 113 and 106.

2. Anthony Giddens, *The Transformation of Intimacy*, pp. 61–63.

3. Anthony Giddens, *The Transformation of Intimacy*, p. 184. See pp. 182–192 for a more extended discussion.

4. Ruth 1.

5. Genesis 38.

6. C. S. Lewis, "Friendship—The Least Necessary Love," in *Friendship: A Philosophical Reader*, ed. Neera Kapur Badhwar (Ithaca, NY: Cornell University Press, 1993), pp. 39–47, see p. 46.

7. Galatians 3:28.

8. Ephesians 2:14 and 19–20.

9. Arthur Schopenhauer, *On the Basis of Morality*, §22, p. 211.

10. Wolfgang Golther, ed., *Richard Wagner an Mathilde Wesendonck: Tagebuchblätter und Briefe 1853–1871* (Berlin: Alexander Duncker, 1904), p. 79. I owe this reference and translation to Christopher Janaway.

11. Cited in Mark Johnston, *Surviving Death* (Princeton, NJ: Princeton University Press, 2010), p. 347, n. 20. I owe this reference to Christopher Janaway.

Chapter 35

1. Hannah Arendt, "On Humanity in Dark Times: Thoughts on Lessing," trans. C. Winston and R. Winston, in *Men in Dark Times* (New York: Harcourt Brace Jovanovich, 1968), pp. 11–12. Cited in Michael P. Steinberg, *Judaism Musical and Unmusical* (Chicago: University of Chicago Press, 2007), p. 30.

2. Michel de Montaigne, "Of Friendship," *The Complete Works*, p. 170.

Chapter 36

1. Harry Frankfurt, *The Reasons of Love*, p. 43.

2. Harry Frankfurt, *The Reasons of Love*, p. 40.

3. Harry Frankfurt, *The Reasons of Love*, p. 39, my italics.

4. Plato, *Symposium*, 206d–206e; cf. 207a3–207a4, 208e1–208e5, 212a.

5. Aristotle, *Nicomachean Ethics*, 1161b28 1161b29, in *The Complete Works of Aristotle*, vol. 2, p. 1836.

6. Marcel Proust, *In Search of Lost Time*, Vol. 2: *Within a Budding Grove*, p. 433.

7. David F. Lancy, *The Anthropology of Childhood*, pp. 29–30.

8. Plato, *Symposium*, 192d, p. 63.

BIBLIOGRAPHY

Allison, Henry E. *Kant's Theory of Freedom*. Cambridge: Cambridge University Press, 1990.

Anderson, Gary. "Celibacy or Consummation in the Garden? Reflections on Early Jewish and Christian Interpretations of the Garden of Eden." *The Harvard Theological Review*, Vol. 82, No. 2, April 1989, pp. 121–148.

Aquinas, Thomas. *Summa Theologiae*, Vol. 5: *God's Will and Providence*. Translated by Thomas Gilby. London: Eyre & Spottiswoode, 1967.

———. *Summa Theologiae*, Vol. 9: *Angels*. Translated by Kenelm Foster. London: Eyre & Spottiswoode, 1968.

———. *Summa Theologiae*, Vol. 16: *Purpose and Happiness*. Translated by Thomas Gilby. London: Eyre & Spottiswoode, 1969.

———. *Summa Theologiae*, Vol. 19: *The Emotions*. Translated by Eric D'Arcy. London: Eyre & Spottiswoode, 1967.

———. *Summa Theologiae*, Vol. 23: *Virtue*. Translated by W. D. Hughes. London: Eyre & Spottiswoode, 1969.

———. *Summa Theologiae*, Vol. 34: *Charity*. Translated by R. J. Batten. London: Eyre & Spottiswoode, 1975.

Arendt, Hannah. *The Human Condition*. Chicago: University of Chicago Press, 1958.

———. *Love and Saint Augustine*. Edited by Joanna Vecchiarelli Scott and Judith Chelius Stark. Chicago: University of Chicago Press, 1996.

———. "Martin Heidegger at Eighty." Translated by Albert Hofstadter. *The New York Review of Books*, October 21, 1971, pp. 50–54.

———. *The Origins of Totalitarianism*. New York: Harcourt Brace Jovanovich, 1973.

Aristotle. *Eudemian Ethics, Nicomachean Ethics, Magna Moralia*, and *Metaphysics*. In *The Complete Works of Aristotle*. Vol. 2. Translated by Jonathan Barnes. Princeton, NJ: Princeton University Press, 1984.

Auden, W. H. *Collected Poems*. Edited by Edward Mendelson. London: Faber & Faber, 1976.

———. *Selected Poems*. Edited by Edward Mendelson. London: Faber & Faber, 1979.

Augustine. *Answer to the Pelagians IV, The Works of St. Augustine, Vol. I/26*. Translated by Roland J. Teske. New York: New City Press, 1999.

———. *City of God*. Translated by William Babcock. New York: New City Press, 2013.

———. *The Confessions*. Translated by Maria Boulding. New York: New City Press, 1997.

———. *Sermons 94A–150, The Works of St. Augustine, Vol. III/4*. Translated by Edmund Hill. New York: New City Press, 1992.

———. *Sermons, The Works of St. Augustine, Vol. III/11*. Translated by Edmund Hill. New York: New City Press, 1997.

———. *The Trinity*. Translated by Edmund Hill. New York: New City Press, 1991.

Babylonian Talmud. Edited and translated by I. Epstein. London: Soncino Press, 1935–48.

Barth, Karl. *Church Dogmatics: The Doctrine of the Word of God*. Vol. 1, Part 2. Edited by G. W. Bromiley and T. F. Torrance. Edinburgh: T&T Clark, 1956.

Bätschmann, Oskar, and Pascal Griener. *Hans Holbein*. London: Reaktion Books, 1997.

Beckett, Samuel. *The Selected Works of Samuel Beckett*. Edited by Paul Auster. New York: Grove Press, 2010.

Benedict XVI. *Deus Caritas Est*. Encyclical letter, Vatican: Libreria Editrice, 2005.

Benjamin, Walter. *Reflections: Essays, Aphorisms, Autobiographical Writings*. Translated by Edmund Jephcott. New York: Schocken Books, 1978.

Bergmann, Michael, Michael. J. Murry, and Michael C. Rea, eds. *Divine Evil? The Moral Character of the God of Abraham*. Oxford: Oxford University Press, 2011.

Berlin, Isaiah. *The Roots of Romanticism*. Edited by Henry Hardy. Princeton, NJ: Princeton University Press, 1999.

Bible, New Revised Standard Edition, Anglicized Edition. Oxford: Oxford University Press, 1995.

Blackburn, Simon. *Mirror, Mirror: The Uses and Abuses of Self-Love*. Princeton, NJ: Princeton University Press, 2014.

Bloom, Harold. *The Western Canon*. New York: Harcourt Brace, 1994.

Bretherton, Inge. "The Origins of Attachment Theory: John Bowlby and Mary Ainsworth." *Developmental Psychology*, Vol. 28, No. 5, September 1992, pp. 759–775.

Bryant, Edwin Francis. *Krishna: A Sourcebook*. New York: Oxford University Press, 2007.

Buber, Martin. *I and Thou*. Translated by Walter Kaufmann. Edinburgh: T&T Clark, 1970.

Burke, Edmund. *A Philosophical Enquiry into the Origin of Our Ideas of the Sublime and Beautiful*. London: Routledge & Kegan Paul, 1958.

Burton, Robert. *The Anatomy of Melancholy*. London: Chatto & Windus, 1891.

Catullus. *The Poems of Catullus*. Edited and translated by Guy Lee. Oxford: Oxford University Press, 2008.

Coan, James A., and John J. B. Allen. *The Handbook of Emotion Elicitation and Assessment*. New York: Oxford University Press, 2007.

Cohn-Sherbok, D., and C. Lewis, eds. *Beyond Death*. London: Macmillan, 1995.

Comte-Sponville, André. *The Book of Atheist Spirituality*. Translated by Nancy Huston. London: Bantam, 2009.

Conrad, Joseph. *The Secret Agent*. London: Penguin Classics, 2007.

Coontz, Stephanie. *Marriage, A History: How Love Conquered Marriage*. New York: Penguin Books, 2006.

Dante Alighieri. *The Divine Comedy*. Translated by Robin Kirkpatrick. London: Penguin, 2012.

———. *La Vita Nuova*. Translated by Barbara Reynolds. Harmondsworth: Penguin, 1969.

Danto, Arthur C. *The Abuse of Beauty: Aesthetics and the Concept of Art*. Chicago: Open Court, 2003.

Darwin, Charles. *The Descent of Man and Selection in Relation to Sex*. London: John Murray, 1901.

Dodds, E. R. *The Ancient Concept of Progress and Other Essays on Greek Literature and Belief*. Oxford: Oxford University Press, 1973.

———. *The Greeks and the Irrational*. Berkeley: University of California Press, 1992.

Dostoevsky, Fyodor. *The Brothers Karamazov*. Translated by Richard Pevear and Larissa Volokhonsky. London: Vintage, 1992.

———. *Devils*. Translated by Michael R. Katz. Oxford: Oxford University Press, 2008.

Dyson, Michael Eric. *Pride*. New York: Oxford University Press, 2006.

Eliade, Mircea. *The Myth of the Eternal Return.* Translated by Willard R. Trask. Princeton, NJ: Princeton University Press, 1974.

Elliot, T. S. *Four Quartets.* London: Faber & Faber, 1959.

Emerson, Ralph Waldo. "Friendship." In *Essays: First Series.* London: Routledge, 1883.

Ferreira, M. Jamie. *Love's Grateful Striving: A Commentary on Kierkegaard's Works of Love.* New York: Oxford University Press, 2001.

Fiddes, Paul S. "Creation Out of Love." In *The Work of Love: Creation as Kenosis.* Edited by John Polkinghorne. Grand Rapids, MI: Wm. B. Eerdmans, 2001, pp. 167–191.

Finley, M. I. *The World of Odysseus.* New York: NYRB Classics, 2002.

Frankfurt, Harry. *Necessity, Volition, and Love.* Cambridge: Cambridge University Press, 1999.

———. *The Reasons of Love.* Princeton, NJ: Princeton University Press, 2004.

Freud, Sigmund. *Standard Edition of the Complete Psychological Works of Sigmund Freud.* Vols. I to XXIV. Translated and edited by James Strachey. London: Hogarth Press, 1953–1974.

———. *Standard Edition,* Vol. XIV: *Some Character-Types Met with in Psycho-Analytic Work* (1957).

———. *Standard Edition,* Vol. XX: *Inhibitions, Symptoms, and Anxiety* (1959).

———. *Standard Edition,* Vol. XXII: *New Introductory Lectures on Psycho-Analysis* (1964).

Fromm, Erich. *The Art of Loving.* London: HarperCollins, 1995.

Geertz, Clifford. *Available Light: Anthropological Reflections on Philosophical Topics.* Princeton, NJ: Princeton University Press, 2000.

Giddens, Anthony. *The Transformation of Intimacy: Sexuality, Love and Eroticism in Modern Societies.* Cambridge: Polity Press, 1992.

Golther, Wolfgang, ed. *Richard Wagner an Mathilde Wesendonck: Tagebuchblätter und Briefe 1853–1871.* Berlin: Alexander Duncker, 1904.

Goodman, Lenn E. *Judaism: A Contemporary Philosophical Investigation.* New York: Routledge, 2017.

Gorfinkle, Joseph I., ed. and trans. *The Sayings of the Jewish Fathers.* New York: Block Publishing, 1923.

Gottfried von Strassburg. *Tristan.* Translated by A. T. Hatto. London: Penguin, 1967.

Gottman, John. *The Science of Trust.* New York: Norton, 2011.

Gottman, J. M., and J. L. Driver. "Dysfunctional Marital Conflict and Everyday Marital Interaction." *Journal of Divorce and Remarriage,* Vol. 43, No. 3–4, 2005, pp. 63–78.

Gottman, John, and Nan Silver. *What Makes Love Last?* New York: Simon and Schuster, 2012.

Griffin, Jasper. *Homer on Life and Death.* Oxford: Oxford University Press, 1980.

Grimm, Jacob, and Wilhelm Grimm. *The Original Folk and Fairy Tales of the Brothers Grimm: The Complete First Edition.* Translated and edited by Jack Zipes. Princeton, NJ: Princeton University Press, 2014.

Haldane, J. B. S. *Possible Worlds and Other Essays.* London: Chatto & Windus, 1927.

Hazm, Ibn. *The Ring of the Dove.* Translated by A. J. Arberry. London: Luzac, 1953.

Heidegger, Martin. *Being and Time.* Translated by John Macquarrie and Edward Robinson. Oxford: Blackwell, 1962.

Hesiod. *Works and Days.* Loeb Classical Library, 57. Edited and translated by Glenn W. Most. Cambridge, MA: Harvard University Press, 2006.

Heubeck, Alfred, Stephanie West, and John B. Hainsworth, eds. *A Commentary on Homer's Odyssey*, Vol. 1: *Introduction and Books I–VIII*. New York: Oxford University Press, 1998.

Heywood, Colin. *A History of Childhood*. Cambridge: Polity Press, 2001.

Hindman, Hugh D. *Child Labor: An American History*. New York: M. E. Sharpe, 2002.

Hobbes, Thomas. *Leviathan*. Edited by J. C. A. Gaskin. Oxford: Oxford University Press, 1996.

Hobson, Harold. "Samuel Beckett: Dramatist of the Year." In *International Theatre Annual*, Vol. I. Edited by Harold Hobson. London: John Calder, 1956, pp. 153–155.

Hoffman, Martin L. *Empathy and Moral Development*. Cambridge: Cambridge University Press, 2000.

Homer. *The Odyssey*. Translated by Robert Fagles. New York: Viking Penguin, 2006.

Hume, David. *A Treatise on Human Nature*. Edited by L. A. Selby-Bigge. New York: Oxford University Press, 1978.

Ignatius of Loyola. "Reminiscences." In *Saint Ignatius of Loyola: Personal Writings*. Translated by Joseph. A. Munitiz. London: Penguin, 1996, pp. 13–17.

Illouz, Eva. *Why Love Hurts: A Sociological Explanation*. Cambridge: Polity Press, 2012.

Irigaray, Luce. *Je, Tu, Nous: Towards a Culture of Difference*. Translated by A. Martin. London: Routledge, 1993.

———. *Sexes and Genealogies*. Translated by Gillian C. Gill. New York: Columbia University Press, 1993.

———. *The Way of Love*. Translated by Heidi Bostic and Stephen Pluhacek. London: Continuum, 2002.

John of the Cross. *The Collected Works of St. John of the Cross*. Translated by Kieran Kavanagh and Otilio Rodriguez. Washington, DC: ICS Publications, 1991.

Johnston, Mark. *Surviving Death*. Princeton, NJ: Princeton University Press, 2010.

Jollimore, Troy. *Love's Vision*. Princeton, NJ: Princeton University Press, 2011.

Joyce, James. *Ulysses*. London: The Bodley Head, 1993.

Kant, Immanuel. *Critique of Judgement*. Translated by J. C. Meredith. Oxford: Oxford University Press, 2007.

———. *Religion and Rational Theology*. Edited and translated by Alan W. Wood and George di Giovanni. Cambridge: Cambridge University Press, 1996.

Katz, Steven T., ed. *Mysticism and Language*. New York: Oxford University Press, 1992.

Kenny, Anthony. *Aristotle on the Perfect Life*. Oxford: Oxford University Press, 1995.

Kerig, P. K., and D. H. Baucom, eds. *Couple Observational Coding Systems*. Mahwah, NJ: Lawrence Erlbaum Associates, 2004.

Kern, Stephen. *The Culture of Love: Victorians to Moderns*. Cambridge, MA: Harvard University Press, 1992.

Kierkegaard, Søren. *Works of Love: Some Christian Deliberations in the Form of Discourses*. Edited and translated by Howard V. Hong and Edna H. Hong. Princeton, NJ: Princeton University Press, 1995.

Kolodny, Niko. "Love as Valuing a Relationship." *Philosophical Review*, Vol. 112, No. 2, April 2003, pp. 135–189.

Korsgaard, Christine M. *The Sources of Normativity*. Cambridge: Cambridge University Press, 1996.

Krebs, Angelika. "Between I and Thou—On the Dialogical Nature of Love." In *Love and Its Objects: What Can We Care For?* Edited by Christian Maurer, Tony Milligan, and Kamila Pacovská. Basingstoke: Palgrave Macmillan, 2014, pp. 7–24.

Lancy, David F. *The Anthropology of Childhood,* 2nd ed. Cambridge: Cambridge University Press, 2015.

Lewis, C. S. *The Four Loves.* London: Collins, 2012.

———. "Friendship—The Least Necessary Love." In *Friendship: A Philosophical Reader.* Edited by Neera Kapur Badhwar. Ithaca, NY: Cornell University Press, 1993, pp. 39–47.

Lucretius. *De Rerum Natura.* Translated by C. H. Sisson. Manchester: Carcanet, 1976.

Luther, Martin. *Lectures on* Romans. Translated and edited by Wilhelm Pauck. London: SCM Press, 1961.

Makrinos, Antonios. *Eustathius' Commentary on Homer's* Odyssey. PhD thesis, London: University College London, 2004.

Mann, Thomas. *Pro and contra Wagner.* Translated by Allan Blunden. London: Faber & Faber, 1985.

Marion, Jean-Luc. *The Erotic Phenomenon.* Chicago: University of Chicago Press, 2007.

May, Simon. *Love: A History.* New Haven, CT: Yale University Press, 2011.

———. *Nietzsche's Ethics and His War on "Morality."* Oxford: Oxford University Press, 1999.

———, ed. *Nietzsche's* On the Genealogy of Morality: *A Critical Guide.* Cambridge: Cambridge University Press, 2011.

———. *Thinking Aloud: A Collection of Aphorisms.* London: Alma Books, 2009.

McDonagh, Josephine. *Child Murder and British Culture, 1720–1900.* Cambridge: Cambridge University Press, 2003.

Mencius. *Mencius.* Translated by D. C. Lau. London: Penguin, 2004.

Moltmann, Jürgen. "God's Kenosis in the Creation and Consummation of the World." In *The Work of Love: Creation as Kenosis.* Edited by John Polkinghorne. Grand Rapids, MI: Wm. B. Eerdmans, 2001, pp. 137–151.

———. *The Trinity and the Kingdom of God.* Translated by Margaret Kohl. London: SCM Press, 1981.

Montaigne, Michel de. "Of Friendship." In *The Complete Works: Essays, Travel Journal, Letters.* Translated by Donald M. Frame. London: Everyman's Library, 2003, pp. 164–176.

Nehamas, Alexander. "The Good of Friendship." *Proceedings of the Aristotelian Society,* Vol. 110, No. 3, Part 3, October 2010, pp. 267–294.

———. *A Promise of Happiness: The Place of Beauty in a World of Art.* The Tanner Lectures on Human Values, delivered at Yale University, April 9–10, 2001.

Nietzsche, Friedrich. *The Antichrist.* In *The Portable Nietzsche.* Edited and translated by Walter Kaufmann. New York: Viking, 1976.

———. *Beyond Good and Evil.* In *Basic Writings of Nietzsche.* Translated by Walter Kaufmann. New York: Modern Library, 1968.

———. *Ecce Homo.* In *On the Genealogy of Morals and Ecce Homo.* Edited and translated by Walter Kaufmann. New York: Random House, 1969.

———. *The Gay Science.* Translated by Walter Kaufmann. New York: Random House, 1974.

———. *On the Genealogy of Morals.* In *On the Genealogy of Morals and Ecce Homo.* Edited and translated by Walter Kaufmann. New York: Random House, 1969.

————. *Twilight of the Idols*. In *The Portable Nietzsche*. Edited and translated by Walter Kaufmann. New York: Viking, 1976. [*Götzendämmerung*. Stuttgart: Alfred Kröner Verlag, 1954.]

Nozick, Robert. *The Examined Life*. New York: Simon & Schuster, 1990.

Nussbaum, Martha C. *Love's Knowledge: Essays on Philosophy and Literature*. New York: Oxford University Press, 1990.

————. *Upheavals of Thought: The Intelligence of Emotions*. Cambridge: Cambridge University Press, 2001.

Nygren, Anders. *Agape and Eros*. Translated by Philip S. Watson. Philadelphia, PA: Westminster Press, 1953.

O'Donovan, Oliver. *The Problem of Self-Love in St. Augustine*. Eugene, OR: Wipf and Stock, 2006.

O'Loughlin, Thomas. "Celibacy in the Catholic Church: A Brief History." *History Ireland*, Vol. 3, No. 4, Winter 1995, pp. 41–46.

Ovid. *Metamorphoses*. Book III. Translated by F. J. Miller. Cambridge, MA: Harvard University Press, 1977.

Pessoa, Fernando. *A Centenary Pessoa*. Edited by Eugénio Lisboa and L. C Taylor. Manchester: Carcanet Press, 1995.

Plato. *Euthyphro, Apology, Crito, Phaedo, Phaedrus*. Translated by Harold North Fowler. Cambridge, MA: Harvard University Press, 2005.

————. *Meno and Other Dialogues*. Translated by Robin Waterfield. Oxford: Oxford University Press, 2005.

————. *Sophist*. Translated by Nicholas P. White. Indianapolis, IN: Hackett, 1993.

————. *The Symposium*. Translated by Walter Hamilton. Harmondsworth: Penguin, 1951.

————. *Theaetetus*. Translated by John McDowell. Oxford: Oxford University Press, 2014.

Plotinus. *Enneads*. Translated by Stephen MacKenna. London: Penguin, 1991.

Poe, Edgar Allen. *The Complete Illustrated Stories and Poems of Edgar Allen Poe*. London: Chancellor Press, 1988.

Polkinghorne, John, ed. *The Work of Love: Creation as Kenosis*. Grand Rapids, MI: Wm. B. Eerdmans, 2001.

Pollock, Linda. *A Lasting Relationship: Parents and Children over Three Centuries*. London: Fourth Estate, 1987.

Proust, Marcel. *In Search of Lost Time*. Translated by C. K. Scott Moncrieff and Terence Kilmartin. London: Chatto & Windus, 1992.

Putnam, Hilary. *Jewish Philosophy as a Guide to Life*. Bloomington: Indiana University Press, 2008.

Richardson, Joanna. *Baudelaire*. London: John Murray, 1994.

Rilke, Rainer Maria. *Duino Elegies and The Sonnets to Orpheus*. Edited and translated by Stephen Mitchell. New York: Vintage, 2009.

————. *Selected Poems*. Translated by Susan Ranson and Marielle Sutherland and edited by Robert Vilain. New York: Oxford University Press, 2011.

————. *The Selected Poetry of Rainer Maria Rilke*. Edited and translated by Stephen Mitchell. London: Picador, 1987.

————. *Sonnets to Orpheus*. Translated by Daniel Joseph Polikoff. Kettering, OH: Angelico Press, 2015.

Rosenzweig, Franz. *The Star of Redemption*. Translated by William W. Hallo. Notre Dame, IN. University of Notre Dame Press, 1985.

Rougemont, Denis de. *Love in the Western World*. Translated by Montgomery Belgion. Princeton, NJ: Princeton University Press, 1983.

Rousseau, Jean-Jacques. "Discourse on the Origins of Inequality." In *Discourse on the Origins of Inequality (Second Discourse), Polemics, and Political Economy*. Translated by Judith Bush, Roger D. Masters, Christopher Kelly, and Terence Marshall. Hanover, NH: University Press of New England, 1992, pp. 1–95.

———. *Julie, or The New Heloise*. Translated by Philip Stewart and Jean Vaché. Hanover, NH: University Press of New England, 1997.

Santayana, George. *The Sense of Beauty*. New York: Dover Publications, 1955.

Sappho. *The Poetry of Sappho*. Translated by Jim Powell. Oxford: Oxford University Press, 2007.

Sartre, Jean-Paul. *Being and Nothingness*. Translated by Hazel Barnes. London: Routledge, 2007.

Scarry, Elaine. *On Beauty and Being Just*. Princeton, NJ: Princeton University Press, 1999.

Scheler, Max. *The Nature of Sympathy*. Translated by Peter Heath. London: Routledge & Kegan Paul, 1954.

Schlegel, Friedrich. *Lucinde*. In *Friedrich Schlegel's* Lucinde *and the Fragments*. Translated by Peter Firchow. Minneapolis: University of Minnesota Press, 1971.

Schopenhauer, Arthur. *On the Basis of Morality*. Translated by E. F. J. Payne. Indianapolis, IN: Bobbs-Merrill, 1965.

———. *The World as Will and Representation*. Vols. I and II. Translated by E. F. J. Payne. New York: Dover Publications, 1966.

Shakespeare, William. *Shakespeare's Sonnets*. Edited by Katherine Duncan-Jones. London: Nelson and Sons, 1997.

Singer, Irving. *The Nature of Love*. Vols. I–III. Chicago: University of Chicago Press, 1984–87.

Smith, Adam. *The Theory of Moral Sentiments*. Edited by Knud Haakonssen. Cambridge: Cambridge University Press, 2002.

Soble, Alan, ed. *Erôs, Agape, and Philia: Readings in the Philosophy of Love*. St. Paul, MN: Paragon House, 1989.

Solomon, Andrew. *Far from the Tree*. London: Chatto & Windus, 2013.

Solomon, Robert C. *About Love: Reinventing Romance for Our Times*. Lanham, MD: Rowman & Littlefield, 1994.

Solomon, Robert C., and Kathleen M. Higgins, eds. *The Philosophy of (Erotic) Love*. Lawrence: University Press of Kansas, 1991.

Spinoza, Baruch. *Ethics*. Edited and translated by G. H. R. Parkinson. London: Everyman, 1992.

Steinberg, Michael P. *Judaism Musical and Unmusical*. Chicago: University of Chicago Press, 2007.

Stendhal. *Love*. Translated by Gilbert and Suzanne Sale. Harmondsworth: Penguin, 1975.

———. *The Private Diaries of Stendhal*. Edited and translated by Robert Sage. London: Victor Gollancz, 1955.

———. *Rome, Naples and Florence*. Translated by Richard N. Coe. Richmond: Calder Publications, 2010.

Studd, John. "A Comparison of 19th Century and Current Attitudes to Female Sexuality." *Gynecological Endocrinology*, Vol. 23, No. 12, December 2007, pp. 673–681.

Teresa of Avila. *The Life of Saint Teresa of Avila by Herself.* Translated by J. M. Cohen. London: Penguin, 1957.

Tillich, Paul. *Dynamics of Faith.* London: Allen & Unwin, 1957.

Trilling, Lionel. *Sincerity and Authenticity.* Cambridge, MA: Harvard University Press, 1971.

Unterman, Jeremiah. *Justice for All: How the Jewish Bible Revolutionized Ethics.* Lincoln: University of Nebraska Press, 2017.

Velleman, J. David. "Love as a Moral Emotion." *Ethics*, Vol. 109, No. 2, January 1999, pp. 338–374.

Virgil. *The Aeneid.* Translated by David West. London: Penguin Books, 1990.

Vlastos, Gregory. *Platonic Studies.* Princeton, NJ: Princeton University Press, 1981.

Wain, John, ed. *The Oxford Anthology of English Poetry*, Vol. 2: *Blake to Heaney.* New York: Oxford University Press, 2002.

Waldron, Jeremy. "When Justice Replaces Affection: The Need for Rights." *Harvard Journal of Law and Public Policy*, Vol. 11, 1988, pp. 625–647.

Ward, Keith. *Religion and Human Nature.* Oxford: Oxford University Press, 1998.

Warneken, Felix, and Michael Tomasello. "The Roots of Human Altruism." *British Journal of Psychology*, Vol. 100, No. 3, August 2009, pp. 455–471.

Weber, Max. "Science as a Vocation." In *Max Weber's "Science as a Vocation."* Edited by Peter Lassman and Irving Velody. London: Unwin Hyman, 1989, pp. 3–31.

Weil, Simone. *Gravity and Grace.* Translated by Emma Crawford and Mario von der Ruhr. London: Routledge, 2002.

———. *The Need for Roots.* Translated by A. F. Wills. London: Routledge, 1997.

———. *The Simone Weil Reader.* Edited by George A. Panichas. New York: McKay, 1977.

Whitman, Walt. *Democratic Vistas.* In *Leaves of Grass (I) and Democratic Vistas.* London: J. M. Dent & Sons, 1912, pp. 301–359.

Woods, Robert. *Children Remembered: Responses to Untimely Death in the Past.* Liverpool: Liverpool University Press, 2006.

Wright, Tamra. "Self, Other, God: 20th Century Jewish Philosophy." *Royal Institute of Philosophy Supplement*, Vol. 74, July 2014, pp. 149–169.

Zelizer, Viviana A. *Pricing the Priceless Child: The Changing Social Value of Children.* Princeton, NJ: Princeton University Press, 1994.

INDEX

Abel, 78, 113, 254n9
Abraham, 42, 43, 49, 85, 142, 157, 159, 197
  covenant with God, 143, 144, 145–46, 148–49,
    150, 151, 194, 195
  exile of, 102
  God's call to, 50, 68
  sacrifice of Isaac, 94, 96, 100
absence. *See also* lack
  of answers to questions about specificity of
    love, 23, 32–35
  of a home, 102
  of the loved one, 65, 75, 78, 143, 151
  of meaning or purpose, 187
Adam and Eve, 35, 86, 87, 197
  exile of, 100–101, 104
  not in love relationship, 100–101
  sexuality and, 101, 253n7
Adler, Felix, 199
Aeneid, The (Virgil), 44, 58
agape, 112, 114, 150, 182, 193. *See also* all-affirming
    love; *caritas*; disinterested love; divine love;
    enduring love; unconditional love
  benevolence distinguished from, 84
  Garden of Eden's absence of, 101
  genuine love posited as, 29–31
  as a mode of attentiveness, 122–23, 124
  parental love compared with, 236
  secularization of, 9, 11–22, 29–31, 34–35, 51, 84,
    173, 191, 236
  specificity test failed by, 34–35
  as a value-creating principle, 10
alienation, 99, 104–9, 178, 195. *See also* exile
  love as a response to, 107–8, 109
  in other eras, 108–9
  Western modernity's proneness to, 109
all-affirming love, 9, 19, 20, 21, 51, 192–93
  divine love not necessarily, 88
  enchantment without, 108
  parental love claimed as, 231, 233, 235, 236
  qualities of, 17–18
altruism, 4, 5, 6. *See also agape*; care; devotion;
    neighbor love; self-giving
Amalekites, 86, 89, 251n20
ambivalence, 77, 122–23
amor fati, 43, 189, 263n15
Anatomy of Melancholy, The (Burton), 71

ancestors, 50, 54, 69, 70, 72, 94, 110, 111, 147, 149,
    150, 236. *See also* love for the dead
animals
  altruism in, 6
Antigone (Sophocles), 78
appraisal theories of love, 11–14
Aquinas, Thomas, 8, 12
  on damnation, 9, 29
  on divine love, 30
  on divine violence, 87–88, 90
  on evil, 187
  on friendship with God, 225, 255n14
  on Heaven as home, 44
  on love for God, 63, 132
  on neighbor love, 132
  on self-interest, 91, 96
  on self-love, 96, 133–34, 257n3
Arendt, Hannah, 18, 95, 134, 218, 228
Aristophanes (*Symposium*), 26, 33, 35, 55, 59,
    67, 102, 177, 245n12. *See also* wholeness,
    yearning for.
Aristotle, 4, 11, 70, 100–101, 138, 147, 150, 193
  on beauty, 177
  on children/love for children, 197, 209, 232, 233
  on the conditionality of *philia*, 18
  on friendship/*philia*, 27, 33–34, 73, 195, 207,
    208, 224, 228, 229
  on the impossibility of loving evil, 185
  on the impossibility of loving the gods, 85
  Nicomachean Ethics, 219, 242n28, 243n21,
    243n22, 252n4, 257n1, 257n15, 258n21, 262n6,
    263n1, 265n39, 266n5
  on self-love, 133, 135
art, 7, 50, 110, 144, 182, 183, 194, 195, 199, 236
"ascent" of love, 32, 101, 131, 132, 245n12.
    See also ladder of love
atheism, 31, 90, 116
attachment theories, 33
attentiveness, 70–72, 96, 118–24
  definition and characteristics of, 118–20
  erôs, agape, and *philia* as modes of, 122–23, 124
  object of, 120–21
  Odyssey on, 160
  patience and, 121
  spirituality as, 124, 125
attunement, 71–72, 120